£7.94

A *High* in the *Andes*

Taking part in the Inca Trail Rally

Vic Quayle

Gold Medal Winner

Published by
Wyntok Ltd

©2002 Vic Quayle
A High in the Andes
ISBN 0-9543540-0-1

Photographs © Vic Quayle 2002
(except where indicated)

The right of Vic Quayle to be identified as the
author of this work has been asserted by him in
accordance with the Copyright, Design and
Patent Act 1988.

Published by:
Wyntok Ltd
Mannin
Wykeham Road Guildford
Surrey GU1 2SE

www.wyntok.co.uk

A CIP catalogue record for this book is available
from the British Library

Design and production co-ordinated by:
The **Better Book** Company Ltd
Warblington Lodge
Havant
Hampshire PO9 2XH

Printed in Great Britain

Ah, but a man's reach should exceed his grasp:
or what's a heaven for?

ROBERT BROWNING 1812 – 1889

Tichio — highest
main road pass in
the world (16,000 ft)

Huancayo
Ayacucho
Lima ● ● Machu Picchu
Ica △ **Cusco**
Nasca · · **Nasca** · · **Puno**
Lines △ Raft Ferry across
Andahuaylas Lake Titicaca
Colca · · **La Paz** — World's highest capital city
Canyon **Arequipa**
Arica

Sucre Bolivia's colonial capital —
World Heritage Site
Atacama **Potosí**
Desert World Heritage Site
Calama
Jujuy
Salta
G
R **Campos**
A **do Jordão**
N **Londrina**
Iguazu **Ouro Preto**
C **Falls** World Heritage Site
H **Paranaguá**
Catamarca A **Guarujá**
C **Corrientes** **Rio de Janeiro**
O **Florianópolis** **START & FINISH**

Aconcagua
highest peak
in Americas **San Juan** **Porto Alegre**

Marbella **Buenos Aires** **Punta**
del Este
Ferry across River Plate
Mar del Plata
Temuco Lake **Bahía Blanca** Balcarce —
District Fangio Museum
Bariloche
The Old **Puerto** · · **Valdés**
Patagonian **Madryn** Peninsula
Express **Esquel** Gaiman · · **Trelew**
Welsh Town · · **Punta Tombo**
Coyhaique penguin reserve
Comodoro
Rivadavia
Lago Posadas
· · **Petrified Forest**
Glaciers
National
Park **El Calafate**
Torres **Río Gallegos**
del Paine
Puerto · · Ferry across Straits of Magellan
Natales **Río Grande**
Tierra del
Ushuaia Fuego
The Southernmost City on Earth

Key

| Route variant for some crew |
| Railway trip |
| Ferry |
| Night halts |
| Part rally night halts |
| Rest days |

My thanks to Pam for being there,
for keeping me on the straight and narrow,
and for telling me where to go.

Foreword

By Hannu Mikkola

The 1960s saw a resurgence in the ultra long distance rallies with the London - Mexico World Cup Rally sponsored by the Daily Mirror being one of the most arduous.

These events revived the challenges set in the old classic reliability trials which required drivers, often with riding mechanics, to race huge distances from city to city, usually on diabolical roads and often in appalling weather conditions.

The 1970 London - Mexico World Cup Rally had all these ingredients. It started in London and toured Europe over classic rallying roads as far east as Yugoslavia before the cars were shipped from Lisbon to Rio de Janeiro.

The crews met up with their cars again and restarted from Rio heading south through Brazil and Uruguay before travelling west across the Argentinean Pampas and heading north through Chile, Bolivia, Peru and eventually to Mexico City. The finish of the rally coincided with the World Cup Football Tournament.

The Inca Trail Rally recreated part of that 1970 rally covering a similar route to that which I followed with my co-driver Gunnar Palm in a Ford Escort. We had the backing of the Ford Motor Company as works drivers and the amazing Escorts came 1st, 3rd, 5th, 6th and 8th as well as winning the Manufacturer's Team prize.

However, participants in the 2001 Inca Trail Rally didn't have the benefit of works service crews and back up. Crews tackling the Classic Reliability Trail had to arrange their own repairs and maintenance often relying on help and assistance from the 4x4 crews who carried their spare parts, personal belongings and regularly helped them out of tricky situations. The 4x4 teams also had their own challenges to tackle.

Events such as the Inca Trail Rally demand dedication, skill, endurance, stamina and determination and the teams that completed the course, especially those who did well, will have been tested to the utmost degree.

The Historic Endurance Rallying Organisation is to be congratulated for organising such an event and Vic's book ably records the event, the countries through which it passed, the wonderful rallying terrain in South America as well as the characters who take part in such challenges.

The book brings back many memories of my rallying in South America and I thank Vic for a good read.

Hannu Mikkola
WINNER 1970 LONDON - MEXICO WORLD CUP RALLY
WORLD RALLY DRIVERS' CHAMPION 1983

Contents

INTRODUCTION 1

BECOMING INVOLVED 3

WHY? 8

COMFY CLASS 12

AUGUST 18

SEPTEMBER 34

OCTOBER 35

INCA TRIAL 4x4 ADVENTURE DRIVE

    DAY 1   In at the deep end .41

    DAY 2   Catching breath 47

    DAY 3   Mud, mud, glorious mud 49

    DAY 4   Getting into a routine 55

    DAY 5   Wet, wet, wet 58

    DAY 6   Jesuit Missions 62

    DAY 7   Chaco 66

    DAY 8   Butch Cassidy and the Sundance Kid 70

    DAY 9   Drive in launderette 78

    DAY 10   Awesome 83

    DAY 11   Lake Titicaca 94

    DAY 12   Into the land of the Incas 99

    DAY 13   R and R 103

    DAY 14   Machu Picchu 105

    DAY 15   The real thing 108

    DAY 16   On top of the world 118

    DAY 17   On top of the railway world 125

    DAY 18   Where is prisoner number 6? 128

    DAY 19   Desert rats 130

    DAY 20   Up, up and away .134

    DAY 21   Invisible condors .141

    DAY 22   Beyond the boondocks 146

DAY 23 Gran Turismo computer games 153
DAY 24 High flying flamingos 159
DAY 25 Wrong slot 164
DAY 26 Red mist 170
DAY 27 Over the Andes again 177
DAY 28 Another town, another garage 182
DAY 29 CD Day 187
DAY 30 Lakeside BBQ 191
DAY 31 Steaming 196
DAY 32 Austral driving 201
DAY 33 We meet Bin Laden 206
DAY 34 Houston, we have a problem 210
DAY 35 A wonder of the world 219
DAY 36 Salmon by the lake 224
DAY 37 We meet a mamba 228
DAY 38 Fin del Mundo 233
DAY 39 Total silence 238
DAY 40 Weird road to gollygosh 244
DAY 41 The loneliest road 248
DAY 42 More flying 253
DAY 43 Wales today.... 257
DAY 44 .... and whales today 262
DAY 45 McDonald's and civilisation again 266
DAY 46 World racing drivers' champion 272
DAY 47 Tango city 276
DAY 48 Dog walkers delight 278
DAY 49 Rain, rain and still more rain 281
DAY 50 Disaster strikes 286
DAY 51 World Cup Rally test 294
DAY 52 Anyone for tennis? 299
DAY 53 Sound of Music 300
DAY 54 Motorway horses 304
DAY 55 Gold and sands beckon 309

REFLECTIONS 312
POSTSCRIPT 319
ACKNOWLEDGEMENTS 321
APPENDICES 323
   TRIALS AND TRIBULATIONS OF A CLASSIC CAR ENTRANT 325
   ENTRY LIST 328
   INCA TRAIL 4x4 ADVENTURE DRIVE - MAJOR AWARD WINNERS . .332
   INCA TRAIL CLASSIC RELIABILITY TRIAL- MAJOR AWARD WINNERS . .333
   TOOLS AND SPARES LIST 334
   FIRST AID AND MEDICAL SUPPLIES 335

A High in the Andes

Introduction

Just how do these things start?

On the start line, as the second hand of the clock ticks those last few segments that signal another minute and our time to begin the journey of a lifetime?

Or is it the time of one's actual birth?

Or along the way of life at some place where strands of interest click together to become the all encompassing urge to undertake some amazing enterprise?

Not that this enterprise, taking part in the Inca Trail Rally, was all that amazing. Many people have undertaken longer and more arduous journeys. Many people have overcome tremendous misfortune or odds to complete far more fantastic feats of endurance. One thinks of Scott or Shackleton and their exploits in Antarctica, of Hilary and Bonnington and their climbing adventures, and many others who have achieved greatness through their willingness to tackle the unknown and succeed.

No, I don't put myself on the pedestals they quite rightly deserve. But for me, in my little life, in my circumstances, the chance to take part in the adventure that was to be the Inca Trail Rally was every bit as thrilling. It would be a trip into the unknown, a test of resolve, endurance, commitment and approached with great anticipation.

The start, the real start of the adventure for me, was when I first became aware that the event was being organised. Immediately I knew I had to be there come what may. The event had all the right ingredients – distance, great roads, marvellous terrain, romantic sounding places, fabulous scenery, and the chance to pit oneself against the unknown.

However there was a need to consider the pluses and minuses. On the down side was cost, potential for real dangers, possible personal injury and serious damage to whatever vehicle we used, and the long absence from home and work and all that they entail.

On the plus side there were great comfort factors. Support by way of the organisation that was being brought to the event with pre-planned accommodation and headaches such as customs and border controls sorted out.

Would it be the trip of a lifetime?

Would we have a high in the Andes?

Becoming involved

It's September 1999 and Pam, my wife, and I have just returned from a holiday in Namibia in south west Africa. Like most active motor sports enthusiasts, my habit on a Wednesday is to get a copy of Motoring News, or Muttering Nudes as the cognoscenti know it, and there is a review of a book called 'Capers' published by HERO, the acronym for the Historic Endurance Rallying Organisation.

It's about a London - Capetown car rally and features the eighty or so entrants and their vehicles, with a short story from each of them about their experiences on the event. The idea of a London - Capetown rally was pure magic to me: a trans-continental rally, different cultures, brilliant scenery and sights, fabulous rally roads and tremendous camaraderie amongst those taking part as well as those organising the event and providing support.

I bought a copy of the book and read it from cover to cover about three times before I came up for air. It was the story of the motoring event I had always wanted to do. And what's more, the one country most of the entrants raved about in their short articles was Namibia. We knew why as we'd just come back from there, in fact the rally must have passed through only a few months before we were there, and, as I was to find out later, used many of the roads we used too.

The story of our trip to Namibia is worthy of comment as it is crucial to us entering the Inca Trail Rally. To celebrate our 25th Wedding Anniversary, Pam and I had planned a holiday trip to Australia, but when Pam's dad was taken seriously ill not long before our due departure we were forced to cancel and claim on the insurance.

The money was fiercely guarded and kept for a future trip and once we felt the time was right we looked around for another holiday destination. For some reason, I can't remember why, we felt like going to somewhere closer to home than Australia and one Sunday I saw a short article in the newspaper about Namibia.

Unlike most people, I had a reasonably good idea about where Namibia was and a little about its geography and culture - some years ago a friend had gone to work out there with Raleigh International and, as is my practice, I had looked up some information about the country and its character.

For our holiday Namibia offered many benefits over Australia. Shorter flying time, no time zones to cross, not too many tourists and plenty of African wildlife to see. And so it was we flew to Windhoek, collected a hire car from Avis and toured the country over three weeks.

Being a rally fan, the country was brilliant. Hardly any tarmac roads, but thousands of miles of beautifully graded gravel roads criss-crossing the desert landscapes from town to town. By most people's standards we did a high mileage during our three weeks, nearly 6,000 kms of which about 90% was on the gravel roads. With our rallying background I usually insisted on going the long way round between our main stops and using some of the more remote roads that in turn led to some terrific experiences.

I should add that it isn't necessary to see this beautiful country and its wildlife by venturing onto the remote gravel roads. Most of the main tourist sites can be reached on sealed tarmac, but one should expect to have to travel on at least some unmetalled roads.

During our time driving a little Toyota Corolla two wheel drive saloon around this desert country, we had no problems whatsoever, not even a puncture, and understood how the entrants in the London - Capetown Rally felt about the country.

Getting back to the plot. With the Capers book came details of a new event being organised by HERO to be called the Inca Trail and using South America as its location.

The name Inca Trail was pinched from the famous trek undertaken by backpackers up to Machu Picchu from Cusco, but the rally would involve far more than the four days usually taken to tackle that Inca

Trail. This version would be over 55 days and 25,000 kms taking in most of South America below the Amazon valley, going as far north as Lima on the Pacific coast and Tierra del Fuego in the south.

My imagination was fired. I had to find a way of doing this event. We had two years to plan and raise the finance and I immediately confirmed my interest in taking part.

A few words about the organiser of the event are needed here. HERO, is headed by John Brown. Its existence stems from a wish by many rally fans to return to the old days of long distance rallying events and to tackle them in cars from the right era.

HERO is one of several organisations, (businesses would be a better way to describe them), holding car rallies exclusively for pre-1964 (or in some cases pre-1976) rally cars and there are many each year. Typically these events have Austin Healey 3000s, various types of Mercedes, old Volvos, Rovers, and MGs taking part.

HERO holds a very tough event called LE JOG (an acronym for Land's End - John O'Groats) each December, a London - Lisbon Rally, the Classic Malts Scottish Reliability Trial each spring and the occasional big one like the London - Capetown or Inca Trail. Other similar organisations hold events to Monte Carlo reliving the days of the classic Monte Carlo Rallies of the fifties and sixties and in recent years there have been round the world events, London - Sydney, Peking - Paris, and others.

The nature of these rallies varies considerably. Recognising many of the cars likely to take part are of considerable vintage, speed is usually not an element in deciding the outcome. More often the results are decided from driving tests of various sorts on private land along the route or regularity sections where the crews need to drive at strictly controlled average speeds between identified points. At the time I didn't know it, but before long I would be doing one of these events.

With the really long events it is difficult to find enough people to put their old rally cars to the test over such huge distances and not everyone is prepared to spend a large part of the trip fettling their vehicle after a long day on the road. So to make these events viable commercially entrants are also encouraged to take part in 4x4s and there were about 40 of these in the London - Capetown Rally. They would also be welcome in the Inca Trail.

From all that was going on my imagination was fired up and in the autumn of 1999 HERO held an open day at the National Motor Cycle Museum near Birmingham to provide information about the forthcoming Inca Trail for potential participants. Several teams from the London - Capetown event were there and I came back totally enthused and became committed to finding a way to take part.

A tour of South America had been chosen because John Brown had been Clerk of the Course in that part of the world for the 1970 London - Mexico World Cup Rally. This rally had been held to coincide with the World Cup football competition in Mexico and started in London, toured many famous rally locations in Europe, before heading for South America and many thousands of miles of motoring before the finish in Mexico City.

The event was a speed event as well as being an ultra long distance rally. It attracted many of the works teams of the day including Ford and British Leyland. It was won by Hannu Mikkola, the Colin McRae of the time, in a works prepared Ford Escort, whilst the England football team (who had hoped to repeat their famous 1966 success) were knocked out in the early rounds.

The new Inca Trail Rally would use some of the same roads but because so many had been tarmaced or otherwise improved, equally challenging sections had been identified and would be included in the new rally route. In addition, the Inca Trail would venture into new rallying territory such as Patagonia and head towards tourist attractions such as Machu Picchu, Iguazu Waterfalls and Colca Canyon.

The new event would have two classes. A Classic Reliability Trial would be open to rally cars built before 1976 and timed to the minute throughout. These entrants would have Regularity Sections where set average speeds would have to be maintained over predetermined distances with secret checks and penalties awarded for early or late arrival. They would also tackle Medal Sections where target times are set and late arrival at the end of the Section is penalised. Some of these sections would be relatively short at 20 kms, whilst others as long as 300 kms.

For the 4x4s there would be Explorer Sections on most days of the rally that would take the cars into remote areas and over testing tracks. Whilst target times for starting and completing these were set, they were advisory only, and there would be no penalty for departing or arriving at other times. Gold medals would be awarded to those who completed all the tests and also complied with the starting and finishing times each day, silver for completing a given percentage and so on.

Thus there would be several threads to this new HERO event. Classes for old rally cars as well as modern 4x4s, a true endurance element often with 500 miles a day being covered and an average daily mileage of 350, good quality accommodation when available, opportunities to visit tourist sites such as Machu Picchu, the Nasca Lines, Iguazu Waterfalls as well as tour romantic sounding places such as Tierra del Fuego, Patagonia and the Atacama Desert.

The trip of a lifetime and it would go high into the Andes.

Why?

People often ask why I am so besotted with rallying. I don't know, is the simple answer, but being born into a motorcycling family on the Isle of Man probably has something to do with it. The Island is the home of the world famous Tourist Trophy (TT) Races - motor cycle races that aren't for the faint hearted as they take place on the Mountain Circuit over 37 miles of closed public roads.

As a family we had moved from the Island to the mainland when I was only months old, but dad worked in the motorcycle industry and every summer we would return to the Isle of Man to visit grandparents for our holiday, always during the racing weeks. I never owned a motorbike, but I had a car as soon as I could and it was a natural progression to join a car club and it wasn't long before I learned about rallying. In fact when I sat down to write this book I realised that the first book I ever bought with my own money after starting work back in 1963 was one about the Peking-Paris Rally held in 1907, a rally that was re-run in more modern vehicles in 1997 to mark its 90th anniversary.

I remember soon after joining the Malden and District Motor Club that I marshalled on an event called the London Gulf Rally. This was a classic of its time taking competitors around mainland Britain over five days with hardly any rest periods. We went to a forest near Camberley in Surrey and the friend I was with drove like mad down the forest tracks to our marshalling point. We then watched the competitors through before we had a chance to drive like them out of the forest again. I was totally smitten but finance and other restrictions meant it would be many years before I could do the same.

I have only ever been an enthusiastic clubman, never achieving great success, but always enjoying competing, organising and marshalling. Rallying has taken me to some wonderful places, almost always off the beaten track because that's where rallies go. As often as possible I would go to watch the big events like the RAC Rally.

Over the years I competed in various cars, mostly Ford Escort Mexicos, a car developed for general sale from the one used by Hannu Mikkola to win the London - Mexico World Cup Rally. Later I rallied a Mazda 626, not a very suitable car, but then obtained a Peugeot 309GTI. There were long gaps in my rally activities as children, work and mortgages intervened.

In 1994 I had an opportunity to take part in the Cape-to-Cape Challenge, an unusual event, which because of its nature was immediately attractive to me. The idea was to break the world record for driving from Cape Tarifa, which is on the Spanish coast near Gibraltar and the southernmost place on mainland Europe, to the northernmost place which is at the top end of Norway and called Nordkapp. To prevent illegal speeding every vehicle had to be fitted with a tachograph, as used by lorries. We broke the old world record and had a brilliant time. The Cape-to-Cape Challenge was completed in an ordinary family car, our Mazda 626 GT, that was ideal for the trip and which is still our day-to-day transport. However, for the Inca Trail Rally we would need something different.

Another event that brought me closer to taking part in the Inca Trail was an opportunity to take part in another HERO event, the Classic Malts. Its full title is the Classic Malts Scottish Reliability Trial and a friend who has an MGC sports car telephoned out of the blue one day early in 2000 to see whether I would like to navigate/co-drive with him. Is the Pope a Catholic?

Although the previous owner had used it for sprint racing Peter had owned the MGC for a couple of years but not used it for proper competitions. In advance of the Malts, Peter had carried out all manner of improvements to the car and being big-engined (there is no substitute for horsepower on events such as these), strong and well prepared it was an ideal choice for the rally.

The event was to take us anti-clockwise around northern Scotland starting and finishing in Edinburgh. It was sponsored by The Classic Malts visiting several of their distilleries en route but there would, of course, be no sampling of their excellent whiskies during the day. Everyone made up for that in the evenings!

And it was at one of these evenings that I met Peter Rushforth a well-known rally navigator from the sixties and seventies who was officiating on the event. We enjoyed a bottle of Dalwhinnie one evening and I learned he was working in the motor trade and had supplied a 4x4 to John Brown to use as a recce vehicle for the Inca Trail. I mentioned my plans to enter and we discussed suitable vehicles for the event.

The Classic Malts Rally was all that we had hoped for. The weather was excellent and the route had plenty of challenges for both the driver and navigator. The social side was just as good and when we had to retire because of damage to the steering, we hired a car to complete the route and help with marshalling.

I continued to keep an eye on progress with preparations for the Inca Trail and bought maps of South America to plot the recces being carried out by John Brown, reports of which were being posted on the HERO website.

Crunch time came in the autumn of 2000 as the entry list for the Inca Trail was filling up and we had to decide whether or not to commit to taking part and send in a cheque to HERO to reserve our place.

Doing events like this isn't cheap. The entry fee covered the general organisation, hotel accommodation, customs clearances and other administrative issues, but not transport for us and the vehicle to and from Rio de Janeiro where the event started and finished, fuel, insurance, general day to day expenses on food etc, nor the cost of a vehicle.

The deadline was close and Pam and I discussed whether or not to take part long into the night on several occasions. My attitude to life is that you are only here once and life's ample opportunities should be grasped whenever possible.

Pam takes a far more serious and responsible attitude to life than I do. She is more reserved, calmer and worries a lot about finances. She has done a fair few rallies as well, having navigated for me on several occasions before our two daughters were born and generally been around helping to officiate on the many other events we ran and took part in with Malden and District and other motor clubs.

Our discussions also turned to what sort of vehicle we might take. Whilst I had done lots of rallying over many years I had never owned a classic, nor did I consider myself especially mechanically competent. I used to work on my own rally cars but it wasn't an aspect of rallying that I enjoyed.

Research in the motoring magazines had revealed that a good second-hand classic rally car could be obtained for a reasonable price and much cheaper than a new or second-hand 4x4 would cost. But added to this would be preparation costs and the need to factor in the resale value after the event.

Another consideration was the increased entry cost for the classics. They would be paying an extra £5,000 for additional insurances, marshalling costs and other related matters, as they would be doing a proper competitive event.

But most important of all, if we took a classic rally car there was greater potential for having to spend many hours working on the car during the rally. Was I prepared or interested in spending lots of time each evening fettling a classic rally car after driving several hundred miles? Basically, no I wasn't.

Pam was eventually convinced that she should join me on the trip , so in September 2000 we sent an initial cheque for £12,500 to HERO to confirm our entry in the Adventure Drive in a 4x4, make yet to be determined.

Comfy Class

I had hardly ever driven a 4x4 and had little experience in deciding what vehicle might be appropriate to use for the Inca Trail.

Visits were paid to all the local dealers to try potential vehicles and I even tried a few letters to see whether I could get a loan vehicle from a manufacturer – "Join the queue sonny". Well you have to try, don't you?

It seemed clear that 4x4s came in a variety of guises. We were on a limited budget for the event and our allocation for a vehicle was about £15,000 plus about £2,500 preparation costs. That ruled out the top end market of Range Rovers, Land Cruisers and the newer, quality 'soft' 4x4s from Lexus, BMW and Mercedes.

It also became clear that Toyota Land Cruisers were the vehicle of choice. Rated top vehicle in places like the Australian Outback and widely used by the United Nations in all manner of difficult situations, they had a reputation for reliability, toughness and availability of spares as well as servicing facilities worldwide.

For us though it meant a middle-range vehicle, something like a Land Rover Discovery, Freelander or Mitsubishi Shogun and probably a second-hand one.

John Brown, head of HERO, was raving about the Mitsubishi L200 pick-up he had used for the route survey and was recommending them to anyone who would listen. They were available as LHD twin cabs with four seats and a hard cover for the back for only £13,500 from Peter Rushforth. These seemed a good backstop option if something more suitable didn't turn up.

Peter runs the Left-hand Drive Place in Basingstoke and specialises not only in supplying new 'lefties', but also trading in any left hand drive vehicles.

A chat with Peter soon revealed that he could also do LHD Mitsubishi Pajeros (Shogun) for only a little more than the price of an L200, and after a test drive this seemed to offer the best solution. It also offered the possibility of a proper saloon as it wasn't a 'builder's truck' and would probably have a better resale value in the future.

A final decision was left till after Christmas 2000 but when I went down to firm up a purchase I found that the Pajeros were becoming more difficult to get and the only alternative was the Hyundai Galloper, an older-bodied version of the Pajero with mostly Mitsubishi running gear that quite frankly looked 'naff'.

It looked like an L200 was going to become ours but on the day I visited Basingstoke Peter also had a second-hand French registered Toyota Land Cruiser Colorado available. A Colorado would have been my first choice of vehicle but was way outside our budget. However being left hand drive its UK value was less than normal. This one was dark green in colour and was in good condition with a minor dent and a little internal wear and tear from 50,000 kilometres of use. A deal was quickly struck with Peter and it soon became ours at a price we could afford.

The main bonus was that we now had a vehicle to do the trip that would otherwise have cost £22-25,000, a major saving. True it was LHD, but that would be ideal in South America and I'm not worried about driving a LHD in the UK. The only disadvantage of LHD in the UK is getting in and out of multi-storey car parks where you have to grab a ticket when you enter. I have to jump out of the car and run round and collect it by hand. In addition the speedometer read in kph rather than mph, something that isn't a problem.

We took delivery of the car in mid-February 2001 and had to decide what preparations we needed to carry out by mid-August as the entries from the UK would be shipped out to Brazil then.

From my research it was clear that tyres and suspension would be crucial, as would weight. On HERO's last big event, London - Capetown, it seems the major problems for 4x4s were punctures and blown shock absorbers. The advice from all those in the know was – keep it simple.

Our Colorado came fitted with Oz alloy wheels and Goodrich Mud Terrain tyres, the tread for which has a large open pattern much like those on tractor tyres. These tyres were too chunky for the Inca Trail so we had All Terrains fitted with a good discount from Guildford Tyre Services. These tyres offered us a good compromise between grip on off-road sections, especially gravelly roads, and an ability to cope with long distances on ordinary highways at a reasonable speed.

Alloy wheels have a reputation for cracking and shattering on arduous events and a couple of people recommended changing them to steel wheels.

On all manner of car rallies over 30 years I have only once had wheel problems, so we decided to keep the alloys and risk it – would these be famous last words? We wanted to take two spare tyres and had an Oz alloy spare, also with an All Terrain tyre, as well as the original manufacturer's spare, a steel rim with a Dunlop road pattern tyre. This one would be used as a 'get you home' wheel if we really got stuck.

Various options for a suitable suspension set-up were considered and we decided to change to Old Man Emu (Australian) shock absorbers and springs on the advice of Chris Bashall at Surrey Off-Road Preparations who was also fitting this suspension to a couple of other Toyotas taking part in the Inca Trail.

Chris had the car for a couple of weeks and also fitted a sump guard (French), extra lighting, a Brantz for navigational purposes, jerry can holder, tie down straps and a few other bits and pieces.

A dog guard was fitted to act as a strong divider between the passenger compartment and the rear storage area where all our spares, tools and tyres would be. The rear seats were taken out and our personal baggage (enough for two months remember) would fit in the space available.

Hella kindly supplied us with a couple of spotlights. The standard Toyota lights are OK for normal driving but the organisers warned us of some 4.00am starts in the dark and if we got delayed we may need to be doing some night driving to keep to schedule. So extra lights were considered a must.

Spares were another important consideration. Our local Toyota dealer, Wadham Kenning (now Inchcape) in Guildford, very generously donated some spares (brake pads, filters and belts etc), a workshop manual, and offered to give the vehicle a full service just prior to departure, which was very good of them. Decisions also needed to be made about other items to take as in 25,000 kms of difficult driving we would undoubtedly have problems and needed to keep the vehicle on the road.

There were many other preparations to make. The paperwork side was worth several acres of trees from the Amazon. I don't know how many passport photos we supplied to HERO, but I am sure my local Sainsbury's manager was getting suspicious about the number of visits Pam and I were paying to their photo booth.

In April 2001 HERO organised a get-together for all the entrants at the Heritage Motor Museum at Gaydon in the Midlands. This was Pam's first real involvement in the event and gave her a chance to meet other people involved and get a proper feel for what it would mean to do the Inca Trail Rally.

There were entries from all over the world and although UK-based teams topped the list, others were from France, Germany, the Netherlands, Switzerland and even Clay Regazzoni, the former F1 driver who is Monaco-based. From further afield there were crews from South Africa, USA, New Zealand, but oddly only one from South America itself. One wonders why – what did they know that we didn't?

There were about two hundred people at the Gaydon meeting and when we first arrived and joined the queue to register I started chatting to the couple in front of us and it turned out that not only did Peter and Carolynn Robinson live within walking distance of us in Guildford, but they would be taking part in a Toyota Colorado as well. Very handy indeed.

The meeting was very useful and much up to date information was given out by John Brown and his team. The dangers of the trip had been identified in the event Regulations where there is a paragraph that clearly states:

This event is potentially dangerous. It passes through areas and uses roads which may be hazardous. It is expressly organised to present a challenge to participants, and to test amongst other things, their stamina, initiative, self-reliance, and resourcefulness. Participants should not enter unless they accept that there is an element of risk to themselves and their vehicle.

However the full impact of this was highlighted by a sharp intake of breath by everyone present when the fatality and serious injury rates on events such as the Inca Trail were made known. It sounded like it was more dangerous than blind/deaf white water rafting.

Following this meeting there was much more to consider in our preparations for the event. Besides the car, we needed to think about all manner of things and in the next couple of months were deciding on how to get the Colorado to and from Rio (by roll on-roll off ferry), insurances, international driving permits (two types would be needed), inoculations, vehicle passport (carnet de passage), and Pam was kept busy preparing lists and lists (and lists of lists).

She, of course, was more worried about what clothing to take.

One of the benefits of having someone like John Brown organise an event such as this, is the work the HERO team do in opening doors that would otherwise remain closed. We learned that many of the towns we would be visiting would invite us to Civic Receptions, there would be some sort of 'do' at the British Embassy in Buenos Aires, and all manner of entrances to places that one can't normally get to. So what to wear?

There was also the climate factor. We would be in South America in their spring, so very warm and humid weather could be expected in Rio. The nearest we would get to the equator would be about 11° south in Lima, but when travelling up to 5,500m (16,500 ft) it would be cold and no doubt icy.

From Lima we were due to pass through the driest places on earth, and then in Patagonia and Tierra del Fuego much colder and windy conditions might be expected.

At the same time we were doing a rally and may need to work on the vehicles, get a push out of mud or sand and thus didn't want to be too overdressed.

The organiser had warned our various hosts about all this and the fact that some participants might not be dressed as one might hope, but nevertheless appropriate clothing would need to be carried for all manner of occasions. We planned to have one bag of best clothes (trousers and jacket for me and posh skirt and top for Pam). After that it would be comfortable clothing with lots of shorts and tee shirts.

We would also be camping for at least one night, and we suspected more. We borrowed a tent from the local Merrow Scouts that was very easy to put up, but we also needed to take sleeping bags, blankets and pillows.

Things were slowly coming together.

August

Whilst at Surrey Off-Road picking up the Colorado I met Chris Elliott, one of the other Toyota drivers, who had had a great deal of work carried out on his 4x4, the larger and heavier Amazon. Whilst there, Chris "Basher" Bashall who ran the place set up some off-road training for us both, and Roger Lucas another Toyota man who was also taking an Amazon to South America.

I had been looking forward to this because with the foot and mouth disease crisis it had been difficult to get off-road experience and I wanted, indeed needed, some instruction. I had joined the All Wheel Drive Club and been to some local meetings, but initially all off-road events were banned because of Government restrictions.

So off we set in convoy for the short trip to a local private estate that Basher had clearance to use and after some photos of the three cars lined up by the lake we set off for the rough stuff.

Chris had had a winch fitted to the front of his Toyota and part of the plan was to try this out so he knew how to use it, so the first track we used was deeply rutted with steep banks on each side, and, we were warned, a big pot-hole about halfway up.

Chris went first with Basher on board and Roger and I watched them as they steadily crept up the steep narrow track. They got stuck at one point but eventually cleared a big lump on the near side rut and headed upwards and out of sight, which was my signal to follow.

The lowest gearing and rear differential lock were applied and I crept up the track, my only worry being the closeness of the banks to the bodywork. The first lump caused a bit of a problem, but after a couple of attempts the car climbed over and then onwards till I saw Chris's car really wedged in.

I chose a suitable place to stop and wandered up to see what was happening to find that the front nearside of Chris's Toyota was in a deep hole and the whole car at an angle of 35° or so from vertical. Basher was unperturbed and claimed the car could climb out but it was a good opportunity to use the winch.

This took quite a long time to set up. The cable was wound out of the front of the car and attached to a sling that had been put round a nearby tree. The winch was engaged and slowly the car was hauled up and out of the hole and onto the track proper.

The whole exercise was very impressive but I wondered whether we would ever be on tracks like this on the Inca Trail and I was more than a bit concerned that I risked damaging my car as the next in line to tackle the track and its hole. Yes, I'm a wimp. Roger and I talked about the prospect of digging at the track to smooth it out a bit, but nothing came of it.

Of course my car was backed up by Roger's anyway, and reversing back down was probably as potentially damaging as going forward, so a bit reluctantly I set forth.

Basher had advised that I could probably get through the hole if, as the front wheel dropped into it, I put on some left lock and drove the tyre into the bank which it would grip and climb. I tried, about four times, but finally had to admit defeat. I probably wasn't prepared to give it full welly and drive at the bank, because each time it felt like it was almost there.

But anyway I was stuck with the left wheel deep in this hole and the right front wheel about three feet in the air.

"No worries," says Basher, "this is an opportunity to try some towing." Out came a tow-rope and Chris, whose car was further up the track, towed me out, and then I was able to follow him to the top of the track, walk back and see how Roger did.

Well he did it didn't he, with no problems! My excuse was that he had a differential lock on his front wheels as well as the back, and yes, as I have admitted already, I'm a wimp anyway.

Basher assured us that we had crossed the worst, and we ventured on to try some more mud and gravel tracks and also some steep hill starts, all of which were great fun and I thoroughly enjoyed. It wasn't until later that I noticed that my nearside wing had taken a belt (presumably when I was charging the bank), and also the rear nearside bodywork was pressed in. That's rallying – as the saying goes. But I wasn't too pleased as the tracks we used were much worse than we were ever likely to get in South America.

Another meeting, this time over two days in early August, was organised by HERO back at the National Motorcycle Museum near Birmingham.

John introduced the organising team who would be out and about on the rally.

Having the worst job on the event would be father and son team of Mike and Anthony Preston who would be driving the Advance Course Car running a couple of days ahead of the rally checking the route was all right and providing route amendments and road condition reports. They would be travelling on their own for most of the seven weeks staying in the various overnight halts we would use, but missing all the high jinks on offer to us. Mike has an honourable rallying background and his son is creating one for himself as a top class navigator on classic rallies in the United Kingdom.

Peter Rushforth was there and would be Assistant Clerk of the Course along with Mark Appleton who works for HERO full time. Mark would be accompanied by Paul Heal, an accountant by trade but rally navigator and organiser as well.

Peter was partnered by Stuart Wood, who is a good navigator himself having taken Phil Surtees to his win on the Peking-Paris Rally in 1998. Stuart would be in charge of the results.

Husband and wife team Don and Pat Griffiths would be Trailmasters for the 4x4 crews and generally look after our interests.

On an event such as the Inca Trail Rally there is clearly a need for medical support, and this responsibility fell on the shoulders of three great individuals - Dr Greg Williams, Dr Mark Human and paramedic Mike Johnson.

Greg would travel with Tim Riley, better known as Jingers to most people. Greg worked in the Accident and Emergency Department at Wrexham Hospital, had been on other similar events as medical adviser as well as on trips with the British Army. Greg was also an expert on altitude sickness, something we would all have to face up to during the rally.

There is only one Jingers. Son of a well-known rallying couple from the fifties, Jingers now runs his own rally car preparation service and is an ace at getting cars fixed quickly and efficiently. Easily identifiable in a crowd, Jingers has never been known to wear long trousers, is always in shorts, and doesn't much like wearing shoes either. But he's your man if you have a technical problem with a classic rally car. It's fixed in no time.

Two expatriate South Africans would make up another of the organising teams travelling round the route with us. Paul Marsh, who also runs a vehicle preparation company specialising in 4x4s for expeditions, would be accompanied by Dr Mark Human, also with expedition and rally experience.

Phil Surtees, mentioned above as winner of the Peking-Paris Rally was in another vehicle with his son Daniel and John Bayliss.

There was also Mike 'Medic' Johnson, an ambulance driver, who with a previous career in engineering in Africa was also a very competent mechanic and who I first met in Scotland on the Classic Malts Rally in 2000. Mike was to be teamed with Bill Price, formerly a member of the BMC Works Rally Team and also a good man to have about.

Oddly there were two Mike Johnsons on the event, the other being 'Paparazzi' Mike Johnson the official photographer for the event. He would travel in the various official support vehicles and we were also advised he might look for the occasional lift in a 4x4 so as to get on-the-spot photos on the road. The thought occurred to me that whilst it would be nice to give Mike a lift we only had two seats in our Colorado so it would be difficult.

I think it was Roger Lucas who stood up and said as he ventured the two-fingered salute to Mike "If we see you thumbing a lift and you see this sign from one of the 4x4s we aren't being rude, but only have two seats because most of us have taken our rear seats out!"

There was much laughter, but Mike was quick enough to reply as he stuck his reversed middle finger in the air, "and if you see this signal, I am reminding you I am only looking for a single seat!"

I took the opportunity to visit the car park a couple of times to see the amazing range of vehicles taking part in the event. During one of these visits we met up with Dave and Carole Angel also doing the Inca Trail in a Toyota Colorado. They run a vehicle dismantling business in Dorset and we discussed forming a team entry with the Robinsons. Together we were the only three long wheel base Colorados on the event, although there was also a short wheel based version entered.

Other teams were being formed as well, amongst these three Toyota Amazon crews who would call themselves the Hooligans. They were Spencer and Carole Flack, John and Jill May, and Mike and Margaret Waterhouse who would regularly drive in convoy at great speed on the rally and keep in touch with each other with CB radios.

I had co-driven the Classic Malts in an MGC Roadster (for the uninitiated an MGB with a bigger engine) and was well aware of how little space there was for storing any spares or clothing on a long trip such as the Inca Trail. Rita Shelley and Mike Knox were doing the event in one so we offered to carry some bags for them and they said they would consider the offer.

I was also looking around the 4x4s to get some preparation ideas especially as I hadn't yet decided how to affix our rally plates, the Colorado not having any obvious space to fit them neatly.

Bill Price, a doyen of rallying and with whom I had a mutual contact through Lions Clubs, was interested in our vehicle as 'it was the one with all the stickers' and I was showing him what we had done to it when I was approached by John Bateson who was driving one of the Classics.

John lives in the Isle of Man, my home country, although he isn't Manx, and was driving a Ford Escort RS2000 in Modena Green, similar to one I once rallied. He said he was looking for someone to carry some spares around and could we carry a gearbox for him?

"Well John, I am actually raising funds for charity, but for a small consideration I am sure we could work something out."

"I don't mind making a £50 donation, just want to make sure it's there if we need it. It's not the whole box, there's no casing, just the innards." A deal was struck and he also arranged for Chris Elliott to take a cylinder head.

That was actually two cylinder heads being taken as spares, as our fellow Guildford Colorado driver, Peter Robinson, also had one that he wangled out of Toyota as, apparently, they have a tendency to give up the ghost at about 100,000 miles.

We met a lovely New Zealand couple David and Patsie Mitchell, both in their sixties, who had already shipped their car, an old Holden to Rio and which as we spoke was probably in Singapore en route. They were in the UK on holiday and had timed their visit to coincide with the Inca Trail Briefing. They had done no rallies previously but were out to enjoy the trip and wouldn't take the competitive aspects too seriously – unlike some others.

During the weekend we had an opportunity to try a short rally route with instructions set out in the same tulip format we would use on the rally. Pam was a bit nervous about this, but once we had been a few miles we were well away and zipped around in no time at all. Prior to the weekend we weren't at all sure whether the whole route would be given in tulips or whether we would need to rely on map reading abilities as well.

In fact, we learned, the whole route would be given as tulips and a set of marked maps provided to supplement them. There would be four books of each, with about 10,000 tulip instructions for the whole trip and 100 individual maps.

Route instructions by tulips are the standard way for providing route instructions on many rallies around the world and are so called because they were first used on the Dutch-run Tulip Rally in the 1950s. Basically a little diagram is provided for each notable junction along the route with a blob indicating the direction of approach and an arrow given on the route of departure. In addition, accurate distance readings are given between each instruction and an accumulative mileage for the whole section of the route, which might be a day's run, or for us an Explorer Section. Where there are no specific junctions a roadside feature may be included and all hazardous places are added too. The distances are given in both metric and imperial.

As the odometer on most cars isn't particularly accurate, to make best use of tulips an accurate distance recorder is needed in the car and we fitted a basic Brantz, and doing the rally section in Birmingham was an opportunity to set it up properly.

We would also get a set of marked maps with the whole route identified clearly, with the separate routes for each class, the various types of controls and some tourist spots all located for us.

Lately we had also given consideration to worst-case scenarios. What would we do if we had a serious accident, or worse, and how should we respond to bad news of a close relative back in the UK? Fortunately we only have one elderly close relative, Pam's mum who was in her late eighties. Basically we decided that we didn't want any news from the UK while we were away and work on the principal that no news was good news. If there was bad news to respond to, we would have to decide according to circumstances and this might include how far from the finish we were, how to get the car back to the UK and much more.

Mention should be made of the shippers, All Ways Forward (AWF) and the insurers for the event. The shippers move the Formula 1 Teams around the globe as well as many other motor racing and rallying entourages. Maybe they are used to dealing with Transport Managers in these teams but for us individuals they weren't geared up at all.

Our vehicle would go to South America by roll on roll off ferry (roro) via Tilbury and we were advised that it needed to be there on Thursday 16th August. By Friday 10th August I had received no confirmation or anything that even said they were expecting my vehicle and I was beginning to worry that we weren't even booked at all. So I called their Cheltenham office on the Friday afternoon before the HERO weekend but could track down no-one. POETS Day I supposed.

It was during the HERO weekend that I learned that the departure date had been put back to Tuesday, 21st August and it was claimed they had been in touch with everyone. From the response from the audience, it was clear I wasn't the only one who didn't know about the date change.

On the Monday I phoned their office to be told they had phoned everyone during the previous week.

"But nobody phoned me, am I actually on your list?" I said.

"Just a moment while I check," came the response while I had kittens wondering if I was going to be told I wasn't included.

"Yes you're on the list as a roro. That's right is it?"

"Yes, but nobody has advised me of the date change. Is there anything else I need to know, like extra charges, times?"

"Well we did manage to contact 98% of customers,"

"But not me, despite having an email address and three telephone numbers for me, all of which have answer phones." However, it wasn't worth pursuing.

"We are sending out an information pack to everyone tonight, first class post, and all the information you need is in the pack. Yes, there is an extra charge of £320 for storage at the Rio docks."

I had expected this as it was mentioned over the HERO weekend, so

I left the matter till I got the information pack that duly arrived on the Wednesday. However, later on the same morning I had a phone call from a lady at AWF "just to advise you that the shipping date has been postponed till 21ˢᵗ August." Make of it what you want!

Yes the invoice was in the information pack, also including another fee of £40 for disinfecting the vehicle before departure due to foot and mouth disease. Dig deeper in the pocket.

The insurers weren't too much better. At the Birmingham weekend, two representatives from L T Clowes, the event insurers, were present and handed out statements of the cover we had supposedly placed with them. A quick glance showed that they hadn't included cover for Marine Transit or contents of the vehicle during the transit both ways.

"Well, Mr Quayle you didn't tell us you wanted cover on the form you returned to us," and he showed us the form we had completed for medical, personal injury and other insurance from a file he was holding.

"Quite right," I replied, "at the time we weren't too sure who we would ship the vehicle with. But once that had been decided I wrote to you with a cheque confirming I wanted Marine Transit and contents insurance," and I showed him my copy. "Are you sure you haven't received it?"

Our man then looked in his file and sure enough my letter was there and a note of the cheque.

"Sorry about that Mr Quayle, we'll sort that out first thing on Monday."

I had expected a further statement of the cover we had, in line with the one handed to me at Birmingham, but by the day before transit nothing had been received, so a call had to be made to confirm the cover.

"All the documents will be sent to you in about a week."

After the car has been handed over and the boat has gone! No doubt I get to read about the exclusion clauses then! But then about three hours later I received a call from the insurers.

"Can we have your credit card number Mr Quayle."

"What for?"

"To pay for the extra insurance you require."

"It's all been paid for. I have sent you cheques and you confirmed that last week when I saw you." From the noises in the background it was clear that someone was talking to him in an office.

"Oh that's right. It's a madhouse here. Please excuse my call."

"I am covered for the Marine Transit aren't I?"

"Yes. Definitely."

Well, maybe!

Another requirement for the event was the need for one of the crew to have had first aid training. The last time either of us had had any first aid training was when we were in the guides and scouts and, I suppose, fortunately, we have never had the need to use the skills we had acquired. We felt that there was little point in one of us having training, as Murphy's Law states that the one with the training is the one who gets knocked unconscious, so we decided we would both attend a local British Red Cross course.

It was a two-day course held over a weekend and both days were long but interspersed with copious practical work such as bandaging each other and giving mouth-to-mouth resuscitation to special dolls called Little Annie. There was a great group of other people on the course all doing their training for a variety of reasons, but we both ended up on the Sunday evening brain dead from all the new information we had taken on board. Fortunately the best treatment for being brain dead is a glass of alcohol, so we treated each other rapidly and in copious quantities.

The course coincided with the last few days before the Colorado was due to be taken to the docks for shipment to Rio and I needed to do a last few little jobs to it before taking it to Tilbury. I had already stopped using the vehicle, just in case something happened to it, and let the fuel run down till I was driving on the warning light.

Pete Malby, who normally services our cars at his MVS garage in Guildford, kindly pop riveted the tin rally plates on the front and back of the vehicle and the existing number plates were repositioned.

And so the Colorado was as ready as it ever would be to be driven to Tilbury in readiness for shipping to Rio. I got the tyres pumped up to 35 psi and the spares to 40 psi (on the basis it is better to let air out if we have to use them, than pump air in), and loaded everything in.

The shippers needed all manner of documentation including a packing list and this was typed up and checked. Everything was photographed as well, as this would provide evidence if anything was stolen en route. And this seemed a real possibility as everything had to be accessible for customs to check and we handed over the keys as well. Somehow it didn't seem right, but we were all in the same boat – pardon the pun.

While all this was going on, we were reading of major financial problems in Argentina where their government was calling in the World Bank and IMF and others to help them cope with huge debts. At the same time the US$ was going down against the pound which might have worked to our advantage as we would be using US$ as our currency when away. We watched this carefully over the next few weeks and tried to pick the right time to buy.

The day to ship the Colorado arrived. The back (boot) area was full up to window height. Everything was strapped down and seemed pretty solid. I had received a tip off that the shippers needed the car to be weighed so I popped down to the local weighbridge to get that done (2040 kgs).

We had to take the car to Tilbury Docks, about 60 miles away around the M25 London orbital motorway and through the Dartford Tunnel and the idea was for Pam to follow me in our Mazda. Of course I forgot to ask the obvious as we left our road. "Do we turn left or right to Tierra del Fuego?"

I had two 5-litre spare fuel canisters on board, and sure enough about

5 miles from Tilbury the car started sputtering and came to a stop on the verge. At least we didn't come to a stop in the Dartford Tunnel. In went 5 litres and in a couple of minutes we were driving into Tilbury Docks and soon found a clutch of rally cars parked up. I guess 'clutch' is the right word for a collection of rally cars?

I introduced myself to one of the AWF shipping agents who told me there were all sorts of problems.

"We're well behind as the shippers wouldn't accept the documents this morning. First they wanted an export licence for each of the vehicles, but of course the vehicles aren't being exported."

"Exactly, hopefully they're all coming back to the UK," I said.

"Yes, and then they said the Carnets are not suitable, although the RAC issue them all the time. However, we have managed to get round that but it held us up for a couple of hours this morning. You've probably done the right thing to come along now, as things are moving much faster. In fact, if all your documentation is in order and you want to get away, I can deal with everything here."

"Sounds like a good idea to me." This is exactly what I had hoped for and why I had left bringing the car to the docks late so that any problems could be ironed out early.

There were several familiar faces around including many of the organising team as their vehicles were amongst the twenty or so cars that were parked up. It seemed that those that arrived earlier on had now been moved to another compound following their paperwork being sorted out. As our man from AWF was happy to take over from us and let us go it seemed the best thing to do and our wedge of paperwork was signed for.

Pam and I had a look round at the other vehicles to see how they were packed and get some idea of what they were taking. There was all manner of ideas. One Toyota had a fridge fitted, whilst several had their kit stored in cardboard boxes in the back of their vehicles. I was content that we had done a good job on ours.

After a couple of photos we were probably back out of the docks within half an hour of arriving, much faster than everyone else, and were soon headed back home in the Mazda. Along the M25 we passed some big rigs from Benneton, McLaren and Arrows Formula 1 teams returning from the Hungarian Grand Prix.

Sending the car away was a major hurdle overcome and with it a sense of relief wafted over us. In essence all we had to do now was approach the trip as we would a foreign holiday – organise some currency, pack some clothes and get to the airport on time for the flight. There was more, of course, especially when the maps and road books arrived, but we now had a few weekends at home to get some DIY completed, catch our breath and prepare mentally for the trip ahead.

One thing I wanted to do now was concentrate on the charity fund raising I was linking to the trip. Like many other participants, I was trying to raise funds for charities and through Guildford Lions Club felt that a reasonable sum could be achieved.

I had been a member of Guildford Lions Club for nearly twenty years and during that time held many of the important posts in the Club culminating in a year as President that ended in June 2001. Guildford is one of the larger, more active Clubs in the UK where (with Eire) there are about 900 Lions Clubs and about 42,000 members. The motto of Lions Clubs is 'We serve' and most Club activities are centred round raising funds for charitable use locally, in the UK and worldwide. All the Clubs in the UK are part of the wider organisation - Lions Clubs International - based in the USA where the organisation first flourished in the early part of the twentieth century. There are now Lions Clubs in almost every country and about 1.25 million members worldwide.

Of course there would be South American based Lions and meeting up with other Lions is always a pleasure, so I decided to try and track down Clubs in the various towns we would be staying at on the Inca Trail. Almost all of these towns had a Club so I wrote to each one telling them about the event and when we would be passing through in the hope that we might make contact. I only heard back from a few by email - all very interested in what we were doing, some actually incredulous at what we were doing, and hoping to meet us.

In addition I put out sponsorship forms and gave a talk about the event and what it involved, both of which were well supported. At the talk somebody asked, "Why?"

"Because it's there of course."

Road Book

A sample page from the road book is shown opposite and is typical of the type of route instructions we used to follow the 25,000 kms route around South America. This page covers the start of the first long Explorer Section in the Andes just after crossing the border into Bolivia.

Each instruction is separately numbered, so that fresh amending instructions can easily be issued and added in or deleted. This happened on an almost daily basis as the Advanced Course Car running ahead of the rally identified changes that were needed, new hazards, or reported on road conditions.

We also added in our own extra information prior to the start of each day. This included reference to the map number, and what the length of a section was, in this case 331 kms (over 200 miles). Pam also added in times at regular intervals, just for the record. We finished this section in the town centre of Potosi at 5.30pm, but had left the Day Start Control in Jujuy at 6.30am.

The nature of the features we passed can also be identified too. We started just outside the town of Villazon and followed a 'main' road, but soon we were on tracks with river crossings. As each feature passed, Pam would tick off the instruction and zero the Brantz.

My thanks to HERO for permission to copy a page from the Road Book. There were four Road Books for the whole event, each with many thousands of individual instructions.

X8S = Start of Explorer Section 8

HERO · Historic Endurance Rallying Organisation

Inca Trail 4x4 Adventure Drive 2001

Road Book

X8S Villazon - DF8 Potosi

MAP 22

Row No	Interval km	Section km	Interval miles	Section miles	Symbol	Landmark/instruction
1	0.00	0.00	0.00	0.00		*11am start* X8S VILLAZON *SECTION 331 KMS.*
2	5.55	5.55	3.45	3.45		Km 240
3	6.48	12.03	4.03	7.48		Follow main road SP Tupiza (Route 702) (SP ↗ Tarija)
4	*.67* 0.75	12.78	0.47	7.94		
5	6.97	19.75	4.33	12.27		
6	0.86	20.61	0.53	12.81		Level crossing - line in use !
7	5.69	26.30	3.54	16.35		River bed crossing around bridge span
8	0.75	27.05	0.47	16.81		River bed - new road being built to L
9	0.81	27.86	0.50	17.32		
10	3.65	31.51	2.27	19.58		Slow

September

With the Colorado now on the high seas heading for the South Atlantic and Rio de Janeiro, preparations changed direction and we now concentrated on getting ourselves ready. By the end of September we had raised about £4,000 for our charities and the goodwill from people who we wouldn't be seeing again before we left was also terrific and very heart warming.

After some delays the first set of maps and road book for the event arrived. They covered the first sector of the rally from the start in Rio de Janeiro as far as Cusco in Peru. There were 36 beautifully prepared maps with the route clearly defined on them. All the controls and sections for the various categories of entrant were marked, together with detailed town maps so we could identify where we were due to stay overnight.

The road book was even more interesting. It covered the first 6,000 kms and there were just under a thousand separate instructions to consider. Every road and junction was described in tulip form with distances given from the previous instruction.

The really 'good' bits started once into Bolivia with a 330 kms (about 200 miles) section on a rough mountain road with dozens of watersplashes/fords identified with comments like:

- Wooden bridge – dodgy' *(and there were four of these in a row!)*
- Follow riverbed for 1200m
- Very rough – keep right
- In village go round bandstand

And did I say level crossing? From the information given in the road book it looked like 'level' crossing was a misnomer and some of them would be anything but level. The rest of the maps and road book would be given out when we were over in South America.

October

On Sunday 30th September we had a family day with both daughters and their boyfriends over for lunch and a briefing of what to do when we were away.

Oddly, on the same day another World Cup Rally started not far from home at the famous Brooklands Motor Museum near Weybridge about 10 miles up the road from us. So it was up and out at about 8.30am to drive up to Brooklands, see the cars start that event and then pick up mother-in-law and back home for about 11.30. Ideal.

This World Cup Rally was being organised by the Classic Rallying Association, the other main rally organisation in the United Kingdom, and was for cars up to 1,400cc (1,700cc for diesels) and although intended to be a clubman's event had attracted some 'works' cars, notably a couple of MGs. The entrants were due to drive through France and Spain, and then cross into Morocco for some fun on the edges of the Sahara Desert before returning home via Portugal.

All the cars were prepared to a minimum specification with all the usual safety gear, but almost everything else was standard. So unlike most rally cars there were no extra spotlights, special tyres and the like. They would be doing special stages and the result based on time, but this World Cup Rally route was about 6,000 miles over 12 days, about a third of what we had to tackle.

I met up with an old rally colleague, Roger Brackfield - we always seem to meet at these events - so it was a chance to catch up on news. Roger navigated for me on many occasions in the past.

I had set aside the last two days in the UK for all the many last minute jobs that inevitably needed to be done. We got up on Monday to find a fence panel had managed to blow over in the wind, and later when Pam put on some washing the machine threw a wobbly and we could smell some rubber burning from inside the machine. That could wait till we got home.

Some months ago our neighbour, Mirak, had volunteered to loan us a video camera to take on the trip, but he had been away on business and holidays for most of the summer and we had only seen him a couple of times since July. He was however home now and confirmed his company would still be interested in loaning us video equipment to take on the trip and make a donation towards the charities in return for use of the material.

I had a call from Mirak mid morning on Monday 1st October asking if I could call into his office at the Research Park adjoining Surrey University to meet his boss and sort something out. I duly met Mirak and Dr Paul Ratcliff and it was agreed that they would supply a video camera and all the necessary ancilliaries together with sufficient tapes to last the trip.

They would use the material produced for their research purposes in developing search and retrieval software for multi media data whilst I could use the recorded material to create our own personal video diary. Great.

Later that evening Mirak arrived with all the gear and 50 cassettes, each one enough to record an hour of material. It was going to take some editing. So we now had two ordinary film cameras, a digital still camera and the video camera to take with us!

My plan had been to put all the electronic equipment into one bag for transporting to South America as my hand baggage, but the awful events in New York and Washington on 11th September 2001 meant that we had to rethink this as the airline wanted everything in the hold. I eventually got agreement from Air France that we could carry my laptop and video camera, without their power supplies, with us in the plane, but everything else would have to be in the hold.

A visit to the barber's was also due. Keith who does lots of odd trips such as John O'Groats to Lands End by bike for charity and who normally cuts my hair had already collected £80 from customers, but unfortunately wasn't there on this visit. However, I learned that he had more funds to hand over which would have to wait for our return.

In the evening besides Mirak, Pam's brother Ian, and my successor as President of Guildford Lions, Andrew Henwood, called in to wish us luck. It was nice of both of them to take the time, and also those who phoned us with good wishes. We also received about a dozen cards and emails with the same message.

We were ready to go.

A High in the Andes

Inca Trail 4 x 4
Adventure Drive

In at the deep end

Day 1 Saturday 6 October
Rio de Janeiro - Ouro Preto (542 kms)

5…4…3…2…1… and at 8.21am we really did start the Inca Trail Adventure Drive as the Brazilian flag was dropped across the bonnet of our 4x4 at the Copacabana Fort with a backdrop of the famous Sugar Loaf Mountain.

We nearly didn't make it to the start at all. We were due to fly out via Paris on the previous Wednesday, 3rd October, but along with some other Inca Trailers were delayed 24 hours when a flight connection in Paris failed. Air France put us up for the night and we had a pleasant evening in Paris in the company of new friends Ted and Judy Howles driving a Reliant Scimitar on the Inca Trail. It was whilst we were on the Paris Metro that we first heard the famous South American pan pipes being played by buskers, not where we expected to hear them! In the end we caught the Thursday flight celebrating Pam's birthday on the flight with some Buck's Fizz, again not what we'd hoped for.

When we finally got to the hotel in Rio on Thursday evening, we had an enthusiastic welcome from other competitors, many of whom had been in Rio for a week or more. This left just 24 hours to make our final arrangements, including getting the car out of the docks and through Customs, but no time for any sightseeing. Fortunately getting the car was painless (although the bag containing our wet weather and winter gear and walking boots had been stolen) and by lunchtime we had it parked on the parade ground at Fort Copacabana with all the other cars taking part.

The Fort was an ideal place from which to start the Inca Trail. It stands on a promontory between the famous Copacabana and Ipanema Beaches, and with the rally headquarters based in the Sofitel Hotel over the road everything was conveniently placed.

We also learned that John Brown was none too well and would have to head back to the UK immediately after the rally started. John is of ample proportions and heart problems demanded investigatory procedures. He had spent three years planning the Inca Trail Rally and it must have been a severe blow to have to do this, leaving the day to day management of the rally to his team, colloquially known as the Red Team as they all wore red T-shirts. John planned to be back for the finish, sooner if he could. At the start line, photos and videos were taken and once out of the Fort the initial run was out of Rio along the waterfront, past the docks on roads taking us north. Naturally we were both nervous at the start, Pam more so than me, and neither of us wanted to make any major mistakes in the first few miles. After leaving the Fort it wasn't long before we caught up with George and Barbel Pollnow who as car number A34 left a minute before us. We followed for a few kilometres but Pam then had a fright whilst we were still on the first page of the road book when they forked left at a junction and she told me to go right.

"Are you sure, A34 has gone left?"

"If this is the right junction we go the other way," Pam confirmed.

"I think that must be correct as we go out of town past the docks and I remember we went right yesterday when we went over to collect the car."

"Go right then," confirmed Pam and I was pleased to hear some certainty in her voice.

I had slowed down just in case we needed to go left, so I now picked up pace. The next junction fitted the instructions properly so we headed on with greater confidence, unlike some crews who ended up doing several circuits of the city trying to find their way out.

Soon afterwards we passed by the Hotel Gloria which had been the headquarters for the original London-Mexico World Cup Rally teams when they had arrived in Rio following a sea crossing from Lisbon back in 1970. Nearly a hundred cars had started that rally too, and following a tour of the best European rallying locations only about 60 cars restarted here. They would go around South America in a clockwise direction, whilst our route, which was common to theirs in a few places, was essentially anti-clockwise. For now we headed north out of Rio, whilst back in 1970 they headed south.

Pam did well and we were soon out of the city and into the countryside, very glad not to be heading the other way back into Rio for there were horrendous traffic jams, at least 15 kms long.

Seeing other entrants on the road boosted the confidence factor and from time to time we ran along with other 4x4s as we headed into the first attraction of the trip, the Mirante do Cristo, a view spot at the top of a 20 kms climb on a twisting dual carriageway. The view across the verdant hillsides was splendid, but we didn't stay long and were on our way again after a few minutes. The route turned off the main road to join that running towards Teresopolis where the classic rally cars would start their first test, a 27 kms Regularity Section they had to complete at a set speed of 50 kph. Marshals were checking their progress at hidden points along the way.

Having started the day before us, the classics were already through and away, but we soon came across a road hazard that was to be all too familiar during the next few weeks - speed humps. In South America they seem to take their speed humps more seriously than we do back at home with our nicely rounded and smooth topped sleeping plods. In South America they can be vicious and they roam in packs, perhaps three or four in close formation. Sleeping policemen they were not, vicious SS thugs they were.

In Teresopolis there were many, often in twos and threes, and it had also started raining, but only for a short while. We were now in the Serra dos Orgaos, mountains with impressive organ pipe stacks of rock and as the weather cleared on our way north so the views became better. This was farming country with many stables and dairy herds.

The small town of Uba was our next target, but not before we managed to head down a one-way street the wrong way, along with several other 4x4s. By now we were travelling with some of the classics – were they having problems and running late, or were we ahead of schedule? We weren't too sure.

Uba marked the start of another test for the classics, a medal section mainly on gravel roads. On this 107 kms section they had to maintain an average of 55 kph. The same farm roads formed the basis for our first test, with the 4x4s turning off onto more rustic roads and going a little further at 127 kms. We had no average speed to maintain, as the finish control would be open to 4x4s for several hours.

Our Explorer Section was a great start to the event. With the rain it was slightly damp, although dust from other vehicles became a problem in some places, and there were occasional patches of mud, puddles and all manner of bends to negotiate. For the most part the road was in good condition, except where we passed through villages. Here the road condition would either deteriorate rapidly, or be constructed of cobbles or stones that were rough to drive over with a 4x4 fitted with stiffish suspension.

My approach to the event was to treat each Explorer Section as a special stage allowing safety margins for possible oncoming traffic, which there was, and for the longevity of the event. No point in blowing it on the first day. So for us it was full speed through the Section and it was thoroughly enjoyable except where, from time to time, we came upon other 4x4s taking it easier. One reason for entering the Inca Trail was that it isn't possible to cover these distances on such challenging, unmade roads in the UK and it was all as good as expected. Already I was having a great time.

One small village was particularly charming with houses spread out around a football pitch with dark green trees acting as an umbrella over them. The road ran round the edge of the pitch, passing a little chapel before crossing a stream on the way out into the countryside again. On the turn was a little shop and outside was the worldwide logo of Wall's ice cream. We didn't stop and buy one.

Several of the bridges over streams were narrow plank affairs and needed particular care as one approached them to be sure the front wheels were in the right place.

The attitude of the locals was mainly indifference. A few waved at us encouragingly, whilst others took no interest at our passing.

All too soon the test ended as we arrived at the finish control in the village of Padre Viegas where a small crowd had gathered around the marshal's car. Here we rejoined the tarmac and were soon heading off towards our overnight stop near the city of Ouro Preto about 40 kms away.

Dusk was falling and the road was reasonably fast and we soon fell in behind the Lancia Flavia Coupe of Roberto Chiodi and decided to follow him to the hotel rather than overtake. The SS intervened here and we watched as Roberto slowed down for a set of humps going very gently over the first, then the second. But he clearly hadn't given a thought to the third hump as he then put his foot down to pick up speed again only to hit a third SS agent at full pace. The front of the car lurched into the air and crashed down again with sparks flying off the undercarriage at the rear of the car, the petrol tank guard taking the full force of the tarmac. He slowed immediately and pulled up to check for damage as we passed by on our way.

Everyone on the rally was due to stay in the same hotel for a couple of nights, but the car park wasn't really up to taking so many cars and they were parked all over the place, many already being worked on after the rigours of the day.

We found a spot for ourselves and before checking in to the hotel had a quick look over our 4x4. All seemed well. The tyres had no damage, we'd used no oil and everything was where it should be. The car was of course very dirty with the mud and dirt of the day's roads, a sure sign that I had had a good day's driving. Normally the dirtier the car gets the more fun I've had and this was an eight day on a scale of one to ten. We'd been on the road for a full ten hours with only short breaks and little food. If this was the Inca Trail we wanted more. We put a large tick against day one; only fifty-four to go.

However in the bar it was a different story as there were already complaints. Many of the classic drivers were moaning about the roughness of the route, especially so early in the event. Many cars hadn't arrived yet and as a result of all the penalties they would thus attract already had no chance of any medal in the final results. Quite rightly they were very disgruntled. Already the number of classics eligible for a Gold medal was down to 14 crews and even one of the Mitsubishi course cars had suffered a problem. A battery cell had caught fire and spread into the engine bay, although it was soon put out.

A Volvo arrived very late at the hotel after it also had a fire when the fan managed to make contact with a fuel line, whilst a lovely Portuguese Porsche suffered a holed fuel tank.

We soon headed for the hotel restaurant for a meal with some of the other 4x4 crews. By comparison everyone was on a high. Many 4x4 crews were novices at any form of rallying and had been worried about the duration of each day and following the road book tulips. These had all been all right. We heard of nobody with any serious mechanical problems although our Guildford friends, Peter and Carolynn, were already suffering with soft shock absorbers. In addition some crews were already complaining about having to drive in the dark.

Catching breath

Day 2 Sunday 7 October
Ouro Preto

Pam and I both woke early and as it had been dark when we arrived the previous evening, I took a walk round to see what condition the various cars were in and to get a feel for our surroundings. Surprisingly many of the cars were very clean, whilst ours was very muddy and dirty. On a walk along the approach road to the hotel I found a building site where there was a hose attached to a tap, so I quickly moved the car up there and gave it a wash. It wasn't brilliant, but it was cleaner than it had been.

We were now in Minas Gerais province and as the hotel was on the side of a hill there should have been a good view to the south but this was shrouded in low cloud that would last all day.

There was no travelling today as all the cars were due to leave the hotel in convoy to drive into the centre of Ouro Preto to be displayed for the general public. It took an age to get the cars together but eventually we were all lined up in the approach road and began the short drive through the hills to the centre of town where we were parked up in the main square. We would all be released again at lunchtime after which the day was our own.

The cloud was still low and as Ouro Preto is perched on a hilltop it often interfered with what should have been excellent views around the area and its many splendid buildings. The town is a World Heritage Site so as to protect the many buildings which date from colonial times and are still in good condition. Many are churches and at one a wedding was in progress adding extra colour to the scene.

Along one side of the square was an official looking building with lots of music, shouting and laughing coming from the upper floor. We went to investigate and found that local schoolchildren were taking dancing and gymnastic examinations. There were a couple of hundred children, mainly dressed in white costumes, together with many parents, examiners and others.

I was taking photos on the stage when Pam called me over as some local Lions had arrived. They knew we were due in town and had seen the 4x4 outside and tracked us down to meet and exchange memorabilia.

The rest of the day was pretty relaxed. We sorted the car out a bit more and felt satisfied we had now caught up with ourselves after the frantic start. It was a chance too for meeting other crews and getting their feel for the event. As we found last evening it depended in which class you entered. David Moffat had the Bentley S2 he uses for classic rallying on the jack and was working underneath it. He wasn't too happy with HERO. As he put it, one expects some rough roads, but in short stretches on non-competitive sections, but not miles and miles of rough and car damaging tracks set against the clock, especially so soon in the event.

The lovely little red Alfa Romeo Guila Sprint of Geoff and Jenny Dorey had serious problems. On a bump it had launched into the air and the engine had pushed up through the bonnet. One of the Porsches had electrical problems.

We began to wonder how long we would last before we had problems to sort out so went and found our 4x4 and checked it over again. The rally had had a baptism of fire and we wanted to last the course. Today's rest day had offered a chance for everyone to catch their breath and consider what lay before them - the next rest day wouldn't be till we reached Cusco in Peru, ten days and 5,580 kms away via some fearsome rally sections.

We were in bed by 8.30pm.

Mud, mud glorious mud

Day 3 Monday 8 October
Ouro Preto - Campos de Jordeo (547 kms)

The day dawned wet and misty again and we were on the road a few minutes after seven. We faced a long run, mainly on tarmac, before an Explorer Section in the late afternoon over a wooded mountain that would lead to our next stop in Campos de Jordeo. We were soon out onto the road and made good progress in rain southwest through arable farmland to a coffee stop in Tiradentes, a little town previously known as Sao Joao del Rei.

This was a sweet little place, although as we approached I doubted where we were actually heading. Having been on main roads all morning with easy driving, the route took us along some fairly poor gravel roads into the back end of the town, but then we were rewarded with a visit to Brazil's version of Bourton on the Water. Like Bourton, Tiradentes is a honey pot and deservedly attracts visitors from around the world.

A stream ran through the village with neat little cobbled stone bridges, one of which led us to a broad green sward where many of the rally cars were parked up. Adjacent to this was a lovely hotel, run by an Englishman - John Parsons, and built in the style of a colonial mansion and overgrown with acacias inhabited by some inquisitive tamarin monkeys. Coffee was being served here, in what is reputedly one of Brazil's finest hotels.

Here we learned that the rally cars continued to have problems. The huge Chrysler Imperial le Baron which carried four spare tyres on brackets cantilevered out over the rear bumper had blown its head gasket, a part not easy to come by. We wouldn't see the car again for some weeks as the driver, Ruedi Mueller, allegedly flew home to have a new one made, returned to Brazil and then drove across Argentina to join us all again in Salta.

In the town square were donkey-drawn carts and taxis, I suspect because the cobbled roads in the immediate area were so rough that local people rarely took their vehicles over them. Rally cars and 4x4s had no alternative.

All too soon we were heading on our way again on fast main roads, mainly along the top of hills. Local wildlife was evident from time to time and we saw a couple of toucans, egrets and many other birds we couldn't identify.

Although the road was generally good tarmac in a couple of places, often with no warning it suddenly became gravel. It maintained main road status and width and we found ourselves overtaking some of the classics, including the Aston Martin of Ralph and Dorothy Jones. With all the recent rain this length of road had suffered badly and on an uphill stretch we had to pick out a passable route between deep trenches cut out of the sandy gravel base by flows of rainwater. The Aston must have had a tough time here.

The classics had a time control at a garage on the edge of the little town of Piranguinho and as the roads had mainly been easy they were well ahead of time and had to wait at the control till their due time came up. They were parked all around the petrol station whilst most people had a spot of lunch or a drink. We decided to stop and join them and I ordered a cheeseburger from a pleasant, blonde, young woman who didn't appear to be Brazilian and spoke very good English. She turned out to be Norwegian on a student exchange!

It was still raining slightly and with so many rally cars around the garage the scene reminded me of November RAC Rally controls in Wales, the main difference being that we were in shorts and tee shirts and it was very warm and humid.

Not far from here our Explorer Section for the day started. This was a gravelly track over the mountains to Campos de Jordeo. With all the rain the track was nice and muddy and we were soon slipping and slithering our way upwards using our lower gearing. Somehow we were in the company of a gaggle of other 4x4s and this seemed to me to be a bit dangerous, as although we were travelling slowly, we were sliding across the whole road and sometimes were too close together.

At the start of a particularly long slope we stopped and watched the fun, letting a couple of 4x4s behind us come past. Once we had a clear run we had our own go and gently made our way up the long slope. This was great and proper 4x4 driving. What I had come for.

The track levelled out and wound through some woods dotted with rustic cottages, many with lovely gardens, and once again we were soon in a convoy. Near one pair of cottages we all came to a stop and in front there was the Toyota Amazon of Chris Elliott and Linda Banks stuck at 45 degrees in a ditch at the side of the track.

We waited in the car for a few moments, but whilst we could all get by there were no plans to leave Chris and Linda stuck, so gradually everyone got out to see how we could help.

The track was very slippery and curved slightly right over a narrow plank bridge. The approach to the bridge was very chewed up and Chris had slipped off on the right, the side of his car resting on a hedge with a fence running through it. It was soon clear he couldn't be pulled out forwards as the ditch drained out into a deep cutting under the bridge, so it would be a reverse job.

Chris tried several times to reverse out under his own steam but without success, although he got very close. Roger Lucas in another Amazon was first up behind Chris so agreed to try and pull him out. With a committee of seven other 4x4 drivers giving instructions, several out with their video cameras recording the whole episode for posterity, the two Amazons were hooked together and Roger gave it a go.

Revving, slithering and sliding by both cars took place for a couple of minutes and again Chris was nearly out, but not quite. The car had been moved further back from the cutting, but was also pulling the fence away.

Roger came close to dropping his own car into the ditch in his attempts to pull Chris's out so decided that he would head on to the next control. Amazons are big cars, probably the heaviest in the event, and we all recognized that the next couple of 4x4s in line weren't man enough to try pulling so they headed on too.

More 4x4s had arrived by now including Sir Terence English's Toyota on which he carried sand ladders. These were tried in an effort to get some grip under the Amazon, again without success.

While this was going on, a VW Beetle arrived from the other direction with four people in it. The track was blocked by about eight 4x4s by now but he was keen to get by, so just went for it, humbling us all as he drove round the queue half in the ditch and half on the track and away. A bit embarrassing really.

We were next in the queue so we took a turn at trying to pull the Amazon out, the idea now being to lift the back of it out of the ditch and onto better ground that had grip. We lined up across the track at 90 degrees and gave it a go, but it was well stuck and, like Roger before us, we risked dropping off the track ourselves. We decided to head on and straightened up very gingerly, offered Linda a lift to Campos which she declined, and bade farewell.

We made our way out of the section and not long after hit tarmac, but with it darkness, rain and thick mist. Rallying is a perverse sport as the worse the conditions are, the greater the challenge is and the greater the enjoyment – masochistic I suppose. But this was great. The road wound its way off the mountain and for about 20 minutes my eyes were on stalks up against the lenses of my glasses as I tried to pick out the road and at the same time maintain a good pace. I'd done this many times on rallies in the UK and previous experience paid off.

In the past several parts of Brazil were colonized by German émigrés and our overnight stop in Campos de Jordeo was one of the towns that has subsequently been developed as a tourist centre and looked like it should have been in Bavaria. Through the persistent heavy rain we could see the buildings clearly followed Germanic architectural styles.

The control was in the town square and it was obvious from all the barriers and plastic tape strung between the trees that earlier there had been a big crowd of people present. However in the rain, and after our hour's delay on the mountain, the only person present was Julie Eaglen, HERO's Press Officer, who had drawn the short straw and had to wait to check us in.

Pam and I had both looked forward to getting to Campos as I had been in touch with the local Lions Club and was assured they would meet with us, and Pam, being a tennis fanatic was keen to enjoy a reception at the local tennis club laid on for the Inca Trailers by the town. Pam had even talked about the possibility of playing some tennis.

We found the club, but there were very few people there and most of the food and drink had been ransacked by the classic crews, who had taken a shorter and smoother route to the town, leaving little behind. We consumed what we could and tried in vain to track down some Lions. They had either gone or forgotten about us.

Our hotel for the night, the Quatre Saison, was back up another hill and was difficult to find in the mist but the tulips in the road book worked a treat as they pinpoint exactly where there is a junction or turning. Once we had tracked it down we were soon inside and settled in our room that was actually a small two-storey apartment with plenty of space. There was an underground car park, but we couldn't find the entrance so left the car outside, the steady rain running down the bodywork washing off the mud onto the car park. By morning there were little piles of mud under all the cars. The mud index today was the best of the trip at 9.5.

For the first time we had a proper four-course meal sharing a table with Dari Shalon and Orph Nachum, both young Israelis. They were in a Mitsubishi L200 they had bought from Peter Rushforth. Dari was a keen Toyota Colorado enthusiast and wanted to know all about ours. He'd taken part in the London - Capetown rally in a Colorado and also the famous Paris - Dakar Rally and used one at home in Israel as his personal transport.

"The best 4x4 in the world," he said. I was beginning to form the same view.

"You mean best 4x4 by far, don't you?" I replied, borrowing the Land Rover slogan.

Getting into a routine

Day 4 Tuesday 9 October
Campos de Jordeo – Londrina (815 kms)

Two Explorer Sections had been planned for today, one just outside Campos and another further on shared with the classics.

Confusion reigned at breakfast about whether or not the first Section up to a local view spot called Bau Rock was being run. First we were told it was cancelled because the tracks were too damaged after the rains, then that it was on, then that we could go through if we wanted to.

We headed off to the Day Start Control and learned that the Chris Elliott Amazon was still stuck in the woods. Further attempts to extract it last night failed, so he and Linda were given a lift down to the hotel and were going back today with some forestry workers to try and get the Amazon out. In the end it took a tracked bulldozer to do it. He'd also learned that he wasn't the first vehicle to go off the road at that point. The course car had slipped off too, but managed to get back on with minimal fuss, and one of the big American 4x4s had also chewed up the road when he struggled to get back onto the straight and narrow. It seems Chris happened to be the next one along and.....

Along the main road through Campos we came across several 4x4s all wanting to know whether or not to give the Section a go and asking what our plans were. We decided to take a look at it to see what was happening, but when we turned up the approach road to the Section we came upon the Israeli lads coming back down. They had been up to the Control, been told it was cancelled and decided to head back down and carry on to the next Section via the main roads. It seemed the best thing for us to do and we followed them.

The second Section, about 60 kms through farmland and forests was a treat. With the recent rain there was plenty of mud and water about and the sandy gravel tracks made for some great driving. For the classics the story was different, and several went off in the mud and others had major mechanical problems. The end of the section came all too soon for us and as Mike Johnson and Bill Price checked our time card we heard of some of the problems encountered.

The A90 of John Blanckley had damaged a wheel, it would suffer much greater problems later, whilst the big Dutch Rover P5 had gone off and been towed into the finish control by a 4x4, and several cars had damaged exhausts.

It was no time before we were back onto main roads. These would make up the rest of the day as we sped across country to reach Londrina for the night.

The countryside was much like Wiltshire at times and the roads were busy with many lorries. Overtaking these was generally easy, but with many hills and blind brows their drivers were usually very helpful in letting us pass. If they used their right indicators the road wasn't clear, but when they started indicating left we could safely go. It took a little while and some tricky experiments to work out this code, but once we had it sussed it hastened our progress.

Along the way we passed around the city of Campinas, passing around three sides on a motorway with lots of roadworks. Here in Brazil, managing traffic flows at roadworks is normally very different to the alternating traffic light flows that we have in the UK. One might have to wait 15 minutes for traffic the other way to cease before getting a chance to make headway. And then it was everyone for themselves.

On one occasion we were stopped at the bottom of a long uphill road being widened into a dual carriageway. We were held up behind a lorry, so once we had the all clear to go, started to overtake him (on his left of course) only to find he was doing the same to another slower moving lorry, that in turn had to pull out to avoid a road digger. In between were other cars and the whole scene was reminiscent of a Le Mans start. We actually ended up on the hard shoulder on the other side of the dual carriageway, the central reservation still not built, as we passed the lorries chugging up the hill.

We also learned another little trick from the locals – overtaking on the nearside hard shoulder. With so many lorries it was inevitable that we followed many up twisting hills, double centre lines and sight lines making it difficult to overtake. Nearly all main roads have a gravel hard shoulder and we noted the locals used this for overtaking in such cases, zipping past on our right. Well, when in Rome...... and soon we followed the same procedure.

Londrina, which takes its name from London, was a sizeable city and we arrived in the dark after 700 kms on the road to a splendid brass band welcome in front of the cathedral. They really laid it on, although the large crowd that gathered to see the classics arrive had largely disappeared.

More classics were in trouble and one of the local garages pulled out all the stops and stayed open all night to help them out.

Wet, wet, wet

Day 5 Wednesday 10 October
Londrina – Foz de Iguacu (530 kms)

Overnight we heard that some 4x4s went through the cancelled section and thoroughly enjoyed the trip leaving us a bit annoyed and wondering why HERO had cancelled it. However we also learned that one of the two Camel Trophy Discoveries had fallen over onto its side, but was soon righted without any significant damage.

Today would be a short drive, only 500 kms, so we could get to Foz de Iguacu with time to take a look at the famous waterfalls. Famous may be the wrong word as like many people I had hardly heard of them till I became involved with the Inca Trail, but the falls are higher and wider than either Niagara or Victoria and most people who have been to the others claim that the Foz de Iguacu are much better.

First, though, we had a cross country run on main roads on which, for the most part, high average speeds were possible. Today would be our last day in Brazil till we were near the end of the Inca Trail on the home run and we felt a touch of foreboding as we would be crossing into Argentina tomorrow to begin the trek across to the Andes in a couple of days time. For now though it was press on to the falls.

With all the problems the classics were having over the last couple of days, they were regularly seen at various garages along the route getting attention. Our friends Ted and Judy Howles in their Reliant Scimitar were one of these and with a need for constant attention to their gearbox we often saw their car up on a ramp with Ted working underneath. Others too would be working on their cars, perhaps not in a workshop but quietly parked up in a corner of a forecourt, car jacked up, tools and spare parts spread around.

We were having a few problems too, the most serious one remained the CD player that was jumping tracks on road humps! The Colorado was going well and Pam and I had settled into a routine.

The areas around the falls, which are on the border between Argentina and Brazil, are national parks and at the entrance we were greeted by a representative from the local tourist office who gave us loads of gifts and then we enjoyed a pleasant drive up to the Cataracts Hotel, overlooking the falls themselves.

The noise from the water crashing over the falls can be heard for miles around and the anticipation of our first sight grew as we approached. We weren't disappointed as the falls were in full flood and there in front of the hotel they were spread out in an arc of crashing white thunder. Amazing is an understatement.

We checked in as quickly as we could and set off with cameras to take a closer look. A walkway leads down in front of the hotel along the cliffs providing exciting views of the falls as well as a gentle shower of spray.

We would learn later that the rain of recent weeks meant the water flow over the falls was more than ten times normal; such was the quantity of water that instead of the usual 275 individual falls over their 2.5 kms width there were far fewer as they were joined together.

From the cliff path a spur has been built leading out to a viewing platform over a natural rock outcrop below some of the falls, in fact Prime Minister Tony Blair had been photographed on it in May 2001 when he made an official visit to Brazil. With the flow of water now, it would have been too dangerous to venture out there and it was closed.

Up in the corner of the falls, nearest the Brazilian bank, another platform enables the public to stand virtually underneath the water coming over the top. I imagine that on normal days the water comes nowhere near the platform itself, but today it was crashing over it. It was stupendous – a curtain of continuous white foaming water thundering down. We were getting very wet.

We wandered back to the hotel as we were due to go on a boat trip on the river below the falls. I was debating whether or not to go as I get motion sickness very easily and really didn't fancy a bout whilst on the rally as it can take me a day or two to get over it. To decide whether or not to go on the boat trip, I tossed a coin - I would be going.

A coach took us a couple of miles along the approach road to Macuco where boat rides start. Macuco is a type of bird found locally which is unique in that the male of the species nests the beautiful blue eggs laid by the female and raises the young. We didn't see any, but instead there were plentiful yellowy-orange butterflies that congregated on salt patches.

After applying liberal doses of mosquito repellent, a jeep with passenger trailers took us down to the riverside and the jetty to board twin-engined rubber inflatables taking about 30 people. After donning life jackets and taking our shoes off, we climbed aboard with other Inca Trailers and Pam and I both managed to get front seats.

I reckon the pilots of such boats have to be adrenalin-seekers as they are there to provide thrills for the tourists several times a day. And, of course, Inca Trailers suffer from the same adrenalin-seeking condition. Put the two together on a river in full flood. Well!

Ride of a lifetime doesn't really do it justice. The boat dipped and rolled through the surging, foaming water as we made our way upstream against the incredibly strong current downstream from the falls. From time to time the pilots made the front of the boat dip under advancing rollers so that about 3 or 4 inches of river water washed over the front – just where we were sitting. We were drenched in seconds and it was impossible to stop the water getting into our mouths. This came nil on the taste scale and it certainly wasn't up to EU drinking water quality standards.

The boat paused in front of the falls where the noise was a roaring crescendo of sound. Then the boat was taken right under the falls, the water crashing down on our heads from about 50 metres. It hurt! They did this about half a dozen times and we now know what it must be like to ride inside a washing machine.

We were wet, very wet, but the buzz was terrific. I was glad I went.

The rest of the day was tame by comparison. A great barbecue in the evening and for those who wanted a talk from one of the medics about the problems arising from altitude we might encounter in a few days time. If we were planning to take it, now was the time to start on medication for altitude sickness. We had weighed up the pros and cons before the trip and decided against, as the side effects appeared to be worse than the sickness.

Despite a continuous roar from the falls we slept well.

Jesuit Missions

Day 6 Thursday 11 October
Foz de Iguacu – Corrientes (640 kms)

Although today's run was due to be nearly 700 kms, we had no Explorer Sections to do so decided we would head back into Iguacu town before hitting the route to try and replace some of the clothing we had had stolen from the car at the docks. We left the hotel at 7.15am having first had another quick glimpse at the falls.

However, they were shrouded in mist which, combined with spray, made them difficult to see.

After about three tours of the town we found an outdoor clothing shop and bought a couple of anoraks, and then Pam found a shoe shop and replaced her missing walking boots.

A word or two about shoe shops is due here, because throughout Brazil, and later Argentina, we noticed a passion for shoe shops in all the towns we visited; and they were all busy too. Is shoe fetishism endemic in South America?

I also needed to get a couple of bits for the car and found an accessory shop that had what I needed - windscreen wiper blades and the local equivalent of WD40. The only 'problem' with the car so far was a stripped wiper blade, whilst WD40 was something I had somehow managed to leave behind.

The chap behind the counter was drinking maté tea, a concoction that we saw being drunk throughout our trip in various guises. His was in a large ornate mug, possibly pewter, from which he drank the tea through a straw, which was pushed through a wad of leaves.

Maté, (the word is taken from Quechua the language of those living in the highlands of Bolivia), is a serious business in this part of the world. It is the national drink of both Argentina and Uruguay and associated with it are various rituals almost as rigid as those of the tea drinking ceremonies in Japan. Herbs and leaves are placed in the maté flask, often ornately carved gourds, and hot water added. It is then drunk through a bombilla, these days a metal straw, but in the past through a reed.

The man had all the paraphernalia of the maté ritual: a special water heater that heats the water without boiling it and an insulated flask to keep top-up water hot.

He sucked regularly through the bombilla as we were doing business. I was inquisitive, hadn't expected to be offered the flask, but couldn't refuse when he did.

I gingerly took a suck and the water was foul. OK it wasn't to my taste, but it was bitter, grainy and had an aftertaste that lasted hours. I smiled politely and handed the maté back, offered a gracias and was glad when business was done.

On today's route the first job of the day was to cross the border into Argentina, this being the first of fifteen border crossings we would undertake in the next few weeks. Help was on hand from Hugo Bogetti from the Automobile Club of Argentina and as we were one of the last cars to reach the border because of our shopping trip, the process had been refined and only took about an hour. Some of the early arrivals had taken over two and a half hours to get through.

We were soon on the way again, the road being through the Argentinean national park around the falls region that was lush and tropical. Soon there was more open countryside, but hillier.

The classics did a short test in the morning and we all stopped for lunch at the ruins of the Jesuit Mission at San Ignacio Mini. The Jesuits were some of the first foreigners to move into the region and this mission was built at the turn of the sixteenth century. There are displays depicting life at the time the Mission was active but the stone buildings are now derelict and well spread out but carefully looked after. This was really quite a pleasant and interesting diversion, but too hot to stay in the sun for long.

The route today wasn't too inspiring although towards the end, perhaps the last 200 kms, we passed along marshland at the edge of the Parana River that forms the border with Paraguay. It was very much like southern Florida with many birds, including heron, and only occasional villages. Strangely there were few lorries on the road, and Pam was glad of that because she had a spell behind the wheel. If lorries were few, the filling stations were a rarer breed still along this road, and several people had problems finding enough fuel.

We came across Chris Denham in his Alvis Grey Lady at one fuel station, but it was money he didn't have, so we loaned him $25.

The Day Finish Control had been set up at a garage on the outskirts of Corrientes and when we got there we found there was a political demonstration going on. There were several hundred people, mainly young, with banners and posters and several bands playing the loud uncoordinated umphaa music so characteristic of South America. Just a noise, not music.

It was all very friendly, but we were rerouted away from another demonstration further in town and led by a roundabout route to the riverside where a special car park had been established for all the Inca Trail vehicles overnight on the Costenera. This was a pleasant shady promenade alongside the river, here about a mile wide. The sun was just setting over the other side and a huge bridge dominated the scene. A large crowd had gathered to watch us arrive and unpack our overnight bags to board a coach that would take us through town to our hotels.

HERO really splashed out on hiring the coach – it was a wreck! The windscreen had numerous cracks, side windows were broken with some replaced by board. The seating was worn and torn. Once we were underway it was no better with 50 mechanical experts second-guessing the noises coming from below the floor.

"Offside wheel bearing, I think," said one.

"No, it's the nearside," came another.

"And the exhaust is blowing badly," from a third.

"Does someone want to check the toilet for leaks?" Said a fourth.

And so it went on. We were all surprised to actually reach our hotels for the night. We ate that night with David and Carole Angel and also Howard Seymour and Ann Bennett for whom trouble with their Range Rover hadn't yet become apparent. However, it would be the last we would see of Howard and Ann for many weeks.

Chaco

Day 7 Friday 12 October
Corrientes – Jujuy (813 kms)

HERO Luxury Coaches picked us up from our hotel as promised to take us to the rally car park on the promenade. They rattled and rolled through the quiet streets of early morning Corrientes, a contrast to the vibrant bustle of last night. We were dropped back on the promenade facing the Parana River and in the shadow of the huge bridge that would take us across to Chaco Province and our day's run to Jujuy.

We set off at 6.35am and were soon onto and over the Belgrano Bridge. Initially the weather was overcast as we skirted Resistancia and headed out onto the arrow straight Ruta 16 that would take us through the Chaco.

The rally route today would be a transport section, one to take us as quickly as possible to the more interesting rallying territory the Andes had to offer. The Chaco is vast and flat, its rivers flowing south, eventually emptying into the Atlantic at Buenos Aires. Initially on our east-west route the scenery was green and if not verdant, certainly there was plenty of growth with colourful flowers and plants, but the further west we travelled the Chaco became drier and more barren, and the vegetation with it.

There were many settlements, more than we imagined, but they seemed meagre, hard places to live and work. At one we saw a very heavily laden pick-up truck turn onto the main road in front of us and then turn off the other side, heading towards some houses. Someone was moving house as it was laden with household goods with a wardrobe strapped to the roof of the cab, and a huge pile of belongings on the back. If the wind had caught it, the whole rig would have toppled over.

We stopped for fuel in one isolated community and were immediately set upon by a dozen children wanting to wash the car. I let them do the screen which they did by climbing on the front wheels to gain height, whilst others did the side and rear window and headlamps. Each got a small sum for their efforts and they awaited the next car with anticipation.

There was little traffic on the road except for lorries and long distance coaches, but such traffic as there was usually drove with little regard for anything else. On one poor quality stretch a white van coming the other way suddenly swung onto our side, ignoring us, so as to avoid some potholes. We had to take avoiding action onto the verge.

At the only significant junction on Ruta 16, about halfway across we stopped again for more fuel and a comfort stop before remembering to take the right fork out from the garage to continue our northwesterly journey. One crew, who must have been having a bad hair day, failed to do this and carried on the other road for over 250 kms before realising their mistake and had to backtrack, taking several hours out of the day.

Eventually we came to Ruta 34, the main north-south road along the eastern side of the Andes and turned north towards a fast four-lane highway that took us towards San Salvador de Jujuy, normally referred to by its last name only, pronounced Hughy-Hughy (as in the boy's name).

As we approached, I was debating whether or not to turn off and follow the classics and try and photograph them on a section they were due to do off the main road. We reached the junction but there was a police control there and all the cars were sent left and advised to enter Jujuy by that route because there had been an accident on the main road.

We followed this new road for some way. It was a good two-lane highway and in a few miles we came upon a turning to the left that led to the start of the classics medal section. It was soon apparent that this was a private or restricted access road and on speaking to Don Griffiths, the marshal, were told we couldn't go any further. The road ran through some vineyards and then around the edge of a reservoir. It then rejoined the road we had been on previously before dropping into Jujuy city.

We stopped for a while but decided to make our way back and into town. This diversion illustrated the importance of being aware of the maps as we were issued with no tulips for this diversion, although a few HERO direction arrows were erected at key junctions.

On the outskirts of Jujuy we pulled into a garage for yet more fuel and supplies so we would be ready for tomorrow's early morning start. As we pulled out of the garage back onto the road, we saw a police car coming from our left with lights ablaze and he sounded a brief burst on his siren as he drove straight through traffic lights set at red. Behind him, in formation, were half a dozen rally cars led by the Bentley of the Moffats and taking the rear were two police outriders.

The outriders saw us and signalled for us to join the end of the cavalcade, which we did, and with police outriders sped into the centre of town through red traffic lights and, at times, against the flow of the traffic. Other police were manning the road junctions holding up other traffic and in moments we were into the main square and the final control for the day. Here in front of the cathedral, a brass band was playing once more and there was a sizeable crowd to greet us. There would be more finishes like this and each of them made us feel very special and welcome.

We soon found our hotel, the Augustus, and parked in the car park that became very crowded as other classics and 4x4s arrived. We checked in and the management advised us we had been given adjoining rooms as they couldn't offer us a King size bed. We decided one room and a Queen size bed was adequate.

We had a wander round town trying to get one of the cameras fixed, something that was eventually done by a computer shop. It was a digital camera on loan to me on which images were stored on floppy disks that I planned to download to my laptop. Unfortunately we had problems with a disk getting stuck.

Like others, we were aware that tomorrow was the first of the big, tough tests so we wanted an early meal. There would also be the altitude to handle and we were feeling pretty tired from several days travel and early starts.

We soon found a pizza place and with a mix of other classic and 4x4 crews had a very enjoyable meal. This was interrupted briefly by a noisy procession that passed right by with groups of dancers, mainly children, in bright costumes jumping up and down like monkeys in time with a raucous band. Despite making enquiries, we never found out what it was all about.

We were fed and watered and in our cosy Queen size bed by 9.30pm.

Butch Cassidy and the Sundance Kid

Day 8 Saturday 13 October
Jujuy - Potosi (631 kms)

We had been on the road for a week and the first of the big long tests would be today. The alarm was set for 4.30am and it was still dark at 6.10am when we left the control set up in the main town square. The road out of town was policed so we had no routing problems and were soon heading north on the main road towards the border with Bolivia.

Just outside town there is a road to the west that leads up to the Sierra de Chani passing the local thermal baths and on which the classics would be doing a Regularity Section. I had originally hoped to go up there to take photographs of the classics as they drove through but, it still being dark, I decided against that in favour of getting up to the border and onto the long Explorer Section we would later share with the classics.

As the day dawned we could make out the colourful mountains that surround this region and soon crossed a sign marking the line of the Tropic of Capricorn. The road was climbing steadily as we were heading up towards the Altiplano and the hues of the rock strata were becoming more striking as the sun rose higher. There were also several stretches of major road works and on one we were diverted onto what was effectively a field that had several deep puddles. One 4x4 actually got stuck here, but was soon pulled out.

The road book recommended the 4x4s take a short diversion off the main road to visit Humahuaca, described as a 'typical' Andean village. We took this and soon found ourselves in a warren of narrow streets and alleys hardly wide enough for the car. After three attempts we found the

A High in the Andes

main square, barely 30 metres each way, the roads leading to and from it with houses built in the local adobe style. The village was indeed pretty and at any other time worthy of a short stay, but at 8.00am on what would be a very long day we felt, like others, we should press on.

Having taken several attempts to find the main square, it also took a couple of attempts to get out of town again as the local Coca Cola lorry was making a delivery and nothing could get past. More back alley diversions enabled us to finally make it out of town, but I wonder what the locals made of so many 4x4s descending on their little town for such a short visit so early in the morning. Mad dogs and Englishmen!

Back on the main road, we continued to climb and rounding one corner came upon dozens of butane gas cylinders strewn across the road and then a large lorry lying on its side. It would seem the accident had only just occurred as some cylinders were still rolling around, although the driver was sitting on the road verge looking very forlorn. Someone else with a bad hair day. Several local vehicles had stopped to help so we headed on.

As we climbed, so the vegetation became less and habitation more isolated. The sky was turning a brilliant blue and we looked towards a pleasant day as we sped on. I had wondered how the vehicle would perform at altitude and so far it was travelling at 140 kph with no ill effects. We were now at an altitude of 3,000m (10,000ft), having climbed up from about 1,500m (5,000ft) at Jujuy and were truly in the Andes.

On reaching the Argentinean side of the border at La Quiaca, we decided to fuel up before heading into the customs post. There were many cars at customs already and it took an hour to complete various forms, have our documents checked and get the necessary stamps on them before we could proceed over the border to the Bolivian side and the little town of Villazon.

What a reception! The main street, (there was little more to the town), was thronged with local people, many of the women wore typical

Bolivian bowler hats and multi layered skirts that made them look like bell tents. They looked quizzical as to what we were doing and no doubt envious, but the reception seemed friendly and warm. Along the road, too, were local uniformed militia with white belts and hats. The Inca Trail Rally was clearly very welcome in Bolivia.

Villazon is an important southern Bolivian town as it is the main border crossing with Argentina. There is also a significant contraband trade between the two countries and many Bolivians emigrate through here to live in the more prosperous province of Jujuy in Argentina. With all the financial problems spreading through Argentina one wondered whether so many would continue to emigrate, but the grass is always greener and we wouldn't find much grass in Bolivia.

The road was soon deteriorating as we headed out of town, and I wasn't sure we were heading in the right direction as it seemed such poor quality so soon. It degraded to rough broken concrete and to gravel in no time, but there ahead was a HERO Course Car parked on the verge marking the start of the Sundance Trail Explorer Section.

This was 330 kms long, about 210 miles, and as it would be tackled by the classics we reckoned wouldn't be too rough. Notes in the Road Book described it as 'gravel varying from good to roughish, with dry river bed crossings, through a succession of valleys and gorges and remote ethnic villages'. I relished the thought and we were soon away.

The section was named after the famous Kid who partnered Butch Cassidy, subjects of the famous film in the 1970s. They spent part of their lives in Bolivia and supposedly the silver mine robbery featured in the film took place near here and the shoot out, (that may never have occurred at all), was not too far away either.

HERO chose to use this road for several reasons. The route between Villazon and Potosi, our stop for the night, had been on the London - Mexico Rally route in 1970 when John Brown was Clerk of the Course for the South American sector. It was also the route taken by the town-to-town road races held on the continent in the 1930s and 40s. Juan

Manuel Fangio, who was to become World Racing Drivers' Champion several times in the 1950s, made his name on these races often driving Chevrolets.

Both those routes used another road that ran parallel and to the west of the one we would use, but which had now deteriorated and was too rough for the Inca Trail Rally. The road we would use was the 'main' road between the two towns.

We set off at 11.00am and like the other Sections, I was intent on tackling it as a special stage. It was terrific.

To start with it reminded us of roads in Namibia, wide sweeping gravel in fairly good condition and which made for good progress. Our first target was Tupiza a small town at about 77 kms into the Section. The local railway line crossed the road several times and when we reached Tupiza we remained on the 'main' road to the east of the river rather than through the town.

This little town is building on its reputation as the centre for Butch Cassidy and the Sundance Kid connections and offers tours and hikes visiting sites supposedly linked to the two robbers. At the main junction where the road into town crosses the river and where there was petrol available, a huge crowd had gathered to see us pass through.

There were numerous water splashes and river crossings identified in the road book but in most there was little or no water, a disappointment to me, but a blessing to the classics. We stopped at one that did have some water and videoed a couple of classics going through and were soon joined by some locals. Sadly, the first thing they did was ask for money, but we declined. More people gradually appeared and two of them started to build a small dam in the stream crossing the road to increase the depth of water to be crossed. It only raised it a little, perhaps from 5 cm to 15 cm but it made a better splash for the video.

Before we left Jujuy in the morning we were issued with route amendments and one near the village of Tumulsa referred to a detour to avoid a broken plank river bridge. On arrival we duly followed a HERO arrow down a long slope towards a river, ending up on a stony bank with the supposedly broken bridge high on our left. This was a proper river about 30 m wide that in front of us looked deep. We couldn't identify any clear crossing point so drove upstream on the bank under the bridge to see if the water was shallower or if there was a better ford. There wasn't.

I drove back to the original point and a classic, the red Sunbeam Alpine of Malcolm Pickering and David McConnell, had arrived and was debating whether or not to cross. On the other bank some children were playing and it was now that we saw another HERO arrow partly obscured from sight by a log it was fixed to. This was the intended crossing point.

With much better ground clearance I agreed to cross first and Malcolm said he would follow if he thought he could make it too. The water was deep, maybe 40cms for about 20 m but I crossed with no problem, so Malcolm decided to follow, only to drown out in the middle at the deepest point, river water flowing into and through the car.

Calls for help soon followed and I got out our towrope and reversed back into the river to the Alpine and they fixed the rope to my tow hook and their car and I pulled them out onto the bank. While all this was going on, a large lorry arrived and he didn't hesitate to go through the river, parking up next to us and the Alpine now unhooking the tow rope.

By now more rally cars had arrived on the other river-bank and watched the goings on and were reluctant to cross over themselves. They were scurrying about like mice on the river-bank looking for a better crossing point and eventually a couple of them drove back up the approach road, scrabbled up a steep bank to the original road and headed for the plank bridge.

This was about 50 m long and about 20 m above the river. It was of steel construction but had planks laid on metal supports as the road surface. A couple of the classic drivers got out of their cars, took a look at the bridge and decided to cross. They did this successfully, then a 4x4 did the same, and thereafter many others followed.

The Alpine started after a couple of turns of the engine and they drove off but stopped a couple of hundred metres down the road to start drying out. For them this was only the start, as it took a couple of days for the interior to dry out properly.

I put the towrope away and debated what I should do. Would the next classic come down to the river and try and cross only to drown out? I decided to take the arrow on our side over to the other side and direct cars back towards the bridge. This seemed to work as I later heard that most cars went over the bridge without any problem, but a couple of cars, including the Cortina MK1 of John and Julie Catt, also drowned in the river, being pulled out by the lorry. In all we crossed the river four times sorting all this out, so the underside of the car was very clean.

We also came upon Chris and Jill Wray in their Hyundai Galloper with what was to be the first of many punctures they would have over the next few weeks. Others had stopped to help them sort it out.

The end of the Section was sited 30 kms before the intended finish as the route deteriorated and cars would need to run slower. We arrived at the control at 4.40pm and headed onto the rougher section till we reached the outskirts of Potosi, approaching from behind the famous Cerro Rico mountain, the main source of silver that has brought prosperity to the region.

We passed over a brow and below us we could see the town and as the houses started, so did a huge crowd of people, for the town's populace was lining all the streets as we headed down into the main square. The police were out in force as well, making sure we weren't bothered by other traffic, and holding back about 50 large lorries that were due to travel south on the same road we had just completed.

We were both delighted by this welcome and as we passed through the town waved back and sounded the air horns to the cheering and waving crowds. It was great. Another good welcome from Bolivia.

And it didn't stop there. The square had a band playing and throngs of people welcomed us onto a proper finishing ramp where we were made to feel that we had finished the whole event, rather than just one Section. The square was closed off and parking reserved for the Inca Trail cars.

We'd finished for the day and had thoroughly enjoyed the roads and the reception from the people of Potosi. Others would feel very differently.

Many classic cars had major problems on this first long stage of the event and they would be arriving throughout the evening and it was the early hours of the next morning before some arrived. The MGC of Rita Shelley and Mike Knox had exhaust problems, the Alpine we had rescued had a problem with their sump, one Mercedes had run into the back of another, whilst yet another Mercedes had hit a local car.

The 4x4s suffered too. Our teammates Peter and Carolynn had broken both rear shock absorbers again, and another 4x4 had shredded a tyre, whilst another was overheating badly. Howard and Ann in their Range Rover started their bothers here with the cylinder head gasket going.

Meanwhile we went off to find our hotel, the Tourista, not what we were used to but an experience nevertheless. We had a super welcome from the owner who offered us coca tea, the best antidote to altitude sickness, and as the dirt factor on the car was eight again, she supplied me with buckets of cold water. I took this gently as the altitude was definitely affecting my breathing but neither Pam nor I would have any other effects during our time at altitude, despite taking no medication.

The hotel was, to say the least, basic. Lonely Planet says the Tourista offers 'sporadically excellent hot showers'. Well, the sporads must have stayed the day before, as the shower looked too dangerous to use and the whole place was freezing. I bought a woollen hat during the evening and wore it and all my clothes when I went to bed.

The welcome from the town hadn't finished either as they held a reception for us in the Treasury Building with much speechifying, drinks and food. It was a pleasant interlude and the city fathers, all dressed in their best suits and wearing bright red satin sashes, were clearly very pleased to have us in town. In the hallway to the Treasury Building where the reception was held, they also set up a craft market and this was where I bought a woollen alpaca hat. I looked very daft in it, but it kept my head warm. Thereafter I was christened as Inca Vic.

Drive in launderette

Day 9 Sunday 14 October
Potosi – Sucre (252 kms)

Today would be far more relaxed as we had the shortest run of the whole Inca Trail, only 160 kms to Sucre. We had a short Explorer Section to undertake, but the classics only had a main road tarmac run before a short test on the outskirts of the next overnight stop.

Our hotel was basic and having woken up early, I decided to make a trip out into town and take some photos. It was a Sunday, so the town was quiet and it provided a chance to take in the superb architecture of many of the city's important buildings in peace. On returning to the hotel, Pam was showering, brave soul (and the water was stone cold!) and after a rather basic breakfast we decided to move the car up to the square, where many other cars had remained for the night, ready for our start at midday.

I had hardly parked up when I was approached by the President of the local Lions Club, whose son was with him and was able to act as an interpreter. He was very interested in the trip we were on and could hardly believe that we could be driving such distances on such a regular basis. We exchanged Lions memorabilia and bade each other good luck and farewell.

Pam and I went off to look for a coffee. Wandering around the local streets admiring the buildings and with no particular schedule to maintain, it was a very pleasant couple of hours after the almost continuous pressure of the last week.

We came across a four-storey office block in one street that identified itself as the *Cies Juvenil – Salud Sexualy Reproductiva.* Our Spanish wasn't good enough to translate, but the mind boggles.

We found a suitable coffee bar and were joined by Colin Francis who was navigating the Ford Escort RS2000 of John Bateson. Colin, a retired civil servant from Wales, is one the top line navigators with an enviable reputation. The Escort they were driving was also identical to one I used to rally many years ago but with a Manx (MN) registration plate and international badge (GBM).

Colin, being a former civil servant, is a meticulous record keeper and he showed Pam his copy of the road book and how it was already marked up with useful information that would help him do well.

Pam delighted in telling him that on Day Three, back in Brazil, she had interpreted a route instruction better than he had. We were travelling in company with several cars and the tulip showed an odd-shaped crossroads where we went straight onto a side road, whereas the 'main' road we were on swung left at about 10 o'clock.

We stopped at the junction to check that we were in fact heading in the right direction, and as we did the Bateson/Francis Escort sped past us, staying on the main road and headed off in the wrong direction. Pam saw where they went, but was confident enough to keep us on the right route. A few minutes later the Escort caught us up and quickly overtook us.

Colin also got out a little notebook in which he had basic details of all the Inca Trail entrants. He didn't have much additional data on us and asked us to add some.

"You never know when it may become useful," was his comment. We await a call.

All too soon it was time to head for the hills again and we were on the main road to Sucre. It was a good asphalt road and we passed a couple of villages where cattle markets were taking place. We also came upon a rope strung across the road at a height of about one metre which was dropped to road level as we got to it by a couple of people standing beside the road. We weren't sure whether this was an attempt to obtain some sort of fee from us, but we didn't have to stop so didn't have to cough up.

We soon arrived at the start of the Explorer Section, Betanzos, which we started at 12.47pm. The tracks led through a couple of modest villages and then up into some hills that offered extensive views over the surrounding mountains. High up in the mountains we were travelling along one track with a steep slope upwards on our left and a similarly steep slope down on the right. We had seen no habitation for many miles but squatting by a small pool at the side of this track was a Bolivian woman doing some washing. We thought about stopping and doing some of our own but decided against this – the services of a hotel seemed preferable.

The Section was only 40 kms long but was an interesting diversion and we returned to the main road. We came across another rope across the road here, this time in a small cluster of houses where there was what might have been a Police Control or Toll House. These ropes weren't easy to see and I only just stopped in time and waited for something to happen. It didn't. So I got out of the car, unhooked the rope and drove on. Other teams later told me that I should have paid a toll, so I guess I am now a fugitive from the Bolivian Road Toll Police.

The reception in Sucre was much the same as in Potosi with an even bigger crowd in the main square where the control was sited. The town had laid on a reception for us in the square, but it seemed the locals had invited themselves as well. There were dancing and music displays but it was difficult to see because of the crowds encircling the display area. We managed to get round to where the reception seemed to be organised and were immediately offered a better view, a drink and empanada, a sort of small, spicy Cornish pasty very popular in South America.

The displays continued and various speeches made and when the Inca Trailers were invited to stand in the open arena everyone clapped and cheered. We then clapped them and they clapped even louder. It was great, but Pam and I didn't oblige with a dance for their benefit, although some Inca Trailers did.

It was at Sucre that we first became aware of the growing disquiet amongst the classics about the route. We knew about the hard time many of them had been having but it seemed things were developing further and crews were starting to talk about retiring, taking alternative routes and even abandoning the event altogether.

In response, the organisers decided to cancel the test for them the next day, a long one described as a 'basic road through the mountains' in the road book, and offered them a smoother route to La Paz back through Potosi again and mainly on tarmac up to the Bolivian capital.

There were also concerns being raised about hotel accommodation. Some people were voicing views about the hotels in Potosi, one describing theirs as 'disgusting', and others claiming they were getting a raw deal when it came to hotel allocations.

One hotel each night was described as the HQ hotel where the organisers were billeted and it was generally considered as the best hotel. Very often we all stayed here, but inevitably other hotels had to be used and HERO claimed that allocations were made as fairly as possible so that one night one might get a less than good hotel, but over the event this would balance out. This seemed fair and equable, but didn't satisfy many people.

For a number of people the issue of hotel accommodation became all-consuming over the next couple of weeks and their only topic of conversation. They were no longer interested in the rally but only in whether or not HERO were making exorbitant profits from that part of the entry fee intended to cover accommodation.

It seemed to us that there were several reasons why this preoccupation might have started. Many classic rally crews already had to consider giving up all chance of enjoying the rally or were looking to just get round as much of the event as they could and get a finish. They needed to take their wrath out on someone.

There were also some very wealthy people on the trip for whom a hotel below five stars was the equivalent to slumming it. Many of the towns we were staying in simply didn't have enough accommodation of such a standard, or if they did, not enough rooms available, so lesser standard hotels had to be used. In a couple of towns we visited later during the event we might be spread out through six or seven hotels, some only being the equivalent of bed and breakfast establishments or apartments, rather than hotels.

Awesome

Day 10 Monday 15 October
Sucre – La Paz (570 kms)

Today would see us tackling the second of the big long Explorer Sections of the event, this one being called Ravelo and covering half the 570 kms from Sucre to La Paz. The Section was also originally intended for the classics as a Medal Section, but with the cries of 'foul' from them and the sorry state of many of their cars only the 4x4s would travel its tortuous path.

I was keen to get started early. This allowed us scope to take any rough parts of the road slowly and if we had mechanical problems there would be plenty of people behind us to lend a hand. This was my policy throughout the event, although only once would we be first on the road.

We arrived at the main control in the square at 6.05am and soon after were on the outskirts of town near the airport where the start of the Explorer Section was sited. The helpfulness of the Bolivian authorities was already evident today as all the junctions up to the airport were manned by local police directing us on our way.

Stuart Wood was at the start control and his comments were enlightening.

"Good morning," I said as we pulled to a stop at the airport control where it was just beginning to get light.

"You thought it was a good morning, but you have seven hours of pure hell ahead of you." There was a hint of glee in his voice.

"That's what we came for," I replied as he marked up our time card and handed it back to us. It was 6.20am.

"Good luck and be good."

We headed off up the track of what was supposed to be a main road and had only travelled a few hundred metres before we saw the Buick

Rendezvous heading back. Not a good sign.

They pulled up beside us and told us they had a puncture already and thought it wise to head back to town and get it fixed before restarting the section. We pressed on.

To begin with it was definitely puncture territory as it was very rough for the first 20 kms or so. And the classics were supposed to come through here!

The road got better, but it twisted and turned up through the mountains with the views improving as the sun rose above them. At a police check-point we were waved through and the road at last became smoother and made for a better pace.

The excellent road book prepared by HERO provides distances to key features such as village signs, junctions, fords and the like, but normally not the nature of the road in between. Thus a 14.52 kms section from a couple of houses and a junction provides no indication of the actual road to be followed. It was classic. Hairpin bend after hairpin bend, huge drops, often to the next piece of the roadway below, and narrow, making no concession to passing possibilities or errors of judgement on the part of the driver. And there was more, much more of this to come, together with oncoming buses and lorries, often overloaded with people clinging on in the back.

And there were liberal doses of fords and river crossings today. In fact the road book mentioned little else for several pages with comments such as:

- Ford
- Rough ford
- Viewpoint
- Summit: 13,300 ft
- Ford
- Archway to ford
- Bandstand

Day 1: *5...4...3...2...1... and at 8.21am on Saturday 6th October 2001 we started the Inca Trail Adventure Drive in Rio de Janeiro*

Day 5: *Foz de Iguacu*

Day 7: *Wash your windscreen, sir?*

Day 8: *Pedro has a bad hair day in northern Argentina*

Day 8: *Bolivian girl in local costume*

Day 11: *Parked up by Lake Titicaca in Bolivia for a breather*

Day 12: *Preventative maintenance in Cusco*

Day 13: *Machu Picchu*

Day 14: *Out with the trolley jack at 5.00am to help the McKane's get their Mustang out of a nasty predicament*

Day 15: *Oops! You don't want to do it like that*

Day 15: *On top of the world at 16,500ft but we decided not to join the 3½ mile high club*

Day 15: *Ted and Judy Howles in their Reliant Scimitar were lucky not to go further off (and down!)*

Day 22: *Southern Peru where the Andes meet the Atacama Desert*

Day 24: *On the back roads between Calama in Chile and Salta in Argentina passing the volcanoes Miscanti and Chiliques*

Day 27: *What rally drivers love. The Ruta del Ano with its 365 bends over the Andes again to Chile*

Day 30: *Left to right: Chris Elliott, Vic, Linda Banks, Judy and Ted Howles, Anna and Jonathan Pelly-Fry provide assistance changing a wheel*

- Ford
- Roughish ford by old mine
- Detour to rough ford
- Summit: 14,170 ft

… and so on. And these few instructions covered only 20 kms.

Yes, there were bandstands. On the road today we passed through several remote villages, (hamlets would be a better word), and their characteristics were much the same. The approach road towards the village would normally be all right, but as we reached the first houses it was normal for the condition of the road to deteriorate dramatically until we reached the village square.

The square would be well looked after and invariably had a bandstand for as we would find out later, band playing is an important cultural activity in these parts. The road around the square was usually good quality concrete, but as we headed out towards the countryside it would become awful again until we were clear of the town and back on 'normal' country roads.

There may be several reasons for this change of road condition. Firstly, it is likely that responsibility for roads is vested in different authorities, the local village having to look after its own roads and streets. Secondly, the village roads were often very rough cobbles and sets indicating their great age and suitability for pack animals rather than vehicles. Anyway it paid to go very slowly through these villages.

Peana was, however, an untypical village being set on the open plain of the Altiplano. Its mud houses were set alongside the main earth road through the village, but set back from it by about 20 m. There was a market taking place with dozens of ladies in their bell tent skirts and tiny bowler hats, the men leading animals about.

There were stalls selling fruit, vegetables and meat as well as the other necessities of life such as hand tools and clothes. Whether by design or coincidence, the road through the village was partly blocked by two lorries leaving only a small gap to squeeze through. We weren't approached at all as we managed to get the car through but one felt that we weren't too welcome and that a charge might have been requested to get through. We'd have liked to have stopped but keeping up the Inca Trail pace was also a worry.

Further on we stopped near another village, Lluchu, where there was a ford we wanted to video the car going through. I dropped Pam and headed back through the water to get the action recorded. Meanwhile Pam was approached by a Bolivian woman carrying a small baby, both in traditional dress, suggesting we pay her for a photograph.

She was joined by another girl, who looked to be a teenager and we obliged with the photograph and made suitable reparations. We were all satisfied. The village was about as remote as we had seen – a cluster of mud houses, just hovels really, with roughly thatched roofs and no evidence of any sanitary facilities at all. In most other villages we had seen separate outside loos, but there were none here.

One wonders what sort of lives these people lived and I later wished we had tried to visit one of the houses. Opportunity missed.

The route continued ever onward up and down mountains, round bends or alongside precipitous drops. At the approach to another village, there was a large body of water across the road and adjacent fields with three men wanting a lift through it. We couldn't oblige with the lift but they insisted on standing where they would get wet as we pressed on. We did our best to keep our wake to a minimum but it was a long stretch of water, about 50 m and quite deep in places. Many classics would have come to grief if they had been on this road.

This village, like others, gave us a rousing reception and many of the local folk were out to wave us through with friendly waves. Perhaps earlier concerns about our reception were misplaced?

Out in the mountains again we turned around a headland to behold an incredible sight. Before us was a lush green valley stretching 10 or 15 kms into the distance with a smattering of houses and fields with a variety of animals grazing. It looked like Shangri La and it might have been. However, I suspect that for the locals it was anything but Shangri La as again there was no evidence of proper sanitation, the wind was bitter and in winter… well? This was springtime at 14,000 ft and although the sun was shining, the wind brought a definite chill.

We came across another such valley later in the day and felt we could have been in Tibet or Nepal in the Himalayas.

The village of Macha offered another surprise. This too had very rough streets, but down a side street we noticed a large group of locals having some sort of meeting. They were all in their bowler hats and warm shawls and again we felt that we should stop and take a photo. We might have had a nasty shock.

Later it seems that several cars passing through here had trouble. The locals set up a barrier across one of the roads leading around their square with its bandstand and started charging a toll. One Inca Trailer took offence at this and drove straight through the barrier, so the next 4x4 through, Sir Terence English in his venerable Toyota Trooper, caught the villagers' wrath and one of his rear windows was stoned.

Ploughing in the fields was done by a wooden plough drawn by an ox and for many hours we had seen no motorised traffic other than the occasional lorry or bus. However on arriving at one village we came upon a tractor and soon a couple of private cars. How the cars came to be there is a mystery as the roads around this village were abysmal and in the village itself they were diabolical. Yet someone had decided a car was what he needed and somehow brought it in from the outside world.

The condition of both cars we saw matched that of the surrounding roads. They were rust heaps, with missing glass and very bashed about. I wondered if they were insured or paid road tax!

In this same village we came upon other signs of help from the outside world. There were two blocks in the village centre identified with metal plaques as being provided by UNICEF. They were public conveniences.

We had a strange incident in the next village along the road. We were driving slowly through on very rough cobbles. Our windows were fortunately closed because as we passed one house a young woman on the front door step suddenly scooped up a bowl of water from a bucket and threw it at the side of the car.

We weren't too sure how to take this. There was no dust from the car, as there had been in other villages and to which she might have taken offence. We pressed on, but we discussed the incident over the next few miles and decided we would enhance the story when we came to recount it later.

> *There's an ancient Bolivian custom, only bestowed on an honoured few, whereby fresh urine is thrown over a traveller to wish him luck on his journey. We had been thus honoured.*

Perhaps our tale is truer than we thought as it must have worked because we made it to the end of the stage and the rally!

The village of Uncea brought another story. This was more of a small town with some private cars around, but the roads they had to drive on were hellish to say the least. We had a good welcome here through the curving main street and on the roads out through the other side of town where many people were waving to us from vantage points on a hillside.

But all around the town were huge mounds of gravel and with them quarries and plant to crush and grade it. However, we saw no sign of any lorries to carry it away, nor any suitable roads that could take the number of lorries that were surely needed. The place remained a puzzle to us, so isolated, yet with a thriving populace and a hint of prosperity. It was a pity they didn't use some of the gravel locally to improve their own roads.

Another sad sight here though was rubbish. We passed several kilometres of rubbish, mainly coloured plastic bags and bottles strewn over the countryside.

It was also here that we saw several people carrying brass band instruments and we had passed several lorries with other people carrying instruments including big bass drums. We reckoned there must be some gathering or competition about to take place. We even saw a small group standing by the roadside practising as they waited for some transport. There were no houses about and we wondered where they came from.

And so after eight and a half hours of hard driving, with only a few stops for photos and calls of nature we came to the finish control above the small town of Huanuni. Mark Appleton, the Clerk of the Course, was at the control and I told him:

"That was awesome – the best day's driving I've ever done."

It was. The roads had been terrific, the driving experience was great, the scenery, the people along the way and the various incidents we had encountered all made the Inca Trail what it was – a super challenge. Just the driving we had done today made the whole trip worthwhile in my judgement.

After a ten minute break to refresh ourselves we headed off again, me not being aware that we still had 270 kms to get to our hotel for the night in La Paz.

Huanuni was where we hit the tarmac again and could make better progress, but as we headed into the next town along the way, Oruro, we came upon another splendid reception. From about 10 kms outside town, soldiers were lined up at 100 m intervals on either side of the road, all waving at us as we passed by, most also waving little Bolivian flags. It was a terrific reception and they were so regimented in their spacing that we could have calibrated the Brantz as we sped by.

In Oruro we stopped for diesel and the reception here was terrific too. The owner wanted a photograph of us and gave us each a baseball cap.

We passed quickly through Oruro but nearly came to grief at one junction where there was a huge manhole cover missing from the top of the shaft it was supposed to protect. I dread to think what might have happened had a wheel dropped in. There was no warning whatsoever.

I was not too pleased when Pam told me that we still had a long way to cover before reaching La Paz. Although we had had a brilliant day, I was tired and hungry and wanted to be there before dark. As we made progress we came across an Inca Trailer 4x4 whose driver had clearly been too far today as he was weaving back and forth across the road as we approached.

I gave him a loud blast of the air horns as we came up behind and as we passed I was pleased to see him pulling up on the verge.

We were tired and had travelled a long way, but still had two challenges to overcome. Getting to our hotel for the night, and also checking in.

HERO had set up a control on the outskirts of La Paz, the idea being that cars could congregate and then be taken to the centre of town with a police escort. This was fine, but we waited for an age for another car to arrive to join us and then still longer in the hope that more would arrive to make up a small group that the police car allocated to us could lead. In the end just two of us headed off into the city with a police 4x4 ahead of us, lights blazing, to announce our importance.

Malcolm McKay in the little red TR2 was ahead of me and we zoomed through red lights and across busy junctions keeping as close as we could to the police car in front.

Such processions attract a certain kind of driver, and all and sundry wanted to join the parade as it offered them too a chance to jump the traffic and perhaps grab some of the attention being given to us. Malcolm tried to keep as close as he dared to the police car, and I to him, but from time to time some interloper would try and spoil the act and we would have to fend him off to maintain our position. Our own headlights, hazard flashers, liberal use of the air horns and sheer bolshyness helped.

The main approach road into La Paz, which sits in a valley below the Altiplano, is dramatic with a six-lane dual carriageway sweeping around the edge of the valley side until it reaches the valley floor. It had been daylight on the top, but by the time we reached the hotel it was dark. There were still many Inca Trail cars behind us and there were already complaints about having to drive in the dark earlier in the event. It would be late into the night before some of them arrived.

We parked up in the basement car park of the Radisson and headed for Reception. Most of the classics were in already and enjoying the benefits of the bar, but we still had to register.

We joined a short queue to check in to the hotel with Chris and Jill Wray who were driving a Hyundai Galloper. We were all knackered and ready for food; we'd had virtually nothing since 5.30am and it was now well past 7.00pm. Not much happened in the queue.

I was getting impatient so tried to get the female receptionist to hurry along, but she seemed indifferent to our request.

"My name is Vic Quayle and we're crew A35."

"Could you please fill in this form."

"I'm very tired, you've got all my details including passport numbers on the list in front of you, could I just sign for a room key."

"I'm sorry sir. All guests must complete a registration form. I'll have one for you in a minute."

Well it was a South American minute, but eventually we got our form, and Chris got his as well. Pam filled in ours and handed it in. It was checked thoroughly against the listing provided by HERO and time marched on together with my patience.

"I'll need a credit card as well please."

"Surely not. Can we just have a room key. We're very tired and been travelling since very early this morning."

She would not be moved, "It's company rules." Of course it was, I wouldn't have doubted it.

While this was going on I could hear that Chris was having similar problems. He was being offered a room on the twelfth floor.

"I'm sorry, but we can't accept this room," said Chris to the receptionist, "My wife cannot deal with heights and HERO will have informed you that we cannot have a room above the eighth floor."

"I'm sorry sir, but that is the room allocated to you."

"But my wife cannot go above the eighth floor." Chris was gently, but gradually losing his rag and standing next to him I was close to doing the same. Chris's wife Jill was getting upset because she was the centre of unwarranted attention and the whole situation was developing into farce. Pam, who hates any fuss and bother, was trying to calm me down and wanted me to do what the female receptionist wanted, in the way she wanted.

Chris stood his ground, but the mounting frustration got to him as he too was tired and wanted to get to a room as quickly as possible. Then he quite literally screamed out loud.

I have never heard a man scream, and not unnaturally it brought the whole of the hotel lobby to a stop. But it had some effect. The hotel Reception Manager appeared in an instant and one of the HERO doctors also made an appearance to check there was no medical problem.

"No. Only high blood pressure."

While all this was going on we reluctantly found a credit card, it was photocopied and after what seemed an age we were handed a room key. Room 607.

"Hang on Chris. We have a solution," I called out to him. "We'll take your room and you have ours."

We should have kept the arrangement to ourselves but the Reception Manager heard us and got involved. He wanted to get more forms signed and checked.

"If you do that, sir, we'll have to re-enter the details on the computer."

I gave Chris my keys and we took his and headed for the lifts leaving the Manager to contemplate his computer.

Pam and I had room service (which I hasten to add we paid for rather than Chris), but I could barely finish my meal before I was sound asleep. I will never stay in a Radisson again. Their customer service is the pits.

Other long distance rallies have much better checking-in procedures at hotels and we learned that other organisers ensured that all hotel registration was carried out in advance and that all a competitor had to do on arrival at a new hotel was show his identification tag and sign for his room key. End of story and no blessed forms to fill in each evening.

A fine arrangement at the end of a long day, but one that HERO never got to grips with. Only towards the end of the event were a few hotels ready to follow a streamlined checking-in arrangement.

Lake Titicaca

Day 11 Tuesday 16 October
La Paz – Puno (272 kms)

Our night in the Radisson wasn't that good because we didn't sleep too well, but the breakfast was excellent and what's more we were able to have a lazy start today. The run up to the Peruvian border and on to our next stop was only about 300 kms and we'd had word that the Explorer test for the day had been cancelled so first thing we went out to a local store to do some shopping for supplies to eat and drink in the car.

The Day Start Control was in the Cathedral Square in La Paz, not far from the hotel, but through some narrow streets with chaotic traffic. The approach to the square was a steep hill and amidst the traffic one of the classics, a Dutch Jaguar, was in trouble, being unable to generate enough power to get up the hill.

We offered them a tow, the initial problem being getting the local traffic to let us pull up in front of the Jaguar to get the towrope hitched up. Once done it was a simple tow into the square. I should have used the low gearing on our car, but forgot and on getting to the square the clutch was burning like mad with clouds of blue smoke coming out from underneath and a burning smell all through the car. I was annoyed with myself for such a small error and also worried I might have destroyed the clutch so we decided to get it checked before leaving town.

HERO had identified a garage willing to work on the rally cars so as it wasn't too far away we headed there, only to find the place full of Inca Trail cars, both classic and 4x4. The owner, a former top racing driver, took my car out and tested the clutch on a couple of steep hills and pronounced it OK, but suggested I get it checked again in Lima. I was relieved, but the burnt clutch smell was to remain in the car for a couple of days.

Satisfied it was safe to head on, we returned to the square and checked out at just after 11.00am and drove out of town via the dual carriageway that swept around the valley edge. There was no police escort this time.

The road north from La Paz across the Altiplano was nothing special except that we began to get some pleasant views of Lake Titicaca, especially when we turned west to Tiquina. The Lake is the highest navigable waterway in the world at 3,810 m and is really two lakes, joined by a narrow passage of water where, at the town of Tiquina, there is a car ferry across the 400 m channel.

The weather was warm and sunny and along the waterside of the Lake we could have been in the Mediterranean; it was lovely. Although we passed along the main tarmac road, we were supposed to have tackled an Explorer Section along a track passing even closer to the waterside. This had been cancelled due to a landslide, something we thought odd as, unless it had been severe, it should have been passable by 4x4s. From the main road we could see the track we should have used and it looked good.

At Tiquina all the wooden ferry boats that cross the channel had been called into service to take the rally across the water. Each boat could only carry one vehicle at a time and ours, crewed by a young lad about 12 years old who took the tiller and his father, soon had us over the other side.

Safely on the western side of the lake we followed a good road till we were near the Peruvian border. However major road works were taking place here and a number of diversions took us round a variety of back doubles, along a track across an allotment, through someone's front garden and around the edge of several fields before we rejoined the 'main' road along the water's edge. Here we could see several of the famous reed boats in use as day to day transport.

The border control was in chaos. Before leaving Bolivia we had to pass through a narrow archway, but rally cars were parked all over the place blocking each other in – nobody had the nouse to park sensibly. Once through the archway the situation at the Peruvian Customs Post was no better and the local customs men were taking an age checking our documentation. A long queue soon formed as most of the details in our vehicle carnets was being copied by hand into a huge ledger. Rumours started in the queue.

"His pen's run out and he doesn't have a replacement."

"He's going to lunch in ten minutes and won't be back till after his siesta."

Eventually we were cleared to drive on into Peru and headed north on a reasonable road towards Puno. We were making good progress until about 20 kms from Puno we began to see one or two rally cars approaching us and heading back the way we had come.

"Have we forgotten anything at the border, Pam?"

"Not that I can think of."

"We've got all the correct stamps in the documents?"

"Yes, as far as I know."

"What's going on then?" We had no idea.

We were soon entering Puno and what a dump it was. It was an absolute wreck of a town and reminded me of pictures I've seen of towns in the back end of China. Dirty, dusty, unkempt, grubby, squalid, bedraggled are just a few of the adjectives that sprang to mind.

The main street was a dual carriageway and in the outside lane on our side was the hulk of a rusted coach, no chassis or wheels or any other part, just the body. At the side of all the roads, dust accumulated so deep the edge couldn't be seen. The concrete roadway was potholed and broken and clearly hadn't been repaired at any time in the last millennium, never mind this one.

The buildings were much the same. Drab, grubby and festooned with electrical cables running in all directions and gaudy advertising hanging listlessly from roofs.

Welcome to Peru! I wondered what sort of tip our hotel would be.

Our route instructions led us out to the docks beside the Lake where a local attraction is the SS Yavari and our Day Finish Control was sited here. The steamship Yavari is one of two similar ships built in England in the 1860s and brought out to the Lake in pieces before being assembled, launched and used as steamships on the Lake. Transporting and building the ships took seven years, having been shipped in pieces to Arica in Chile and transported by mule to the Lake. The Yavari was launched on Christmas Day 1870.

Originally the boilers of the Yavari used dried llama dung as fuel but some time ago this was changed to diesel. The ship was unused for many years but now a Trust has been established to renovate it and start reusing it on the lake as a tourist attraction. Its sister ship has been transported back to the Pacific and is still used by the Peruvian navy as a hospital ship.

We had a chance to look at the Yavari and it was straight out of a film about Scott or Shackleton. Sumptuous wooden panelling, aged and heavily worn by years of use, brass fittings and ancient maps. While we were there the boilers were lit, but as yet the ship doesn't sail, more funds are needed to complete the renovation.

When we checked in to the control, Don Griffiths advised us of a hotel change, and that we would now be staying at the Libertador. He said there was a problem with the hotels, and the reason we had seen other cars heading in the opposite direction was that crews had had to be farmed out to hotels all around the area.

The Libertador turned out to be a haven in the tip that was Puno and a much better hotel than we had expected. Approached across a causeway, it was really on an island in the bay and was a five star establishment. Our room had a view across the lake, by now in darkness, and was clearly at the upper end of the hotel scale. Initially we couldn't work out why there was a demand for a hotel such as this in Puno, but it turned out it relies heavily on tourists brought direct to the hotel from Cusco by the local version of the Orient Express – the train stops almost right outside. The tourists visit the reed boats and reed islands and are then coached out to the airport to fly out of the region. The town itself doesn't feature on their itinerary.

In the restaurant later we ate with Dari and Orph, the Israelis we had eaten with previously. Dari told us they had tried the Explorer Section in the morning, and apart from a short section where he had had to take care, it was all right.

Why was it cancelled?

Into the land of the Incas

Day 12 Wednesday 17 October
Puno – Cusco (512 kms)

If Puno was a tip, then Juliaca, the next town up the road to Cusco, was even worse. One guidebook describes it as 'one of the globe's least desirable places' and we can confirm that opinion. And getting through it wasn't easy either as the town was full of tricycles used as taxis and for carting goods.

They were everywhere, never gave way and barged their way in and out of the traffic with little regard for life or limb. Most were pedal powered, but some were petrol driven with little motorcycle engines, this type usually having a canopy and side panels to protect the passengers from the elements. In the Far East they are called tuktuks. We found both types of tricycle throughout Peru, especially in the Andes region and even where the roads were dreadful. In such cases they tipped and rolled over the bumps and looked like they were likely to topple over, but never obliged.

From Juliaca we followed the line of the Cusco to Puno railway up into the Abra La Raya Pass with snow capped mountains all around and scattered settlements here and there. The road crossed the railway in several places but as usual the level crossings were anything but. However, we did see the Orient Express climbing towards the pass, its splendid paintwork somewhat out of place in this drab and barren environment.

We dropped down towards Urcos where our next Explorer Section would take us back up into the mountains to the east, finishing at the Inca ruins at Pisac. Having left the tarmac of the main road, the gravel track turned up and up into the mountains twisting and turning backwards and forwards on itself to the top of a pass at 3,900m before entering the village of Ccatca.

This was larger than expected with a wide range of buildings and, on the outskirts, a full size football pitch and other sports facilities, all in good condition and clearly in regular use. We found this was common to most Peruvian villages as they take their inter village sports seriously, although getting between them must be difficult at times. Ccatca had a typical square and over the road out of town that we used was an archway with ornate paintings on it.

Our rally nearly ended here as we were passing through some houses, (village might be too bold a word to use), when we came upon a group of school children who had placed a line of boulders across the road. I considered getting out of the car to move them, (but had the feeling we might be stoned and the car get damaged), or driving over the boulders risking punctures. I decided that I would drive around them, none too quickly to avoid the kids, who unbeknown to me were next to a gully into which I dropped. The car crashed down, the sump guard taking most of the impact with the back soon following. We didn't get stuck at all, but I was none too pleased.

Once away from habitation, in the mountains the route became much like parts of Wales with small white furry cacti growing at the side of the road. The second part of the section was shared with the rally cars who joined our road and from here on for the next 60 kms the road was smoother.

A motorcyclist in the village of Chocpia posed another hazard. He was carrying a wooden plough, the shaft of which was about 4m long making him very difficult to overtake. If you've seen the police videos shown on television in the UK with the man carrying a plank on a moped, you'll know what I mean.

From the end of the Section it was only a short way into Pisac, passing some Inca terracing on the way. Pisac was a typical Andean town with narrow streets and with a busy market taking place in the main square. Many of the classics were parked up as they had a control here, so we joined them in the local hotel for a bite to eat.

The itinerant caravan that was the Inca Trail Rally was ever moving on and we had to move with it, so after some refreshment we were soon on the road again, this time heading for Cusco, but first passing some excellent ruins at Saqsaywaman (or as we called it Sexy Woman).

Sexy Woman was a well preserved and laid out site with plenty to see and little need to clamber up and down flights of steps to see the best bits (as we would find was necessary at Machu Picchu). Such things are important at altitude.

Having given Sexy Woman a good looking over, we were back in the car and dropping down the last few kilometres into Cusco where we would be stopping for two days, a very welcome break after an almost non-stop run from Rio.

The dirt factor on the car was about six and when an opportunity came to have it washed by some kids in a garage, we took it and they enthusiastically swamped it in buckets of water to get rid of the grime. We failed however to agree a price before they started and got ripped off when it came to pay up. You live and learn; anyway they did a good job.

Like most crews we were due to stay in another Libertador Hotel in the centre of Cusco and chaos reigned outside. There was little parking on the busy street that passed by and dozens of rally cars were trying to park and unload their cases. All around we came upon our first signs of the begging that is universal in Peru. Tours, postcards, woollen clothing, jewellery and shoe cleaning were pressed upon us by men, women and children. One kid selling postcards even claimed his name was Michael Owen. We unloaded and got into the hotel without any problem, but we heard that other crews had cases and other personal items stolen in the melee outside the hotel. The police presence wasn't too helpful and they only seemed bemused by what was going on.

Later, at the request of the police, we moved the car into an alley running alongside the hotel and next to the famous Inca Wall in Romeritos.

In the evening we went out to investigate the town with friends Dave and Carole who were also having a trouble-free run in their Toyota Colorado. Pestering for restaurant custom as well as begging was a nuisance and we were glad to seek sanctuary in a restaurant where alpaca and guinea pig, a local delicacy, were tried. Alpaca was eatable but nothing special, whilst guinea pig was a waste of time, too many bones and not enough meat. Such that there was tasted a bit like dark chicken meat.

R and R

Day 13 Thursday 18 October
Cusco – Rest day

When we arrived in Cusco there was a reasonable-sized crowd at the control in the Plaza de Armas, including a woman from the local Toyota garage offering service facilities for the rally cars. I had originally intended to have the car checked over once we arrived at Lima, approximately a third of the way through the rally, but as that was only three rally days away it seemed a good idea to take up the offer in Cusco. She told me they opened at 7.30am so I said I would be there. And I was.

Finding the garage in the one-way system of Cusco wasn't easy, but once there I explained what I wanted done, which was to change the engine oil, renew all the filters, check the brakes and tighten up all the suspension and steering bolts. I had filters and brake pads for them and they said return at 12.30pm. Whilst I was content to leave my car there, the situation at the garage struck me as a little odd, for there were hardly any cars in the workshop at all and the office area seemed largely empty and unused.

I made my way back to the hotel by taxi and joined Pam for some breakfast, which we took at a leisurely pace. Later we went for a walk round town to look at the terrific architecture, which was both Inca and from the later Spanish colonisation of the country.

We made our way back to the garage at the appointed time to find the workshop was now full of Inca Trail cars, both classics and 4x4s, some being worked on, others awaiting their turn. Mine was up on axle stands and the mechanic showed me that he had renewed all the filters and oil and he was now checking the brakes. He had one of the brake callipers unbolted.

Most of the other cars in the garage were there for similar routine maintenance. The Discovery of Rolf and Inis Pritz was next to ours, but awaiting attention, Alastair Caldwell had his Ferrari up in the air, as usual working on it himself, the sump guard laying on the garage floor nearby. You don't see many Ferrari sump guards!

The MGC, the Austin Healey, the 4x4 Buick Rendezvous, the Irish boys' Hyundai Galloper, a couple of Amazons, John Blankley's A90 and other rally cars were all around in various states of activity. For a garage that was empty that morning it was now very busy. The problem was that ours would be some time so we left it there and went to find some lunch.

We went back again at about 3.30pm to find it still wasn't ready, but this time we decided to wait, which we did for nearly an hour until they finally released it. They seemed to have done a good job as the brakes were much better, they had been bled, and the price was a very reasonable £27.00 including the oil. You'd pay more than that just for the oil in the UK.

Our evening was fairly low key with a meal in and an early night.

Machu Picchu

Day 14 Friday 19 October

The lost Inca city of Machu Picchu is said to be one of the true wonders of the world. Hidden in the jungle till the early 1900s when it was 'found' by an American explorer, Hiram Bingham, the city is perched high in the Andes above the Urambamba River.

Like many of the Inca Trailers we had pre-booked an all-inclusive day trip to this World Heritage Site. Another early start was demanded, with a 4.30am alarm, and a coach trip to Cusco railway station to catch a train that would take us on a three and a half hour journey to the nearest station at Aguas Calientes. The trip started with the train zigzagging up the side of the valley as it went backwards and forwards through some of the suburbs of Cusco.

As all train journeys do, this offered an almost voyeuristic insight into the town waking up and getting about its business. The train was so close to houses one could see into the rooms with people getting their first meal of the day, drinking coffee, and setting off to work or buy food. Animals too were awakening. Dogs curled up in scrubby hollows lifted their heads at the noisy intrusion of the train, sat up, stretched and wandered off to do their ablutions. Pigs, cattle and the occasional llama too, did much the same.

The greatest intrusion was the squealing as the wheels rubbed against the rails on the tight bends, a noise I found particularly irritating. I was pleased when we reached the top of the valley and the train gathered pace on more regular tracks across farming countryside.

Once the train reached the Urambamba valley, the scenery changed to scrubby hills and mountains and once more some zigzags were needed to keep pace with the falling river valley.

Breakfast was served on the train, much like on an aircraft, but once this was over most fell asleep for at least some of the journey. At Aguas Calientes we detrained and the plan was to board coaches to take us up to Machu Picchu. Somehow things went very wrong here, as it seemed a large proportion of the group, ourselves included, didn't have the all-inclusive tickets that would take us up to the city and get us in.

An age was wasted while this was sorted out, with nobody seemingly taking any initiative to get us onto the coaches and away. Finally we were advised to pay for the tickets ourselves and we were promised that HERO would reimburse us later. This was fine if we had money to buy the coach ticket and entry, but many people had not thought to carry much cash with them, credit cards weren't acceptable at the coach terminal, so a lot of hasty borrowing was going on.

Once we started, the coach trip was very impressive, up a steep track with about 15 hairpins to the main entrance to Machu Picchu. A guide was included in the package and soon we were meandering our way around the site.

Despite being at 2,400 m it was very warm and humid and with the altitude I was sweltering and a bit short of breath. The sand flies were having a go at my bare legs and within minutes I was bitten from ankle to somewhere private well north of my knees. An application of cream helped but the damage was done, and it was a week before the evidence of these bites cleared completely.

The site is very impressive, built as it is on a saddle of rock so high in the mountains. The end of the other Inca Trail was pointed out to us, the one that is a trek over the mountains to the site. Generally this takes three or four days with camping along the way, and such is its popularity that access is now strictly controlled to prevent wear and tear to the route. The record for running the route we were told was under four hours, and what we saw later would give rise to believing in this remarkable feat.

Our tour covered all the main features of the city but in the sweltering heat and high altitude I wasn't really taking it all in. One didn't walk around the place but clambered, as there were many steps and steep walkways to negotiate.

Soon it was time to leave and we boarded a coach to take us back to Aguas Calientes. The coach left the hotel and entrance complex and as we backtracked to the second hairpin there was a young lad dressed up in bright red Inca costume standing at the side of the road shouting an extended "G - o – o – d – b – y – e" to us as we passed.

Two hairpins later, he was there again with the shout of "A – d – i – o – s" as we went by, and these were repeated alternately all the way back to the bottom of the valley as he ran down a footpath between his calling points. At the bottom, of course, the coach stopped to pick him up, he was only about ten years old, and he went round with a collecting tin. By my reckoning he had earned every penny he collected and as I assume he was in training for a world record attempt at the Inca Trail route I fully expect to hear he's lowered that record to two hours very soon.

Back in the Aguas Calientes more chaos reigned as there was uncertainty about where lunch was being served, and whether we had to pay for it or not. Having found the location, we had a very quick turnaround having to scoff our meal so as to be back at the station for the train. This left no time to visit what looked like an excellent market in the main street of the town and which oddly the coaches had driven straight through, rather than stop so people could wander through.

The train ride back to Cusco was much the same as in the morning, another three and a half hours and my abiding memory of both journeys was the diesel fumes from the engine. If they converted the train to steam they'd have a real winner.

As you might have guessed, I hadn't enjoyed the day too much. We were both very tired so we ate in the hotel and had an early night as we had the two most demanding days of the rally starting tomorrow.

The real thing

Day 15 Saturday 20 October
Cusco – Ayacucho (684 kms)

The next few days would be the toughest of the event. The region was at the heart of the 1970 World Cup Rally that had prompted the creation of the Inca Trail Rally and our route would now take us up into the high Andes again and eventually down to the coast in Lima.

But here where the real rallying was beginning, a significant number of the entrants were forced to turn east to the coast to preserve their cars for the rest of the event – and it wasn't till we reached Lima that we would be a third of the way through the Inca Trail Rally.

Only seventeen classic rally cars and thirty one 4x4s would take the proper route, and even amongst these many would avoid as much of the competitive Sections as was practicable so as to preserve their cars, or themselves.

The number of cars going 'off piste' as it was described was so great that HERO allocated a support vehicle to them and we wouldn't see them again till we reached the rest day in Lima. 'Off piste' was a word they used but not one that those doing the proper route thought appropriate. 'Off piste' is a skiing term applied to someone going off the official piste to try something more challenging; this was hardly relevant to those heading to Lima by the coast route. To be fair the route available to them wasn't too easy either as road travel in these parts never is, but they were most definitely taking the much easier option.

The New Zealander David Mitchell driving a Holden Kingswood had a better word for them – *woosies* – roughly translated to English from Kiwi colloquial being – softies. Over dinner, we developed this thought and it eventually became the WRC, Woosies Rally Club. In the rally world WRC more usually refers to the World Rally Championship.

A High in the Andes

The woosies would drive with the rest of us to Abencay, all tarmac, then head east down to the coast and stay in the Nasca region, before turning north up the Pan American Highway to Lima. Once we were all together again in Lima we would retrace much of this route back to Nasca as we started to head south after our rest day.

It would be a tough day for us so we made an early start. The alarm was set for 3.45am (ugh, and we paid to do this!) and we were on the road at 5.00am when it was still dark.

The Kanes' Ford Mustang was in trouble early on. The route out of Cusco took us up through some side streets and out onto a main road at a T-junction. This had a steep uphill approach, and as the road book stated – "Care! – Deep gullies". The main road had a deep gully about one foot across and a foot deep running along its edge. This was bridged by the side road, but coming up this to the T-junction, especially with a long bonnet such as that on the Mustang, it wasn't possible to see where the bridge started and finished.

The Kanes had dropped their front wheels into the gully and even at this time of the morning a small crowd had gathered. We were next car along and offered help, getting our trolley jack out to put under their sump guard to jack the front up sufficiently for the car to be reversed back onto firm ground. This didn't take too long and once the Mustang was away, the locals put a small pile of stones at each end of the bridge as markers for those that would come along later.

The Kanes probably saved us from the same fate as I suspect that if they hadn't dropped into the gully we would have done, as it was an easy mistake to make.

We had only just got going again when we very nearly hit a dog. Dogs were a pain in the backside during the Inca Trail Rally as they would persistently run out into the road as we approached and run alongside the car. It would happen five or ten times a day in towns and villages and even miles from anywhere in open countryside. As often as not, we never knew where they came from and although many were probably owned, a lot were strays. Sometimes they would be in packs of four or more and initially, when we were back in Brazil, the natural reaction was to swerve away from them.

This was itself dangerous and we learned to ignore them and if we hit one – well, we hit one. In fact we never did, more by luck than any skill or judgement on my part, but several rally cars did.

Pam was always worried that we might. I was more realistic about it and whilst I wasn't going to go out of my way to hit one, if we did, well tough. Many dogs we saw had clearly lost an argument with a car, as they had withered or missing limbs but still wouldn't give up.

Often we would see some dogs a few hundred yards ahead and Pam would tense and take hold of one of the grab handles.

My reaction would be, "It's OK I've seen it."

"Take it easy."

"No. We are in a hurry and he's off the road anyway. I can't slow for every dog we see, we'll never get anywhere."

"But what if……."

"The chances are he'll chase us for a few yards and in doggy thoughts we clear out of his patch and he thinks he's a clever dog as we are gone. And then he'll do it again for the next car and the same thing will happen." Pam was never really happy about this, but we had no alternative but to keep going.

Our first port of call would be Abencay and a superb road took us up and up in glorious sunshine with views of surrounding snow-capped mountains. Although the road was good tarmac with fast sweeping bends and curves, from time to time it would change to gravel for short stretches where it crossed a stream, or in places where there had been landslides or earthquakes. The area was very reminiscent of the European Alps and in the company of some of the classics and fine sunny weather it was a very enjoyable drive.

Coming the opposite way were occasional groups of cyclists as this road offers a very long coast down with very little effort, probably

60 kms, from the top of the highest pass at about 4,300 m (14,000 ft). If you try it make sure the brakes are OK!

For us, the descent on the other side of the pass was spectacular too, but the bends far tighter, frequently hairpins, and from about 35 kms it was possible to see the town of Abencay.

On the way down we came across yet another lorry driver having a bad hair day. He had clearly been descending in an articulated lorry of cut timber and failed to take a right hand bend, ending up across the other side of the road where his lorry was stuffed into a steep bank. No one seemed to be injured and other vehicles had stopped to assist so we carried on.

Abencay was nothing special, in fact despite its size, most of the roads were gravel and there was only one petrol station. For those having a business or house on the main road, the dust was a serious problem and hosing down the road to help minimise it was a regular occupation here and at many other places along the route.

Having negotiated Abencay, the road dropped down further until the official route turned off over a bridge to begin a long steep climb north toward Ayacucho. The road narrowed here as it began to climb and we were once again in amongst the classics. They started a Medal Section here and we all used the same road that had formed part of the Caminos de los Incas, a local city-to-city road race, held a few days earlier. I expected to see some evidence of this event, but nothing came to light over the next few hundred kilometres to Ayacucho.

As the road wound up into the mountains again we came upon a series of hairpin bends, so I stopped the car and videoed some of the rally cars as they passed by below us, and then again when they reached us.

In a village, we nearly had a coming together with a donkey. It just wandered out into the road in front of me. I swerved and brushed the side of it, but no damage was done to either of us.

Up at the top of a pass we came across a Time Control at a tiny little restaurant. Jingers, Dan and Greg were on duty clocking in the rally cars and sending them on their way again. Dan was having some chicken and rice as breakfast and we stopped, along with a couple of other 4x4s for a few minutes breather. I was desperate for a pee and across the road was a roughly-built structure with sacking walls and banyo (toilet) scrawled on the outside. I went to investigate and it was just a pit and little else. I did what I had to, but suggested to Pam that we drive on down the road and find a more appropriate ladies rural loo. However she used this one as she couldn't wait any longer. Quite an experience she said!

We headed on towards Andahuaylas, our next port of call on our way to Ayacucho, and dropped down for mile upon mile, often able to see the road ahead for ten or fifteen kilometres and with it cars and 4x4s ahead of us. Along here we came upon many adults and children waving madly at us, to which we gave a friendly toot in return.

In Andahuaylas we stopped for 10 minutes to stretch our legs before heading on. The area was very Alpine again and generally there was little growth beside the roads, in fact hardly at all.

Once up in the mountains again, we were waved down by Mike *Paparazzi* Johnson who was getting a lift with Anna and Jonathan Pelly-Fry in their Audi All Road. He wanted to take some head-on photos of them and asked if we could give him a lift for a few kilometres so he could find a suitable location for shooting. It was a squash as we had no rear seats but he managed to sit on some cushions after we'd moved some luggage.

Our car was running well, but I was always aware of squeaks and rattles that might start up.

My Colorado was built to French specifications and the dog guard I had bought from the local dealer didn't fit the existing seat belt bolts as it should have done. Surrey-Off Road had fabricated some brackets to suit and from time to time I was finding that these came loose, started squeaking and needed attention. This was one of those days and we stopped for a few minutes to tighten the bolts up.

Again we started to drop down into a river valley and this time there was quite a bit of shrubbery on each side of the road. Here we nearly had a nasty accident as a blue lorry coming the other way was taking rather more of the road than he should and I was left with a very narrow gap between him and thick bushes across the drain-off ditch from the road. I braked as hard as possible and we got a bit twisted up, with loads of opposite lock. I managed to miss the rear end of the truck by about three centimetres, and of course he was on my side. We were lucky! Pam hadn't seen this as her head was in the road book – just as well!

Soon afterwards we came across John Blanckley in his A90 Westminster stopped by the road, so we pulled over to see what the problem was. It turned out a shock absorber had gone but he needed no help to fix it, so we were soon on our way again.

We were now travelling in a river valley, a river that for once actually had water in it that was fast flowing. We followed it for some time before crossing over on a steel bridge and heading off towards the control for our Explorer Section start.

We'd had the air conditioning on and when I got out of the car here, the heat hit me like a wall. It was really hot, I guess in the upper 30s centigrade with no wind to speak of. Fortunately the control was set under the trees, marshals aren't half as daft as they look!

This Section, called Ninabamba, would be 100 kms long and take us up more mountains and on some of the narrowest tracks we would come across on the whole event. We left the Control at 3.20pm and headed up the mountains through a series of sandy hairpins, letting John Bateson and Colin Francis pass in the Ford Escort.

It was very twisty and at times the late afternoon sun would disappear behind the hills making it very difficult to see. Regularly we would turn around a headland straight into the low sun and could hardly see anything. The drops, on Pam's side of course, were often many hundreds of metres and a couple of times I just came to a stop trying to work out where the road actually went, it was so difficult to see. It was some of the most difficult driving I have ever done.

I was particularly conscious of the huge drops and remembered the comment Brian Culcheth, a works Triumph driver, made at the time of the original London - Mexico Rally - "The drops are so big that if you fell over the edge your clothes would be out of fashion before you hit the bottom." He was right.

We rounded one corner and there in front of us was Ann Locks waving us down, with the blue Porsche 911 she was sharing with Lady Pauline Harris over the edge of the road balanced precariously on some bushes.

"Can you help us?" asked Ann. "We got caught out by the sun and just couldn't see where the road went."

"Yes. I know what you mean. Can we tow you back onto the road?"

"Yes, but we'll need to be careful as Pauline is still in the car and it's balanced on some bushes. She doesn't want to risk getting out."

"Let's take a look," I said as I pulled over and got out of the car. Pam went to get the warning triangle out and put it down the road.

I walked up to the Porsche and took a look. The right hand rear wheel was still just about on the road edge, but the left hand front and rear of the car were well off and down the side of the track. Ann said it looked like the near side front wheel was perched on top of a bush. The slope down, away from the road was much more than 60 degrees and fell away for several hundred metres. Pauline looked shocked.

By now Pam had put out the warning triangle, retrieved the tow-rope from the back of our car and got the video out to record the incident.

Pauline couldn't get out of her car. Using the driver's door could have caused the centre of gravity of the Porsche to tip outwards and the car would have slipped off the bush and down who knows where. It might have been possible to climb over the centre console and get out of the passenger door, but I know how hard that is as I used to own a similar 911 myself and it isn't an easy manoeuvre to make, especially on a mountainside. I think Pauline was worried about creating any movement in the car, just in case it caused it to slip from its current predicament.

"Pulling the car straight back won't achieve much, so I'll pull right across the road so as to get the Porsche back onto terra firma," I said to Ann as I jumped back into our car and manoeuvred it into position. I closed up on the Porsche and between us Ann and I hooked up the tow-rope to the towing hitch at the front of the Colorado and to a sump guard mounting on the back of the Porsche.

I took up the slack and Ann checked with Pauline that she was ready and I pulled the Porsche backwards onto the roadway again. It was a simple manoeuvre, but when I stopped, the Porsche didn't and it nearly rolled back into our Colorado. A shout from Ann got Pauline to stamp on the brakes.

That done we unhooked the tow-rope, Ann thanked us quickly, jumped back into the Porsche and they were away. We soon headed after them, once we had sorted out the towrope and warning triangle, but quickly came upon them as they were travelling very slowly. They let us pass with a friendly wave.

We reached the end of the Section in the dark at 5.40pm after 12 hours 40 minutes on the road and still had a further 40 kms to do to get to the hotel. Back in 1970, Hannu Mikkola in his works Ford Escort had driven from the Bolivia/Peru border south of Puno to Ayacucho on a *prime* of 560 miles in almost the same time as I had done just a part of that distance, his *prime* being set at a 50 mph average. After such a trip he then had to drive on to Lima, (we would take another couple of days) following a route very similar to ours where he arrived 1 hour and 20 minutes early, having completed the trip from the border with Bolivia in just less than 24 hours of non-stop driving.

Another Ford Escort driver, Zasada, had taken somewhat longer on this *prime* as he wrote off a front strut and not having a spare 'borrowed' one from a standard 1,100cc Escort with drum brakes. The imbalance between a standard strut with drum brakes and a state-of-the-art works strut with disc brakes must have made for interesting driving.

Part of this route was also in the Peruvian Rally held the previous year, 1969, when allegedly a local driver had gone over the edge and neither the crew nor the car were ever seen again. I didn't think it appropriate to mention this to Pauline and Ann.

With it becoming dark, I stopped to take the plastic protective covers off the spot lamps and started using them as well as the normal standard lights. The road dropped down towards Ayacucho, still on gravel and we reached the edge of town.

Pam asked me to turn left into what seemed a back alley. I hesitated on the corner. "Are you sure this is the right road?"

"According to the road book it is. And the distance on the Brantz is right," came the response.

"The main road goes straight on and, well, this doesn't look right."

"Let's try it. There should be another turning on the left in a couple of hundred yards, a football pitch and then a school."

I headed off down the rough lane, picking my way through the ruts. Sure enough there was the football pitch and the school, and soon after we came to a junction and turned out onto a busy tarmac road and in a few minutes we had finished our day in the main square, the Plaza de Armas. Pam was well pleased with herself.

We had been on the road for a solid fourteen hours. We had found our way into town in the dark and had no problems with the car. There was a good crowd and Don and Pat Griffiths were marshalling and told us to leave the car where it was and walk to the hotel. They also mentioned there would be a firework display later in our honour.

The car was parked up at the side of the square with other Inca Trail cars as the authorities had closed the square to other traffic. Some young lads approached us wanting to wash the car, which wasn't dirty, only dusty. They had no water with them and I doubted they could do a good job, I didn't want the dust smeared around the bodywork. I said no, but they persisted, indicating plastic ice cream boxes they had and a small fountain a few yards away that they planned to use as a water supply. I still doubted their ability to do a reasonable job and repeated my no.

They moved on to someone else's car.

We checked in to the Playa Hotel, a bit run down and basic but it seemed OK for the one night, and headed for the bar for a couple of drinks – we felt we'd earned them today. It was already busy as there was a good atmosphere with rally and 4x4 drivers well mixed together with busy chat about the day's drive. It had been tough and long for all of us and we'd made it. The woosies didn't know what they'd missed.

Outside the bar window in the side street was a crowd of people and while chatting and drinking I could see that something was afoot. Some people were dressed in costumes and there was a big framework construction that was clearly for fireworks.

Soon there was a lot of excited dancing and prancing about and the fireworks were lit and the framework set alight. It was bedlam, flashes and bangs, whizzes and whooshes mixed with tall flames, and all very close to our hotel and another building across the street. The whole display lasted only a couple of minutes, but was very impressive, if rather frenzied. But it wasn't for us.

It seemed that the Peruvians need no excuse to use fireworks and the display held in honour of the rally would take place later. Pam and I wandered back down to the square at the appointed hour and waited around for twenty minutes for the firework display for us. Another wooden tower was there, along with fireworks tied to various places of the structure.

However, nothing happened so we went to find a meal back at the hotel.

On top of the world

Day 16 Sunday 21 October
Ayacucho – Huancayo (395 kms)

This would be a slightly shorter day but it was due to be slow and tough. The 4x4s would be tackling the highest road in the western world - only the Himalayas have a few higher roads - which would offer us another first.

The first 20 kms out of Ayacucho were on tarmac which had suffered from earthquakes and was what was called a 'deformed' road. From time to time there would be a crack across the road with, perhaps, a six inch drop, or the road would have rolls in it caused by the heave from earthquakes.

Soon we turned off onto narrow twisting roads in desert landscapes. The road pitched and turned alongside a dried-up riverbed with high cliffs on our left and nasty drops to the right. It soon got very warm too and as the road wound its way around headlands it was hard to keep up a decent pace.

We were steadily climbing and the road book was littered with remarks about crossing fords. We reached a summit at over 4,600 m (15,000 ft) and dropped down again before entering the small town of Lircay where the route would split, the classics taking a lower, easier road to Huancayo.

On leaving Lircay we arrived at the supposed control point to find nobody there. We decided to wait whilst other 4x4s carried on, and within ten minutes Peter Rushforth arrived and soon had our time cards marked and we headed on.

This was the start of the road up to the Abra Huayraccasa at 5,059 m (16,593 ft). Initially it was very rough, certainly compared to any road we had used so far, and I used the low gearing on the Colorado. We crossed an awkward bridge and then the going became better with the track crossing green fields and meadows.

We were only five kilometres into the test and making good progress on the track across meadowland when I made my big mistake. I guess I lost concentration for a moment, or was watching the scenery out to our left, but all of a sudden we were halfway off the track and the nearside of the car was sinking into a mire. I think I had taken to the edge of the track to avoid a deep puddle on the left side, thinking the edge was good grassland. But it wasn't. There was a green sludgy top to muddy waters underneath and the car sank straight in, ending up at about 45° from horizontal.

Of course Pam was nearest the mire and was a bit shocked. She confirmed she was all right, that she wasn't injured in any way, but I knew I had to keep her busy over the next few minutes to avoid her thinking too much about what had happened. I wasn't worried about the state of the car or getting out, as it had been a very soft 'landing' and we would soon get a tow out from another 4x4.

Getting out of the car was another matter. That had to be on my side, and with the car over at 45° it was very difficult getting the door open, and then once it was open, holding it open, almost vertically, while I climbed out. Pam then followed after squirming over the central console and we had a look round to assess the situation.

As I thought the car was all right, it was just the right hand pair of wheels that were in the mire, the others were still on firm ground. It was obvious that we would not be able to get out under our own steam, frontwards or backwards, as I was certain we would only get ourselves in deeper.

By now George and Barbara Pollnow had stopped, and behind them Dave and Carole. The tow rope was clearly needed, but getting that out too was a job and a half, as the rear door of the Colorado opened downwards towards the mire and was quite a weight. Having got the tow rope out, I nearly fell into the mire myself trying to pull the door back up again to close it.

Phil Surtees in one of the Course Cars had now arrived as well and suggested it would be best to pull the car out backwards, rather then forwards, the original plan, so George agreed to line up his Daimler-Chrysler G461 and we hooked the two vehicles together.

To keep Pam busy, I had retrieved the video camera from the Colorado and she was filming the whole operation for the record.

A couple of minutes later, and no more than 10 minutes after I first went off, our truck was back on terra firma, we had unhooked the tow rope and George was on his way again after a few thank yous.

Pam and I sorted ourselves out, checked for any damage, but there was none, just a lot of mud on the two wheels that dropped in, and headed for the hills once more.

Quite properly, I was feeling somewhat embarrassed at what I'd done, and I took it carefully for the next half hour, but we were soon in the groove again and back to normal.

The track carried onwards and upwards and was the narrowest, roughest and slowest we'd tackled so far on the Inca Trail, but no problem for a 4x4. We were soon passing through the small village of Huachocolpa.

The quality of the road improved a little and we passed several waterfalls with strongly coloured water, and beside them, red and green deposits, although we couldn't tell whether these were natural deposits or from a mine working.

The road headed on and soon entered a large mine working area where zinc, lead and copper are worked. There was a maze of roads leading around a grey tailings pond, a weighbridge and various mine buildings and offices. The whole area was strangely quiet with no vehicles and people and we supposed this was because it was a Sunday.

Upwards we continued, the road clearing the mine working area, but twisting up a huge mountain slope with the road cut across its whole width. From below we could see tiny dots crossing this road, and before long we were doing the same. To the left we could see a steep sandy slope up to the mountain top, to the right a huge drop way down to the valley floor, the mine and other 4x4s meandering their way through the workings.

The higher we went, the worse the weather became. We had had some showers, but as we reached the summit so it began to get very windy with light snow blowing hard across the track.

An arched sign marked the top of Abra Huayraccasa and we parked underneath it for the obligatory photographs standing there in our shorts getting freezing cold in the winds and snow. There was a HERO control soon afterwards which we reached at 2.23pm.

We were at 5,030 m about $3\frac{1}{2}$ miles straight up. Pam and I thought about joining the $3\frac{1}{2}$ mile high club, but in the rarefied atmosphere decided we didn't have the energy!

The road now was much better. It headed down the mountains, mainly straight and was generally better engineered and smoother. However it occurred to us that we were fortunate it had been a Sunday when we tackled this road as there were no mining trucks on it – they would have made an interesting obstacle to our progress.

There was, however, one set of bends, and amongst these an 'impossible' right hand hairpin where the terrain prevented a wider road so that a full bend could be constructed. To overcome this the engineers had built a small roundabout about 80 m further on, where cars did a full circle so they then came back on themselves and turned down the lower part of the bend.

We were following Dave and Carole on this road and held back as they reached the junction, only to notice that as he arrived at the roundabout he went round English style (starting on the left) rather than Peruvian style on the right hand side. This wouldn't have mattered if the only car we had seen in ages hadn't arrived from the other direction and they met in the middle of the roundabout!

Lower down, we drove into Huancavelica hitting a proper asphalt road for a short while but were then stopped by a policeman standing next to diversion signs. The road ahead was blocked by piles of earth, so we followed his directions across some open ground till we reached the river where it was obvious we had to cross via a deep ford. This was no problem and on the other side, another policeman on a moped signalled us to follow him along the river bank for a couple of hundred metres, back across the river over a bridge, around the back of a walled sports ground and then onto the main road again where he waved us goodbye.

It was still over 100 kms to get to the outskirts of Huancayo and it was getting dark as we came upon a new road that swept through the countryside with virtually no traffic on it. Nor were there any road markings or signs, so when the road abruptly stopped and reverted to gravel, as it did on two or three occasions, the driving became interesting to say the least!

It was dark now and Pam was doing her stuff with the road book and Brantz. We came to a T-junction in a cluster of houses where we expected to see a Course Car as the Classics were due to have a time control here. There was none, but we managed to pick out a HERO arrow on a far telegraph pole and turned right. This matched the instruction in the road book, but Pam was doubtful because there was no marshal there.

In between road book tulips, no indication is given about the road so we just had to press on. Usually there was no doubt about which way to go, but the road we were on now seemed very rural and dived down into a dry river bed and out again with no road book instruction, although we would have expected one.

We pressed on and the next instruction seemed right. We joined a poor quality dual carriageway.

"3.2 turn right off the dual carriageway," said Pam, "there'll be a building on the far corner."

"3.2 turn right off dual carriageway," I repeated.

We got to 3.0 on the Brantz and I slowed to find the turning. There was no advance warning and little evidence of any turning right. In the gloom a building emerged on the right, and in front of it a narrow lane leading away to the right between stone walls. At the junction itself was a huge puddle.

"There's a turning here Pam, is it the right one? It looks a bit grotty."

"That's the instruction."

I was still doubtful, as we were heading into a sizeable town, with not far to go to the centre, and here we were turning off a dual carriageway onto a dirt track.

I looked around and from what I could see in the dark, the dual carriageway actually ended here, there was nowhere else to go. It was one of those roads that they start building, run out of money and just stop.

I turned into the track and through the puddles, but got no further than a few yards as there were two huge coaches heading towards me and the track wasn't wide enough to pass. Well I guessed it was the right road if the local coaches used it. I reversed back out onto the dual carriageway, let them by, and headed on in again.

In 200 metres the track widened out, we bumped over another not-so-level crossing and came out in another few hundred metres to a main road to turn left. This turned out to be the main road into town and a few minutes later we were outside the Town Hall and being directed onto the pavement and the control that was sited on the plaza to the side of the building.

We got out to get our bearings and see whether there were any Lions about. There weren't so we headed for the hotel which was sited on a road at the back of the square and which had its own car park. I drove into the car park and it was jam packed with classics and some 4x4s that had taken the easy route for the day. We found a space and unloaded to check in.

We had a meal in the hotel with Anna, Jonathan, David and Patsie. The New Zealanders were finding the going a bit tough, never having competed on a rally previously, and weren't taking the time keeping too seriously, just enjoying themselves. I asked David how he'd heard about the event.

"I opened a car magazine one day and there was a short piece about HERO organising a rally. I thought "Oh no. They're not getting in on that as well are they.""

"What do you mean?" I asked.

"Well HERO is the main gay rights group in Maori land and they organise all sorts of parades and events to promote their causes and it looked like they were getting in on car rallies as well. Only when I read it more carefully did I see that this HERO was rather different."

I complimented David on his driving the previous day when we'd followed him for many miles up the tarmac pass out of Cusco. I hadn't tried to overtake as he was doing a good pace.

"You pedal that old car very well."

"Thanks, it goes quite well once you get it going. And down hill it's even better – we use Maori overdrive a lot."

"Maori overdrive?"

"Yes, freewheeling in neutral." Hoots of laughter all round the table.

It was a good evening as we all knew that we had probably tackled the worst roads we would traverse on the Inca Trail and made it in one piece. Well, most of us had. We heard that the Lucas's had managed to damage the step rail on the side of their Amazon, whilst the sandy coloured Toyota of Arnold Meier had dropped into a ditch and bent some bodywork but was still going.

On top of the railway world

Day 17 Monday 22 October
Huancayo - Lima (389 kms)

There was a slight sense of euphoria as we set off this morning. We had, by all accounts covered the worst sections and come through unscathed, and whilst we still had a long way to go, the next few days would be fairly straightforward, and tomorrow would be a rest day anyway.

We set off at about 8.30am, a late start, and were soon out of town heading north towards La Oroya through a fertile river valley, the worst hazards being potholes that proliferated along this stretch of road. This caused the usual problems of lorry avoidance as they ducked left or right without notice around holes they saw or were familiar with. We passed through Mucqui (which it wasn't) and on through a string of farming communities, before heading into the hills at a major junction where there were at least a dozen police on duty.

The only car we saw in difficulty along here was the Ferrari that once more was jacked up with Alastair underneath, checking something out. The Camels had stopped to offer help so we kept going.

As we headed into the hills on our way to La Oroya we were joined through the river valley by the railway line that runs from Huancayo through to La Oroya and then over the Ticlio Pass and down to Lima. It is the highest railway line in the world, far higher than anything in the Himalayas, and 1,500 m higher than the Jungfrau in Switzerland, but these days is only used for freight traffic.

As the road headed into higher territory, so the landscape became bleaker, but in total contrast our arrival in La Oroya was marked by tall industrial chimneys spewing smoke. La Oroya is a mining town 3,700 m above sea level and the town is spread out along the River Manteo.

We now turned west to climb up over the Ticlio Pass, passing the highest golf course in the world, and overtaking dozens of lorries climbing slowly up the same road as well. At the top of the pass, which is said to be the highest asphalted road in the world, we turned off for a few minutes to check out a monument commemorating the railway that passes here at 4,818 m (15,806 ft).

It was downhill all the way now as the road tumbled through numerous bends, with a river and the railway never far away, until we reached the suburbs of Lima and with it a nasty aggravating smog. The roads were much busier now and as we hit a wide dual carriageway heading into town we joined several other Inca Trail 4x4s driving in echelon weaving through the traffic.

Soon we had arrived at El Pueblo las Americas, a resort hotel, that would be our home for a couple of days and we enjoyed a pisco sour as we checked in. We parked up and got our bags to our room, and as it was still only early afternoon, found a restaurant in the complex for some lunch.

We took it easy in the afternoon, but made a point of turning up for a special meeting at which the problem with Peruvian hotels was due to be aired, as a statement had been issued by HERO earlier.

HERO had engaged a company called Hirca as their agent yet, unbeknown to HERO, during the whole of the time they had been dealing with them, they had been in administration (bankrupt). Very significant sums had been handed to Hirca yet these hadn't been used to pay hotel deposits, as a result of which problems had occurred at various hotel locations in recent days. Some hotels had had to be changed at short notice, sometimes participants had unexpectedly had to pay for their rooms and there was often doubt about whether or not any particular hotel would accept crews when they arrived to take their rooms.

In the absence of John, Joanna Brown spoke to the gathered rally crews in the conference centre of the complex. She explained the problems and how they were trying to deal with them – not easy when the rally entourage of 300 plus people is moving on day by day. She sought our indulgence with assurances that they were doing all they could and so far everyone had been found accommodation.

Several questions and statements were then made from the floor, not always complimentary of HERO, but in a timely manner, Jonathan Pelly-Fry stood up and congratulated Joanna on her handling of the matter, confirming that many Inca Trailers were sympathetic to her predicament, and suggesting that the majority of participants in the Inca Trail wished to offer their support and understanding. This received, quite correctly, a round of applause, but I noticed a few who failed to put their hands together and shook their heads in disagreement. They were mainly woosies.

A short break ensued before the next item on the agenda, a party thrown by the Automobile Club of Peru and most people headed for the bar to warm up for the festivities.

The party took the form of a barbecue, with demonstrations by local dancers and two firework displays. The food and drink was good, the dancers were colourful and vibrant putting on a terrific display, the music was loud and raucous, and as expected the fireworks seemed to last for ever.

Where is prisoner Number 6?

Day 18 Tuesday 23 October
Lima rest day

We reckoned we'd earned our rest day and as the car was running well, felt we should take it as easy as possible. The alarm went off at 7.30am but Pam switched it off. I didn't hear it at all. She got up later and breakfasted on her own while I slept in till about 11.00am.

It was still smoggy and the air caught our breath and whilst there were opportunities to go into Lima we decided to stay and potter about at El Pueblo. The resort reminded us of Portmeirion, the North Wales village built in Italianate style by Sir Clough Williams-Ellis and used as a location for the Patrick McGoohan television series, 'The Prisoner'. There were lots of little passageways and alleyways leading to new areas of accommodation and the main facilities. We expected the big, soft white ball that was forever chasing Prisoner No 6 to appear at any time, but it never did.

In a tented area, a bit like a mini Millennium Dome, the local motor club had set up an exhibition of Peruvian-owned classic cars. These ranged from small British saloons and sports cars to big American automobiles, and most were in good condition. We were both pleased to see an old Mini, Pam's first car, and an Austin A35, very similar to my first ever car, an A30.

All entrants had been encouraged to raise funds for charity and one of the 4x4 woosy teams, Wendy and Tim Franey had managed to raise £50,000 for a local children's charity and a presentation was made with the British Ambassador present.

I spent some time checking the Colorado and unpacked most of our gear to sort it out. David Mitchell borrowed our trolley jack as he was rebuilding his rear brakes and in return Pam borrowed his brush to sweep out some of the rubbish and dust that had accumulated in our car.

In the evening there was a grand dinner held in our honour, and we had the first prize giving for the event. The prizes were given for performance on the first sector of the Inca Trail Rally and were predominantly given to the classics.

These were divided into four Categories; Category A being those produced before 1950; Category B built before 1958, Category C before 1968 and Category D being those built between 1968 and 1976. These categories were further subdivided into classes based on engine size and type of car – sports or touring.

In all, there were twelve classes for the fifty-four classic rally car entries, and for most of these, awards were given out to those leading and in second place in each class. It was a long, boring affair that would be repeated later in the event as prizes were presented again after the completion of further sectors.

By contrast, only two awards were given to the 4x4s. Admittedly we weren't engaged in any competitive event so the awards were presented, quite rightly, to the Irish lads, Barry Aughey, Gerry McGuigan and Eugene Courtney in their Hyundai for sportingly helping out several classics, in particular the Aston Martin; and the American father and son team of Robert and Ryan Lowe in the Land Rover for their Spirit of Adventure; but the balance seemed wrong to me and I made my views known to Don Griffiths at the end of the evening.

Once the award presentations were over, a good band and singer kept us entertained late into the evening as the piscos flowed.

Desert rats

Day 19 Wednesday 24 October
Lima - Ica (477 kms)

The nature of the Inca Trail would change dramatically today, for instead of mountains, we would be heading into the desert to begin our long three week trek south to Tierra del Fuego. We left El Pueblo at about 8.00am and headed towards Lima, before hitting the equivalent of their M25 to avoid the city centre and head out south and onto the Pan American Highway. These roads had a hotch potch of vehicles on them, grossly overladen lorries struggling to do 30 kph, old wrecks of cars that had been patched up a thousand times, and bicycles – everywhere.

The pollution was no better, if anything worse, as we headed further down towards the coast. It rasped at the throat leaving a choking feeling. One wonders what the long-term effects are for the locals.

However we were soon heading south away from Lima, and glad to be doing so as we started to hit the Atacama Desert that would dominate our driving conditions for the next week or so. Gradually the pollution diminished the further we headed into the desert on a good tarmac road, through sand dunes and small seaside resorts. Initially the sand was dark and polluted in places with rubbish, but this too steadily gave way to cleaner, whiter sand. The Pacific Ocean also came into view and added a new freshness to the climate.

Our initial target for the day was the Paracas National Park where we were due to have an Explorer Section across the desert. We needed to be there promptly as HERO wanted to check all the cars in and out at both ends of the Section so they could be sure nobody went missing.

The Section started near the town of Pisco, about 250 kms into our day, that has given its name to the brandy liquor made locally and which we had been sampling in pisco sours in copious quanitities over the last week or so.

We started the Explorer Section at 11.20am and immediately left the tarmac to take a series of desert tracks, at first along the coastline. We stopped at one particularly pleasant bay and went down to the edge of the sea to have a paddle and take a couple of photos before heading on. We'd now achieved one of our principle aims on the Inca Trail Rally, getting from coast to coast.

I had hoped we would pass near the famous Candelabra sand drawing that is etched into the side of a hill facing the sea. It is 200 m high by 60 m wide, but nobody really knows why it's there or who created it. Although it is called the Candelabra, it is said to be more likely a representation of a cactus or the Southern Cross, although the idea of it being a beacon for sailors is more appealing to most people. However, this was well off the route we would follow, and, as I learned later, is best seen either from the air or a boat.

On this Section, the tulip instructions were often very different to those we had been used to. Now we had instructions such as:

- Keep left round base of hill
- Head towards low hill in middle of valley
- Large dune ahead to left
- 3 low pointed rocky outcrops to R
- Keep close to shore

and if there wasn't a track we made our own route through the desert sand.

The sand was hard and although we kicked up a trail behind us, grip wasn't a problem as we sped along. About 40 kms into the Section we came to a lovely sweeping bay with a small village away to our right where the road book recommended a stop for a fish lunch. The route took us into the village, but one look at the shacks that claimed to be restaurants soon determined that we would keep going. The setting however was a delight. The sun was shining, the sky was blue and the sea sparkled. It was very warm with a pleasant breeze blowing off the sea and but for the quality of the eateries, we could have stayed and chilled out for many hours.

We were in company with several other 4x4s and the route back out to the main road was less easy to follow. At one time there had been a proper road, but the sand had reclaimed much of it and the main features to follow were kilometre markers and piles of sea shells the locals had deposited to help their own navigation.

It was easy to lose the main route though, and 4x4s were careering around all over the place trying to pick out the track. It was great fun and we could keep a good pace as we bucked and rolled across the sand back to the main road. It was one of the best sections we did on the whole event and as the finish was quite close to the start point, I was nearly tempted to go around again.

All that remained for the day was a straightforward run down the Pan American again to Ica, an oasis in the middle of the desert, where all the 4x4s would stay the night at Las Dunas Hotel. The classics went on down to Nasca.

The hotel was a lovely place, and as we arrived early in the afternoon we all flopped out in front of the pool catching up on post cards, swimming and enjoying a drink. It was a pleasant few hours and we all felt much less pressured than during the previous couple of weeks.

We had a good dinner in the evening too, joining with an elderly English couple Edwin and Carolyn Hammond and toasting Edwin, as it was his birthday.

They were in a Land Rover Discovery to which they had had a roll cage fitted, one of the few in a 4x4. There had been much discussion before and during the event about the benefits of fitting a roll cage to the 4x4s for safety reasons.

The benefits were obvious, there was considerably more protection if one had a bad accident, but the downside was cost, intrusion into the passenger compartment of the car and risk of head injury as they tended to be closer to the body than the normal bodywork and the crew wouldn't be wearing crash helmets.

We were in bed early, at 10.00pm, as it would be another early start tomorrow.

Up, up and away

Day 20 Thursday 25 October
Ica - Arequipa (574 kms)

Today would be action packed as besides having two Explorer Sections to do in the desert, we had also booked a flight over the famous Nasca Lines.

The first Section started just off the Pan American Highway near the lost city of Hoayuri. We decided not to visit the city but to go straight to the start of the Section where the control was sited, next to a 1,000-year-old carob tree. For the first 20 kms this Section was much like yesterday's one in the Paracas National Park although the main tracks to follow were better defined and more frequently used. However, rather than being sunny and bright, the day was overcast and murky and the sand was much darker than at Paracas. The tracks flowed much better too, and dipped and dived between river valleys with sweeping bends.

The second part was a great contrast as we passed through some villages and along tracks between walled fields and enclosures. In one village the instruction was:

• Pass across football pitch, to the left of the goal posts.

The villagers were out to watch and there were many friendly waves. As in Bolivia and Peru, we wondered what they thought of us in our expensive, high-powered 4x4s zooming through their villages, leaving a trail of dust, vanishing in seconds. What would we think if a Peruvian motor club came to do a rally in the back lanes around Guildford? I would welcome them with open arms, but I suspect the local authorities would be horrified, as would local residents. Shame really.

We crossed a couple of riverbeds though there wasn't too much water in them and all too soon we were at the control ready to join the main road again.

Next on the agenda for the day was a visit to the famous Nasca Lines. The main road climbs up onto the Nasca Plain and very soon we came upon a Mirador, a viewing tower, built very close to one of the key features of the plain, and got out to take a look. I had been looking forward to this visit as the lines are something of an enigma; nobody really knows what they are for or who made them. All manner of hypotheses have been put forward but none adequately explains their purpose. There are hundreds of arrow straight lines across the desert as well as hieroglyphs of various animals and birds.

We left the tower and headed on into Nasca itself where, like many of the Inca Trailers, we had booked a flight over the lines. As I have explained before, I don't like flying, but having taken some pills decided that my wish to see the lines from the air overrode any discomfort I might feel.

The flights were in small four-seater planes. Pam went up with Carol and Roland Guille, both from Guernsey who were in the event in a Land Rover Discovery. I took a flight a few minutes later accompanied by David and Carole who sat in the back whilst I sat next to the pilot, a chap called Carlo. He produced a small map and showed us the figures he would take us to, including representations of a humming bird, whale, eagle and others.

Admittedly the weather wasn't the best, but I had a job picking them out from all the other lines etched into the desert surface. We flew from one to another and he did a tight turn over each, circling around at almost vertical position before levelling out again.

For the first few I felt fine, but gradually I was feeling worse and worse and I was getting really queasy. I didn't want to embarrass myself but prepared myself just in case – I planned to slide open the window and spew out what might come.

I suspect Carlo knew how I was feeling because I managed to last out till the final figure and he said we would be flying back to Nasca now. I was very pleased about this. He turned to me and asked, "Would you like to fly the plane?"

"Well, yes please."

He showed me how to use the joy stick and pedals that control the throttle for the single engine and took his hands off his joystick and left me to it. I jiggled the joystick a little to judge the reaction and Carlo showed me how to maintain the right bearing and the correct height.

To be fair I wasn't doing much, Carlo adjusted the trim regularly and we flew along for 5 minutes or so back towards Nasca. In the murk, I could see the runway over to our right, sorry starboard, and Carlo asked if I wanted to land the plane too.

"Sounds OK to me."

"You make sure plane flies like this," and he showed me with his hands how the plane needed to swoop round to the right and lose height towards the runway. I did my best to do his bidding, but I noticed he was using his joystick now as well, and also adjusting all sorts of knobs and buttons. But we were soon lined up for the runway and in no time had landed and taxied to the hard standing. I didn't do much really, but it took my mind off the queasiness.

We jumped down from the plane and although I felt better than I had earlier, I really felt awful and couldn't get away quick enough. I was very close to being sick and didn't want to do so in public. I gathered Pam up and we jumped into the car and I headed away from the airport. Even writing this now I begin to feel queasy again and it took me a full twenty-four hours to get back to normal. Unlike Iguacu Waterfalls, I wished I hadn't.

And the Nasca Lines? I was very disappointed. They are probably a wonder of the world, but I wasn't impressed, perhaps the condition of my stomach influenced my thoughts. Someone said they were just "scratchings in the desert", and sadly I have to agree.

But the day wasn't over yet, not by a long way. Pam and I stopped a few miles down the road and I took a walk to get some fresh air into my lungs and stabilise my stomach. It was still only 10.15am but we had a 300 kms thrash to the next Explorer Section, and after that another 160 kms to our overnight stop at Arequipa.

It was a great road, mainly running alongside and on cliffs above the Pacific and with little traffic we made good progress. The weather didn't improve and although it was sunny, it was still dull and we couldn't see far out to sea. There were, however, plenty of fishing boats near to the coast and the little villages we passed through clearly based their economy on what they could glean from the sea.

From time to time the road climbed high over the ocean, with sand dunes on the left and huge drops to our right down to the sea. Occasionally we would drop down into quebradas, valleys usually with settlements, where there was often some fertile soil and water with rice growing, before climbing back out again onto the desert plateau. In several places the sand was blowing very strongly across the road and fingers of sand spread out into the road, shielded by small bushes.

I needed to have something to eat to settle my stomach and we found a little roadside café perched on top of a cliff where I had some rice and fish. We couldn't see far out towards the ocean, so watched the traffic going by, the occasional compatriot in a 4x4 and huge lorries, mostly Volvos, Mercedes and Scanias.

Another sight on the road were long-distance coaches typically driving from Lima to Santiago in Chile and we wondered how much longer they would take to complete their trips compared to our high speed runs from town to town.

In Camana we turned away from the ocean and off the Pan American to tackle another Explorer Section, this one being only 14 kms long. We had been told it ran up a sandstone valley with weird rock formations and so it did, but only after the following instruction in the road book:

   • Through rubbish dump to scenic sand canyon for c1km

Sure enough, along the first few hundred metres of the track, rubbish was strewn around and blowing about in the wind. This was the local rubbish dump.

Further on, though, the wind blowing through the canyon had caused the sandstone to wear away and form lacy filigree overhangs on the rock. They were indeed very scenic and almost anywhere else in the world would be a major tourist attraction with parking lots, kiosks and tour guides. But here there was a rough old 4x4 track through a rubbish dump. Sad really.

We stopped and took photos at the outcrops and headed onto the rest of the Section that was a series of desert tracks, mainly with soft sand which blew up in huge trails behind the car and laid on the roof too, running off once we hit the main road again.

The run into Arequipa was fairly straightforward, we were back on the Pan American and but for the lorries there was little traffic. At one point the road dropped down into a deep, dried-up river valley about 250 m wide, the River Chili I think. Having dropped down one side, the road crossed the river and headed directly into a tunnel at river bed level, leading on for another 200 m and out into desert terrain again. Given the tunnel is at the same level as the river bed, one wonders what happens should it ever rain!

Further on we came to an area where there were a series of barcan sand dunes blowing across the road. The sand was a very light grey and it is said the dunes move forward at the annual rate of about 15 m. Unlike Namibia where we once came across a barcan dune about 15 m high blocking our road, these were only a few metres high.

A main control for the classics had been set up at a Shell garage on the way into town so we stopped there to refuel and check the car over. With so much sand and dust on the trip a regular part of the maintenance programme was to take out the air filter and use an airline to clear the dust. Today huge quantities of sand came out, probably as much as a teacup full – I just hoped none had reached the engine.

While at the garage a strange sight befell us. An ancient Datsun came into the garage packed to the gunnels with at least four people and all manner of personal gear. However, on the roof were the skinned carcases of two animals, llamas I think, still bleeding, the blood running down the bodywork. The heads were still attached to the bodies and draped over the sides of the car. Fresh meat for a barbecue, I suppose.

Nearby several classics were getting attention at various garages and workshops. Yet again John Bateson was in a tyre shop getting replacements, and a Mercedes was in an auto electricians with the bonnet up.

It was now dark and like most of our final controls, this one was set up in the Plaza de Armas, the main town square. Getting to it, though, was a real challenge; it was closed to normal traffic and chaos reigned in the surrounding streets as lorries, vans and the numerous black and yellow taxis tried to find a way round. Police were stationed on most corners and tried to help us thread our way through this mêlée, but it was twenty minutes of frustration at the end of a long day that we could have done without.

Our welcome in the square was very nice, with gifts given to us from the town, a drink and some promotional material. One side of the square is taken up with the famous white stone cathedral which was so badly damaged in the earthquake that hit the region during the summer of 2001. In fact at the time Don and Pat, the 4x4 Trailmasters, were in Arequipa checking the Inca Trail route. The earthquake caused enormous damage in the region, as well as fatalities and serious injuries to many Peruvians. It registered 8 on the Richter Scale – pretty high.

Our hotel for the night, the Portal, also adjoined the square, but to get to it we faced another circuit of the adjoining roads and their congestion or a neat loop around against the flow of traffic for a few yards. The policeman didn't like it but it was the obvious solution. We unpacked and checked in and found we had been allocated a huge suite overlooking the cathedral and square.

Don Griffiths and the police had recommended we didn't leave the car in the square overnight and directed us to the hotel parking a couple of streets away. This turned out to be an old Audi garage with a very deep underground car park. We drove down several floors from the street to park and felt like we were on a journey to the centre of the earth. I didn't like to think what might happen if there was another earthquake.

Another charity cheque presentation was planned for this evening. Inca Trail entrants had been encouraged to donate to a special earthquake fund for those people who were so tragically affected by the disaster. In all the rally had managed to raise £10,000 and a presentation 'do' had been arranged at the headquarters hotel, the Libertador for 7.30pm. So we jumped into a taxi to go over there aiming for an 8.00pm start, but still arrived far too early as the speeches didn't get going till 8.30pm. There was a good turn out, probably because there were free drinks and rallyists have a nose for such things.

Back at the Portal, rumours were circulating that the Hammonds had rolled their Discovery in one of the desert Sections, fortunately with only minor injuries, but would be retiring from the event as their vehicle was a write-off. Theirs was one of the few with a roll cage! We had a meal with Linda Banks and Chris Elliott and as we were feeling very weary headed for bed.

Invisible condors

Day 21 Friday 26 October
Arequipa - Colca Canyon - Arequipa (462 kms)

An early start was demanded today so as to be at the Colca Canyon in time to see condors, the huge Andean birds of prey, who use the thermals in the canyon to gain height. The best time to see this was said to be before 9.00am and it was 200 kms away.

For us the day's run was necessary as there was also an Explorer Section on the way back to Arequipa and missing it would drop us from the gold standard which we intended to maintain. Many crews, however, took the day off, either to fettle their cars or to visit the many tourist attractions in and around the city.

For the second, and last time the alarm was set for 3.45am, but we could get no breakfast at the hotel, so made our way up to the car park only to find the entrance ramp barred by a padlocked grill. We shouted out several times in the hope there might be someone down in the depths and had nearly given up when a dark apparition emerged from the gloom to unlock the gate.

As the route instructions out of town to the Day Start Control began at the headquarters hotel, we headed out there first and then on to the control at a garage at the edge of town. It was just before 5.00am. Paul Marsh and Greg Human were marshalling and several classics were ready to go, together with a growing number of 4x4s.

Technically, because we weren't in any competition we could have just driven on, however the Time Card recommended an earliest start of 4.45am and here we were. However Paul was concerned about the 4x4s mixing it with the classics and wouldn't sign our Time Cards till 5.15am, another twenty minutes or so. We agreed to wait but couldn't see the purpose of the delay, as we would surely catch up with many of them and it delayed our journey to the canyon to see the condors.

Needless to say, once we did start we soon caught up with some of the classics and because so many of us had been held up, we were travelling in convoy. Initially it was dark, but dawn soon arrived and with it superb views of the three mountains that surround the town. Most notable is the steaming volcano El Misti (5,822 m) which has an almost perfect cone, but it must be a menacing backdrop to those who live near it. Also visible were two other mountains, Chachani, a little higher, and Pachu-Pachu, slightly shorter, and all three silhouetted snow-capped peaks were tinged with pink from the dawn sky.

Once away from the city, the road soon deteriorated from smooth (ish) tarmac to some that was diabolically potholed. In fact there was probably less tarmac than holes and even in the 4x4 it was a dreadful road to use. There were several river bed crossings again and much of the route was similar to that we had passed in the Andes a week back. We crossed the railway line to Juliaca several times, but saw no trains.

The road climbed steadily, at times on gravel, and we crested four passes in quick succession at 4,350 m, 4,291 m, 4,219 m and 4,900 m, the car suffering by chucking out dark plumes of unburned diesel. There was snow around and also fog and low cloud which slowed our pace at times.

Throughout the trip we hadn't seen much wildlife, but along this road we saw a small kangaroo-like creature near the road which we think was a Peruvian hare. Another feature were hundreds of cairns alongside the road, built from small stones, and which we learned later were erected by locals as an offering to their gods for safe passage.

We stopped with several other 4x4s at the Mirador del Mismi where the clear mountain air offered views across the valley of the Rio Sihuas and the village of Chivay far below which was our next port of call.

In Arequipa, most of the local people dressed western style, but up here traditional costumes were much in evidence, the women in their short bell tent style skirts and always with hats, the men often suited although working in the fields.

Through Chivay and on up to the small villages of Yanque and Achoma there were signs of increasing tourist facilities and along the road up here we passed several mini buses bringing tourists up for one day or overnight trips to the canyon. It was pleasing to see, though, that all these developments were tasteful and in keeping with the local environment. Another feature here was evidence of Inca terracing and ancient irrigation channels feeding water to fields.

Near Macha we passed a lovely looking Baroque church, sadly surrounded by scaffolding as a result of the recent earthquake. This village was also badly damaged by an earthquake in 1991 and one can only guess at the effect on day to day life such a disaster can have. This part of southern Peru is one of the most active areas worldwide for earthquakes and the road for the next few kilometres was under repair as a result of damage.

We arrived at Cruz del Condor, the main viewing spot above the canyon, at 9.00am. There were many coaches there together with Inca Trailers, but sadly no evidence of condors. We took a wander around and got into conversation with some English people on a package tour who had been in Cusco when the rally was there and were interested to hear all about our adventures. They found our itinerary and the required daily mileages hard to comprehend and, I think, thought we were all mad. They were probably right!

The canyon is said to be the deepest in the world, although it didn't seem to be as deep as the Fish River Canyon in southern Namibia. I suppose it depends from where one measures these things. The Fish River Canyon and the Grand Canyon have a clear edge from which to make a measurement, whereas this canyon didn't, as it is surrounded by mountain peaks. The guidebooks tell you it is twice as deep as the Grand Canyon in the United States.

We stayed an hour but there was no sign of any condors. Together with many other people, we were pretty cheesed off. Would we have seen them if we hadn't been delayed at Arequipa, or not stopped for photos and looking at the stunning views? We'll never know. We managed to track down the local warden who told us the condors had flown at about 8.30am, but would they fly later? Was it worth waiting? He didn't know. But he did point out two condors to us that were flying above a ridge high up and miles away. So far as we were concerned they didn't count. At the Cruz, the condors are reported to rise on the thermals created in the canyon in the early morning and fly so close to the mountain it seems almost possible to touch them. Certainly photographs I have seen confirm this. We decided, reluctantly, to head back to Arequipa.

The road back improved and just before we reached the start of the Explorer Section at Cabanaconde we stopped to gaze upon a huge area of Inca terracing still in use by local farmers and providing valuable farmland in what would otherwise be a steep hillside. The return journey to Arequipa was uneventful and my notes on it are sketchy, but I remember it was very enjoyable, and much better than the road up. We were back in the city by 3.00pm but were very tired and hungry.

We took the car back to the underground car park and on the walk back sought out some food and found a burger bar. John Bateson and Colin Francis joined us again and some of the Americans also came in to eat. The need to catch some zeds came next so I napped in the room until we made our way to the hotel bar to meet with others.

The talk was all about the problems HERO was having with hotels and Carol and Roland Guille had had to pay their own room bill at another hotel. It was suggested we might have to do the same before leaving in the morning as there was no funding from HERO because of the problem with Hirca. It was also reported that Jo Brown would be round later to explain what might happen.

There was no sign of Jo, so Pam and I went out to do some shopping for souvenirs and restock our nose-bag for the car and later met up with the Guilles again for a meal.

It had been a frustrating day. We'd done a 500 km loop for no particularly good reason, whilst those who stayed behind had rested and enjoyed the tourist attractions, raving especially about the beautiful architecture at Santa Catalina Convent, a haven of peace and tranquillity in the middle of the city. On top of this, the hotel situation was still tricky and many people were 'slagging off' HERO at every opportunity over this and the roughness of the route. Tomorrow, however, we were due to leave Peru for Chile.

Beyond the boondocks

Day 22 Saturday 27 October
Arequipa - Arica (475 kms)

Today's Explorer Section at 210 kms had been intended for use by the classics, but due to earthquake damage they missed it and headed straight down the Pan American to the border with Chile and on to Arica by the Pacific coast.

The Omate Section was described in the road-book as… "the last of the challenging Peruvian and Bolivian mountain roads with a variety of super scenery and gravel surfaces." It was to turn out to be a brilliant section!

The run out of Arequipa in the growing dawn was average, although Pam admitted to being lost and was relying on me as she thought I knew where we should be going. With her nose in the road book, she didn't see that I was following Arnold and Melanie Meier in their sand yellow Toyota 4 Runner they'd previously used on the London - Capetown event.

The start of the Section was soon reached however and I gave them a few minutes start to avoid running in their dust and left at about 8.00am. Very soon we came upon the two former Camel Trophy Discoveries parked up at the side of the road with their OK board displayed. They were parked nose to nose at 90 degrees to the road, both with their bonnets up and looked as if they were trying to mate. It turned out that one had electrical problems.

We climbed and climbed through scrubby countryside passing around the edge of the village of Pocsi ("no rude comments" said the road book!). The road twisted and turned in every direction and although a bit rough in places, the driving was great and a good pace was maintained. As we progressed, the countryside became more remote and settlements rare, but people still emerged at the side of the road to wave. It was hard to work out where they came from.

We had a close call near Pucquina, where I rounded a corner to find a huge white Volvo truck careering towards me. He was clearly stopping for no-one but fortunately the track was wide enough for us to pass, but not for his mate in an identical truck a couple of minutes later. We screeched to a halt on the very edge of the track as he sped by without any lessening of speed and millimetres from our bodywork. I slowed a bit for a while, half expecting another truck to arrive, but none did.

The road started to go through a very sandy area, with huge sand hills with sparse tufts of grass growing on them. A strong wind was blowing and the sand was streaming across from the hills onto the road, which, although it had a hard gravel base, was covered with about five to ten centimetres of sand. It made for great driving and once more huge sand trails billowed out behind us.

In Omate, which must rank as one of the remotest villages in this part of Peru, everyone was out to wave us through. There was a short piece of concrete roadway here and parked up in a corner a bus that presumably was their lifeline to civilisation.

The nature of the Section changed here as we dropped down into a dried up river valley between very high mountains and beautiful coloured rock faces. There was every hue of khaki, brown, sand, rust, auburn, copper, tan and many more and although one might think of them as being drab, the scenery and its colouring was quite stunning for many miles to come. We were in an area where the Andes and Atacama Desert meet and I think the colours were influenced by this conjunction. For me, this moment was one of the most memorable of the whole event, almost religious in its significance.

Dwellings continued to be few and very far between, but all of a sudden there was a modern saloon car parked at the side of the road, and way below, close to the dried up river, a small house surrounded by a patch of greenery.

A dog too, also suddenly appeared further on, apparently from nowhere, and yet again we did his bidding and cleared out of his territory as fast as we arrived.

The road ran along the left edge of the valley, at times cutting into the cliff face, and there was much evidence of recent rock falls. On the right hand side of the valley in what seemed like a perpendicular face, a road was cut climbing steadily up towards a pass along the face. This would be our next challenge.

The road swept right over the riverbed far below and almost immediately the nature of the track changed from sandy gravel to rock. It was here, and over the next 30 kms, that the earthquake damage to the road had been worst and as the road climbed the cliff face so it was evident that much of the way was newly created. We picked our way through fallen rocks, some as big as houses, the track-way at times only just wide enough to squeeze through. About halfway up we came upon two workmen, one driving a mechanical digger, working on the road and still further on, an impossible hairpin.

Here the terrain demanded the road climb steeply left and uphill from our approach, but the turning was almost impossible to make without a lot of to-ing and fro-ing. However the road builders had kindly created a short flat run to the right where about 100 m away was a full turning circle. A neat solution to an awkward problem. This road hadn't been checked in the summer when Don and Pat were here as it was impassable due to the earthquake damage.

Once over the top of the climb of the cliff face, the landscape became very bleak, much as I imagine the badlands of Wyoming look. The road however, where there was no damage, was fast and sweeping, a joy to drive on.

Frequently it climbed up and over mountains and for a long time we saw nobody but a 4x4 in the distance ahead of us, and occasional glimpses of another, way behind us. Then all of a sudden we came upon a white Daewoo 4x4 taxi saloon going the same way as us. It's hard to imagine what journey might be necessary in a taxi from these parts, but he was trundling along at a reasonable pace with two up in the back. Imagine a London taxicab doing this – they won't even go south of the River Thames after midnight!

The taxi soon let us pass and we continued on, again suddenly coming upon clumps of lilac-coloured heather at the side of the road and on nearby hillsides. In the bleak landscape they stood out like dazzling beacons. The road continued to be brilliant as a driving experience, much like an Acropolis Rally.

The weather was very warm and sunny and I guess my eyes were strained somewhat as when we reached the Finish Control, where the track joined a main road, I had trouble taking in the bright red of the marshals' 4x4, and then the bright blue of two coaches that passed by on the adjoining main road. The effect was surreal in such parched surroundings.

Although we hadn't wasted any time, we only made the control with a few minutes to spare and we soon headed off after the two coaches towards Moquegua. The road was very twisty and I was struggling to get past them when I thought I saw my chance and went for it. However as I got alongside the front of the second coach, the road changed from tarmac to gravel, narrowed and dropped about a foot into big puddles. Oops! It was a close call getting past the leading coach, but I was committed anyway, and we missed sideswiping it by only a few millimetres. I headed off into the distance.

There were still 250 kms to our hotel and a border crossing to Chile to do yet, so we pressed on down to the Pan American Highway again and south for Tacna, the last major town in Peru.

The road was fast two-lane tarmac and most of the other traffic was lorries and coaches. It was flat and straight and we whizzed along unheeded with flat desert on both sides of the road until we crested a rise and came upon a settlement built around a police control point.

There was no need for us to stop, the police weren't out (or at least we didn't see them), but as we drove through we noticed Arnold Meier just pulling away from a hard standing towing a Land Rover Discovery. We signalled to him whether he needed any assistance, which he didn't, and we went on our way again.

At several places along this stretch of road, and in Chile over the next few days, the road across the Atacama plateau drops down steeply to river valleys, quebradas. The roads were mostly well engineered with sweeping bends and the uphill lane was often broadened to twin lanes to make passing easier. Once across the valley, the road would climb up again to the desert plateau.

We dropped down into one, Lucumbo I think, and swung right around a mound onto the flat plain only to find our way ahead immediately blocked. I saw no warnings and other evidence of any road works and had to jam on the brakes to avoid hitting a mound of earth across the road, behind which was a bright yellow mechanical digger shifting earth. On top of the mound was a Desvio sign, local parlance for a diversion, and we followed a rough track across some fields and the river bank to the solid road on the other side of the valley.

We soon reached the town of Tacna, skirting the edge and out into the desert again but not without misreading a tulip and paying a quick visit to what appeared to be the local council lorry depot.

The customs clearance into Chile was very straightforward, but we were obliged to put our clocks on by 2 hours, making it almost 7.00pm rather than 5.00pm. An English-speaking representative of the Chile Motor Club was present here, making life easier and he turned out to be a customs officer anyway.

Arica, the most northerly town in Chile, is set beside the ocean and a major port, much cargo unloaded here actually heading into Peru and up into Andean cities such as Puno and Cusco. It is reputedly the driest city in the world although by chance we were to find out differently.

The night we returned home to England, we had done some unpacking and Pam had started some washing when we sat exhausted in our armchairs after our flight from Rio and put on the television. By who knows what coincidence, the programme was all about the Atacama and whether or not Arica was in fact the driest place. The researcher, some chap from a UK university, was gadding about the desert trying to check out records of rainfall in various towns. He finally decided that a little village near Maria Elena was the driest place, not Arica. We would pass by the village tomorrow.

For now we were in Arica, and our digs for the night was the Pan American Hotel right on the coast. Our room overlooked the sea and had a well laid-out seating area with a couple of sofas. The only downside was an infestation of some tiny, almost colourless creepy crawlies in the bathroom, the only time in the whole trip that we had any problem such as this, and this wasn't a problem, merely noteworthy.

The car park hardly had any 4x4s in it and it seemed we were in with the classics and ended up joining with Geoff and Jennie Dorey for dinner. They were driving an Alpha Romeo Giulia Sprint. They were from Guernsey, Jennie running the only Internet café there, in St Peter Port, and Geoff having some sort of business he didn't elaborate on. It was a very pleasant meal with good company, in the open with the ocean beside us.

Jennie and Geoff had taken part in the Peking - Paris Rally with few problems but on the Inca Trail had suffered all manner of difficulties. They had holed the sump early on, the engine had bounced through the bonnet and these two episodes had led to various other mechanical nightmares. They had missed out great chunks of the route already, had taken the short cut from Cusco and were debating where to go from here as they didn't fancy a trip over the Andes and back to Chile which was planned over the next week.

I suggested they do what Peter and Carolynn were doing. They had also given up on the event and had told us in Arequipa they would be heading straight down through Chile to Santiago and staying there waiting for the rally to arrive. Why didn't Jennie and Geoff do the same?

Rumours were circulating in the evening that a rally car had been in an accident with an articulated lorry and that the crew was possibly seriously hurt. This put something of a dampener on the evening till the details became clearer. It seemed that our Kiwi friends Patsie and David in the Holden Estate had been involved, and whilst David was more or less all right, Patsie had a broken ankle and collar bone. Her injuries might have been much worse, as it later transpired that one of the HERO doctors was on the scene quickly and saved her foot from further damage. At the time, the news was that the car was a write-off, and they were being flown up to Lima (the accident had happened while they were still in Peru), before heading back to New Zealand once Patsie was fit to travel.

As we were in the headquarters hotel, Jo Brown was around but as we had found previously, wasn't all that communicative. We knew that John was due to have his angioplasty on Monday back in the UK and that she would be worried about that as much as anything to do with the rally. We decided to prepare a short good luck and 'thinking of you' note and put it in her pigeonhole at reception.

I had had a good day. The driving coupled with the lovely hotel and good meal rated it the best twenty-four hours of the whole event for me. I slept well with the balcony doors open so I could hear and smell the ocean.

Gran Turismo computer games

Day 23 Sunday 28 October
Arica - Calama (705 kms)

As may be apparent already, I am very fond of desert landscapes and as today would be wholly in the Atacama Desert, we decided to leave early and make the most of the day. It would be a long day anyway, with over 700 kms to drive and included a chance to visit the largest open cast mine in the world.

Peter Rushforth was marshalling the Day Start Control on the road out of Arica and it was still dark when we arrived. He'd only just arrived himself to set it up and was surprised to see us so early.

"Good morning to you Peter."

"A bit prompt aren't you?"

"Yes, on purpose. I love the desert and want to see the dawn as we drive along." Pam gave him our time card to sign. It was 6.30am and our recommended start time for the day was 6.45am.

"If I sign you out now you'll be 15 minutes early and get penalties. It's up to you."

"That's alright Peter, we don't get penalties anyway."

"Well it's up to you," and he gave us our time card back duly signed and bade us good luck. We were the first car on the road.

It was a good half hour before dawn started breaking and as we sped along the Atacama plateau its beauty was everything I'd hoped for. From deep navy, the sky gradually changed colour through every shade of blue over perhaps three quarters of an hour till it was properly light. Long shadows in the desert grew shorter as the sun rose over the Andes as we headed south. The colours of the desert changed too until the full brightness of the day.

As happened, yesterday we dropped down into several quebradas and at the first we came upon a police control at Cuyal. We stopped and being first on the road were questioned carefully about what we were doing, about the rally and also whether we were carrying any fruit. The Chileans are very careful about protecting their fruit crops from disease and there were regular checks for this, especially at the borders where, in addition, the wheels of our vehicles were sprayed with insecticide. We had none, of course, and we pressed on, the road running along a river valley for perhaps 50 kms on the river bed.

Now the Atacama Desert is one of the driest regions in the world, but one can but wonder what would happen if there was ever sufficient rain to cause the river to flow. One of their main arterial roads would be destroyed.

Our early start meant we were even ahead of the Course Car and this passed us shortly before the turn off to Iquique at about the 250 kms mark and where we decided to stop for a breather at Humberstone, a mining ghost town now being turned into a tourist attraction. This was formerly a nitrite mining area and the town was similar to Kolmanskop, another derelict mining town we'd visited in Namibia.

Humberstone had been a completely self-contained town with residential areas for all levels of management and for the miners, as well as shops, a sports ground and even a cinema. Most of it was in surprisingly good condition. A notable little find was in the cinema where, in the entrance hall, we found several large posters of film stars of the day, their colours still strong and vibrant as they were protected from the sun.

By the time we left Humberstone, we were driving along with the classic rally cars and followed a couple into Iquique, a large, busy port on the coast that is approached via a long descent traversing the escarpment and edge of the desert. The road offered stunning views over the city and out to sea where many cargo and fishing boats were anchored in the roads.

At the bottom of the hill, at a large roundabout, we were stopped once more by the police who wanted to know all about the rally and where we would be heading. HERO had produced programmes of the event in Spanish and Portuguese and we always carried a few of these to hand out at appropriate occasions and this was one. Our friendly policeman was well pleased and waved us on our way.

Our route skirted the back of the city and we were soon heading south along the coast road towards Tocopilla another 250 kms away. This was a good quality tarmac road often running alongside the beach, at other times climbing to pass over headlands. With the weather so good, (there was only a little haze), it was a splendid drive and with little traffic the whole road could be used to straighten out corners. I have never been to California, but someone said it was much like the drive of the Big Sur only much better.

Heading south out of Iquique we passed a time control for the classics that was set up in a beach bar. The road book encouraged us to stop for lunch, but it was still far too early so we headed on. Being Sunday the locals were out and about and we passed a golf course set out in the sand, the fairways edged with white painted stones and the 'greens' covered with tar or oil. No bunkers of course. The local cycling club was also out and we saw about 50 cyclists on racing bikes at various places along the road.

Very soon we passed the last of several beach resorts serving Iquique, after which there was very little habitation till we arrived at Tocopilla. What we did see on several occasions though, were condors soaring above the cliffs, but they were high up.

We were caught and passed by Alastair Caldwell's red Ferrari and the Kanes' white and blue Mustang which often drove along together in convoy and I followed them for about 30 kms on the run into Tocopilla. They swung backwards and forwards across the road straightening out corners and bends and I did my best to keep up with them, the sea on our right and high sand dunes on our left. We passed around little bays with glorious beaches and crested small headlands, and it was great to watch the two cars in front, just like a GTO car racing computer game one sees in an amusement arcade.

On the approach to Tocopilla we turned inland to climb back up onto the Atacama plateau, and the two cars soon had the advantage and vanished from sight through a series of bends. One can't miss this town as fish canning is the major industry and an all-pervading smell reaches the parts normal smells don't.

Over the next 100 kms and for about an hour, we would rise sharply from sea level up to 10,400 ft crossing the Pan American Highway (Ruta 5) and a railway that also makes the same climb up as far as the plateau. This caused us no problems, but we learned later that many of the classics, and a fair few 4x4s had overheating problems on this road. However the road from the crossroads with the Pan American was spoiled by several strings of power lines scarring the landscape.

We arrived at the Chuquicamata mine, a few kilometres on from the top of the pass, to find that we were far too early for the planned visit and needed to wait an hour and a half. Calama, our stop for the night, was only about 15 kms away, we could see it below on the desert plain, so we decided to head down there and check in to our hotel, the Hosteria Calama.

First we drove to the headquarters hotel, The Park, to get our time card signed, a nice hotel with a swimming pool, before heading to ours, a three star that was perfectly adequate, also with a swimming pool and which had an underground car park. In the car park there were already several classics, mainly those who were now in the touring class and had taken a short cut to Calama avoiding the coast road.

We checked in and I got in touch with and met a local Lion who arrived with his wife and we had a pleasant chat for half an hour, made somewhat difficult by their lack of English and our lack of Spanish.

At the due time, we headed back to the Chuquicamata mine and found a tour coach waiting to go. It took us through the mine service buildings and on to a viewing platform from where we could see the main workings. The hole in the ground was enormous, about 2 km wide, 4 km long and over 650 m deep with terracing around each side and roadways built into them so the equally huge trucks could bring out the copper ore.

The trucks, and they have over 100 of them at $2 million apiece, work 24 hours a day, carrying 225 tonnes of ore on each trip, crawling up the sides of the opening, a steady convoy of them feeding the extensive ore-crushing and extraction works around the mine. Standing next to one of the trucks, my shoulders barely came up to the hub of the front wheel. Needless to say, we all wanted to try driving one, but that was out of the question.

We watched for some time as a dynamite explosion to loosen more ore was due at 5.00pm, but when it did blow, a little late, the puff of dust was so far down into the bottom of the mine it was a bit of a disappointment.

Once more we headed back to Calama, this time noticing some activity in the desert at the side of the road which turned out to be a local motor cycle scramble meeting, with motor bikes racing round an inner track and four-wheeled dune buggies doing the same on an outer track. We watched for a while, but it was clearly the end of their day and as they were heading away, so did we.

One of the problems of not staying at the headquarters hotel was that all official notices were displayed there, and usually not at other hotels. Most of these notices applied to the classics alone, but sometimes they were specifically for the 4x4s or for everyone. So if there was time, and there was today, we would usually try and find the notice board to check it out.

The lobby of the Park Hotel was overflowing with Inca Trailers when we arrived. The day had been long, but fairly easy and the bar was busy. However, it was obvious within a couple of minutes that the main conversation was about hotel allocations; many people weren't happy. One couple announced that they weren't staying at the hotel they had been sent to (ours as it happened), it was a dump, and they had checked themselves into the Park telling Reception to charge the room to HERO. This from a 4x4 crew who had been in the touring class of the rally for a couple of weeks already. They were complaining about previous hotels, that they alleged were also dumps, and about the way HERO was supposedly ripping everyone off. They were never at the headquarters hotel and both felt they were getting a raw deal.

Poor Jo Brown was trying to deal with the situation as best she could, but in the circumstances there didn't seem to be much she could do. Because John had had to return to the UK, she was doing her best to hold things together, and so far as we were concerned, managing fairly well with the help of the other headquarters team. The whole scene at the hotel was deplorable and we decided to leave. We later learned that the wife had suffered a breakdown, bursting into tears in the hotel lounge because she reckoned she was getting a raw deal. 'Rot' is all I can say to that, and that's being polite.

Back at our hotel, we had fun and games during the evening with the classics now parked furthest from the entranceway to the underground car park and blocked in by 4x4s. Would the late arriving 4x4s move to provide some space? Yes of course, but the following 20 minutes were a farce, as half a dozen experts all decided on who should park where and next to whom and we all reversed up and down a very steep ramp to get into position. Car park manoeuvres in the dark, and the diesel fumes in the basement once we finished were enough to give everyone cancer within days. I managed to arrange to park mine last, on the ramp, and promised to move it in time for the departing classics in the morning.

Getting a meal in the hotel was a slow process, but we ate with Margaret and Mike Waterhouse and the food was good once we got it.

High flying flamingos

Day 24 Monday 29 October
Calama - Salta (613 kms)

As promised, I was up early to get my car out of the car park so various classics could get onto the road and away, and then went back to get my breakfast. However it was still dark when we left, made our way up to the Park Hotel to get our time card signed and headed out of Calama into the desert once more.

Yesterday I had left early to enjoy the dawn, but today we made no special effort to start promptly yet witnessed an even better dawn. We were travelling in convoy with several other 4x4s and classics, and the road headed east towards the Andes which we would cross to get back into Argentina for a few days. The sun began to make its appearance and the silhouette it created behind the mountains was stunning. As the colour of the sky changed once more from almost black, through shades of navy to lighter blues and even off-white, so the shape of the jagged mountain tops looked like a printout from a seismograph. It was beautiful.

First stop would be San Pedro de Atacama where the road book suggested we take a walk through a pretty covered market to the right of the main road – at 6.20am in the gloom of dawn, needless to say there was nobody there. Another suggestion, however, was worth following up, as fuel today would be difficult to get and a supply was available from the only pumps in the town. San Pedro looked like a lovely little town, all adobe buildings and the sandy streets bounded by high walls made it something of a maze to find our way to the pumps. We eventually did, finding a short queue of others, and by the time we filled up there were more cars behind us.

Next stop was the advanced customs post where our paperwork was due to be checked prior to leaving the town for the actual border with Argentina high up in the mountains. When we arrived, only a few hundred metres from the town there was a long queue of cars and a dejected look from many of the crews. Some had been there for an hour already and the word was that the customs officer had been told the rally would be through at about 9.00am and it was barely 7.00am. He'd been woken from his bed by some early crews, had a 'strop' and slammed a few doors, but gone back to bed. There was nothing more to be done.

We learned also that some cars had driven straight through the control and were being stopped up the road and sent back. One by one they reappeared too, so that by 7.30am the whole caravan of cars was parked up higgledy piggledy outside the customs post. These included the Course Cars and the organising team were trying to see what could be done. Eventually, with a little bribery and corruption, they managed to get one office open, but Mr Big wouldn't be moved. He'd been told it would be 9.00am and 9.00am it would be.

The office that did open was for the carnets and a huge melee of drivers huddled round the door to get theirs checked and stamped, the sensible ones sending their navigators to queue at the other door in readiness for Mr Big. I wasn't too bothered and was spending my time wandering around the area chatting to all and sundry and investigating a tyre repair shop nearby. Here, the owner was fixing a puncture on a trailer tyre of a huge blue articulated lorry with Paraguayan registration plates. From what I could gather, the lorry had travelled from Paraguay to Salta in Argentina, our destination for the day, and over the Paso Sico to San Pedro on the rough mountain road we would travel later. That's one hell of a journey and I was mightily impressed by these drivers and the journeys they undertook with their rigs.

Mr Big finally arrived at about 8.30am, an Inca Trail T shirt and threats to tell his supervisors of his unhelpfulness probably doing the trick, and he set about stamping passports. Pam and I were in the middle of the queue and about 20 minutes later we duly put our passports out for him to stamp, but we didn't have our Customs entry form with us that needed to be handed in.

These entry forms were a source of nuisance and comedy to us as each border needed one filled out, or handed in, always with the same information on it. As often as not, a telephone number would be entered for passport number, and all manner of job titles were entered – the best I heard of being HM Executioner.

It was Pam's job to keep track of our paperwork, so we went back to the car to retrieve them, but now joined the back of the queue. We were the last rally crew to get our form signed and I was not too pleased. There was a stony silence in the car as we headed off at last with Pam calling out the minimum of instructions about where to go. I wanted to tell her where to go too, I was fuming.

The atmosphere eased after a while and we gradually started to resume normal relations. The road was gravel now, with odd patches of tarmac as we went through a couple of villages, and on our right was the Solar de Atacama, huge salt flats that I had hoped there might be time to visit, but certainly not now.

The road was climbing steadily up into the mountains that stood in relief in the early dawn. We had a short Explorer Section to do on the east side of the 'main' road which took us past some small soda lakes and close to some mountains. The road was fairly rough in places and needed some careful attention and Chris Wray was in trouble once more with his Hyundai overheating. We stopped a couple of times as the track passed the lakes, variously coloured white and blue with reflections of the mountains behind. It was by now a beautiful day and the scenery was once more stunning. Although we missed them, there were apparently flamingos in one of the lakes.

We were soon out again onto the main road and heading on upwards to the mountains and the Paso Sico that would take us into Argentina. The road was very dusty and by now we were catching several of the classics, some of whom were having trouble with the altitude, the dust and the many sandy sections of road.

We arrived at the proper border post at about 12.30pm and were through in a few minutes, but the surface was deteriorating rapidly and we came upon more classics in trouble. We were waved down by one of the Mercedes who was stuck and who already had his tow-rope out for us to hook onto. In half a minute we had him out of the sand onto harder ground. Soon after, we came on the MGC of Rita Shelley and Mike Knox. They had been in the touring class for some time but had to come through the pass to get to Argentina and the rallying offered for the next few days. They didn't look happy as the car was overheating badly and they needed some water which we were able to supply. We had done 350 kms by now and still had a similar distance to travel to the hotels in Salta. The entrance to Argentina posed no problems and the road soon began to drop now amidst high mountains on either side and although we were still high up, it was very warm. The gravel occasionally gave way to asphalt, but often changed back again with little warning.

From time to time we crossed a railway line, the one used for the Train of the Clouds, a tourist railway that takes passengers from Salta up into the Andes and passing over many bridges, viaducts and through many tunnels. The train stops at San Antonio de los Cobres, and many rally crews did too as there was fuel here. We bypassed this meagre, dusty village and headed on into the hills again, but not before passing two boys who were perched on some rocks on the way out of town with a grandstand view of the rally passing through. They were so enthusiastic jumping up and down and waving their arms about, we thought they might fall off their perch.

The road headed into a long gorge and the condition of the road deteriorated into poor gravel, was narrow and had plenty of blind bends and steep drops to the river bed below. On a tarmac section prior to getting here, Ian Brawn in his Porsche overtook us, but once on the gravel we had the advantage and we were soon in front of him again.

The final run into the outskirts of Salta was through luxuriant green wine-growing countryside, so different from earlier in the day, and any we'd had since we were last in Argentina in Jujuy only 50 kms north of here over a fortnight ago.

A main control for the classics had been set up at a Shell garage on the main road into town, so we filled up and planned to have the car washed too as it was filthy with dust. The car wash bay had a long queue already and with just one man with a hose doing the work it looked like it would be ages before our turn. We decided to give this a miss and headed off into town and on inspiration turned into a YPF garage and low and behold they had two fully equipped car washing bays at the back, one of which was already occupied by the Toyota Amazon of Willie and Barbara Lambertz.

I drove into the adjoining bay and very soon we had two men hosing, brushing, washing and thoroughly cleaning the car. They did a really good job, even doing some of the inside, which over the weeks had also become pretty grubby. They were so keen we had to pull them away as we were worried about reaching the time control before it closed, so we paid up, gave them a tip and headed off for the centre of town.

We left the car in the main square, Plaza 9 de Julio, along with many others and walked to our hotel, the Provincial, and checked in.

Salta seemed a busy, bustling place and later the shops became very busy too as the townsfolk finished work and went window shopping. We decided to eat in the hotel and joined Mike and Jenny Barnes who were rallying in a Porsche 911 RS, a fairly rare model with a 2.7 litre engine. Mike wasn't happy with John Brown and HERO at all as he had had reassurances that the route was suitable for his car which he considered was a classic he was prepared to rally, rather than a classic rally car.

Wrong slot

Day 25 Tuesday 30 October
Salta - Catamarca (647 kms)

There were major route changes announced for today's run as a long loop for the 4x4s through Santa Maria and Andalgala was cancelled as the Advance Course Car had found the road conditions to be too bad. From the road book it looked like a real challenge as there would be loads of river crossings and the guide books identified it as a difficult road with fearsome drops and challenging motoring. That's what we wanted.

In addition, two sections which had been planned for the rally cars were cancelled because they were also deemed too rough, but as we would now be following their route we could take advantage of their loss.

So initially we would follow the same route as the rally cars, almost all on tarmac, and then in the company of just the other 4x4s we would tackle the Cuesta del Clavillo Section, and then the Valle del Singuil, before reaching our overnight stop.

There was quite a bit of head scratching at the morning control as the navigators tried to make the revised route fit in with the road book, but we were on our way just before 6.30am and drove out south from Salta passing through several pretty villages comprising not much more than a small square and some side streets.

One of these, which hadn't been mentioned by John Brown in any of his published material, was a small, unremarkable little place called La Vina. It's a place that has a little rallying history attached to it, as back in 1970 one of the London-Mexico World Cup Rally *prime* ended in the village. The 1970 Rally had approached La Vina from the south and reached it after leaving Santiago in Chile where crews had enjoyed a well-earned rest. They were routed over the Andes via the Paso del Agua

A HIGH IN THE ANDES

Negra to start the *prime* north of San Juan (where we would stay in a couple of days) and then north via Belen and Santa Maria to follow the reverse of our route today to La Vina. The World Cup Rally would then head north through Salta and Jujuy to Bolivia and the sections in the Andes we had already covered on the Inca Trail Rally.

We hardly blinked as we passed through La Vina but I was disappointed not to be following the reverse route through the mountains and hill towns as had originally been planned for the Inca Trail. The drivers in 1970 had an almost impossible challenge. The organisers were worried that they wouldn't get a clear result as the works crews were doing so well, so for this and some other *prime* they lopped off an hour from the target time. The section from Rodeo to La Vina originally had a target time of 9 hours and to prove the point Hannu Mikkola completed it in just 8 h 45 mins and would have cleaned it but for the new target time.

A notable accident on the *prime* was that to Andrew Cowan, now rally supremo at Mitsubishi, who was driving a Triumph 2.5 PI. He went off the road and had a bad crash. Cowan cracked a neck bone, co-driver Brian Coyle broke a wrist and the travelling mechanic, a Peruvian, suffered crushed vertebrae. Rallying is dangerous, but all recovered. One car took 22 hours to complete the *prime*.

Soon our road started passing through the Quebrada de Cafayette, a river valley with remarkable rock formations on either side. Many of these had been given names such as the Stone House, Devil's Gorge, Mushroom and the Frog. The latter was one of the few we could actually relate to the feature and we suspected that it had had a chisel to it at some stage to make it look more froglike.

An easing of the pace meant we had time to stop for a break occasionally and as the rally cars had a control at a café in the town of Cafayate we decided to join them. We weren't the only ones, and soon the car park was jam packed with cars and 4x4s. The route turned onto Ruta 40 very soon after we restarted, a road we used again many times, especially when we went further south into Patagonia.

We stopped at Quilmes, the site of some ruins believed to date from the 9th century but which the Spanish decimated in the 17th century, the population of 3,000 either dying or leaving the area. It was stifling hot and whilst Pam, Dave and Carole went to have a look around the site, I stayed in the cool of the very good craft shop.

Our route through the mountains should have started soon afterwards, but we now turned south east through the village of Amaicha and then down the first part of the Tafi del Valle, a twisting and tortuous road dropping down a very steep valley with dense green foliage on either side. This valley had a Welsh sounding name and, but for the warm humid weather we could have been in central Wales, perhaps near Devil's Bridge. Besides the weather, the other difference was the distances we covered going down through the steep gorges, it went on for ever, twisting down and down.

The road levelled out near the Dique de Angostura, a reservoir, where we paid a short visit to some ancient menhuires (stone carvings). Then the road started dropping down again, through another series of tight bends and hairpins before settling out into much flatter country near Monteros.

However, we were soon heading for the hills again to go over the Cuesta Del Clavillo, the first of the sections the rally cars would now miss. This was approached via a very long cobbled section of road passing through fields and woodland. There wasn't much traffic except for some large lorries going in our direction but which were determined not to pull over and let us pass. As they were heavily laden and going very slowly we had to get by somehow, so it was horn, lights and a few prayers, as well as some very close looks at the ditches on my side of the road.

I mentioned the road was cobbled. It was about 4 metres wide and stretched for perhaps 20 kms, so in a quiet moment later in the day we tried to estimate the number of cobbles that might have been laid. We reached 20 million and wondered where they had come from and who had laid them out, and why, because the road didn't lead anywhere particularly special to demand such effort.

Cobbles gave way to gravel and the start of a wonderful series of hairpins, upwards, that had featured as a special stage in the 1980 Codasur Rally. A well-known rally photograph by Hugh Bishop was taken here and shows Walter Rohl, reputedly one of the all-time great rally drivers, heading up through the hairpins in a Fiat Abarth with a trail of dust tracing the bends below.

At the top were the ruins of a view point where we would have stopped, but we had just overtaken another couple of lorries loaded with building materials and we would have ended up behind them again. It was just as well we did carry on, as the road, now clinging to the edge of the mountain with dense green foliage growing on the upper and lower sides, was a narrow earth road and very muddy in patches. It made for interesting driving though.

We started down again and headed towards the Valle de Singuil our next Section. This started with the crossing of a dried up river bed, but then headed through lush green meadows, much like upland pasture in somewhere like Switzerland or Austria. It was a good road and I put the pedal to the floor for some fun, but slowed for some llamas, including some babies, that were crossing the road. We took a couple of 'Arrrrr' photos and headed off again.

About halfway through the section, as we were heading into a small settlement, a policeman ran out into the road and signalled us to stop. He seemed friendly and wanted to know what was going on. As best we could, we told him about the rally; he was happy so we headed on.

This lovely section was all too short at just 60 kms and Phil Surtees and Roberto Filho were at the end, where we decided to stop for a breather as we only had about 80 kms to the end of the day in Catamarca.

The story of Phil's fingers is one that had been circulating at HERO events prior to the rally and I wanted to find out the truth from the man himself. Phil has only stumps for the two middle fingers of his left hand. Basically it seems he had been preparing an old Jeep to use in the Peking-Paris Rally and was testing it when it rolled and his hand became caught between the ground and the edge of the windscreen and all the fingers on his left hand were severed.

A rapid visit to hospital followed where they were stitched back on but only the two outer ones took, the two middle ones not healing properly. Phil went back to the consultant who advised him that they could operate again and try and get them to reattach.

"I'm due to do the Peking-Paris Rally soon. How long will they take to heal?" asked Phil.

"Oh quite a while," replied the consultant, "There's no chance of doing a rally."

"Then what is the likely success rate of the operation?" asked Phil.

"About 20%."

"Then amputate the middle two and patch them up as best you can."

Phil went on to do the rally *sans* two fingers and what's more, win it.

The run into Catamarca was mainly on a smooth concrete road and at one water splash we stopped so Pam could video me racing through it at speed. It looks good.

Once more we finished the day in the Plaza 25 de Mayo, but whereas on many previous occasions there had been a brass band playing, here Don and Pat Griffiths were being blasted by pop music from a local restaurant. It was deafening. Having checked in, we pulled over and parked up and took a stroll to get the lie of the land. The hotel was just around the corner and had its own parking area so we moved the car there and squeezed it into a small spot between Malcolm McKay's TR2 and another 4x4.

On our stroll we noticed a long line of young people in a queue leading up to the door of another hotel next door to ours. It looked like they were queuing for tickets for a pop concert, but on discussion with a couple of them who could speak English, it transpired there were some jobs on offer, the first ones for many weeks in Catamarca, and such was the unemployment in the area an estimated 1,000 people were queueing for interview. This was to be our first insight into the economic problems in Argentina, one that became much more evident towards the end of the Inca Trail Rally, and even more once we were home.

In the hotel reception was a notice advising us that the local council were holding an official reception for the rally crews later on and everyone was recommended to attend. We duly made ourselves available and, later than anticipated, various city dignitaries made speeches welcoming us to the area and then presented us all with gift-wrapped parcels. We left ours intact, but others opened theirs and each one contained two pots of local preserve, a piece of local cake and some sweets.

This was very nice of them, but not necessarily what you want to carry round on a rally, especially in a small car. As we were sitting with John Bateson and Colin Francis they asked if we could carry their parcels for them, which we did until we got to Rio de Janeiro.

It also turned out to be Colin's birthday and a nice touch from HERO was to present him with a big birthday cake. He was, of course, totally embarrassed when we all sang Happy Birthday to him, but in return he divided up the cake amongst those around.

Later, we went out to get a meal and even when we returned to the hotel at about 11.00pm there was still a small queue of young people waiting for their interview.

Red mist

Day 26 Wednesday 31 October
Catamarca - San Juan (725 kms)

A few kilometres outside Catamarca is a steep escarpment up which a narrow tarmac road winds its tortuous way to the top. El Portezuelo hill, near St Isidora, is regularly used for hill climbs and from time to time as a special stage for rallies. The Inca Trail would use it today with the rally cars having a regularity section from the base to the top, over a thousand metres higher, along which they would be timed at secret checks along the sixteen kilometre length of road.

This meant that they would have to make good progress but would suffer severe penalties if they went too quickly and had a good 'thrash' up the hill. Such restrictions didn't apply to the 4x4s who could take their own pace, fast or slow as they wished. Needless to say, some of us gave it a good crack.

The 4x4s were requested to wait till the rally cars had tackled the hill, so when we arrived at the control at the bottom, there was a short queue of 4x4s, as well as a reasonable crowd of people, some watching the action, others waiting to use the road themselves.

The red mist descended within 100 metres of getting the all clear to go, and on the kilometre run to the base of the hill proper I had already overtaken one 4x4. The tarmac was in good condition but it was narrow with very few passing places, a steep rock face on the inside, low wall protecting the steep drops on the outside.

We soon came up behind Sir Terence English in his white Toyota and I flashed my lights so he was aware I was there. As soon as he came to a suitable spot he pulled over to let me through. Thanks Terence. On and on upwards we went, mostly in second gear twisting left and right, with frequent tight hairpin bends.

We came upon a more open hairpin right and saw Mike Johnson, the official photographer, standing on the outside edge, camera at the ready, so gave the Colorado maximum welly. It felt like it was going round on two wheels – there was certainly plenty of tyre squeal, but I suspect it was fairly unimpressive to watch.

I mentioned that marshals were sited at several places as secret checks for the rally cars, and although the 4x4s were now coming up the hill, they were still in place. At one hairpin left there was a shortcut across the end which I took, although the tulip indicated we were supposed to go the full distance around the bend. Peter Rushforth must have seen this from his vantage point further up because as we arrived at his bend he called out to us as we sped by.

"I saw you Quayle, taking a short cut. That should be a wrong direction of approach. I'll get you next time."

Without stopping, I responded with a friendly two-fingered gesture. We of course didn't have any such restrictions on us.

Further on we came up behind another 4x4, this time Angus Stamper in his Toyota Amazon, who also pulled over promptly so we could dart through the tight gap.

All too soon we crested the top of the hill where there was also a good crowd of people and we pulled over and stopped to catch our breath. The car was hot and the exhaust was clicking as the metal cooled down and contracted. We hadn't been timed on the road but I suspect that we were the fastest ever diesel vehicle to get up that hill, although the Pelly-Fry's in their Audi might contest that claim as they had a good crack at the road too.

It was still only 7.30am – it's a good way to wake up, and the view back down into the valley was great.

For the next hour or so we had a pleasant run on gravel roads through scenery very reminiscent of Exmoor, the road rolling up and down small valleys, cresting ridges at regular intervals and passing through little farming communities.

At Icano we had a control and then hit the tarmac again for a long session on roads across flat featureless countryside northwest of Cordoba with little more than dense scrub on either side of the road.

It was here that we made our only significant navigational error on the whole event. The road book was quite clear, but somehow we missed a left turning that should have been easily picked up. We entered the small village of Casa de Piedra, a spread-out sort of place with the few buildings set well back from the road. We should have turned left next to a bus shelter onto a gravel road, but whether Pam called it out and I ignored her instruction, or she missed it we can't remember. In any case, we kept on the tarmac road and drove along quite happily for some time thinking we were on the proper route.

We had no reason to suspect something was wrong as the next instruction was not for another 66 kms, but we suddenly saw another Inca Trail 4x4 coming the other way, the driver gesticulating, trying to indicate to us that we were heading the wrong way. We pulled up at the side of the road and soon realised our error, so turned around and headed back. We were 35 kms off route, so had another 35 kms to get back to the bus shelter and wasted about an hour.

It seems several other people made the same mistake, although most realised their error sooner, but there seemed no good reason for missing such an obvious route instruction at a prominent junction.

Once on the gravel road it soon deteriorated, with lots of potholes and sand traps. We didn't come across anyone stuck, but we heard that some of the classics got caught out in sand and were rescued by 4x4s.

From time to time the road changed to new tarmac which meant we could make much faster progress, but there was almost no other traffic besides the occasional rally car and as the route crossed the Salina la Antigua it seemed a lonely and desolate part of the world.

In the middle of nowhere, we came upon a Police Post and it seems the two policemen figured this was their chance to make a few bob. As we slowed to a stop there were three cars in front and long animated conversations were going on between the policemen and the crews. One of them eventually came up to us as he signalled the car in front to drive away, and from what we heard later we got the better of the two policemen.

Although we couldn't understand his Spanish, it was clear he wanted money, but we feigned ignorance and shrugged our shoulders. He got upset at this and made his demands stronger, waving a post card he had been given by one of the earlier rally cars. It was becoming obvious we would have to give him something before he would let us get away and finally let him have a Spanish language copy of the rally programme. He seemed very happy with this and let us go.

By comparison the other policeman was being a real b*****d and wanted money and nothing else. We pulled around Greg Stanley's Toyota which was still being held up by this chap and Greg asked us if we could loan him a few US dollars as there was no way he was going to get away without some 'donation'. We obliged and headed on.

The route now took us to a group of low hills, the Sierra de Malanzan, with interesting rock formations and soft sandy gravel tracks. Here we did another 46 kms Explorer Section, which was great fun because there were lots of shallow river bed crossings and the soft sand on the road made for some smooth motoring. The marshals at the finish control had it good too, as it was sited at a set of picnic tables under some trees just outside a small village. With a beer in the hand and somewhere to sit out in the shade they seemed satisfied.

But there was no control car! On enquiry we were told it had been taken down to the local river, only a few yards away and the local children were washing it. The local children were out in force just down the road too, for we drove past the school and they were all out waving and cheering as we drove by.

The rest of the day was taken up with a run on main roads to our next overnight stop at San Juan. The roads continued to be mostly flat and boring until quite suddenly on approaching San Juan they became lush and green and vineyards became the predominant activity. This is one of Argentina's principal wine growing regions and whilst we'd already sampled plenty, we would do our best to sample more later in the evening.

San Juan is a large city with a motorway running right round the outside, something like the M25 only shorter. We had news that there would be a demonstration in the main square in the middle of town and that the rally was being rerouted away from the area because the authorities thought we might be at risk. So we were sent out and round this ring road to a big shopping complex where the local motor club had quickly reorganised themselves and set up a proper finishing ramp and, once we were parked, offered us a drink and snack in the restaurant of one of the stores in the complex. There were even taxis on hand to take us to our hotels in the centre of town.

Our taxi driver spoke a little English and started telling us of the woes of Argentina's economy. The demonstration was by public sector workers who either weren't getting paid at all, or only getting part of their pay. And this had been going on for some time. He blamed the Government of course, and wanted former President Menem back in power as he felt that at least he was trying to solve the economic problems, whereas the current Government were thrashing around. Menem was currently under house arrest in Buenos Aires.

Taxi drivers everywhere drive fast, but in San Juan they take speeding to a fine art form. We careered along the streets at break neck speed while he was telling us his stories, and seemed to play chicken run with other drivers at cross roads. Everyone was at it, and one either joined in or never got anywhere. We got to our hotel in one piece and he convinced us that we should use him again in the morning to get back to the shopping complex, so we agreed a time.

The hotel, Nogaro, was nothing special and was only just off the Plaza 25 de Mayo but we never saw any sign of any demonstration either when we arrived or later in the evening when we went out for a meal. But the

A HIGH IN THE ANDES

incident, together with that in Catamarca the previous night, reminded us again of the sorry state that Argentina was in and we wondered whether we might get some further reactions when we returned to Argentina in a couple of weeks' time.

On the taxi ride in, I noticed that as usual the city was laid out in a grid format, but all the streets, (avenues would be a better description), were wide and spacious and lined with mature trees. But most notable were the buildings, hardly any being more than two storeys high.

Once we settled into our room, I checked up our copy of Lonely Planet to find that San Juan had suffered a severe earthquake in 1944 destroying nearly every building in the city and killing an estimated 10,000 people. That explained the low buildings, but I was reading this on the sixth floor of our hotel!

San Juan is also one of the hottest places in South America. Whilst we were there it was pretty warm and we'd had the air conditioning on for most of the day in the car, but heard that a few days previously it had been 42°C and sometimes it went even hotter. This is due to the Zonda, a hot dry wind that hikes the temperature up by many degrees. Fortunately, today Zonda was having a day off.

We went to investigate the town and took a walk round the local streets which seemed to be the main shopping area, bumped into Dave and Carole doing the same, and found a café overlooking the Plaza for a beer. We enquired about eating but couldn't make much progress as it seemed this was another of those towns where nothing much happens in the evenings till at least 10.00pm so we went back to the hotel for a doze.

Later we happened to meet up with Chris and Jill Wray, the Pelly-Fry's, the Lucas's and joined them for a meal at a restaurant Chris had been advised about. This was a mile or so away, but in the cool of the evening it was a pleasant walk and with so much sitting in the car it was enjoyable exercise. We were soon settled at a long table on a grassy patch in the open, but on what appeared to be a car park during the day time.

The meal was good, as was the local wine, and once he had had a few drinks, Chris was soon regaling us with stories of his past. He's one of those unmistakable characters, short and round and full of beans. The Irish boys on the Inca Trail christened him '*Wee pear-shaped man*' a sobriquet he was proud of. Chris was also proud of being an Essex boy made good, having been a student at the Italia Conti stage school, worked in entertainment whilst moonlighting with one of the first minicab firms in London, and now owning a well-known lighting company in the West End.

We were all well lubricated for the walk back to the hotel and for our part fell asleep within seconds of hitting the pillow, without a thought in the world about what might happen if there was an earthquake.

Over the Andes again

Day 27 Thursday 1 November
San Juan - Marbella (640 kms)

At the appointed hour, our taxi driver was ready to take us back out of town to the shopping complex where we learned there would be further route changes today because of problems with the planned route. Rather than head west out of San Juan towards Tamberias and then south to Uspallata, we would now go south almost to Mendoza, another major town in the region, then head north to Villavicencio and over the Paso and then back down to Uspallata to regain the original routing over the mountains to Chile.

The new road south was mostly fast dual carriageway but then we turned off by a quarry on a long straight road (RP52) up into the hills. This was a concrete road in very poor condition, and it was difficult to overtake some lorries as they would veer around all over the road without warning to avoid bad cracks and broken sections. The road climbed, arrow straight, into the mountains and we passed some racing cyclists out training.

Once into the mountains proper, the road was in still worse condition and twisted and turned with many of the tight bends very steeply banked, much like the famous Karousel Corner on the Nurburgring motor racing circuit in Germany.

The rally cars had a time control at a mountain inn, so we decided to stop for a break and were very glad we did. We were in Villavicencio, a name that we had seen frequently on bottles of water we had bought over recent weeks. They all originated from a spring near here and the refreshing spa water was sold all over South America. The inn was very Alpine and they served huge mugs of coffee and the greatest bacon sandwiches you'll ever taste. Made from locally smoked ham and their own bread they were huge slabs of food that filled us for the rest of the day.

From here the road turned to gravel, but as it climbed, so the weather closed in with light rain and poor visibility. The locals have given the road two nicknames, the Ruta del Ano, (The One Year Road as supposedly there are 365 hairpin bends), or the Caracoles de Villavicencio (Snails of Villavicencio) referring to the way the road spirals upwards. There are said to be fantastic views of the Mendoza region, but the weather spoiled that. But it was a great driver's road.

We came up behind David and Jenny Bishop in their Mitsi L200 as we got towards the top of the pass. They were in the touring class and not doing many of the Explorer Sections, in fact Jenny had her golf clubs in the back of their 4x4 in the hope of finding a course to play on. They, in turn, were behind a local in a Ford Escort but seemed unwilling to overtake it; they just drove close behind.

From time to time they pulled over, as if to say, come through, but didn't indicate so we knew they knew we were there, nor were they leaving any space into which we could slot between them and the Escort, they were too close to it. We had to wait till we could overtake both cars in one go which wasn't too easy on a narrow mountain road.

After passing the summit, the weather cleared and the run down the west side of the pass was much straighter with fast sweeping bends. There was a plaque on the side of the road here that marked a visit to the region by Charles Darwin in 1853.

On the run in towards Uspallata we fell in behind the Inca Trail Special, a 1929 open top Chrysler in which both Richard Newman and Robert O'Hara were well wrapped up in what looked like Arctic clothing. They pedalled this car at a good rate of knots so when we turned out onto the main road up towards the Chilean border we followed them for many miles before they pulled over in the warmer weather to strip off.

It was sunny now with bright blue sky and ahead of us were the Andes once more and standing out from the lower peaks was snow-capped Aconcagua, at almost 7,000 m (23,000 ft) the highest mountain in the whole of the Americas. It was another hour's motoring before we reached the border posts, but not before passing dozens of joggers in grey track suits running alongside the road uphill, also heading towards the Argentinean Customs buildings. We knew not why.

Soon afterwards we were driving through the Cristo Redentor Tunnel at 3,200 m (10,400 ft) which marks the actual border and then had to queue for 25 minutes to get into Chile. Another collection was being made here, for as we left the Customs area, the local fire brigade had a collecting tin to which we duly added a few coins.

The trip down out of the Andes into Chile was wholly different to the road up the other side. Almost immediately we were twisting down the twenty nine hairpins at Portillo, diving in and out of the gaps between huge lorries either descending in low crawler gears, to save their brakes, or creeping up, also in low gears and at painfully slow speeds. Later the road was faster and more flowing, but not as well engineered as in Argentina.

Over the last few days I had become concerned about the state of our front tyres. They were wearing much quicker than those on other 4x4s and the tracking was clearly out as the greatest wear was on the inside edges. I had originally hoped that we would get all the way around on a single set of tyres, but we needed new ones for the front, at least, so decided we should sort out this problem before heading down south and the remoter regions of southern Chile and Patagonia.

So rather than drive straight through Los Andes, the first sizeable town we came to, we took a tour to try and find a tyre shop. Everywhere seemed closed, but as it was only 2.00pm we thought it might be siesta time. We headed on, now in wine growing country again and soon after we turned right to join the Pan American Highway, now a dual carriageway, this time heading north.

The map showed that Quillota was the largest town in the area, so we decided to head there and see what tyre supplies we could organise. A tour round the town, and a few requests for directions later, we found a Goodyear depot, but it was closed. The staff in a petrol station over the road were very helpful and they even rang their boss, who was also the boss of the tyre depot, who told us everywhere was closed today because it was a saint's day, but he could help us tomorrow. This seemed the best option as tomorrow would be a rest day for us, although we were some way from our hotel.

We headed back to the Pan American and then a little further north, before heading off west on a toll road over the mountains to the coast north of Valparaiso and Vina del Mar. The weather worsened as we crossed the mountains and soon it was misty and drizzling, a nice welcome to our halfway stop at the resort hotel complex at Marbella.

With our off-route trip to Quillota, we were one of the last crews to arrive and we found the car park full of damp rally cars and crews already unpacked and settled into their rooms. We sorted ourselves out, unpacking not only all our bags, but also emptying the car of the extra ones we were carrying for Ted and Judy and Rita and Mike.

We were halfway round the Inca Trail Rally and this called for a celebration so we soon headed for the bar, which was packed out, and had a couple of celebratory drinks. It was very welcome. Our euphoria was soon dispelled, however, as we wanted to tell our good news to our family. We phoned Jenny, our eldest daughter, only to find she had been in hospital for a few days recovering from a serious bout of food poisoning. She'd been left very dehydrated so had been kept in hospital for a few days on a drip before being released. She was now home but feeling very debilitated.

We had been invited to join Chris Wray's party at his step-brother's house nearby, but we were somewhat taken aback by our news, so declined when they phoned to remind us of the leaving time

However later on, having decided there wasn't much we could do to help Jenny from so far away, and knowing she was clearly getting the best medical attention, we accepted an invitation to join Peter and Carolynn, 'Big' Jim Taylor and Herby Boger, the Franeys and their friend Colin Forster and went by taxi to a beachside restaurant a few miles away.

Another town, another garage

Day 28 Friday 2 November
Rest day, Marbella

On the last rest day back in Lima we had a long lie in and I missed breakfast altogether, but as I wanted to sort out the tyres we made a reasonably prompt start and headed to La Calera, a town where we had been advised the evening before we could get tyres. It was about a half hour run back over to the main north/south road from where we turned off into La Calera and almost immediately came upon a Goodyear tyre depot.

I pulled in and there was Alastair Caldwell using one of the workshop car hoists to work on his Ferrari. The hubs were off and he had a young tyre fitter helping him out.

My need was for two new Goodrich All Terrain tyres and I had this written on a piece of paper that I gave to the reception desk. A fitter came out to look at the car and indicated that it would be no problem, but it became evident they would have to be brought from another depot. This would take about 20 minutes. So we waited and chatted to Alastair who told us that Chris Wray's step-brother, Paul, had sorted out a workshop for the rally cars about half a mile away and about a dozen were round there being worked on. Alastair said he'd been there as well initially, but the workshop was fairly small and felt he was unlikely to get any work done to his car for some time, so came here to do it himself.

The 20 minutes soon became half an hour, then forty five minutes and an hour with continued reassurances that the tyres were on their way. Paul called round to see what was going on and, with his Spanish, was able to find out that there was a bad accident on the main road and traffic was being held up. Our tyres would be available as soon as possible. We had heard sirens, so this made sense.

A few minutes later we looked out onto the road where a strange and unexpected sight occurred. Two red Dennis fire engines sped by, bells ringing and the sign writing on the side telling us they were from the Cheshire Fire Brigade. There's dedication to duty we thought, and we'd come a long way! And Dennis fire engines are built in our home town, Guildford. Once we got home to the UK, I checked with the Cheshire Fire Brigade and found out that the fire engines we saw were obsolete tenders donated to Chile a few years ago.

It was nearly two hours before a white van arrived at the depot with a load of tyres including the ones intended for us. It had come from Quillota the town we had visited yesterday and the depot we would have visited had it been open. But the tyres on board were not All Terrains, but Goodyears – I wasn't very pleased. I was put on the telephone and spoke in English to the owner of the business who told me they only did Goodyear tyres and no other, and also that the tyres offered were more than adequate for the job and would last for the rest of the event.

I debated what we should do. It seemed that All Terrains weren't available in this part of the world at all. We had already done the worst part of the route and the second half of the Inca Trail was supposedly easier on the car and therefore the tyres. We had already eaten well into our rest day and wanted to be sure we were ready to restart tomorrow. I agreed to have the tyres fitted, although wasn't really too happy about it and had the All Terrains from the back, which were still in pretty good shape, put on the front, and the new Goodyear road tyres fitted on the back.

This didn't take long and then the fitter asked me to put the car onto the rig to have the tracking checked. Here he found that the steering rack was loose, the problem, he said, was that the vertical and horizontal bushes were worn, as well as those of the anti-roll bar. The tracking couldn't be done until that was sorted out, but that would need a visit to a workshop as they couldn't do it at the Goodyear depot.

We settled up and headed round to the rally workshop that Alastair had told us about. This was in a residential street and entered via a narrow lane beside a bungalow behind which was a covered yard and workshop. There were Inca Trail rally cars and 4x4s all over the place, some being worked on, others waiting for their turn.

Rick Dyke Price was just leaving with his Austin Healey 3000 having had it over the workshop pit for several hours. The Inca Special was parked out the back with both Richard Newman and Robert O'Hara underneath it. They were having a new shock absorber mounting made. Lady Pauline Harris was asleep in Chris Wray's Galloper. She was waiting for the Porsche to be looked at, as was Chris who wanted the overheating problems he was suffering resolved.

Roberto Chiodi was busy on his Lancia trying to rectify all manner of problems. He wasn't a happy man at all and told me that the Inca Trail was the roughest and toughest event he had ever done. This from a rally man who did the Peking to Paris and the 2000 Round the World Rally in his Lancia. He said his car was now 'very tired' and this would be its last event.

Sue Shoosmith was busy on her A90 Westminster with the hubs off and plans to replace the disk brakes. Of course these cars never had disk brakes as original, but in modified form for historic rallying they are allowed to upgrade using parts that would have been fitted to other models in the manufacturer's product range. The disk brakes were those from an MGC and had been shipped out during the rally as replacements for the originals.

The owner of the workshop had a quick look at mine and said he could replace the bushes but that it would be a while before they could do it. I had little choice but to wait…. and wait…… and wait.

One by one, the other cars had attention and then departed. Paul called in a couple of times to see how things were progressing and also made apologies to me for Goodyear not having the tyres I was expecting. In discussion with him I found out he actually worked for

Goodyear in Chile in the division supplying tyres for mining vehicles such as those we had seen further north at the mine at Chuquicamata.

Time marched on and Pam and I were getting colder and colder. They still hadn't started work on the Porsche or mine and most of the rest of the workshop was emptying. Paul was planning to go back to Marbella with Pauline (navigator Ann Locks was staying with the car) so I made sure Pam went with them. She had been very patient waiting with me all day.

Work started on my car, and a mechanic, David, had it over the pit and was stripping down the steering in no time. The anti-roll bar bushes were certainly shot to pieces and these could easily be replaced, those in the steering rack being more difficult to extract. Once done, the owner then went away in the van to try and get replacements. I waited some more.

It was about six o'clock before he came back and it was clear the bushes for the steering rack were non standard, but 'should fit'. They started work replacing them, eventually finishing at about 8.30pm. It was now dark and misty, I was cold and hadn't eaten all day. Ann was the only other Inca Trailer left and the Porsche was still on jacks but we learned they planned to finish soon and I agreed to wait and travel back to Marbella with Ann who was worried about knowing the way.

We finally settled up our bills and left at about 9.15pm. I led and Ann followed, but as always in these situations it is difficult to know whether the car behind is actually the one you hope it is. The first major junction to negotiate was a left turn out onto the far carriageway of the main north/south motorway in the dark, but I saw Ann dart out after me and then fall in behind me.

We travelled together till our turning off the motorway and then to the pay booth for the toll road that led to the coast. Ann was still behind me, but the road now was over some mountains and it was raining and very misty. I soon lost Ann, although a car did pull behind me at one stage which I supposed was her. My worry was that the Porsche might break down, but I knew that Ann had a phone and could call for help if needed.

At a major turn off to the right I pulled up on the verge, but Ann was nowhere to be seen. I waited a while but there was still no sign of her so headed on to Marbella. There was little point in turning back as I wouldn't have been able to see her in the dark, rain and mist.

I arrived back at the hotel at 10.30pm. Ann had dropped behind because of the mist and also missed the turning where I had stopped and travelled on a few miles before realising her mistake, but finally made it by about 11.00pm.

I tracked down Pam who had been an angel and put aside some food and a beer for me in our room. I ate some of it, had a shower to warm up and flopped into bed. It had been a long, boring day involving standing around getting cold in various garages – not a rest day at all. It was past midnight by now and the alarm was set for 4.00am.

CD Day

Day 29 Saturday 3 November
Marbella - Temuco (845 kms)

Today would be a transport section to take us down south and more interesting rally terrain in southern Chile and back in Argentina. Our 4.00am alarm enabled us to get sorted out promptly, but not before some more dealings with the local dog population.

The hotel was built on sloping ground and our room was on the ground floor with a covered passageway leading to the stairwell and lifts that in turn led to reception and the restaurant two floors up. Overnight it had been wet and misty again and when I took the first set of bits out to the car the passageway and stairwell were occupied by about a dozen scraggy strays who had slept there overnight. They had left their mark too, with damp patches from their wet fur on the carpet and on the white painted walls.

I must have been the first person along that morning as the dogs clearly hadn't expected anyone so early and were taken aback to see me. However, they looked wretched and were also very frightened by me arriving and once up on their feet cowered away and vanished into the wet gloom. I felt very guilty at disturbing their short interlude in the dry.

We'd unpacked most of our bags at Marbella, but hadn't had a chance to sort them out, so they all needed repacking before we had breakfast. This was a subdued affair. It was early, most people were only half awake and we all faced a long day's drive, whether or not we were still rallying or just touring.

We now had a new entrant in the 4x4 class. Leo Schildkamp and Cees Willense who had written-off their Volvo back in Bolivia were now driving a Daihatsu they had purchased in Lima. They would eventually get back to Rio in one piece.

We checked out of the control at 5.30am and headed south around the back of Vina del Mar and Valparaiso, two of Chile's major cities, and then south east passing around Santiago via a couple of gravel road passes.

It was just over 200 kms and three hours before we joined the Pan American Highway, Ruta 5, arriving at 8.30am and we would follow this for a further 400 kms today to get to our next stop, Temuco.

We'd been warned to watch out for police activity and sure enough at regular intervals down this dual carriageway they were out with their radar guns. During the day several people got stopped, a few were fined, and others had warnings, but despite doing my share of 'just over the speed limit' driving we were only stopped once.

I pulled over and the policeman who had waved us down walked up to the car with a smile on his face and spoke to me in Spanish.

"Jabber, jabber, jabber, jabber," he said.

"Sorry. I don't speak Spanish," I replied courteously.

"Jabber, jabber, jabber, jabber," he said again.

I shrugged my shoulders and showed him my Inca Trail identity tag.

"Jabber, jabber, jabber, jabber. You no Spanish?" he continued, beginning to realise he wasn't getting anywhere.

"No Spanish, English. No speak Spanish."

He gave me a broad smile and waved us on and I gave him a friendly toot in return. He and I both knew I had gotten away with speeding and probably a fine.

Initially the road was very busy with dozens of lorries, as usual many of them grossly overloaded, but many others clearly operated by proper transport firms that took pride in their fleet. They were clean, well maintained and professional looking. White van man is also known in these parts and there were plenty of Fords, Renaults and other white vans speeding to their next drop off.

We hadn't used our CD player for a long time, (they don't like rough roads), but today we decided to work our way through all fourteen CDs we'd brought with us. They helped to pass the time and we enjoyed the sing-song as well.

A lunch stop was planned for today and we turned off the main road to visit the Salta del Laja. Here a waterfall fed by the Rio Laja drops 47 metres and although nothing like as spectacular as the Foz de Iguacu the stop was a pleasant break from the long journey.

In the restaurant we shared a table with a local family on holiday. He was an English teacher in a Santiago school and his wife and son spoke English quite well too. They were keen to know all about the rally and we had a chance to find out a bit about their life in Chile. The steak we both had was excellent, and for the first time it was served with mashed potato, something we found very appetising and a nice change from the ubiquitous fries. We found that mashed potato was very common as an accompaniment to steak, and with us eating more and more steaks from now on mash would become a regular part of our diet.

Once we were clear of Santiago, the weather had improved and eventually the sun came out. This region is known as the Central Valley and is fertile so farming is the main activity. There were many rice fields at the side of the road, often being ploughed by a horse-drawn contraption that seemed to be a flat board that floated on the water of the rice field with the farmer perched on top of it. There were also vineyards and fruit growing in abundance but the further south we went, so forestry became more significant, and there were miles and miles of fir trees growing alongside the road with wood yards and saw mills at frequent intervals.

The mountains of the Andes on our left to the east also became visible again with their snow-capped peaks once more contrasting with the blue sky. We passed by numerous towns, their names being a blur on the sign posts – Ranagua, San Fernando, Talca, Linares, Chillan and Los Angeles before heading into Temuco the major city in the region.

The rally was spread between two hotels placed either side on a street just off the main square with plenty of safe parking nearby. Just for once there was hardly anyone working on their cars as the day's run had been easy and all the fettling had been done yesterday.

In the lobby of our hotel we met Ian Green who had flown out from the UK in the last couple of days to join his brother in a Land Rover Discovery for a couple of weeks navigating. Work commitments with IBM prevented any longer involvement in this rally, but together they had done the London - Capetown. Ian later joined us for a meal at a local restaurant that had been recommended to us by the hotel receptionist and once more the place was well supported by other Inca Trailers. We all had steak again but decided against a local delicacy called craidillo – testicles!

It had been another long day and I was glad to get to my bed again promptly as the real rallying would start again tomorrow.

Lakeside BBQ

Day 30 Sunday 4 November
Temuco - Bariloche (491 kms)

We were able to make a reasonably leisurely start today and were on the road at 7.30am but not before telephoning home to check on Jenny's health. It was Sunday and a bit early even at home so the response we had was sleepy, but we were pleased to hear she was on the mend.

Before leaving, we also said cheerio to Sue Shoosmith. She was still set for a Gold Medal in her A90 she was sharing with Alexa Scott Plummer, but family problems at home demanded she return immediately and she was to fly back to Santiago and then on to the UK. Alexa was to take over driving the car and had recruited Tony Humphrey to navigate.

Tony had originally started the event in a Mercedes 250SE that he and David Garrett had bought especially for the event, a car that was beautifully prepared and looked impressive. However the pairing had parted company at the halfway in Marbella as there were disagreements between them about David's driving. To keep going, David had recruited Sarah Born who had completed the first half of the event with her parents in a Land Rover Discovery.

On the road, we were soon heading for the Chilean Lake District and arrived in the small town of Villarrica. This was a lovely place set alongside a lake of the same name and with its Alpine-style buildings, we could have been on the shore of Lake Geneva or Lucerne. Now apparent on the skyline behind the town was the Lanin volcano and in various places all the rally cars vied for position to get the right photo of their car in front of the smoking mountain. Capped in snow, it looked like a slumbering giant – I wouldn't want to be around when it erupted. The whole area around this part of southern Chile is very prone to both earthquake and volcanic activity.

We were steadily climbing and the views of the snow-capped mountains through the pine forests were breathtaking as we headed for the 1,250 m Paso Malhuil Malal, described as one of the most scenic Andean crossings, and the border with Argentina.

We were now on a gravel road, much like a British forest track and having passed through the Chilean customs post we went round a corner and I felt a rear tyre going soft, one of the wheels with the new Goodyears on. I pulled up at the side of the road just above a beautiful blue-watered lake with mountains and forests surrounding it. We were actually just under the Lanin Volcano too, but it was too close to see through the trees.

I checked the wheel and the left hand one was flat, so it was out with the trolley jack and wheel brace and on with the remaining unused alloy spare that still had an All Terrain fitted. The job only took about five minutes but the location and weather couldn't have been better.

It was also encouraging to see our friends stop whilst I was changing the wheel, including Ted and Judy in their Reliant, as well as Chris and Linda (Toyota Amazon) and Jonathan and Anna (Audi Allroad). Of course they didn't stop to help, merely to make sure I was doing it right and also take the proverbial. It was good to know they were there though and that help was on hand should we have needed it. Although I didn't notice, Pam told me later that several more cars both classic and 4x4s also stopped to see if we needed any help. It was a lovely spot and as I was finishing off and packing up I regretted not having a barbecue with us as it would have made for a pleasant interlude in the rally.

We headed on again and came across Rick Dyke Price (Austin Healey 3000) who was parked up checking a front wheel. He didn't need any assistance, but later we heard he had had steering problems and returned back to Chile to get repairs carried out rather than head on.

Out of no-mans land we soon crossed the border back into Argentina, our third visit so far, into the Parque Nacional Lanin and down towards

Junin de los Andes and tarmac roads once more. For the first time we began to see monkey puzzle trees that are very common in this region.

I was now worried about our tyre situation. Were the Goodyears up to the job? We still had about 6,000 kms of gravel roads to do yet and I'd had a puncture after only a few miles of gravel. I had retained the two All Terrains that had been removed at La Calera, just in case, so decided to rearrange the tyres as soon as possible.

This was sooner than I thought, as in Junin de los Andes we came across a gomeria (tyre shop) that was open, even though it was Sunday. Here I had both Goodyears taken off the rims and the well-worn All Terrains put back, but on the rear wheels, leaving those with the better tread on the front. And the Goodyear that I thought had punctured, no, it had rolled off the rim!

The route now took us south towards San Martin de los Andes, a larger town than its neighbour and winter sports centre with lots of ski boutiques and kitsch restaurants. Many 4x4s decided to stop here for lunch, yet another indication of the slowing pace of the Inca Trail, as lunch would have been a real luxury in the early stages.

Out of San Martin we climbed alongside a lake with sailing boats on it and headed up into mountains again and also back onto gravel and over the Paso del Cordoba (4,200 m). We also passed back into a national park, this time the Parque Nacional Nahuel Huapi, with its rock pinnacle.

We hit the main asphalt road towards Bariloche at Confluencia and almost immediately saw a car transporter heading the other way with a load of very nice looking cars on the back. There were Jaguar E Types, various older BMWs, and some open topped cars and we discovered later they would have been on their way home having taken part in a local classic car touring-style rally that finished in Bariloche the day before. On the way to town we passed several more transporters with similar loads.

Bariloche, or San Carlos de Bariloche, to give it its formal name, is

Argentina's premier ski resort and attracts thousands of visitors all year round. Sited on the southern edge of Lago Nahuel it too has the air of an alpine resort but was very windy when we arrived. We sought out a petrol station to top up and also to get guidance on tyre availability in town. We were given directions to the local Michelin depot, but with the very complicated one-way system operating in the town, found ourselves going the wrong way down a one-way street, with a police car coming the other way! Oops!

We pulled up, and they pulled up, and fortunately it was a quiet side street with no traffic, but I took the wind out of their sails by immediately asking the way to the Michelin depot. They indicated the one-way street and I acknowledged I was in the wrong and apologised. They were all right about it and indicated for us to follow them so they turned around to face the wrong way too and led us down to the next junction and around some more streets to the depot that they said would be open at about 8.00am the next day. We thanked them and off they went.

There was nothing else we could do so we hit the road again out of town to the west and on to our hotel for the night, the Llao Llao Resort Hotel. This was approached via a roundabout route to take advantage of the scenic drive around the edge of the lake and through pine forests.

The hotel has a stunning setting on a high isthmus overlooking Lago Perito Moreno on the one side and Lago Nahuel Huapi on the other and a backdrop of snow-capped mountains both ways. The hotel is surrounded by its own golf course and has a yacht marina sited on the larger lake.

For marketing purposes there is a group of hotels who brand themselves the 'Leading Hotels in the World' and this is one of them. HERO had clearly blown the accommodation budget here as it was a beautiful and luxurious place. Built in the 1920s, mainly of timber, it is a hotel on the grand scale. Our room on the second floor facing forward was the finest we stayed in during the whole trip, if a bit frilly, and we had a balcony overlooking the northern lake and the distant mountains behind. Pam enquired about staying a month – it was very tempting! Blow the rally.

Having settled, we took a walk around and I quite fancied a game of golf, but we knew it would soon be dark. I wasn't the only one who fancied some golf as Jenny Bishop managed a round the next morning before heading on.

The hotel had laid on a buffet for the rally, (it was too far to think about going into Bariloche to eat), but we joined David and Carole for a beer beforehand in the main lounge area. This was like a large baronial hall with a high ceiling, fireplaces at each end and dark wood and leather artefacts on the walls.

It reminded me of the hotel in the Jack Nicholson film, The Shining, where he plays a deranged caretaker stalking the corridors and rooms. Carole said she had had the same thought and it made her shiver.

The meal lived up to expectations with the food exquisitely laid out and tasting just as good as it looked. We slept well in our softly mattressed bed.

Steaming

Day 31 Monday 5 November
Bariloche to Esquel (372 kms)

It wasn't easy to drag ourselves away from the luxurious splendour of the Llao Llao Resort Hotel but the caravan of cars that is the rally moved on relentlessly, and so did we.

I had lost confidence with the Goodyear tyres I had fitted in La Calera and we were running on a mixture of three tyres, something I didn't intend to continue for long. So rather than take the official route away from Llao Llao we decided to backtrack to Bariloche and see what tyres we could get there. There would be no penalty for this as the official route through the main skiing area in the mountains of La Catedral behind the town was not an official test for the 4x4s, only for the classics.

We quickly found the Michelin/Bridgestone tyre shop the police had directed us to the previous night, but it was shut and didn't look much like it was due to open. We waited a while until enquiring of a chap in an office over the road who told us the place was permanently closed – "Kaput" as he described it. Perhaps this was another sign of times to come in Argentina.

I thought I had seen some tyre places on my way into town the previous day so we decided to try and track them down. We soon found the Goodyear tyre depot, though I wasn't keen to use them again, but they pointed out another depot across the road, so we went there (only after many meanderings around more one-way streets to approach the main set of traffic lights from the right direction).

At this new place we found other Inca Trailers. Phil Surtees was there with one of the Course Cars getting new rubber boots, as well as Mike and Jenny Barnes trying to get suitable tyres for their Porsche 911. My first question was whether we could get All Terrains, but it seemed they aren't available in South America, so we settled for a couple of Firestones that we were assured would be suitable for the many miles of gravel yet to come.

Mike Barnes still wasn't in a good mood, 'slagging off' John Brown over the advice he'd been given about the suitability of his 911 for the rally. Although it had full protection underneath and up-rated suspension, the rear of his car was still very low to the ground.

Mike didn't go on many more gravel roads, as he was one of the crews that were cutting and running wherever possible to avoid them. "I'm sending a bill to the Chilean Government when I get back as I'm regrading all their gravel roads as I go along," was Mike's comment.

I left the existing All Terrains on the front, putting the new Firestones on the back and the spare All Terrain that had been in use went into the boot. I retained the two Goodyears just in case and they remained in the back of the Colorado until we got home to the UK.

It was gone 10.00am before we had completed all this tyre business, so we quickly found the main road out of town to the south to get back on route, which we did by about 10.40am.

However our rally nearly came to an end on the way out of town. Whilst the weather was warm and sunny, and we were still wearing shorts, there was a very strong wind blowing south off the lake. We were following an open-backed lorry carrying a load of building materials when the wind caught a sheet of corrugated roofing material, carrying it onto the bonnet of our car. The lorry driver knew nothing of this and didn't stop, but fortunately there was no lasting damage to us and we carried on our way. However it could easily have broken our windscreen, or worse.

The route followed fast tarmac on Ruta 258 for about 100 kms before turning off onto gravel and the way to our initial destination for the day, El Maiten, where we were promised a steam railway engine treat.

We were not to be disappointed. The car park of the La Trochita railway station was already full of rally cars and there was a railway engine in full steam surrounded by Inca Trailers taking photographs or just taking a look; mainly the guys of course. La Trochita was made famous by Paul Theroux in his book "*The Old Patagonia Express*", but express it is no longer, as it only runs occasionally as a tourist treat to Esquel where we would end the day.

The whole town had turned out and many of the children were seeking autographs from whoever would oblige. As we were now heading into Patagonia the wind blew strong and it was very dusty.

Clay Regazzoni was getting a lot of attention and it was the first time we had seen him on the road as he had only just joined the Inca Trail. Clay used to drive for Ferrari in Formula 1 racing during the 1970s and won the British Grand Prix in 1979 in a Williams Ford. He had taken part in an Argentinean classic car event that finished in Bariloche the day before we arrived there.

Clay is now paraplegic as a result of a motor racing accident in the USA many years ago, but regularly competes on rallies in the Mercedes 300 Coupe he was now using on the Inca Trail, and which has hand controls. He was also being supported from here to the finish in Rio by two French teams entered in other Mercedes classics.

But the locomotive was hissing steam and the sweet smell of steam is the same the world over – great! We had time to stop for some coffee in the buffet car and a walk round the station area and adjoining depot where there was plenty of interest for railway buffs.

All too soon we needed to get underway again and head on south to Esquel where we would be stopping the night. From the railway, the classics had a Medal Section on gravel for about 90 kms so we headed off with them down yet another dusty track.

We let Kermit, the Wignalls and some others pass through on our left even though our dust was blowing from right to left. Later I was travelling down the middle of the track when all of a sudden the lights of the white Mercedes of David Garrett were in my mirror on the nearside (right). Initially I pulled over, but this only made his potential overtaking manoeuvre more difficult, so, as the road was clear, I made for the wrong side so he could come through on the nearside which he quickly did, smothering us in his dust as he went by.

The section ended near the entrance to the Los Alerces National Park, but before that we passed by the small village of Cholila just a couple of kilometres off our route. The exploits of Butch Cassidy and the Sundance Kid were referred to earlier during our passage through Bolivia but before that they also lived for some time in Cholila.

They emigrated from the United States because the authorities were gradually catching up with them and they had heard that there were new opportunities in Argentina. The scenery around Cholila is much like that in the mid west of the States and perhaps it attracted them to stay. Even here they ran into problems and eventually had to move on, which is why they probably ended up in Bolivia attracted by talk of fortunes being made in the silver mines.

And their death in a shoot out as depicted in the famous film? According to the Lonely Planet that probably didn't occur. They either died in a shoot out in southern Argentina or far less romantically Butch may have returned to the United States and died in an old people's home in 1937. The Kid may well have been killed as a result of his nefarious activities. Whichever is correct, I prefer the film version.

The next 60 kms through the park were taken at a gentle pace alongside Lagos Rivadavia and Futalaufquen that were very pretty and across which were dramatic views of nearby forests and steep, craggy mountains.

The park takes its name from the alerce tree, also known as the Patagonian cypress. It is highly valued for its resistance to rot and infestation by bugs and it has been so heavily harvested that in modern times its existence has largely been confined to a few restricted areas. The park also has a reserve for the huemul and the pudu, the smallest deer in the world, but not unexpectedly we didn't see either.

A fairly short run into Esquel was all that remained after we left the park. Esquel is a quiet little place with about 25,000 inhabitants and the feel of a frontier town about it. But at the finish in the main square all the local school children seemed to be present, once more looking for autographs. We provided a few but the children were very hyped up for some reason and we were glad to leave the square once we had our time card signed.

Our digs for tonight were a modest bed and breakfast establishment, a far cry from the five star splendiforousness of Llao Llao. But it was clean and adequate and the owner was very obliging in letting us use his hose to clean the car and recommended a super parilla (steak bar) to eat at, one that was dedicated to the steam railway we had visited earlier.

What happened at La Trochita Parilla was typical of so many evenings on the Inca Trail. Three hundred or so people arrive in town for one night and are looking for a meal. In a small town like Esquel there are only so many places to eat, and for them all their Christmases come at once. We arrived at the parilla relatively promptly and there was one other small group of Inca Trailers there before us. However, within an hour the place was completely packed out, probably for the first time in weeks (or maybe longer) and the restaurant management was under more and more of a strain as the evening went by.

They coped as best they could, but will happily recall the evening the Inca Trail came to town.

Austral driving

Day 32 Tuesday 6 November
Esquel - Coyhaique (503 kms)

Over the last week or so we had trekked a long way south, long trousers were in order and our shorts were packed away for the time being. We made a leisurely start and had a good breakfast at our B and B with lots of home made jams, and were soon heading south out of town back towards Chile again.

As far as Trevelin, a small settlement whose name reflects the Welsh ancestry of the inhabitants, the road was asphalt, but for the rest of the day as far as the approaches to Coyhaique, about 500 kms, we would be on gravel roads.

The Welsh influence in this part of the world would become more evident as we travelled around the southern tip of the continent. Many settlers came here in the 19th century to escape the poverty in Wales and seek new opportunities. In the southern Andean regions they found countryside that was very reminiscent of home and, as so many settlers do, named their towns and villages after familiar places back home.

Trevelin, which in Welsh translates as *village of the mill,* was originally settled by Welsh immigrants from the Chubut Valley on the eastern side of Argentina, which we would visit at a later stage on the Inca Trail. We found a John Daniel Evans Street, and just up the road we came upon the Cascada Nant y Fall.

We pressed on, passing the border controls at about 8.30am, and then headed on through the pretty settlement of Futaleutu where most of the houses are wooden built in the Alpine style and where white water rafting is becoming a tourist attraction. The local police were out in force here, all two of them, helpfully directing us through the maze of little streets and out into the countryside again. The village also marked the start of our Explorer Section that would take us all the way into Coyhaique. The rally cars were also supposed to be doing this section, but had been rerouted due to road works towards the end of the section. They missed a super road.

Soon we skirted the southern edge of Lago Espolon, the first of many lakes we would travel beside over the next few days, before turning south onto the Carretera Austral (Ruta 7) at Villa Santa Lucia. The road is the continuation of the Pan American Highway although this southern section is gravel, mostly single track and has little traffic.

The Carretera has been built in the last 30 years or so to link up the various small settlements down in this remote region of Chile. Previously they had had to rely on sea transport or the occasional excursion through the mountains to Argentina. Troubled by the possibility that the Argentineans might try to occupy the region, the Juntas construction of the road was a strategic move to make troop movements easier. The road is now often referred to as Pinochet's Folly as it has few links to other parts of the country in the north except by slow and often infrequent ferries, some key sections never being completed.

However, it is bringing with it better communications and also tourism to the area, but the settlements that do exist are very small and fuel is generally hard to obtain.

Ruta 7 was much like a British forestry road, mostly single track and steeply cambered with gravelly ditches at either side. It had fast sweeping bends, but along most of its length, the trees and bushes grew close to the road, making bends especially dangerous because there was, just occasionally, some traffic, but not much. Mostly it was large lorries, often carrying timber, but also fuel tankers and we even followed a small refrigerated delivery van for a few miles.

It was a joy to drive on and before we knew it, we were at the village of La Junta which had the only fuel for many hundreds of kilometres in either direction. We stopped for a breather, joining a couple of other 4x4 crews in restocking our nose bag from the small shop. The name of the village suggests it was named after the former political leaders of the country, and there was a large sign commemorating the name of the town and the Carretera, but we could find no firm evidence of this. I suggest it was built as a construction camp originally and has developed since.

There were fields in some places, particularly near the settlements, but mostly the area was forested. The shrubbery growing close to the road caused us a problem somewhere along here. We came across a road crew cutting back the shrubs and trees, leaving stubbly ends of shoots and branches in their wake. Further down the road we suddenly came upon a lorry coming the other way, and I had to dive into the right hand ditch to avoid hitting him. We must have caught one of these branches as we sped past, although I don't remember anything happening, but Pam saw it, too late, and it hit the front right hand lights and scraped along the side of the car.

I didn't stop, but later found that the plastic headlight cover was badly cracked, the side lamp glass broken and there was a light mark along the side of the car. The plastic was taped up with duct tape which, although it needed renewal a couple of times, got back to the UK.

Further south at the little village of Puyuguapi, we had been warned there was a barrier across the road that wouldn't be opened by the local police until the middle of the afternoon. The barrier seems to work as a means of controlling traffic on the next section that was very narrow alongside a fjord, but we arrived at 12.15pm and it was open.

The scenery continued to be stunning, with the mountains reflected on the mirror-still waters of the fjord and the forests providing a beautiful backdrop to occasional farms and dwellings. The road itself was great to drive on, offering relative smoothness with the slippery thrill of gravel, some of which was wet.

There was a small fishing boat sailing down the fjord making progress south and with the flat calm it left a long but low wake across the whole expanse of water.

Not far from Puerto Cisnes we turned away from the fjord and climbed up a river valley into the snow-capped mountains again. Over the last few days we had seen many gauchos on their horses and along here we saw one chap dressed in a wide-brimmed black hat and black cloak, looking much like Zorro.

Towards Manholes major road works started. They were no bother to us in a 4x4, but the road was under considerable reconstruction and there were graders and diggers all over the place. The weather had deteriorated somewhat over the latter part of the day, in fact since we left the fjord, and it was raining and getting much cooler, justifying our warmer clothing.

It wasn't long before we reached the tarmac and had two options in the road book. One was to take a short cut on gravel to Coyhaique, the other to do a slightly longer tarmac route. We chose the latter which was actually mostly concrete, but was a good road over most of its length.

We were driving along and I happened to remember that Coyhaique had been in the news at home not so many months previously when Prince William had come here to undertake some gap year work with Raleigh International. And if Raleigh International were here it was worth seeing if my old work colleague, Dominic O'Neill, was as well. The last I had heard of him was that he'd left Namibia, where we had a chance meeting with him, to become Operations Director in Mongolia. We determined to see whether we could make contact with Raleigh once we got to town.

On the final run into Coyhaique we followed a small bus which was going along very quickly indeed. Overtaking was possible, but the driver seemed to know the road well so I decided to stay behind him. It was a good move. The road had suffered from landslips in many places and suddenly Tojo up front (all drivers up front were Tojo) would dive across onto the other side of the road to avoid a large step or crack in the road surface. We followed him. Two of the Hooligans came up behind us and decided to overtake me and Tojo, doing so at a place where there was a large landslip. Tojo had to keep his lane, but the Amazons had a tricky moment as they both went by, and didn't make too much distance on him along the next length.

The police directed us to the main town square in Coyhaique and a large crowd was gathered to welcome us. We were approached by the local radio station for an interview, but they wanted people who spoke Spanish, and although I was learning a little as we ventured round the continent, it was nothing like good enough for a public broadcast.

Coyhaique is the major town in the region and was another to have a frontier feel to it, but also had a slightly dingy, grubby, unfinished ambiance, unlike Esquel which was a bright and breezy sort of place. I wouldn't have wanted to live here.

We were due to stay in the Hotel Austral which was a bit basic, but adequate, and having settled in, took a walk round town. We found a café and had a coffee but there wasn't much else. It was much colder than we had been used to and we now had our new anoraks on.

Back in our hotel we tried the phone book to see whether we could track down a telephone number for Raleigh International, but without success; the owner of the hotel couldn't help either. We'd planned to visit the headquarters hotel anyway and there we made contact with Lisa, the Spanish-speaking member of the HERO headquarters team who helped us get the right telephone number.

Amazingly we found that Dominic was now based in Coyhaique, but sadly out of town with a party undertaking a project. I wished we had found out about his presence earlier and made arrangements to meet. I left a message and wondered where we would catch up with him next. (Back home in the UK, I emailed Dominic to find that he hadn't received any message that we were in the region.)

We ventured out again later, found a fairly ordinary pizza restaurant and had an early night.

We meet Bin Laden

Day 33 Wednesday 7 November
Coyhaique - Lago Posadas (498 kms)

The morning control was sited on the edge of town in the car park of the local football field, which at 7.00am on a cool overcast morning wasn't too appealing. We were soon on the road however, but the first hazard was a very rough and narrow road works about 2 kms from the start.

The road south out of Coyhaique, still on Ruta 7, was tarmac and we made good progress in the company of other 4x4s. Those that were avoiding gravel and sticking to tarmac whenever possible, and the number doing this was growing, took a diversion east here. But for us we had a steady climb up a river valley on newly constructed concrete road with lovely sweeping bends before we hit gravel again and the Explorer Section for the day.

The countryside was more open now, someone described it as 'big country' and we were soon travelling alongside another lake, this time along the western edge of Lago General Carrera. This lake straddles the border with Argentina and was very badly polluted back in 1991 when nearby Mt Hudson erupted and huge quantities of volcanic ash were washed into the lake. There is still a heavy deposit of ash everywhere.

We stopped briefly at Puerto Tranquilo where Clay Regazzoni was getting fuel for his Mercedes with his supporters team. However, as on other days, they weren't running in their rally order and I think were just on the rally 'for the beer'.

Soon after we were buzzing along nicely, when the big wide nose of the Mercedes appeared in my rear view mirror, so we let him pass, and very soon he was gone from our view. We also stopped to take the obligatory photo of the car with a waterfall backdrop. In fact the car was so dirty with dust that had we been able, we would have driven it under the waterfall to clean it, but that wasn't practical.

With the more relaxed pace of the event, we decided to take a break for lunch and once we had left Lago General Carrera we came upon Lago Bertrand on our right so pulled up and sat on the beach for a while.

After a half hour break we headed on into low mountains once more and it wasn't long before we came upon the turning to our right to Cochrane. We had an option to take this and return, but decided not to, but now left the Ruta 7, the Pan American Highway, for the last time. We had been on the road since leaving Lima back in Peru nearly three weeks ago and it was like a friend. The road ends just past Cochrane at Puerto Yungay anyway.

The nature of the road changed somewhat along here and became narrower and the surface softer, the countryside being very much like a Welsh moorland. I liked this a lot and we stepped up the pace to enjoy the terrain over about 30 kms. We learned later that Kermit, the bright green Volvo of Bart and Jolijn Reitbergen, had slipped off the road here and nose dived into a bog. The car and occupants were fine and soon regained the road with the help of a passing 4x4 and a road grader.

We were now heading east towards the border with Argentina and our next visit to that country. Like some of the other border posts in the last few days, in these very rural areas they didn't amount to very much. One building for the customs and a couple of others for the staff was about it.

There was little wait as there were only a couple of other rally cars about, but at the Argentinean control we joined a short queue in the company of a small black Labrador puppy, who of course had everyone's attention. It seemed he belonged to one of the customs officers who had christened him Bin Laden. Pam also found and made friends with a little lamb with unusual grey colouring.

Soon afterwards the route split, the 4x4s being offered a narrow track over some mountains to the next valley. This was much better 4x4 territory with the need to negotiate all sorts of hazards, from rocky outcrops to salt lakes which we crossed. The views were some of the best yet and matched the cowboy films seen on television.

The salt lake was nearly the undoing of a couple of 4x4s as they got stuck and sank in quite deeply. However the next one along learned from their errors and took a safer passage and then helped pull them out.

We dropped down to a causeway between Lagos de Furioso and Lago Pueyrredon, crossed to the other side and headed back west towards Estancia Suyai where we would be camping for the night.

The Estancia was sited hard up against the border with Chile, although there is no formal crossing point and looked back east across the mirror-smooth Lago Pueyrredon. We were directed to the camping field and found that most of the classics had already arrived and bagged the best spots, but we found a slot next to Malcolm McKay and Nicholas Hall who were struggling round the Inca Trail with a TR2.

We'd been loaned a tent by our local scouts and tried putting it up in the garden back home. It was easy and Pam now did her bit by videoing the whole procedure. Malcolm mentioned that in one of the cabins facing the lake there were some refreshments, so once the tent was up and equipped for the night, we headed over there and had some locally prepared lamb stew and a coffee.

With so much beautiful scenery on the Inca Trail it is difficult to find fresh words to describe somewhere that was even better, but on our arrival at Suyai the sun was still fairly high in the blue sky, dusk wouldn't be until about 8.30pm in these climes, and the whole landscape was absolutely stunningly beautiful. A complete delight.

Having supped, I decided to chill out for a while and went and sat by the lake for half an hour contemplating the meaning of life; I didn't get any answers (surprise, surprise), but it was one of those sort of places.

Later we had a barbecue laid on, the lamb being cooked in the Argentinean style. The carcase is split backwards and hooked onto a metal frame, a bit like a crucifix that is pushed into the ground around a fire. The fire was surrounded by about twenty lamb carcases. There was plenty of red wine and beer available as well and as much meat and salad as we needed so we had a good feed. We also had an odd sweet here – crème caramel on a slice of cheese – it didn't taste too bad.

There is something about a bonfire that's past its maturity and is being allowed to burn down that is so nice to stand by. There's a wistful distant comfortableness about it that I like. We caught up with Ted and Judy here, they were still having all manner of problems with their less than reliable Reliant, and stood next to the fire with them chatting with a cup of sweet coffee.

All too soon it was time to try out the tent and having squirmed our way into our sleeping bags, neither of which had been used for about fifteen years, we were soon asleep. Pam didn't even use the hot water bottle she'd brought with her.

Houston, we have a problem

Day 34 Thursday 8 November
Lago Posadas - El Calafate (634 kms)

We both slept well but being under canvas we were soon woken, as some others began to stir and started dismantling their tents. The morning was very fresh and bright and as I crept bleary-eyed out of our tent, having extricated myself from the sleeping bag, I looked up at the mountains behind us and noted snow in some of the crevices that didn't get the sun.

Like most people it takes me a while to get going in the morning, but when camping you do it in public, rather than the privacy of your own home or hotel room. It was nice, however, to see some other Inca Trailers wandering around looking like half wound-up zombies as well, and like me grunting good mornings to each other.

Breakfast was a bit basic, but we were soon packed up and ready for the off at about 7.00am. Today we were due to do over 500 kms on gravel followed by a short run on tarmac into our next stop in El Calafate, and the road was mostly down Ruta 40, Argentina's main north/south road.

Like the Pan American in Chile, we'd been on Ruta 40 before as it starts up in Salta and runs down the eastern flank of the Andes. Down here in Patagonia there is only very light traffic and fuel and any form of habitation is well spaced out. In fact for several days we had been warned about the scarcity of fuel and the need to make sure we always kept our tanks and spare cans topped up.

We headed out of the camp site and passed back along the lakeside saying cheerio to this lovely place. Initially, the road on the south side of the lake was in deep shadow as it was protected from the low sun by the mountains. Here it was still very cold and a slight sheen of ice formed on the windscreen. We were glad we didn't stay here in colder weather. We crossed the causeway once more and headed into fresh territory and our first destination, the tiny settlement at Lagos Posadas, also known as Hipolito Yrigoyen. There was a small hotel here and some Inca Trailers who felt that camping was beneath their dignity had stayed here for the night.

Nearby we were also offered the opportunity of visiting some rock paintings estimated to be about 10,000 years old. We took the track and parked up as directed with some other 4x4s but despite wandering around the rocks for about half an hour, failed to find them. However the view from the hill where the paintings were supposed to be was fabulous and we could see other Inca Trailers speeding across the plain in front of us, leaving a long rooster tail of dust behind them.

We regained the proper route out of Lago Posadas and soon came upon a big 4x4 army lorry heading in the same direction, one of the few vehicles we would see all day. He was bowling along quite happily and saw us approaching behind him and soon flicked across to his right to let us through.

We were heading generally east to start with so as to join Route 40 at Bajo Caracoles where the time control for us and the classics was established. Mike 'Medic' Johnson and Bill Price were in charge and well wrapped up as, despite it being a pleasant sunny morning, the Patagonian wind was blowing strongly. We could get fuel here so topped up and refreshed our nose bag once more and headed out into Patagonia proper.

We headed south, often in the company of other 4x4s and classics, for those that were still rallying were following the same route. We hadn't gone far when we came on our army chums again as they had clearly taken a short cut across country to get in front of us – we could see the dust trail they'd left on our right. We passed them once more with a friendly beep and kept on trucking. Given that there is virtually nothing on the road ahead we wondered where they might have been heading.

This was now Patagonia as I had always imagined it. Vast flat landscapes with scrubby growth and what I call Microsoft Windows sky – baby blue with white cotton wool clouds. And it went on forever. We would drive for ages with a wide landscape either way, eventually crest a low hill or ridge and it would be the same again, and twenty minutes later the same again. It's the sort of territory you either like or don't, but I very much fall for it. In fact it was very like Namibia except that it was less red, more greyish in colouring. And there was some wildlife. We saw our first rheas and even three vicuna near the Hotel Rio Olnie, one of the few buildings alongside the road and clearly closed up for many years.

What is it about Patagonia that draws the imagination? The region conjures up desolation, bleak nothingness, an arid territory where little of anything grows, but where, somehow, people manage to eke out a livelihood.

Patagonia has no official boundaries or borders, its limits are undefined, although generally it is considered to stretch south from the 40th parallel, a line roughly between Bariloche to San Antonio Oeste on the Atlantic coast.

On the east it is bordered by the Atlantic, whilst in the west the cordillera forms a natural barrier to other regions, although some include these too within the confines of Patagonia. In the south, the Magellan Straits are generally considered the southern border, thus leaving out Tierra del Fuego.

There is no capital city to Patagonia, nor even a region of Argentina that has its name, although we did see a Bank of Patagonia in several towns.

The historian Michael Mainwaring described Patagonia as a fictional country like Ruritania, and 'unspeakably remote', and Jules Verne took delight in modelling his book 'The Lost World' on Patagonia.

Charles Darwin perhaps summed it up best in his diaries he wrote whilst on The Beagle:

Day 30: *Bart and Jolijn Rietbergen press on in Kermit, their green Volvo*

Day 32: *Our Colorado needed a car wash, but I couldn't get it close enough to the water*

Day 33: *A heavy duty wooden cattle grid on the northern edge of Patagonia*

Day 34: *John Blankley's A90 in a sorry state at the filling station at Tres Lagos after rolling during a dice with a Ferrari!*

Day 35: *Perito Moreno Glacier*

Day 37: *This way for Tierra del Fuego and the Straits of Magellan*

Day 38: *Fin del Mundo, the rally control at Ushuaia where I completed a double, having driven to the northern and southernmost roads on Earth*

Day 39: *Enjoying the company of fellow members of Lions Clubs International in Rio Grande at the rally parilla*

Day 43: *Gerallt Williams (left) and his Welsh speaking family outside Capel Bethesda in the Chubut Valley*

Day 44: *BBQ Argentinean style on the Valdes Peninsula*

Day 45: *One of the more interesting views of Patagonia, but what a place to rally in*

Day 46: *One of Juan Manuel Fangio's Chevrolet racing cars used for the city to city road races of the 1930s and 40s*

Day 47: *The battle scarred Ford Escort of David Liddell/Mark l'Anson*

Day 50: *The naked truth is revealed about rally marshals Jingers, Daniel and Greg at their rally control in Uruguay*

Day 52: *Pam enjoys her tennis match in Florianopolis, home of tennis idol Gustavo Kuerten, with (left to right) Jill Wray, Anna Pelly-Fry and Angela Fenhalls*

Award ceremony: The Gold Medal team of David Angel, Pam, Carole Angel and Vic

In calling up images of the past, I find that the plains of Patagonia frequently cross before my eyes; yet these plains are pronounced by all wretched and useless. They can be described only by negative characteristics; without habitations, without water, without trees, without mountains, they support only a few dwarf plants. Why, then, and the case is not peculiar to myself, have these arid wastes taken so firm a hold on my memory? Why have not the still more level, the greener and more fertile Pampas, which are serviceable to mankind, produced an equal impression? I can scarcely analyse these feelings; but it must be partly owing to the free scope given to the imagination. The plains of Patagonia are boundless, for they are scarcely passable, and hence unknown; they bear the stamp of having thus lasted, as they are now, for ages, and there appears no limit to their duration through future time. If, as the ancients supposed, the flat earth was surrounded by an impassable breadth of water, or by deserts heated to an intolerable excess, who would not look at these boundaries to man's knowledge with deep but ill-defined sensations?

A hundred and fifty years have changed the region a little, but from what we saw during our several weeks in the region, Darwin had it fairly well summed up.

There was very little to distract us from the driving, which actually needed a lot of concentration to maintain a reasonable pace. There was so little of interest that the road book instructions were very sparse. In one part there were only three instructions over a 150 kms stretch, and they all referred to rough stretches of road rather than any special feature such as a bridge or sign.

We came across some horses in the middle of nowhere, and whereas we'd seen other rather scraggy looking equines at other places, these two were well fed and looked pretty good specimens. But there were no buildings, no vehicles or any other form of human activity and one can't help wondering how come they were there.

The road was quite wide, the top surface being loose gravel which, with the passage of vehicles, had channelled into a series of wheel tracks. This was common on all the gravel roads. Most of the time it was easy to speed along with each set of wheels in a set of tracks, the small pile of stones running under the car, and on each side. On this road there were usually about five or seven sets of tracks and to ease the boredom I would jump wheel tracks from time to time.

This seems easy, but getting the tyres to climb the stones was tricky and once running on the top the grip was all but non-existent which made life fun for a few moments before the car settled into the next set of wheel tracks. Sometimes it would get a bit out of line, making life even more interesting, but it was a practice we'd become used to in Namibia and was what driving on these roads was all about. Great fun!

We were trolling along quite happily when in the far distance I could see, on the right hand side of the road, what looked like a large box laying on the road. As we got nearer it looked more and more like a vehicle.

"I think we may have a problem here," I said to Pam, "It's a 4x4 on its side isn't it?"

"Certainly looks like it. How much of the first aid course do you remember?"

I was beginning to slow down now. I could see nobody further ahead, or coming towards us, and there was nobody behind us.

"We're on our own here. If it's bad get the warning triangle out quickly and then the first aid kit. I'll leave the hazard flashers on and then take a look and see what's what."

"OK. It's times like this I wish we had a satellite phone."

I was now getting very close to the object and it still looked like a 4x4 on its side, but as we pulled to a stop it thankfully became apparent that it wasn't a vehicle at all but an old vehicle trailer that looked like it had had a puncture and been left to rot there.

"That had us worried," I said.

"Too right, I wonder how many other people fell for the same trick," replied Pam. We both breathed a sigh of relief and mentally stored away our limited first aid knowledge for another time.

Nearly everyone it seems had the same thought as us as they approached this obstacle, as when we caught up with other Inca Trailers in the evening they had all thought the worst too, and like us were very thankful it was only an abandoned trailer.

We'd come across a couple of vehicles with car trouble along here. In both cases it was punctures and help wasn't needed, and we also passed a couple of classics too. Ian Brawn and Jan Smith were taking it very easy in their 911 and the Jaguar XK140 of Do and Ans Meeus was pulled up and Do was underneath checking the shock absorbers.

About 280 kms into the day's run, the classics peeled off left to head into Gobernador Gregores where it seems they had a splendid welcome from the local mayor and the townsfolk. They headed that way to get fuel, while we stayed on the 'main' road, where they rejoined us about 65 kms later. Along here we had a big moment as there was a series of bumps for which I slowed down, but as I hit the throttle again we hit another unexpectedly and nose dived into the road ahead. Everything was all right but the heart fluttered a little until we settled down again.

Having come across one optical illusion today, the capsized 4x4, I soon thought we'd seen another because in the distance I thought I saw a series of brightly coloured specks, blue, red, yellow on bicycles. This time our eyes weren't deceiving us, because in the middle of nowhere there were half a dozen cyclists, heading south like us, pedalling away for all they were worth and presumably like us heading for Ushuaia. Patagonia is a hell of a place to cycle - there are strong winds, a flat, bleak and mostly featureless landscape and with so many gravel roads punctures must be a major problem.

These guys seemed to be properly equipped for the job, riding mountain-style bikes with all the gear and we slowed as we passed them to check they were all right. We got a thumbs up so left them to their pedalling. And I thought we were mad!

About another 80 kms further on there was another series of bumps in the road, *ripios* they are called locally. We could see from the tyre marks in the road that something had happened and someone had had some sort of big moment, and very soon we came across John Blankley in his now somewhat remodelled A90 Westminster travelling along very slowly.

We pulled alongside and could see that most of the glass was missing and all the body panels were bent and bashed. Their rear wheels were also at an odd angle too. Pam wound down the window and asked if they were all right, to which they replied they were and would be heading slowly on. They said they needed no assistance.

Soon afterwards we came to Tres Lagos, a tiny settlement with a fuel station, and there was a small collection of rally cars spread about the site. A couple were just refuelling, but the Discovery of Rolf and Inis Pritz was backed into the small workshop.

Rolf was not a happy bunny. He'd had a puncture earlier and was getting it fixed, but had found out his second spare didn't actually fit the vehicle. As he said, he'd bought the vehicle specially for the Inca Trail, and the spare didn't fit. He dumped it there and then.

We got fuel and had a sandwich as it was now gone 2.00pm and soon the A90 crept into the station at a very gentle pace. It seems they had been having a bit of a dice with the Alastair Caldwell Ferrari (I know it seems improbable an A90 and a Ferrari racing together, but that's what they said) and failed to see the bumps in the road. The car flipped over, the roll cage saving all of them from injury.

They were happy to sort themselves out so we headed on again, before long seeing our first armadillo crossing the road in front of us and then coming upon Lago Viedma to our right. The wind had been blowing strongly all day and here the waves on the lake were really rough with white horses rolling onto the beach beside the road with a great deal of force.

Just past the lake I noticed that the car was running much noisier than previous; and very soon it became obvious that we had a problem with the exhaust. I pulled over and had a look underneath and could see that there was a hole in the exhaust pipe more or less under the passenger seat. There was little I could do there and being satisfied the joints were all right and the system wasn't about to fall off, decided to head on. We still had about 100 kms to go.

Pam also warned me that we were running out of time as well. Whilst timing for the 4x4s wasn't too important, we'd kept within the recommended time schedule for the whole event so far and I wanted to maintain our 100% record. We hadn't stopped much today and were rather surprised that we were up against it. I suspected the abortive visit to the rock paintings had slipped us back.

Anyway, with a need to think about getting the exhaust fixed and to reach the control before it closed, I put my foot down and had a good crack over the next 60 kms or so till we hit the tarmac again, and then headed on the road into El Calafate.

The approach to this town was much like that into Bariloche, along the southern edge of a huge lake, this one being Lago Argentino. Again like Bariloche, the sky was blue and the sun shining, but the wind made it very chilly and the waves here had white horses riding them too.

The control was sited just off the main thoroughfare and once we had checked in, we retraced our tracks to a petrol station and workshop we'd seen on the way in where several other rally cars were getting attention. The pumps were free, so I got fuel first and then went round the back to see whether I could get the exhaust fixed. The mechanic had a look and suggested I go elsewhere and gave me instructions to another workshop.

Off we went up some side streets and it was obvious where the workshop was, for there were another clutch of rally cars all waiting for attention. As I arrived it was clear what my problem was and I was sent round the back where there was a little welding shop.

Bart Reitbergen was already there with Kermit, waiting outside for his turn whilst a Mercedes was getting some attention. I would need to wait, so decided that I would go and find the hotel, drop Pam and return.

This only took a few minutes as the hotel, the Posada Los Alamos, was easy to find.

Back at the workshop Bart was now inside having the rear exhaust pipe and box replaced. The mechanic seemed to know what he was doing and worked efficiently.

It was a chance to speak to Bart and find out what he thought of the rally, as he is an event organiser himself. Like most others I had spoken to, he felt the rally was too rough for the classics and generally the days had been too long. His view was that the rough stages at the beginning of the event had spoilt any medal chance for many people and inevitably these competitors would start complaining about anything they could.

He wasn't happy with the hotel procedures either. He told me that for his events he subcontracts the hotel arrangements out so that all the paperwork is completed before the competitors arrive, all they have to do is show their identification tag at reception to get a room key, and that's it. So much simpler than the copious form filling we were having to complete each night.

Bart also felt that the running order of cars could be changed from time to time so that competitors weren't running with the same people every day. He felt it made for a better, more convivial event as one got to meet and speak with a wider range of people.

With Bart's Volvo fixed and out of the way it wasn't long before our Colorado was over the pit and the exhaust was being checked. After we took off the protective shields we found a mounting bracket had come away leaving a hole where it was attached to the exhaust. Ten minutes and $10 had it mended and I was on my way back to the hotel, noting that there were still three rally cars in the main workshop round at the front.

Later we had a very enjoyable, if expensive, meal with Linda and Chris and Ted and Judy, hearing more tales of woe of the Reliant Scimitar. Tomorrow would be a rest day with an opportunity to visit the Perito Moreno Glacier.

A wonder of the world

Day 35 Friday 9 November
Perito Moreno Glacier

El Calafate's existence largely relies on the Perito Moreno Glacier about 75 kms to the west. We had been told it was a stunning spectacle and whilst some Inca Trailers had booked a combined coach and boat trip to see the glacier, we had decided to book just the boat trip in the early afternoon and drive ourselves there and back.

We made a leisurely start in the morning and had a wander round the town to see whether it was a good place to get some souvenirs. This is a tourist town and sadly has attracted kitsch little tourist shops with prices to match. We had a look, but held onto our wallets and decided to wait for some other opportunity to get some presents for home.

The glacier is special because of its unique location and geographical features that cause it to move forward at about 2 metres a day, the speed of light for a glacier, thus enabling visitors to see great slabs of ice fall away from the face of the glacier into the water. There are a couple of other glaciers where this also happens, but they are in remote locations and not easily reached by normal tourists. We have seen other glaciers in the Alps, but whilst they are terrific sights, the ice on them melts away rather than falling away as it does here.

The face of the Perito Moreno is about 4 km wide and it is fed by a huge ice field, partly in Chile as well as in Argentina, the size of Israel. The height of the glacier is about 60 – 90 m at the face so the ice chunks that fall away from the front are often the size of the average house and can weigh several hundred tons.

Another special feature of the glacier is the closeness of public viewing platforms on a V-shaped promontory right opposite the glacier face. To the right from here is a wide spur of Lago Argentino, and on the left, further expanses of water known as Brazo Rico and Brazo Sur. The outflow from these two lakes flows into Lago Argentino, but if the glacier has pushed well forward towards the promontory, as it does from time to time, the flow is blocked and the water backs up. Eventually the pressure against the ice is too great and the water breaks through, causing the water and ice to explode in a huge commotion and land all over the place.

And the viewing platforms can be dangerous too. With such huge slabs of ice falling away from the face of the glacier, the risk from small tidal waves and flying chunks of ice is a very real one for anyone daft enough to venture to the waters edge, which, it has to be said, is very tempting. However, a sign near the viewing platform states clearly that 32 people have been killed between 1968 and 1988.

We headed off for the Parque Argentino los Glaciares and before long we were in sight of the glacier and parked up at the landing stage for the boat trip at Bahia Bajo de las Sombras where many other Inca Trailers were waiting too. Soon we were on the cruiser and heading for the glacier, and in no time the boat was surrounded by small icebergs created from ice that had fallen from the face. It was very cold on deck from where the best viewing was to be had, and we were glad to have worn our cold weather gear.

As we approached the glacier, we began to hear the cracks and groans that signal the movement in the ice field. It often sounded like pistol shots, and then sometimes we would notice pieces of ice falling from the face of the glacier, now towering above us, into the water. The boat doesn't get too close to the glacier face for obvious safety reasons. Whilst the face of the glacier is clearly visible, there is also much ice below the water line. The boat cruised up and down across the southern face as we watched the awe inspiring sight of the ice. One would think it would be white, and the bulk of it is, but much is a translucent blue and in the sunlight, quite beautiful. From the boat we saw many pieces of ice break away, mostly quite small, but nevertheless probably weighing many hundreds of kilos and creating quite a splash and wash.

The trip lasted an hour, and we were both in wonderment at what we'd seen so decided to drive up to the viewing platforms to watch the spectacle from dry land. From here we could see above the face of the glacier and the extent of the ice field stretching for perhaps ten kilometres back up into the mountains. The ice was not smooth and worn as expected, but jagged and rough, looking like a mass of soldiers very, very slowly marching forwards.

We concentrated our glacier watching on the other face of the glacier, although we could tell from the noise that there was plenty of ice activity on the other face, the one we had looked at earlier from the boat. But we weren't to be disappointed. In the warmth of the afternoon, there was a steady fall of ice chunks from the face, preceded by pistol shots or groans from deep within the mass.

Some falls were quite modest, some much bigger, but one crash, about 200 m from us, led to a remarkable scene. A small amount of ice seemed to fall from the face, but a few seconds after it hit the green freezing water, perhaps five seconds in all, a gigantic blue finger of ice appeared from under the water, like Excalibur, rising over a period of twenty seconds to the full height of the ice face, about 75 metres, and then falling very slowly over for another thirty seconds to lay gently in the water.

Now, over perhaps an hour, the blue chunk of ice, much bigger than another tourist cruiser we'd seen on this part of the lake earlier, settled in the water finding its own level and gradually moving away from the ice face with a wake of white ice spreading out around it.

This was nature in the raw like we'd never seen before, and we both found the experience truly remarkable, one we will cherish for the rest of our lives.

We were rooted to the spot and stayed watching as long as we dared and well after most people had departed. The spectacle was just so amazing and so continuous that we could not bring ourselves to leave.

But we had to, and reluctantly returned to El Calafate to get ourselves ready for the next few days. In the scheme of things we reckoned the glacier was better than the waterfalls at Foz de Iguacu, but it was a close run thing.

Back at the hotel, while Pam was washing a few things, I had a few jobs to do to the Colorado, so was busying myself outside when an elderly chap walking his dog stopped next to me looking at the car and said to me in perfect English, "Sounds like an amazing trip you're all on."

"It certainly is," I responded, "and we're hardly halfway through yet. We've seen some remarkable sights."

"I would imagine you have."

In the back of my mind I knew I recognised the man, and then I remembered where I'd seen him before.

"Weren't you on the boat trip to the glacier earlier this afternoon?" I asked.

"Yes, I'm the manager, collect the tickets, make sure we keep to time, that sort of thing."

"Well the glacier is the most remarkable thing we've seen so far on the trip, quite amazing."

"Yes, most people are impressed."

His English was excellent with hardly a hint of an accent, and I thought perhaps he'd learned it for the tourists.

"Your English is very good," I said," where did you learn to speak it so well?"

"Oh, my father was English, and came out here to work on the railways, whilst my mother was half-English too. Her mother was Argentinean, and her father an Englishman.

He went on, "My family originates from South Petherton, Somerset. Do you know it?"

"Certainly, it's just off one of the main roads to the West Country. Been through there many times. So, are you Argentinean?"

"Oh yes, just happen to be of English stock."

"Do you get back to the UK at all?"

"No, I've never been." I was surprised he spoke such good English having never been there.

With that we parted, and we finished by shaking hands and exchanging names. He said, "I'm Ronny Lambert." Such an English name. What a day!

Salmon by the lake

Day 36 Saturday 10 November
El Calafate - Torres del Paine - Puerto Natales (434 kms)

It was 6.45am and a fine sunny morning when we left El Calafate to head still further south, mainly on Ruta 40, then over the border to Puerto Natales. Initially we were motoring on asphalt and Pam was very pleased to spot a couple of condors floating on thermals high above us. We soon hit dirt where Ruta 40 turns south west at El Carito and both the rally cars and the 4x4s had sections starting here.

There were still many crews who had taken decisions to avoid further gravel and were taking routes that would enable them to stay on tarmac. Here they would head east towards Rio Gallegos and wait there for us to join them in another four days, or take the route from there to Ushuaia and back, which meant some gravel, but not as much as following the official route involved.

In fact, when we arrived at the control there were three official vehicles present as well as some 4x4s and rally cars. We let the classics go and then followed a couple of 4x4s down the track and out onto the desolate prairie.

The section was called Tapi Aike and was a fairly straightforward 65 kms thrash, the only real hazard being a tendency for the wheel tracks to vanish into gullies. If one chose the wrong pair to follow, one track would suddenly drop into a gully in the middle of the road, and the other petered out. Bill Price and Mike 'Medic' Johnson were marshalling at the end of the section at a tiny collection of what looked like government housing and a fuel station.

Another 50 kms and we were at the Argentinean border with Chile and soon through to the Chilean Custom House in the village of Cerro Castillo. There was a sizeable crowd here, probably because we were still travelling with the classics which always attracted a lot of attention, while crowds usually dissipated once they had passed and the 4x4s came along. We now headed towards the Torres del Paine National Park where we would do a circuit to a lunch stop, retrace our route back to Cerro Castillo, and then head on south once more to our overnight stop in Puerto Natales.

For no particular reason we seemed to be travelling very bunched up today, so we were always in someone else's dust and they were in ours. We tried to hold back a couple of times, but it made little difference as we then became mixed up in another group. So today we lived with it and made gentle progress around the park.

The Torres are impressive granite peaks favoured as a real challenge by climbers, but today they were mostly shrouded in cloud, only making occasional, but nevertheless, dramatic appearances. For the first time we saw vicuna in numbers, the smallest and slightest of the cameloids and closely related to llamas. They seemed to be dainty, delicate creatures and hardly able to thrive in what must be a harsh environment, but they clearly do.

Today we also saw black necked swans and more condors, but failed to see any puma, unlike Brian Keenan and John McCarthy (the Beirut hostages) who saw a pair of puma on this road when they came by on a trip described in their book – *Between Extremes*. Such a sighting is very, very rare, but it would have been nice to see just one.

Our route finished at Lago Pehoe where there is a restaurant on an island approached by a hundred metre walkway across the water. The whole rally descended on the place, but they were ready for us, even at 11.45am when we arrived and we were by no means the first. Beautifully barbecued salmon steaks were ready for us, which we scoffed in the restaurant overlooking the lake and mountains beyond.

As I mentioned, our set route was to retrace our way back to Cerro Castillo, but on the map there seemed to be a way to continue west and south around Lago del Toro. However, enquiries with reception brought voluble remarks about the way being closed, private roads and incomplete anyway. We went back the way we came!

In the Torres del Paine there had been quite a bit of non rally traffic, something we weren't used to, and this increased as we made our way south to Puerto Natales, another 60 kms.

The town lies on Gulfo Almirante Montt and has access to the Pacific via narrow channels and fjords. It reminded me of several Norwegian towns I visited on the Cape to Cape Challenge, windy, spread out, low buildings mostly painted in pastel shades of lemon, orange, light blue.

A sign mounted on a concrete plinth reminded me that there was a Lions Club here, and when we checked into our hotel for the night, the Glaciares, a Lions certificate, was mounted in a frame behind the reception. It seemed that the Local Club President who ran the hotel was away in Puerto Montt but they suggested I visit the Lions Hall, just up the road.

But first the car needed attention. It was only 3.00pm when we checked in, so we found a car wash and had it cleaned and then in the next bay at the garage had the oil changed. We timed our visit right as we were the only car there initially, but Clay Regazzoni joined us for an oil change, and then half a dozen more rally cars and 4x4s were soon lined up.

We also met up here with some of the disenchanted Inca Trailers who had been looking for easier routes to get into the deep south. A regular steam ship service operates from Puerto Montt south to Puerto Natales over a three day passage. Several classics and even some 4x4 crews took this option and had been in Puerto Natales for several days awaiting our arrival. The passage is much akin to the Hurtigruten that ply up and down the Norwegian coast calling in at small towns and villages along the way, and was originally included in the programme for the Inca Trail until John Brown found that road routes could be used.

We then went off to find the Lion Hall. From other information we had, it seems one of the main functions of Lions Clubs in South America is to run the equivalent of village halls that can be used for all manner of activities. The caretaker of this one didn't understand our attempts at Spanish, but soon a local Lion came round who spoke English. The caretaker had invited us to come back in the evening as there was due to be a party in progress and we would be very welcome, however the local Lion told us it was a private party, an 18th party celebration, and whilst we would have been welcome, it might not have been to our taste.

We had a walk round town later and bought some souvenirs, mainly books, and then after freshening up at the hotel joined a crowd in the restaurant for a meal. Several of us ordered fish from the menu but typical of the mañana style of service in South America an hour later we were told there was none and would we order something else. We were in bed before midnight though.

We meet a mamba

Day 37 Sunday 11 November
Puerto Natales - Río Grande (580 kms)

Today we would say goodbye to the Andes, the massive cordillera that had been so much a part of our lives over the last few weeks. We had seen its majesty and splendour and witnessed, at Perito Moreno and at various volcanoes and earthquake sites, the colossal power that such huge mountains can create. We had also driven its wonderful roads and visited the people and villages of the mountains.

Now we were in for a total change. The far south of Chile is flat, bleak and featureless, and although there are mountains on Tierra del Fuego, geologically they are separate to the Andes. Today would be the introduction to our new environment.

We needed to start early today, as we would be travelling south close to the border with Argentina, then east on an Explorer Section, before making for the Straits of Magellan and a ferry to take us to Tierra del Fuego.

I had really been looking forward to today's run because when I first entered the Inca Trail I paid a visit to Stanford's, the leading map supplier in London, and bought some maps of South America to trace the route we would be following. The best map I was able to get, by far, was a good map of this region and it showed all the roads, including the more rural ones likely to be used by the rally. And sure enough today's Inca Trail route maps showed us going on the very roads I had second guessed.

Heading out of Puerto Natales, the low sun caused us driving problems to start with, but the road was mainly concrete and in good condition. We noticed here that they had a very impressive type of pedestrian shelter at all the minor junctions off the road, presumably for those waiting for lifts or the occasional bus. They were much like Dr Who's Tardis, only painted cream, with blue roof, and given the atrocious weather that can occur in these parts are probably very welcome.

Until we reached the ferry we would never be far from the Argentinean border, in fact for most of the time only a couple of kilometres, and the Explorer Section would take the road leading alongside the border where it turns due east on the 52nd Parallel.

HERO had christened this section Mamba Patagonica, Mamba being the acronym for *miles and miles of b***** all*, and it was the perfect description for the route we took. It was a narrow track, more earthy than gravel and just went on and on and on. For 130 kms the landscape was bare grassland and fairly flat and there was nothing, absolutely nothing. We saw no other vehicles, very occasional buildings, there were estancias about a kilometre off towards the border at a couple of places along the way. The only features of any consequence along the road were cattle grids, and there were plenty of these, but no cattle or sheep. We did see a few guanacos and rhea, but that was it. It was Patagonia at its bleakest best - fabulous.

The Section finished at Punta Delgada village, a ramshackle collection of buildings just off the main road leading to the ferry, and within minutes we were at the terminal waiting for the next sailing.

In front of us lay the Straits of Magellan, the place of long-past history lessons at school, of tiny 16th century sailing boats venturing across oceans in search of new continents, of royal commands to go forth and explore.

Ferdinand Magellan, although born Portuguese, was given command of a Spanish fleet and charged by the Monarch to find a westerly route to the East Indies. He discovered the Straits in 1520 and became the first European to sail into the Pacific Ocean, which he named. The fleet sailed on to the east where he was killed in the Philippines a year later, but one of his ships, the Vittoria, returned to Spain, becoming the first to circumnavigate the globe. Now Tierra del Fuego and its southern outcrop of rock, Cape Horn, is still synonymous with round the world sailings.

Today the scene was much the same as Magellan found, except for a collection of coastguard buildings and a café. It was a fine day, but the wind was blowing a gale from the nearby Atlantic and the 10 kms crossing looked like it might be a bit rough. Gradually a collection of Inca Trailers joined the small group of local cars and big articulated lorries to await the next sailing and it wasn't long before we were loaded and away.

The crossing was rough but only lasted about half an hour and although I felt a little ill, I managed it to the other side. We stood on deck most of the time, but somehow missed sightings of penguins and dolphins that some others saw as we sailed along.

Once drawn up against the ramp at Puerto Espora on the shore of Tierra del Fuego, there was a mad dash to be first off the ferry and onto the road, for we knew it would be gravel and the first cars would have a significant advantage driving along without any dust.

We weren't too lucky but made good progress, but while overtaking the Buick Rendezvous of Patrick Brooks/Kevin Clemens we caught a stone on the windscreen that left a sizeable chip on Pam's side. The first fuel station along here was out of fuel, so we took a side road to another one about a kilometre off the route which didn't look like it had been used at all for about 20 years. A dishevelled old man came out of the little office to serve us, and other Inca Trailers who stopped here too. He probably did more business in an hour than he'd done in a year. Pam needed a loo visit, and investigated the one here. There was no door, so we decided we would drive on and find a rural loo.

Tierra del Fuego is divided vertically between Chile and Argentina and soon we were at the border and onto the Argentinean side where the road improved to asphalt.

Tonight we would be staying in Rio Grande, a sizeable town that was heavily involved in the Falklands War, as the islands are only a few hundred kilometres off the coast. The first evidence of this was the rusted aircraft hangars that we saw along the road, and then the widening of the main road to accommodate emergency runways, but once close to Rio Grande itself, there was much more.

On the main approach roundabout to town, a jet fighter had been mounted on a plinth in the middle, and nearby was a statue representing Argentinean soldiery. There were several commemorative sites for their fallen, which were far greater than British losses, and we did begin to wonder what sort of reception a group of mainly British rallyists would get. In fact, no mention was ever made about the Falklands War to anyone we spoke to, and the locals couldn't have been friendlier.

I had been in touch with the local Lions Club here by email, but when we reached the control, no one was there to meet us. However we were told we had had a hotel upgrade and should go to the Hotel Frederico Ibarra. A short run along Rio Grande's wide streets soon led us to the hotel which turned out to be a medium range commercial hotel, not bad, not especially good, but certainly clean and with everything we needed for a night. It was however only lunchtime, and a Sunday.

There seemed little to do, so as the tourist representative at the control had recommended a parilla, we decided to go and have some lunch. The place was much akin to a UK Harvester and was on the upper floor of what appeared to be a sports centre. There were lots of children about being treated by their parents, but although it was noisy we had a reasonable meal. The starter was self service, and the main course was huge chunks of meat brought to the table on a metal tray heated with charcoal pieces from the barbecue.

I had considered trying to get the car checked out, but couldn't find anywhere open. Thankfully it was still running faultlessly, so I checked the oil and tightness of the wheel nuts, refilled the washer bottle and left it at that. Back at the hotel, I also tried again to make contact with the Lions, and whilst the hotel reception were very helpful, they couldn't point me in the right direction.

At the hotel it was once more obvious that concerns were being raised about the quality of the hotels. Rio Grande is hardly the hub of anyone's empire and although quite a large town didn't seem to have much to justify its existence. Apparently its main activities are linked to the local farming community, fishing and supporting the nearby oil rigs in the Atlantic. There are no tourist attractions, so there is no need for any upmarket hotels, and there were none. The rally was dispersed around six modest hotels and a set of apartments.

Most people we spoke to were moaning about their billet. They were either poor quality, poor standard, 'not up to much', or dirty.

One Inca Trailer walked into the reception of our hotel and said, "Bloody awful hotels here. What's this like?"

"A bit basic, but OK," I responded. He looked around, grunted and left.

With time on our hands, and in the hope that the Lions Club might meet at one of the other hotels and have contact details posted somewhere, we decided to do a tour and went round to the Atlantida, Los Yaganes, Isle de Mar and the Posada de los Sauces. This latter place was the only one we went into, but seemed the best of all and matched anything we had stayed in elsewhere on the trip. However, most people we met weren't happy at all, and HERO, once more was being 'slagged off'.

Worst of all, it seemed, was the Rawson Hotel. It was dirty and there were no lampshades. A couple of people posted there had taken a look and refused to stay.

We were content with our hotel, so went back for a doze and later met up with our friends Dave and Carole again to have a pasta meal. The hotels may or may not have been bad, but the restaurant was one of the best, a real find. The pasta was some of the best I've ever tasted and the chef, who was in a wheelchair, was a dead ringer for the Swedish chef on The Muppet Show and wheeled himself around the customers taking the proverbial. Together with the large group of Dutch Inca Trailers who were also there, we planned to return in a couple of days after our visit to Ushuaia.

Fin del Mundo

Day 38 Monday 12 November
Rio Grande - Ushuaia (257 kms)

We slept well in our hotel, but set the alarm early so we could make a prompt start and get onto the Explorer Section and then into Ushuaia before the classic rally cars. They would be doing a Regularity Section on the same stretch of road, so we were likely to catch them if we started behind and weren't supposed to overtake them anyway. We wanted our fun too.

There were only 250 kms to do today, allowing time for sightseeing in Ushuaia, so it was barely dawn when we started the car and headed out to the morning control on the edge of town.

There followed a fairly short run out into the countryside, south on the Ushuaia road before the start of the Explorer Section for the day, on gravel roads serving a number of estancias. We weren't the first cars on the road - as usual Big Jim had gone before everyone, and the 'Hooligans', the three Amazons of the Waterhouses, Mays and Spencers, (all members of the Bentley Drivers Club), were already away.

The Section was to be one of my favourites of the event. A smooth surface with flowing bends but also many crests and falls – it reminded me of several forest sections in Wales, especially Dyfnant a forest that is regularly used for UK special stage rallying.

There was no other traffic either and as the route we needed to follow was obvious, Pam was able to take plenty of in-car video. Nor were there many animals about, although we did see some sheep all of whom had black bottoms – some sort of local design problem I suppose.

Normally I wouldn't expect to catch up with the Hooligans as they were very swift in their cars, but today I was up behind them on several occasions and to avoid dust problems, stopped and let them get away before having another go. It was a great Section.

At the end of the Section there was no marshal, but the three Amazons were waiting for one to arrive. We were all early and as the control wasn't due to open for another ten minutes we decided to wait until at least five minutes after the control was due to open before moving on.

It was a super few minutes. We were surrounded by meadows and behind was a wool shearing shed. On a hill a mile away was an estancia, and while we waited, a gaucho rode out from the stables with about fifteen loose horses and led them to a field adjacent to where we were standing. Here they then ran off in various directions in free abandon. The weather was fine and we chatted away as if we were standing in a pub garden in Sussex; it was however only 9.00am and we were in rural Tierra del Fuego.

The Amazons decided to move on after a while, but Pam and I stayed for a few more minutes. We both wanted to savour the beauty and tranquillity of the place. The horses had now moved down to another field and were crossing a river and enjoying their freedom by cantering here and there at will.

And then a stranger event took place. A Ford Fiesta appeared from along the rally route with a middle-aged lady driving it. We nodded to each other as she drove by, but soon she'd crossed the river and disappeared from view. She was obviously used to seeing a British registered 4x4 covered in advertising decals parked up by the side of the road. Maybe she had more important things on her mind and was on her way to a Women's Institute coffee morning. Who knows?

We left the spot and soon caught up with the Fiesta and passed it before rejoining the main road south. This was tarmac again, but on reaching Tolquin it became gravel once more and the overtaking problems started again.

This was the main road south to Ushuaia and there were many big lorries, most with two trailers, and this demanded special overtaking procedures. Unfortunately the dust was blowing away from the lorries from our right towards the left (east), thus the overtaking zone beside the lorry was obliterated from behind. So by keeping close to the edge of the road, we could often see past the lorries and get some idea of approaching traffic. This also warned the driver that we were on his tail as he could see us in his nearside mirror. The view of their offside mirrors was of course obscured by the dust.

Most drivers were helpful and started to use their indicators to let us know when, and when not, to make the move, because this involved accelerating into the dusty void alongside the lorry and praying nothing was coming the other way. Lights ablaze and horn a-hooting we did this time and time again, each time a few more hairs on my thinning pate going grey. Once alongside the cab of the lorry, there would be an exchange of friendly hoots by way of thanks and we would be on our way.

The other danger from all this overtaking was stones. The tyres from the lorries threw up a great deal of gravel and it was dangerous to get too close to them at the start of the manoeuvre, or whilst overtaking. This kept us well over to the left and, of course, any traffic that might be hidden in the dust cloud and coming the other way. Had the wind been blowing east to west, it would have made life a little easier, but then we would get the dust from lorries coming towards us and the thought that possibly there was an overtaking car heading straight towards us in the dust. The occasional wreck at the side of the road reminded us that things didn't always work out as planned. I cringe at the thought of it now, but it was the only way to make steady progress on these roads.

Soon after overtaking one of these lorries, we came across the Toyota of the film crew on the event, parked up at the side of the road and we were being waved down by one of the crew. We pulled up beside them.

"Have you got a hammer and chisel?" came an urgent request, but not one you expect.

"We have a hammer, but I don't think we have a chisel."

"No worries. We need both." And we were on our way before the lorry we had just overtaken reached us.

It all went wrong here for the German crew of Willie and Barbara Lambertz. When we reached Ushuaia we heard they had rolled their Toyota Amazon on this road, fortunately without injury to themselves, but with significant damage to their car.

At first they planned to give up the rally and have the car shipped back home from Ushuaia, but it became clear that the car was driveable, and the missing glazing could be replaced with perspex. Suitably refurbished, they restarted the event the next day and eventually got safely back to Rio. All part of the driving experience that was the Inca Trail.

After passing alongside Lago Fagnano, the Ushuaia road climbs over the Passo Garibaldi, a real challenge for the lorry drivers, before a drop down to the city which sits on the Beagle Channel. The approach road runs along the back of the city and provides a lovely view towards the channel named after Charles Darwin's ship, and on towards the island of Navarino which is actually part of Chile.

For us, the finish of the day's rallying was on the sea front and it was still only 10.35am. Don and Pat Griffiths were there and as we pulled up Don stood to attention and saluted us. Another goal reached – the southernmost city on earth, or as they called it locally – Fin del Mundo – end of the world.

Being one of the early cars on the road, we had plenty of time to take some video and photos at the finish control where a banner welcoming the Inca Trail Rally to the city was also set up. That done we had the rest of the day to ourselves, so parked up and walked into town and had a coffee.

We found Ushuaia to be a bigger and much busier city than expected. Although it is only as far south of the Equator as Newcastle (UK) is north, it does have a special location and is becoming something of a honey-pot destination.

The town is clearly building on the tourist trade that is growing in the region but unlike us, most tourists rely on air travel to come and go. There is also a growing cruise ship trade although none were in dock over the two days we were there. Cruises arrive from other parts of Chile and Argentina and also head off for Antarctica, the nearest part of which is only about 1,000 kms away. There were tourist shops by the dozen, with tourist prices to match, but we did our bit for the local economy before heading for our hotel.

Most of the rally was booked into two hotels up behind the town, but along with a few other crews, we were at a brand new hotel just out of town to the west and alongside the Channel. Also staying there were all the Red Team and Joanna Brown.

The city has a lovely setting with the Beagle Channel and Chilean Navarino opposite and all around the three other sides of the city were high snow-capped mountains. The air is fresh and the views enchanting.

We had a light lunch in the hotel with Rolf and Ines Pritz. It was the first time we had spent any time with them and we had a good chat. They are both from South Africa, but Rolf originates from Germany and Ines from Italy. They had bought their Disco especially for the trip and were desperately looking for a second spare wheel to replace the one they'd thrown away in disgust at Tres Lagos. Otherwise, unlike some of the other Land Rovers in the event, they were running OK, but had decided some time ago to cut and run, as they found the going a bit tough in the early stages of the event.

In the evening we were planning to eat in the hotel, but decided at the last minute to head into town and try a fish restaurant. Where better to try fish – and we ended up at Tia Elvira on the recommendation of Lonely Planet. Yet again half the rally was there too but we managed to get a window table and eat a lovely meal while watching a container ship being loaded. How romantic. I recommend the King Crab.

Total silence

Day 39 Tuesday 13 November
Ushuaia - Río Grande (311 kms)

Before heading back to Rio Grande we would have a couple of diversions to occupy us today. Whilst Ushuaia is the southernmost city on earth, Ruta 3, the main road that runs all the way south through eastern Argentina, actually ends in the Parque Nacional Tierra del Fuego at Lapataia, and a rally control was set up there. In addition, we would have an Explorer Section along a track to Estancia Harburton, the most historic estancia on the island.

But even before this we were obliged to head back into Ushuaia and to the Glaciers Hotel up a steep hill at the rear of the town so as to visit the morning control. This seemed pointless to me as we then had to reverse our journey all the way back, past our hotel, and back out on the road to Lapataia.

This was a pleasant run on which we also passed El Tren del Fin del Mundo, the world's most southerly railway, a little tourist train that runs on 5 kms of track through local woodland. Although a tourist train now, it was originally built to transport timber, but whatever its use, we were too early for the management and there was no train on hand to see.

We expected to be one of the first at Lapataia and we were, although somehow a party of schoolchildren aged about 6-7 years managed to beat all of us; there were dozens of them with their teachers doing some sort of nature walk.

HERO wanted to make something of this place and had set up a couple of banners and arranged for someone dressed as King Penguin to be present so we could all have our photo taken. This was the southernmost rally control ever, and we would get a certificate to confirm our visit.

King Penguin had a rather ample form and a rumour was going around that it wasn't a local in fancy dress at all, but John Brown. Nobody was able to prove or disprove it!

For me this site marked the completion of an almost unique double, a visit to the southernmost and northernmost roads on Earth. In 1994, I had competed in the Cape to Cape Challenge which, in those days, finished at Nordkapp in northern Norway. Whilst it is probable that there are other more northerly roads in Russia, Nordkapp is generally considered to be the most northerly place it is possible to drive to. When I was there, I bought the tee shirt and I wore it today to mark the occasion.

My double was also matched by Greg Stanley and some of his team who have also taken part in the Cape to Cape Challenge, in fact one of the two Toyotas they were using had been to Nordkapp earlier in 2001; a unique double?

Although this may be the southernmost road on Earth, the Argentineans don't seem to have made much of a feature of it. There was a turning circle for vehicles, a small car park and a couple of signs explaining its significance and that's about it. By comparison, the Norwegians have built an extensive visitor centre at Nordkapp with a restaurant and displays about the history and significance of the place.

We took some photographs of the car parked next to the 3085 kms marker, the distance from Buenos Aires, and after a walk around got ready to head off.

"Which way?" I asked.

"North, there's no alternative. Head for home Vic, and don't spare the horses," was the reply.

We drove back to Ushuaia, stopping on the way at the local motor racing circuit where the rally cars were having a speed test. I was glad to visit this circuit, although we weren't allowed to drive around it, because it is one of the very few worldwide that is licensed for racing yet has a gravel base.

We said our goodbyes to Fin del Mundo and headed out of Ushuaia on Ruta 3 for about 30 kms before starting our Explorer Section down the track to Estancia Harburton. This was a lovely track, for most of the time clinging to the side of a hill, but it had lots of dips and crests, and with two way traffic, (we would return the same way), we needed to be on our guard. A couple of times the road came out alongside the Beagle Channel and on an inlet from the Channel we came to Harburton itself.

This was the first European farm to be established on Tierra del Fuego and is still run by descendants of the original family. We met one of these, Tom Goodall, in the little tea room at the farm and he showed us a display of information about the farm and his ancestors. There were close connections with the Falkland Islands, which aren't too far from here, and British Territory of course, and he had lived there and had relations there. This was also as close as we were likely to get to Cape Horn, the outcrop of rock that identifies the spot where the southern oceans meet, and made famous by so many sailing races. It is about 100 kms due south of the farm.

Nearby was a large hangar-style building that identified itself as the Maritime Mammal Museum, and which, when we first arrived, was locked up.

However while we were in the tea room, a party of tourists from Ushuaia had arrived by catamaran and were being shown round the farm and then the Museum. We tagged on the back of this group and joined them to have a look round. Besides having displays explaining the life cycle, food etc of the various sea mammals in the southern oceans, the library and research rooms were also open to inspection, although nobody was actually working there at the time.

We started the journey back up the track to rejoin the main road, but as it passed the Beagle Channel decided to stop for a few minutes and enjoy the scenery. I parked the Colorado up on the beach and we faced a little bay where the water was mirror-still and inky black. Across the

Channel we could see the mountains on Navarino, as well as Puerto Williams, a village which is even further south than Ushuaia.

We were sitting there enjoying the view when something struck me. The place was so quiet. There was no wind, and once a couple of birds stopped their song, there was no sound whatsoever. It was really quite weird because we are so unused to hearing nothing.

In years gone by, I have had occasion to use a noise meter and I would have loved to have had one now to see what it recorded. At a wild guess, I suggest it might have been as low as 20 dBa, but who knows.

The magic of the moment was broken by one of our 4x4s passing by, but once he was out of range, that same stillness returned. There was absolutely nothing and we enjoyed the special experience for several minutes, our ears feeling quite strange as they expect to hear something and there was nothing there. It was a rare moment – no cars, trains or planes that normally impose their presence on our environment, and we sat there for half an hour soaking up the stillness.

The run back up to Rio Grande was uneventful but we weren't too sure where we would be staying. We went back to the Hotel Frederick Ibarro to see whether they had a room allocated to us, but they didn't, so headed on to the Apart Hotel Keyuk'm where we should have been two nights ago. They had an apartment for us, it was pretty basic and whilst we wouldn't have wanted to stay for long, everything we needed was there and it was clean.

I was still keen to meet the Lions here and asked the owner if he could help, and sure enough he came back to us to say that they would be round at 7.00pm. And at a few minutes after the due time, three guys arrived to meet us, representatives from Rio Grande Lions Club.

Lion President Alberto Luna introduced himself, but as he couldn't speak any English, handed us on to Lion Jorge Zarazaga and Lion Daniel Merlo. We made good conversation for a while and exchanged items from our respective Clubs. We only had a Guildford Lions bannerette and some badges, but they loaded us up with briefcases full of Lions material, their own bannerettes, pens and an ashtray in the shape of Tierra del Fuego.

I noticed that Jorge was wearing an anorak with a Ralliart logo on it. Ralliart are involved with the World Rally Championship and are based at Rugby, Warwickshire in the United Kingdom. They prepare the rally cars for the Mitsubishi team, driven until late 2001 by World Rally Champion Tommi Makinen and Freddy Loix, amongst others. So I wasn't too surprised to hear from him that besides being a Vice President of Rio Grande Lions Club, he was also President of the Rally Clubs of Tierra del Fuego. Jorge had recently met the Mitsubishi Team Manager, Andrew Cowan, when he came to Tierra del Fuego to see a rally and do some fishing.

Rallying, it seems, is the national sport on the island and they run an annual championship with numerous events in the forests and on the roads, some of which we had used. A couple of events were on the mainland, and another took place on the Chilean side of the island. Jorge also told me of one event that comprised just two stages, a 400 kms stage on a Saturday, with another in the opposite direction the following day. It sounded a great event, and in the true spirit of South American rallying that we were now doing ourselves.

We accepted their invitation to go out for a meal, and they took us to a less than reputable-looking establishment, only a few steps from one of the hotels being used by other Inca Trailers, but not an eatery they were likely to try. It was a parilla, and Jorge told us that he and Daniel ate there two or three times a week.

Parilla are common in Argentina and are a variation on a steak bar. We sat at a counter with a central area where El Patron brought us food from a barbecue at regular intervals. There was a standard price to pay and for that we got a choice of starter, help yourself from the fridge, as much meat as you could eat from what was on offer, plenty of salad dishes to go with it, a sweet and plenty of wine and beer.

I had a Parma ham starter and then the meat was served. The cheaper cuts come first and we had chorilla (sausage) carotid gland (served with mayonnaise spread on top of it) before getting to pieces of pork, chicken and beef.

It soon became obvious why they had chosen this restaurant to come to. It was a rally bar. On the walls were lots of rally memorabilia, including many photographs of rally cars.

Jorge was a man of many talents, as he told us he worked for a local radio station hosting a programme every morning and he promised to give us a mention next day and wish us luck in English.

Weird road to gollygosh

Day 40 Wednesday 14 November
Río Grande - Río Gallegos (376 kms)

Breakfast at our digs had been a pleasant surprise. It being an apartment, we were sleeping upstairs, but when we came down in the morning, the dining room table was covered with almost every combination of breakfast foods it is possible to imagine, except cooked foods. We assume the owner/manager had crept in via the back door at some unearthly hour and set it all up. Whatever, it was a pleasant surprise and set us up for the day ahead.

Today we would pay our last visit to Chile, as we headed back to take the ferry over to the mainland and then head north east to re-enter Argentina again. There would then be a short run on to Rio Gallegos, or Gollygosh as we called it. However, once in Chile, and before reaching the ferry, we would have an Explorer Section covering similar ground to a Medal Section for the classic rally cars.

The border crossing passed without incident and we were at the start control for the Section by 9.00am. The road book, as published, had no route instructions for the Section which would be about 75 kms long but instead these were handed out at the start. Off we went, and soon turned off the road the classics were using to take other roads around Estancia China Creek.

On a normal Section such as this, we would get fresh road book instructions every couple of kilometres, but as the instructions for this were prepared late, there were only about a dozen for the whole Section. Thus, whereas potential hazardous parts of the road were usually identified, this time they weren't, and this made things interesting. We came upon cattle grids much faster than intended, and at one T-junction, just over a blind brow, it was more than obvious that others had had 'moments' as they came to a stop and tried to do a left turn. Good fun though.

We had a long wait for the ferry and it was clear from the white horses in the Magellan Straits that we were in for a rough trip. I had no alternative but to go, so took some pills and hoped for the best. For anyone who doesn't suffer from seasickness, the fear and dread one gets prior to a trip such as this is hard to credit. It's very real and where there is no alternative, the thought of the horrendous queasiness that accompanies seasickness, as well as the embarrassment and aftertaste if one is sick - well it's not much fun. Thank God for the Channel Tunnel, I bought a ticket the very first day they went on sale, and haven't used a Channel ferry since.

Our Magellan ferry arrived, discharged its small cargo of cars and lorries, and we loaded till it was completely full. There were still some Inca Trailers behind, but the ferry runs hourly. The crossing was very rough, but this time we saw some penguins and black and white porpoises who swam beside the boat, and I even managed to get to the other side in one piece, although my equilibrium was a bit flaky. I was, however, glad it was over.

The run up to the border post was on one of the weirdest roads I have travelled anywhere in the world. This is the main road in the area, but the cost of fully improving it is probably not justified as it is little used. So rather than a fully-engineered road, the Chilean authorities have built a single strip of concrete and alongside it ensured there is good quality gravel to make it a two-carriageway road. All traffic uses the concrete strip unless, of course, something is coming the other way when you take the right hand carriageway, concrete or gravel, according to which way you are going. Dealing with bends in the road, brows over hills and overtaking are another story I will leave to your imagination. We did about 50 kms on here before reaching the border where formalities were perfunctory.

Rio Gollygosh came soon, but on a gravel road, and we found the time control in a city centre car park where a group of disabled people in wheelchairs were assisting with car park duties. Our hotel was next, the Alonso, and this was a joy.

I am sure some Inca Trailers would have turned their noses up at the sight of it, but it was straight out of another era. It seemed to exist in a time warp. From the photographs on the reception wall, it looked like it had been built in the early 1950s when there were very few cars in Rio Gollygosh. Nothing had changed.

The phone system wouldn't have coped with the Internet, being all of the old, bulky, black variety with twisted cord. The corridors, the faded green paintwork, the furnishings in our room, all evoked a time when men slicked their hair with Brylcreem and wore Oxford bags, whilst the women had hats with large feathers and wore high heels. And off they went to tango the night away.

With time on our hands it gave us a chance to get the car checked over and as I'd seen the sign 'Frenos' (brakes) on a wall nearby on our meanderings around the maze of one way streets, we headed off there. It turned out the owner was a motor racing enthusiast and had a single-seater racer and VW Sirocco racing car in the workshop. I wanted them to check the brakes for me and have the steering looked at once more. The brakes were no problem, but he took us up the road to another Goodyear tyre depot to have the steering looked at. After our previous experience I wasn't too keen on stopping here, but there seemed little alternative and there were several other rally and 4x4 cars there already.

My turn came, and yes there was a problem again. The steering bushes were no good, and despite a trip to the local Toyota garage, no replacements could be obtained. The ones put in at La Calera in Chile were now useless, so there was no alternative but to put back the originals which I still had. Then they did a tracking check and made a minor adjustment and that was about it.

There was bad news though for Roland and Carol Guille. Their Discovery was having major engine troubles and it looked like they would have to get it trailered to Buenos Aires for a replacement to be fitted. However, they had spoken to the insurance company back in London, and it wasn't too clear who was to pay for it.

Hanging around in the garages had left us rather chilly, so we next went to eat, and what was an almost empty restaurant when we went in was soon full of rallyists. Someone else's Christmas again.

Tomorrow would be the longest day.

The loneliest road

Day 41 Thursday 15 November
Río Gallegos - Comodoro Rivadavia (906 kms)

Our journey today would be nearly 600 miles with a long Explorer Section in the middle along the 'Loneliest Road', so we were clearly due to head into the boondocks.

We checked out of the control at 6.00am and were soon on Ruta 3 heading north across vast plains of empty Patagonian landscapes, the sky once more looking like my computer screen at home. The road stretched before us for as far as we could see, and on gentle slopes this must have been 60-80 kms yet there was nothing to see except the traffic, which as usual was light and mainly consisted of lorries and long-distance coaches.

We stopped for fuel near Puerto San Julian and Pam took over the driving for a while across this vast emptiness. True, at intervals, there were entrances to estancias on either side of the road, but we could see few buildings and the only continuous feature along the road was the fence on either side. Like the road, it seemed to stretch forever into the distance, and we wondered what it was for. We saw no animals behind it, no gauchos as we had seen in various places before, and then I remembered the plans that John McCarthy and Brian Keenan hatched when they were held hostage in Beirut.

They dreamt of Patagonia, and knowing that it was a hard territory on which to farm because of its semi-desert character, formulated a fanciful plan to raise yak. They postulated that if yak could survive the hard and similarly difficult environment of the Himalayas, then they would do well in Patagonia. They subsequently visited South America and travelled down through Chile from the Peruvian border covering similar territory to the rally, ending up by horse riding in the Torres del

Paine. Whether they, or anyone else, ever developed the idea of raising yak here any further we don't know, but we didn't see any behind the endless fences. The car was however running fine.

We were now entering the sparsest region of Argentina. A look at the map for the area west of Puerto Deseado, which was many kilometres to our east, shows very little. There is the occasional road, a few estancias, many of which we could see were derelict, and great holes of nothing, even the rivers are shown dotted on the map. We might have been in nowhere land, but as seems to happen here, out of the blue we came across a man spraying the verge of the main road, presumably with weed killer.

One road that does exist, turns off Ruta 3 for about 50 kms leading to the Monumento Nacional Bosques Petrificados and our road book led us this way. The park is famous for its petrified tree trunks, which look like ordinary fallen trees, that have been turned to stone. The araucarias trees originally grew 150 million years ago, long before the Andes and Patagonia, as we know them now, existed. In a period of intensive volcanic activity, the timbers were buried in ash and preserved in their current position.

The preserved trees now lay around a barren, almost Martian landscape, all within a few hundred metres of the car park and small visitor centre. What was once timber is now a hard copper-coloured stone and the largest stones, representing whole trees are perhaps 50 m long. Around the site are broken pieces and it was tempting to pick one up as a momento, but the park wardens are vigilant and keep a close watch on visitors.

The view around the rest of the park is of desert, a barren, stony, sandy-yellow panorama, and in the distance several bluffs reminiscent of Monument Valley in the USA. I had always thought that the puma, one of South Americas big cats, only inhabited the Andes, yet according to the park warden they also live in these remote parts of Argentina, but again we failed to see one.

Other wildlife getting a lot of attention in the car park were a couple of grey foxes, semi-tame and keen to enjoy any food that was thrown to them.

We now started an Explorer Section which took us out of the park by a back way, on roads not normally available for the public to use. The sandy tracks twisted and turned up and down small canyons and around bluffs until we climbed up over a low escarpment, exited the park and joined a very rural track. This was great to drive on, wide and sweeping and clearly little used, but occasionally narrowing to rough sections that we needed to creep over at slow speed.

Another 30 kms and we turned out onto the so-called Loneliest Road, the only road of any significance that crosses the vast emptiness of this part of Argentina. It was clearly little used, as although it had a normal gravel surface and was quite wide, only the central portion was being used, and here there were just two wheel tracks with scruffy grass growing in the middle. It would be called a three-ply road in UK road rallying circles.

Once more this was canyon country, with huge sculptured outcrops, often with rocks of glorious sandy colours. But there was no traffic. No one at all until we came towards the end of the section as we approached the town of Pico Truncado. And alongside the road, any previous attempts to farm or create any industry had clearly failed, as such buildings as we saw were all derelict.

An armadillo scuttled across the road in front of us and stopped on the verge, so I got out to take a close up photograph. He'd moved on into the scrub by the time I got there, but I soon caught up with him and got my photo and also touched him, a rough wiry skin, whereas I'd expected scales.

Driving these roads at a fast pace demands steady concentration and the eye gets used to the colours and nature of the scenery. So as we drove towards the town of Pico Truncado it seemed out of place. The straight gravel road leading to it was no different to any other, but another road ran across ours at ninety degrees and there were a couple of lorries and cars on this, and beyond them a large town of neat houses and other buildings. What brought them here to the middle of nowhere? It all seemed rather odd and somewhat surreal.

Don and Pat were parked up about 100 metres before the cross roads and we pulled up beside them to get our time card signed.

"Did you enjoy that one?" asked Don.

"Yes, a great road, especially coming out of the Park."

"That's some place isn't it," said Don. "To think those trees are over a thousand years old."

A thousand years old, I thought to myself, more like millions of years old. You're having me on Don.

"Surely they are older than that," I responded, "Here, we've got the brochure," and I opened it up," Yes, they're more like 150 million years old."

Don didn't reply, but his face said it all. We'd been had.

"So what's with this place ahead? Why create such a town in the middle of nowhere? I asked.

"It's a spa town," came the reply, "and Pat's only just got back from taking the waters."

Oh yes, I thought. "I think we'll go and find out for ourselves. See you later." And we drove off.

We drove into town, a neatly laid out place with the usual grid patterned streets lined with bungalows and little corner shops, but no indication of why it should be there. The people here had to be doing something with their time. We found a fuel station and topped up, and then everything became clear.

Alongside the road, stretching as far as the eye could see, were hundreds of nodding donkeys. We had reached the southern limits of Argentina's oil fields and for the time being everything we saw was in some way linked to oil extraction. In Caleta Olivia where we rejoined the Ruta 3 once more, there was even a huge statue of an oil worker, about 25 m high, on the middle of a roundabout, very Soviet. In joining Ruta 3 again we were also travelling along the coast and the road was right above the beach, the cold blue Atlantic washing up its waves below us.

Just up the road was Comodoro Rivadavia, our base for the night, and we soon found the Austral Hotel where we would be staying. It looked impressive from the outside, and the entrance hall, reception and bar were too, but once we took the lift to our rooms, we were ejected into a narrow corridor, and the rooms were small with a bathroom which should best be described as compact, very compact!

We hadn't got long to get ready to go out, as the local motor club had prepared a barbecue for us at their motor racing circuit on the outskirts of town and coaches were waiting for us. They laid on an excellent evening, and in a very crowded clubhouse we ate masses of meat washed down with Argentinean wine. They also provided some entertainment and first we had tango demonstrations followed by a very impressive and entertaining local equivalent of a marching band.

We slept well.

More flying

We had sore heads this morning after the excesses of last night, but it had been good fun though. We were back onto Ruta 3 this morning, with a climb out of Comodoro Rivadavia onto the Patagonian plain for a run of about 200 kms, before turning off towards the coast at Camarones. At the junction, we stopped for diesel and watched a big lorry rig arrive, the driver then making an agreement with the fuel station manager to leave behind a trailer, while he took the same road as us with just a single load.

We soon overtook him and dropped down again to the coast where, after taking a few back roads around the small town of Camerones, we arrived at the start of the Cabo Raso Explorer Section. This was set up close to the beach where a sandy road headed north along the coast in the dunes. There was a sizeable crowd, nearly all school children in a very excited state, running round asking us in English what our names were. They were also writing comments in the dust on the side of the car.

Chris and Linda set off in front of us and I was planning to leave a good distance between, but a lorry pulled up beside us and was about to head off down the road himself, so I decided to go, to avoid having to overtake him later.

The road was a treat. With a sandy gravel surface, it dipped and dived with lots of bends, both tight and sweeping, plenty of short climbs and brows – all along the coastline with no other traffic. I decided to really enjoy myself here and very soon we were up behind Chris and Linda, so stopped for a few minutes to let them get away.

Off we went again, really enjoying the drive, the 4x4 getting just about the right amount of grip on the loose surface. About halfway through, Chris and Linda stopped so we had a clear road in front of us, but then, unexpectedly, there were some lights in the dust behind me. Thinking a rally car may be running late, I pulled over to let it through, only to find it was the Pelly-Fry's in their Audi. They should be able to travel a good bit quicker than us, but with them in front and a clear road, the opportunity for a good 'crack' wasn't going to be missed and I drove the Colorado for all it was worth.

All was going great, I was having a super time, and Pam was hanging onto the grab handle – she was used to this sort of thing. We were belting along with the Audi gradually pulling away from us, when I powered the Colorado up a low hill to find at the brow that the road fell away abruptly and all of a sudden we yumped, all four wheels were in the air for about 5 metres, Pam's feet left the floor and her body parted company with the seat, the car landing very gently and keeping going very nicely.

However, I was conscious of the need to curb my enthusiasm, especially as we had at least three or four thousand kilometres to go yet – Rio was still a long way away. We slowed down a bit and finished the rest of the Section at a rather more sedate (for me) pace. But it had been one of the best, a thoroughly enjoyable drive in lovely territory.

There followed a short run to the Punta Tombo Penguin Reserve, and what a treat this would be. The reserve is home to about a million black and white Magellan penguins who nest in scrubland behind the beaches. Our visit to the reserve was nearly a disaster, as having paid our entrance fee, I was driving very gently along the road to the car park, (there were already penguins waddling about), when a huge armadillo sprinted from behind a bush across my path. I jammed on the brakes, praying we hadn't hit him and was pleased to see him scuttling away about his business.

Cars are a secondary consideration to penguins here, for as we drove into the car park we had to drive around groups of penguins waddling about, oblivious to the cars, either heading to the beach and a foraging trip, or coming back home to their nests. These were spread out amongst the low bushes, or in burrows in the soft sandy ground, often as far as a kilometre from the beach, and uphill.

We parked and took a walk round. Penguins were everywhere, and as it was nesting time, many were sitting on two or three eggs. They were wholly unconcerned about the presence of humans, and on looking closer, we could see some eggs already cracked with tiny black feathery penguins smeared with albumen beginning to emerge. Like all the other visitors, we were entranced, and in other nests we soon saw chicks, about 100 cm high, snuggled up under a parent to keep warm and sometimes being fed with regurgitated food from their parent's beak.

The place was noisy, for there was lots of braying and snuffling from the penguins as they went about their daily business. At one place there was a wide path leading down to the beach. Public access was prohibited, but the penguins used it as a 'motorway' to and from their nests. They would waddle along, occasionally stopping to catch their breath or face out another heading straight for them. A low bridge over this path for us humans provided a grandstand view of activities and it was both comical and enchanting.

Nearby, a cliff top viewpoint looked down on a wide beach where hundreds of penguins were either heading into the water for a fishing trip, or arriving back with food for their young. In the sea, penguins are in their element swishing along at speed, sometimes jumping out of the water like porpoises. But on land, as we had seen already, they are comical in their efforts to cope with a strange environment. But the fascinating stage is where they arrive at the shoreline and deal with the transition from swimming to walking. They beached themselves, often rolling their beaks into the sand as they tipped forward on their stomachs, and then hopped up onto their feet and tried to balance so they could then walk up the beach. However, if they beached too soon and then caught an incoming wave, they would often roll forward again on to their fronts and maybe try two or three times to get upright.

Comical and entertaining. Our daughter Jenny is a penguin nut, and she was very envious of our visit.

Two hours and a roll of film later, we dragged ourselves away and headed towards Trelew, our overnight stop for the night. The control was set up next to the Museo Paleontologico Egidio Feruglia, a modern museum where we later attended a reception in our honour hosted by the local town. This region of Patagonia has become very important in recent years as a source of fossils from the dinosaur era and the opportunity to have a look round the museum gave us a great insight into the work being carried out here and the lifecycle of these great beasts and their cousins.

Chris and Jill in their Hyundai Galloper had had a bad day. Their engine problems had become much worse and they had been towed for most of the day by the Hooligans, each taking a turn, but the stones being thrown up by the towing vehicles had all but destroyed the front end of the Galloper. The paintwork was a mess, the lights all blown out and the windscreen cracked. But Chris had got it to a garage and they promised to work for as long as it needed to get it running again. And they did - it was ready to roll again in the morning.

Wales today........

Day 43 Saturday 17 November
Trelew - Gaiman - Puerto Madryn (250 kms)

Today would be a complete contrast to anything that had gone before, more of a treasure hunt than an adventure drive. The Chubut valley, a few miles up the road from Trelew was settled by Welsh immigrants back in the nineteenth century, who built a series of chapels where they could maintain their religious worship. As we would see, they were just like any chapel one might see in the Welsh valleys.

We headed out of town at a fairly leisurely time of 9.00am, keen to keep ahead of the rally cars who would visit the race circuit at Trelew before starting their tour of the chapels.

The first, Capel Moriah, was on the outskirts of Trelew, down a side road, and the custodian was just opening up as we arrived, before heading off to tend the Argentinean equivalent of an allotment. It was a modest, almost frugal building and as we could see from the memorials in the building and in the adjoining graveyard, Welsh names were very common. In Welsh, Trelew means *the town of Lewis* and in the graveyard was the grave of Lewis Jones who gave his name to the town.

When we entered the rally, the plan had been that I would be the main driver, although I had hoped that Pam would be keen to do some driving. So far she hadn't done much, but as today promised to be a gentle day driving around some country lanes, it seemed a good chance for her to get behind the wheel for a while, so from here she took over.

Soon after, we passed what we took to be a dog rescue home. I've mentioned the occasional dog problem we'd had around the route, but as we passed a house set in about an acre of ground, a dozen dogs came running out to greet us and chase us along the fence. There were more dogs in the road, and although we didn't stop, we felt sure it was some sort of rescue centre, the first indication of such a place we'd seen.

Ten kilometres down grey gravelly farm lanes, past green fields, we came upon the second chapel of the day, Capel Nazareth set in a copse of low trees, but sadly locked up and surrounded by long grass so we couldn't get access.

The route was much like a road rally in the United Kingdom, narrow lanes between the fields, lots of junctions and twists and turns, this way and that. It would have been nice to try these lanes at night, but right now it was glorious sunshine with a blue sky.

The next stop was Capel Sion, but this too was closed, as was the next one at Capel Salem, built next to a school constructed from sheets of corrugated iron. This reminded me of a church we used to pass when I visited my grandmother's in the Isle of Man as a child, known locally as the Tin Tab (Tabernacle).

Our route continued with lots of narrow bridges over irrigation channels built to feed water to the green fields, before we headed into the town of Dolovon for a coffee break at Molino Marinero, a working mill that is also a museum. Here we had a pleasant break doing a tour of the mill and also joining a family group in the garden who invited us to have some of their food.

Back on the road again, and out into the valley once more, we stopped briefly at Igleasia Angelicana San David, a proper church with spire and perhaps the prettiest we would see today, with a lovely setting surrounded by poplar and willow trees. Completed in 1917, it replaced a small chapel built by one Hugh Davies, who came to Chubut with the South American Missionary Society in 1883. His chapel blew down in a tornado and this new brick built structure now stood in his memory. It even had a bell tower, and a bell taken originally from Llanllyfni, near Caernafon where it had previously rung for 300 years.

Capel Bethesda was next, before we headed to Capel Bryn Crwyn where we had a little reception committee waiting to meet us. This chapel had a couple of flag poles and a centenary plaque commemorating celebrations only a few years ago. Inside, we met three generations of the Williams family and grandpa Gerallt showed us round. We spent a lot of time looking at a series of photographs they had kindly displayed on the walls of the chapel.

These had been prepared for the centenary of the chapel in 1997 and depicted various activities in the neighbourhood over the last 100 years, especially those linked to the church, such as picnics, outings, fairs and weddings. Gerallt explained each one in detail pointing out to us various relations of his. We were enthralled.

Gerrallt apologised for his English because, as he explained, he had little opportunity to talk in English, but he spoke it pretty well. Day to day, he told us, he spoke Spanish, but also spoke fluent Welsh, as did all the members of his family. The youngest actually get Welsh lessons and the Welsh Office in the United Kingdom sponsor student and teacher exchanges to maintain links with the old country.

Use of the church has dwindled in recent years. Whereas there used to be three services a week, congregations can only be gathered once or twice a month these days, and only number about twenty people.

Williams is, of course, a Welsh name, in fact my mother's maiden name was Williams and she was born in north Wales. It occurred to me that I might be distantly related to these lovely people farming in a remote region of South America. Other Welsh surnames were common here too, Evans, Jones, Lewis etc.

We bade farewell to our new friends and felt we had had a very special visit indeed. Other crews had looked into the chapel, but while we were there we had had Gerallt's complete attention. Chris and Linda had also spent a lot of time with Gerallt's son showing them round.

This was our last chapel and we now headed for Gaiman, a small farming town where we were recommended to visit a tea shop. Like many other Inca Trailers, we headed to the Ty Nain Tea Shop, the outside walls of which were covered in ivy. Inside it was charming, more of a museum than a tea room, with Welsh memorabilia on the walls, cabinets of little knick knacks and tables covered in lacy table cloths linking it all to bygone times. We could have been in Llandrindod Wells. The tea came in proper tea pots with woollen cosies and the cakes were pure Welsh too. Potato cakes, Barabreath. All very nice – but rather expensive.

The next treat on the agenda for the day should have been a visit to the Welsh Museum, set up in the old station building, but when we got there it was closed and apparently wasn't going to be opened for another couple of hours. We headed on, the road book sending us through an old railway tunnel nearby, before we twisted up onto a proper road and headed back to Trelew, but only after I had directed Pam into a brickyard by mistake. We returned to our normal crew positions now as we were due to travel up to Puerto Madryn, our next night stop, about 70 kms away by main road.

The Welsh influence was strong here as well, as the finish control for the day was set up on the main promenade adjacent to a memorial to the first Welsh settlers who arrived here in 1865. Puerto Madryn is a seaside resort town with a lovely sweeping bay and wide promenade with shady gardens. It was still warm and after settling into our hotel, the Bahia Nueva at the north end of the promenade, we took a walk round.

Back at home, before we came out to South America, we had learned that some old friends would also be in the Puerto Madryn area about now. Vivien and Peter Harrison were on a trip organised by the Dolphin Society, focusing on the various sea mammals for which the region is famous, especially on the Valdes Peninsula which we would visit tomorrow. Prior to our trips we had exchanged details, but neither of us knew then where we would be staying, so on our walk around I checked out a few hotels to see whether we could track them down. I had no success.

Later we joined Americans Robert Lowe and his son Ryan as well as Rolf and Inis for a meal. Robert was driving the only proper Land Rover on the event, a Landy Series 11a that was going well, but with a low top speed was struggling a bit on the long main road sections that were now a feature of the rally. We went to a steak restaurant, on a corner in the town dressed out to look like the bow of an old sailing ship, and had an excellent meal. The steak I had was the best of the whole trip and literally melted in my mouth. Sadly I have no record of the name of the restaurant.

.....and whales today

Day 44 Sunday 18 November
Puerto Madryn - Valdés Peninsula (430 kms)

Today there would be no rallying as we were given the day off to visit the Valdes Peninsula to see the large marine life, by whatever method we chose. Many had booked a coach tour, but we had decided to use the car again and had also chosen to stay on the Peninsula overnight and camp out for a second time.

Just up the road from Puerto Madryn, we took a dirt road leading off along the southern edge of the Peninsula where a number of whale watching places had been identified. And sure enough there was a southern right whale, a female with her calf, in the water just below us and so close we felt we could reach out and touch them. They were both making slow headway through the dark blue water, with no sign of any effort on their part, just drifting along effortlessly. It's the sort of moment one wants to last forever, but they had soon drifted away to our right, and we also had a deadline to make as Pam was due to go on a whale watching trip.

We headed on and soon dropped from the main plateau down to Puerto Pyramides where Pam was to take her boat trip. Then as we drove down to the boat terminal, we saw a couple of people waving at us, our friends from the United Kingdom, Peter and Vivien.

"I'm very impressed Vic. We saw some other Inca Trail cars and asked about you and they said you'd be along in about twenty minutes. And here you are."

"How are you both? Good to see you."

I parked the car and we had a few minutes chat. They wanted to know all about the Inca Trail, and we wanted to know about their holiday too. They'd already been on a boat trip that morning, so as Pam went on hers,

I joined them at their hotel just up the road and while they had breakfast I had a cup of coffee.

All of a sudden I was the centre of attention, and I felt for Pam as she was missing the occasion. However I knew that my stomach wouldn't last on a boat trip and she would enjoy that and had taken our cameras to record her sightings.

Peter and Vivien introduced me to their holiday companions and they too wanted to know about the rally. They could hardly miss it as the rally cars were parked all around the port and they now had a rally driver in their midst. They were all from the UK and had a local guide who gave me useful advice on where to watch for whales on the peninsula, and where best to see the orcas (killer whales).

It was a very pleasant diversion from the pressure of the rally. We promised to get in touch with Peter and Vivien once we returned home so we could swap holiday stories.

Pam's trip on the boat was good too, but she felt that they hadn't seen as much as some other boats. A right whale had come alongside and they had some good viewing, but they hadn't seen the classic tail roll she wanted to photograph.

For now we decided to head off east across the Peninsula to Punta Delgado, where a set of steps took us down to the beach and a sighting of perhaps a hundred sleepy elephant seals, huge great animals weighing anything up to 150 kgs.

Next we headed north, up the eastern coast of the peninsula, where the track follows the coast up to Punta Norte passing on the way the very long lagoon that runs parallel to the sea, and another good viewing point at Punta Caleta.

Here we came across Ted and Judy who had parked up alongside the lagoon where we understood that whales sometimes came in to feed and bask. Miguel, Peter and Vivien's guide, had told us the best time was at high tide, and that there was a pod of orcas who regularly came into the lagoon on the prowl for food.

"They are regularly seen in the first few kilometres of the lagoon, but don't go any further north than the radio mast as the water is too shallow for them there," Miguel had said. "You can also see them up at Punta Norte."

But we had missed high tide and there were only a few seals about, so we decided to pop back to Punta Caleta, only about three kilometres, and did some viewing there before having a snack in their restaurant. Here there were more elephant seals.

We were still both very keen to try and catch sight of some orcas, so decided it was worth the trip up to Punta Norte, about 70 kms, and by the time we got there it was nearly 5.00pm and the car park was empty. In a small round building, a converted gun emplacement by the look of it, I found a museum dedicated to the wildlife of the area, most of it written in English, which was helpful.

We walked out to the point and met a young Swiss couple at a small platform with a pair of powerful binoculars mounted on a stand. The binoculars weren't very good as, they had been somewhat vandalised, but with a mixture of the telephoto lens on my camera, and our binoculars we soon saw a pod of about five orcas well in the distance, but their black and white bodies rolling through the waters of the Atlantic unmistakable nevertheless.

Our drive back south was a joy, as the area has abundant wildlife and in the quiet of the evening, there was now little traffic. We saw dozens of Patagonian hares (which look like a cross between a deer and a hare), rheas, including a mother and about six young ones, and gauchos too still working their horses and dogs rounding up sheep.

Our destination was right in the centre of the Valdes Peninsula, Salina Grande, a salt pan well below sea level where camping and a barbecue had been arrange for those who didn't want to return to Puerto Madryn. In the evening light as we arrived, the salt pan stretched out before us and as we drove down the steep road to the farm, its colour changed through all the ranges from white to deep pink. A stunning sight.

About half the Inca Trailers were at the estancia but many of them were in a coach that would take them back to town after the barbecue had finished, leaving a hardcore of perhaps twenty people to camp out. We pitched our tent and readied ourselves for the night whilst the barbecue was started, much the same as at Lagos Posada, lamb and salad with copious quantities of wine.

I noticed a Land Rover Discovery parked up nearby, (it turned out that it belonged to the owner of the estancia), and what attracted me to it were the tyres, brand new All Terrains. Yes you can get them, he told me, they are standard wear on 4x4s around here, and the tyre shops in Puerto Madryn have them. I pondered on whether to get some tomorrow, but my tyres seemed to be doing all right now, and with the worst of the trip over, felt I could complete the route without the need for yet more tyres.

The barbecue was soon in full swing and we had a great evening, especially once the coach came to pick up the bulk of the group to take them back to town. This left a group of about twenty and we sat round the dying embers for a couple of hours putting the world to rights and doing our best to make sure none of the wine was left over.

On this chore we were all aided and abetted by Don, who walked round and round the circle in front of the fire with bottle after bottle of the stuff, and if your glass wasn't empty by the time he had circulated the group and returned to you, there was trouble. It was a terrible job to do, but, hey, someone had to! We did our best and later slept very well indeed!

McDonald's and civilisation again

Day 45 Monday 19 November
Valdes Peninsula - Bahía Blanca (646 kms)

Once again I realised how public getting up is when one is camping. We had slept well and were very comfortable in our little tent and at first light we could hear other crews stirring and getting up, so we followed their lead. Breakfast was laid on for us in one of the buildings nearby and because so few people had actually stayed on to camp, there was more than enough for everyone present.

We were due to tackle a transport section up the Argentinean coast to Bahia Blanca today, all on tarmac except for the run off the Valdes Peninsula, and whilst is was a long way, it promised to be an easy run.

Pam and I were still keen to take advantage of the opportunity for whale watching and mentioned to Don that we planned to remain on the Peninsula and leave late for the run up north. We also spoke of our plans to a few others, some of whom were aiming to go back to Puerto Pyramides and take another whale watching boat trip before starting their journey north.

We packed up and headed back through the interior of the Peninsula to our favoured viewing spot at the lagoon, just below the headland and visitor centre at Caleta Valdes. We arrived about 8.30am and settled down to watch till about midday when we planned to head off.

Parked up about 200 m away was a big, German-registered Bedford 4x4 also clearly intent on watching for whales. We both overlooked the lagoon which is about 20 kms long and between 50 and 100 m across. The end we were watching from had the only opening to the sea, this being about one kilometre to our right, and immediately below the visitor centre. Across the lagoon from our spot was a spit about 20 m high and beyond that the Atlantic Ocean.

We hadn't been parked long when we were joined by Howard and Ann with their Range Rover. They had suffered all manner of problems on the Inca Trail and had been doing their own event for much of the time, chasing us a day or two in arrears after having to stop and get mechanical assistance. It was a lovely spot and we spent the time scanning the horizon with our binoculars, chatting and tinkering with the cars.

But we didn't see any whales! Well that's not wholly true, we did see one or two at a great distance out in the ocean, but even with the rising tide we saw nothing come into the lagoon nor any other action. What we did get was a windswept tan, but that's it.

At midday we decided it was time to go. Howard and Ann had been getting a bit anxious and were keen to leave earlier, but didn't want to leave us behind and later find we'd seen some spectacular display that they had missed. So at noon I confirmed with Howard that we would indeed leave in a few minutes and he drove off.

As promised we followed soon after, only to be stopped by a couple who got out of the Bedford 4x4 that had been parked along the way all morning. They were German, but spoke good English and had also been told the spot was a good one to see whales. Did we know something they didn't? Did we have radio contact with anyone else?

I explained why we had stayed and that we had to leave to get to Bahia Blanca and left them to it. They had also been keen to know all about the Inca Trail, once more being amazed at the distance and range we were covering. We left them with a programme of the event which they were very pleased to get and said they would check progress on the internet.

In my calculations, working out what time we should leave the Peninsula to get to our next overnight stop, I hadn't really factored in the time it would take to get from our morning viewing place to the main road, Ruta 3. It was nearly 200 kms on gravel which made the total distance for the day nearly 900 kms and we had to stop for fuel at Puerto Pyramid. It was almost 2.00pm when we hit the tarmac 16 kms out of Puerto Madryn and we had 650 kms to do.

Just as it was in the days leading up to Puerto Madryn, the road was fairly good two lane tarmac with little traffic, what there was being mainly lorries and long distance coaches. The countryside was mostly flat and sparse with scrubby bushes and little or no wildlife or domesticated animals.

In fact we wondered about the fencing again, as once more it ran alongside the road for hundreds of kilometres, and had done for days, but there was nothing on the other side of the fence. What did the fence keep in?

As the driving was boring, this was just one of life's unanswered questions that we tried to resolve as we drove along. We came across the occasional estancia or a farm worker's house, but no animals. Why have such a long fence? More important still, who had the contract to erect it and repair it? Making a nice few bob probably.

In the village of Sierra Grande, together with some other vehicles, we were flagged down by some ladies standing on the central reservation. They were collecting money for something, which turned out to be a new ambulance – they pointed to the old one, a wreck parked up by the road. As we found a few pesos and handed them over I said jokingly, "Daylight robbery."

"Si, si. Senor," she said with a smile. We drove off.

We soon got bored again. The road was straight and we sped onwards and northwards. We started a new game based on the kilometre posts and what they might represent.

- 1269 - Sir Jimmy Young born
- 1240 - Liverpool train leaves Euston, late of course
- 1642 - Sir Walter Raleigh bought a cloak that he didn't expect to spread out over a puddle for Queen Elizabeth

- 1040 - Over and out
- 1100 - Coffee time
- 1216 - I'm having an early lunch
- 1199 - I could never eat that many 99s
- 1191 - Adds up to twelve
- 1182 - Something's wrong with my watch
- 888 - Three fat ladies

and so on. Well it kept us amused while we motored on.

We also remembered that the day before had been the Argentinean Census Day and wondered whether or not we'd been counted. We were interested in this because we had both worked on the United Kingdom Census earlier in the year.

About 80 kms north of Sierra Grande, not long before we came to the town of San Antonio Oeste, we came upon a small turning to our left which wasn't identified in the road book, but which was a fairly main road leading more or less due west to Bariloche. There was nothing remarkable in this except that it also marked the point where we rejoined some of the route of the original London - Mexico World Cup Rally.

That rally had come south from Buenos Aires to here and then headed out on the road to Bariloche on a *prime*. All the leading cars had cleaned the section, although the winning car, that of Hannu Mikkola/Gunnar Palm, had had to change a wheel and a fan belt on the way.

We pressed on with our boring day, at last leaving Patagonia after about two weeks travel there, mostly very enjoyable. We crossed the Rio Salado at General Conesa and this seemed to signal the change in the geography and very slowly the countryside was becoming lusher and more verdant; we were heading for the Pampas.

It was now becoming more overcast and several times we saw sheet lightning to the north, and gradually dark grey skies as well. After travelling almost due north on the Ruta 251 for many hours we at last reached a junction and headed east towards Rio Colorado and beyond it Bahia Blanca. The clouds were darker grey here, and we had some light rain but nothing too bad – for us the first for several weeks. However someone was getting it much worse than us. Behind us the sun was very bright as it dropped low in the sky and we saw that the many long distance lorries heading that way had elaborate shading arrangements built into their windscreens to shield the drivers from the strong sun.

It was obvious that we had now left the sparse bleakness of Patagonia behind. This was farming country and beef cattle were everywhere to be seen and there were also clumps of trees with lots of growth, hedges as well as some arable farming.

We caught up with Howard and Ann in the Range Rover and also saw the two Camel Trophy Discoveries who had been taking it in turns to tow Roland and Carol in their Discovery. Investigations had revealed they were unlikely to get any repairs done until Bahia Blanca, so the Camels had towed them for the whole 650 kms.

Soon after, we pulled into a petrol station to refuel. It was just getting dark and it was a big petrol station but was all in darkness. We couldn't raise anyone interested in serving us, we think there was a power cut, so we left.

On the outskirts of Bahia Blanca we found another garage that was open and, as usual, topped up so we were ready for the next day. It had stopped raining now, but the sky to the north was still very dark, the remainder a silvery yellow as the sunset battled out the colour scheme with the dark rain clouds.

The city seemed busy and prosperous and we knew we were back in civilisation after our sojourn in the south as they even had a McDonald's!

As usual, the city was laid out on a grid pattern and we went round and round a few times to find our way to the rally car park which was on a piece of derelict land opposite the Hotel Argos where we thought we were staying. The gate to the site was closed but eventually a policemen who had been sitting in his car wandered over. I signalled that

I wanted to get in.

"You have papers?" He asked. Well we did, but these were buried in a bag somewhere.

"Here, see," I pointed to the rally number panel on the side of the car. "We are on the rally too."

"OK you come in."

How come he didn't work out we were part of the rally in the first place I couldn't begin to guess. Maybe he was after some cash.

We parked up and grabbed our overnight bags and wandered off for a wet walk to the hotel, only to find we were staying elsewhere, a taxi ride away. Here at the Hotel Austral we were soon settled in but headed off soon afterwards to find a restaurant to eat at. Another steak meal followed, by chance accompanied by Howard and Ann who'd wandered in soon after us, but it was nothing special.

World racing drivers' champion

Day 46 Tuesday 20 November
Bahía Blanca - Balcarce - Mar del Plata (527 kms)

With the rain that had fallen in the region over the last few days, rumour was circulating that some of the Explorer Sections in the next couple of days might be cancelled. We were now in the Pampas and from what we'd seen yesterday there was a lot of water laying around, and a glance at a couple of farm roads leading away from the main roads made it clear that there was plenty of mud about.

However, when we checked out we were advised to head for the test and get an update there, so we headed out of Bahia Blanca in the company of several other 4x4s, and some rally cars. The going was easy, we were back on Ruta 3 again, until we reached Tres Arroyos. Here the rally crews had already been advised to take a southerly route through Necochea, as the Section, which started just up the road, had already been identified as unsuitable for them.

We went straight on, but had hardly covered another kilometre when we saw Paul Marsh, one of the officials, heading the other way. We stopped and he told us they had had to cancel the Section because the going was too bad. We should retrace our steps and follow the southerly route to get to our next target, the Fangio Foundation near Balcarce. I was disappointed with this, as the road book instructions gave the impression it would be a superb test, with ghost towns to pass through, old railway lines to cross and the like.

We had no choice though. It wasn't just that the road was so muddy, but with the potential for thirty or forty 4x4s going through it would become very churned up and potentially impassable for locals. We heard that the Camels had ventured in together but had turned back quite quickly when it became obvious that a lot of sliding about, towing and

A HIGH IN THE ANDES

potential body damage was on the cards if they continued.

Angus Stamper in his Amazon did drive the whole way through the Section, but not without having to be towed out by a farmer at one stage. When we saw his car in the evening it looked like it had spent a month on the Somme in World War 1.

On our new route at a roundabout near Energia, we were pulled up by a local policeman. He probably had no warning of the event passing this way, as originally only a few of the Category A cars would be on this road; now, all of a sudden, about a hundred were passing through. We explained as best we could and showed him the map, and he was quite understanding and wished us luck when we left him.

At Necochea we passed around the back of the town on a bypass which must rank as one of the worst roads in the world. Over the last few weeks we'd been on all sorts of roads, but this one scored very high on the diabolical scale. It was built of concrete slabs, but these had broken up and been filled with anything handy – sand, asphalt, rubble. The slabs were uneven, often with a step of 50 or 60 cm between each. It was awful.

Before long we reached El Casco, an estancia on the outskirts of Balcarce, the home town of Juan Manuel Fangio. The estancia was bought for Fangio as a gift and to provide him with somewhere to receive the many famous guests who came to the area to see him. It was here that the Fangio Foundation had kindly offered us a lunch and having parked up in a paddock in pouring rain, we were all shown into a hall and served a splendid meal. Meat was a key part of the menu of course.

Nearby is the Autodromo J M Fangio and the classics were due to have a test here, so as we hadn't seen many of these tests, we decided we should have a look. The entrance road was earthy gravel, but in the heavy rain it was more like a fast flowing river with the rainwater washing out deep gulleys in the road, often 30 cm deep. At the circuit which is built on the side of a hill and which would normally have splendid viewing, the rain was even worse. We watched the classics heading off on the test for a few minutes but decided to move on to avoid a soaking.

Next we headed into the town centre of Balcarce where we were due to visit the Fangio Museum. This could quite easily have been a third-rate affair, with dusty exhibits and a modicum of objects on display; we've all been to museums like it. But, no, Argentina clearly has the highest regard for Fangio, quite rightly too, as he is probably their foremost sportsman, and the museum was a treat. Although housed in an older building, the interior has been gutted and the displays are spread out over four floors. They are modern, colourful, informative (although in Spanish only), and there is a cafeteria and cinema. It was all a pleasant surprise.

Fangio was born in Balcarce in 1911 and at an early age showed the talent he had for being a future great racing driver. His first ever race was in Necochea, and soon he was racing the town-to-town races on public roads favoured in South America at the time. His first major win was in 1940 when he was first home in the Gran Premio del Norte, a race over a period of a week from Buenos Aires through Bolivia and Peru to the capital of Venezuela, Caracas. And much of this route was on the same roads we had travelled only weeks before.

Fangio achieved many more wins in similar races all around South America until he came to Europe in the late 1940s and his talent was spotted by the Formula 1 teams of the day. In the 1950s he subsequently became Drivers World Champion no less than five times, and he hadn't started in his new career till his forties. He retired to Argentina in the 1960s, a national hero.

The museum had numerous displays. His cars were foremost amongst these, all well looked after and in good condition. In particular there were several Chevrolets he raced in the 1940s with spindly steering wheels, low backed bucket seats and petrol tanks mounted where the rear seats would normally be. In those days men were men, and the cars had few safety features!

Around the walls were dozens of cabinets with trophies and mementos from his racing days - maps, newspaper cuttings, various honours he received, and he was bestowed with many. There was a marvellous display and I soaked it up. I can just remember seeing him on television racing at the Goodwood Race Circuit in Sussex.

And while we were there, a request was called up from reception for a Mr Vic, me. Outside when we had parked we had been approached by a chap who was a local Lion and who had seen the logos on our car. We had chatted for a while as best we could without a common language, and I had given him the Guildford Lions bannerette and some badges.

Well, he had gone off to get the local club President and they were now in the museum looking for me. We made contact and had our photographs taken in front of a racing car. A more suitable place to meet it was hard to imagine.

All that remained was a fairly short run into Mar del Plata, Argentina's premier beach and holiday resort where we were staying at a Sheraton. However, in the bar not long after I arrived I began to feel ill, and retired to my bed soon after, although I managed some food we ordered through room service later.

I don't recall too much of the rest of the day.

Tango city

Day 47 Wednesday 21 November
Mar del Plata - Buenos Aires (517 kms)

We were now getting withdrawal symptoms with so many 4x4 Explorer Sections being cancelled and the one for today was reported to be impassable too, so no fun driving to do. But there was little we could do about it, so we faced a straightforward run up a motorway to the capital of Argentina, Buenos Aires.

I felt a bit better today and took a good walk before breakfast which helped to clear my head and, I suspect, get the circulation going in various parts of the body that hadn't been getting too much exercise in recent weeks.

On getting out of Mar del Plata, it was obvious there had been serious rain in recent days for vast areas alongside the road were flooded, and the flood plains of rivers were also awash with water.

The traffic was fairly light, but on reaching the suburbs of Buenos Aires we had a bit of a shock to the system as we suddenly joined another motorway and it was bedlam. Over the weeks we had become used to little traffic, especially cars, but all of a sudden we were right in the thick of fast moving city traffic hurtling along the motorway with little or no courtesy.

We soon got used to it again, though, and in no time were negotiating the city centre and arriving at our hotel, another Sheraton. This was a huge hotel and conference centre and all the cars were allocated to an underground car park below the sports centre that served the hotel.

Our room was on the ninth floor and looked out over the main ferry terminal for Uruguay and the River Plata beyond.

In the evening we went out with Dave and Carole again, and not having any particular aim in mind, got a taxi to the St Elmo district and had a walk round. We came upon a couple of tango clubs and debated about trying them, but realised that somehow none of us had brought enough money with us, nor had any credit cards.

Our walk was, however, enjoyable seeing the Portenõs, as natives of Buenos Aires are known. St Elmo was fairly run down but very busy with people going about their daily routines; it struck us it was a bit like Soho in London.

One sight, though, was particularly sad. We came upon a young couple, perhaps late twenties, pushing a supermarket trolley in which a youngster, maybe aged three, was trying to sleep. However she was surrounded by tatty plastics bags being filled from time to time with items her parents were pilfering from rubbish bags they found in the street.

We needed to eat and found a chiviteria, a restaurant specialising in Uruguayan cooking, and we all had a Chivito al plato which was basically chicken and chips but with potato salad and green salad, stuffed into the chicken and a fried egg on top. Highlight of the evening were two elderly male singers who insisted on regaling the diners with songs. They went from table to table in the hope of getting a tip, but they were hopeless singers, nothing they sang was familiar to us. Their tip was small.

Dog walkers delight

Day 48 Thursday 22 November
Rest day, Buenos Aires

As the car was running well and, unlike others, didn't need any serious attention, we booked a coach tour of the city for this morning and were ready in the hotel reception at 9.30am to act as proper tourists for a day. The coach took us all round the main sights of the city and it was easy to see why it is commonly called the Paris of the southern hemisphere.

The weather helps of course, yet again there were bright blue skies, but the city was well laid out with pleasant open spaces and wide avenues with striking buildings. We spent a quarter of an hour in the Plaza de Mayo, the local equivalent of London's Parliament Square, which, when we were back at home, we would soon see on news programmes with riots taking place following the collapse of the Argentinean economy.

The coach drove on to La Boca, a somewhat seedy and run down area, where we were all warned about the dangers of pickpockets and muggers. The coach stopped at a tacky souvenir store, on the basis that those in need could visit their toilets, and we were left to wander around the area on our own. The buildings are built from old ships timbers that have been covered in sheets of corrugated iron and then brightly painted. They looked as dreadful as they sound and I wasn't too impressed.

Being dog owners, we took note of a local custom of Porteños who employ dog walkers to look after their mutts. Some of these people walk as many as twenty dogs at a time, and as they stroll in the parks are surrounded by dog leads and dogs of all shapes and sizes, like tangled and bedraggled maypole decorations. Apparently they don't clear up the animal mess and some of the parks are becoming more and more fouled as a result, especially under the large trees where these people and their charges rest up in the shade.

We left the coach in the middle of town to take a walk and soon found a city centre restaurant for an excellent lunch and then walked back to the hotel. I had a couple of things to check on the car so went down to the basement to fiddle about and couldn't help thinking about big boys and their toys. All the rally cars and 4x4s were parked up in serried ranks all packed up neatly in the toy cupboard for the day.

In the evening, all the Inca Trailers were invited to a reception held in the gardens of the British Embassy in Buenos Aires, courtesy of Bank Leu, a Swiss Bank represented on the classic rally by one of the Mercedes.

This was a chance for the ladies to dress up and for us all to be a bit posh for a few hours. The reception was held in a large marquee in the gardens of the Embassy and we were all served with canapés and champagne. The Ambassador gave a pleasant welcome speech and there was yet another prize giving which went on for far too long and was followed by some dramatic and sensual tango dancing, and then a local band and singer.

We met some interesting people at this function. An English-speaking Pampas farmer told us of his problems with foot and mouth disease, which as best as we could understand, is not uncommon but is dealt with by vaccination. He was very concerned about the local economy but was reconciled with having to live with the situation.

We also met the Ambassador's secretary, a lively Yorkshire lass called Pat. She told us about life in the Diplomatic Service and about postings she'd had, but she was also keen to know about the Inca Trail Rally.

The conversation got round to punctures and how many people had reason to visit gomerias to get punctures repaired and tyres changed. There were gomerias all over the place, every little hamlet had one and we were never far from one along any main road.

"Gomerias can be a little embarrassing for women," Pat offered.

"How do you mean? we asked.

"Well the word 'gomeria' in Spanish is the same as that for the female bust," she explained, "and when a young woman has to go to the garage to get her tyres inflated she has to be careful to ensure she doesn't ask for her bust to be inflated and cause all the men in the workshop to fall about laughing."

"Women will go to almost any lengths to avoid having to get their tyres inflated because of the embarrassment it causes. They either get their men folk to do it, or if there is no alternative, will avoid using the usual words. The trouble is most men in the workshop will know what the lady is trying to avoid saying and it causes just as much mirth."

She also explained a misnomer associated with the River Plata. The famous film of the sinking the Graff Spee during World War II was called the *Battle of the River Plate*, and the word plate seems to have become stuck in English minds as the name for the river. However its name is plata, Spanish for silver, so the river should really be called, in English, the Silver River.

We had a pleasant evening in magnificent surroundings and good company and it was all too soon that we were boarding our coaches again to head back to the hotel.

Tomorrow we would finally say goodbye to Argentina and it was a fitting way to say cheerio to this amazing country. We had been in and out of Argentina over many weeks, first in the north when we crossed the Chaco to Jujuy, then on a three-day excursion from Chile when we stayed in Salta, Catamarca and San Juan before heading west again over the mountains. More recently, we had travelled the whole of the eastern coast of Argentina up to the capital city.

The country seems to have so much to offer. It has huge areas that are very fertile, wine growing regions, cattle rearing areas, and sheep reared in their millions in the less fertile southern districts. There is a growing tourist trade, although this must suffer because of the collapsed infrastructure, for example the railways, yet the country is destitute and faces economic collapse. It seems such a shame – it needs a saviour to bring it back on the rails again.

Rain, rain and still more rain

Day 49 Friday 23 November
Buenos Aires - Colonia del Sacramento - Montevideo - Punta del Este (337 kms)

The plan for today was for all the vehicles to be ferried across the River Plata to Uruguay on a high speed catamaran, after which we would travel eastwards through Montevideo, the capital, and on to Punte del Este where we were due to stay. On the way, both the 4x4s and the classics would have tests, and a visit to a vehicle renovation garage was also on the agenda.

The day dawned wet, and due to my seasickness problems I wasn't looking forward to the river crossing which would take about an hour. We headed for the port, which was only a few minutes away, and there was bedlam. It was clear they weren't ready to receive us and with three rows of cars quickly formed on the dockside it was nigh on impossible to move any vehicle once parked.

Nobody could tell us what we were supposed to do, who would issue our tickets, who would process the vehicle carnets, for we were finally leaving Argentina, and the damp conditions only made matters worse. Finally we were asked to leave the cars and queue for passport control. We waited and waited but they wouldn't process us until we had a ticket and these were being issued in what appeared to be random order with each participant's name on it.

Once through passport control, we were parted from our crew. Drivers returned to their car, whilst crew boarded the ship via the pedestrian gangplank. This caused problems for some as we understood a catamaran had been specially reserved for the Inca Trail, but in the mêlée several local vehicles were loaded which meant that several Inca Trail crews quite literally had to miss the boat. And as the drivers had to remain with their cars prior to loading, and then join the others once on board, several navigators crossed on the ferry, leaving their driver and vehicle behind on the dockside. For these crews it would turn into a very long day, as the next ferry wasn't a high-speed catamaran but a normal steamer which took four hours to cross, and for the crews to be reunited.

Our catamaran finally left, but this was probably an occasion when the presence of John Brown would have been beneficial. With his size and bearing he has a presence that nobody else in HERO can match and I suspect that had he been there, the whole process might have worked better, and we'd all have been on the same ferry.

Matters weren't much better on the other side at Colonia del Sacramento. We unloaded the cars into the main parking area and were then stopped by the police. Again nobody seemed to know what was happening, although there were a few 'suits' wandering about and I started talking to one of these who turned out to be the Minister of Tourism, who hoped we would enjoy our stay. Diplomacy isn't normally my strong point, but I said I was looking forward to seeing more of his country. What I didn't say was, the sooner the better!

Eventually it became clear that we were to move in convoy to the old part of Colonia, the Barrio Historica, about a mile away through some side streets where we would be processed. The Barrio is clearly a very nice part of Colonia, with a ruined castle, lovely Spanish colonial buildings and a green, but not enough room to park up 100 rally cars and process their documents. I am sure John Brown's plan was for us to have a good look round and leave with memories that would encourage us to return and/or sell the place to our family and friends. In essence this is fine, but the weather had by now warmed up considerably and it was very, very humid. The only thing the rallyists wanted to do was get going.

A band appeared together with some scantily dressed drum majorettes (it wasn't all bad!) and they marched up and down, but it took an age for the customs people to get organised, and then of course there was a rugger scrum to be first, and then get on the road and try and get cool again.

We didn't do too badly at this, the three ladies from the local customs using the bonnet of a car as their 'office', but a long queue formed near the rally control so we found a back way out of the Barrio and made our own way to the main road and off to Montevideo.

Uruguay was green and verdant, very much like home, but it was really hot. Our route took us across country to Montevideo where we skirted around the city on the waterfront, passing at one point the remnants of a road racing circuit that uses the sea front roads and side streets and which I had seen on television a couple of days ago. Armco and other paraphernalia were being dismantled as we drove through.

Uruguay is noted for its ancient motor vehicles. This stems from a time when it was nigh on impossible to import vehicles from abroad due to an outrageous taxation system. This left a high volume of existing vehicles, especially American and English cars from the 1940s and 1950s, in need of extended lives. Many are still used as day to day transport and as we drove along we would see Hillman Hunters, Austin 10s, Austin Farinas, Vauxhalls, as well as big American models. Many were rusted hulks, but just as many were in fine condition, although we heard that it is not uncommon to install modern Japanese car engines in them. We also passed several vehicle scrap yards and at many of these, cars were displayed by the road side, and in one there was even a Dakota airplane. For the classic car enthusiast, and of course there were many on the rally, it was heaven, so John Brown had arranged a visit to a specialist vehicle renovator on the outskirts of Montevideo, near Atlantida.

Here the local motor club had set up a big marquee and laid on some food and drink for us to enjoy while we had a look round. The place was a joy. On display were all manner of renovated European and American cars, whilst in the workshop and nearby barns were models awaiting attention. Although they were frowned upon by the true enthusiasts, there were also a couple of replica Mercedes SS Coupes that the owner of the yard builds.

As we had headed east, so the rain had appeared and by the time we left the yard it was throwing it down with thunder and lightning added for good measure. The roads were awash with water although fortunately they were well engineered and had hardly any traffic.

At last we had an Explorer Section to do, the first for about a week, but when we finished it we were somewhat disappointed. It was 65 kms and called the Ruta Panoramica which was a nice wet gravel road for the first 25 kms, but then joined a normal asphalt country road for the final 40 kms. The weather had closed in and besides the rain it was also very misty, so we missed the geographical feature identified in the road book as '*The Cleavage – you'll know it when you see it!*' The roads had been very like the UK, the later section being much like roads I've rallied in Devon, especially on Exmoor. But it was nothing special.

Punta del Este is a smart up-market resort, sited on a small peninsula jutting out into the water where the estuary of the Rive Plata is at its widest as it meets the Atlantic Ocean. Certainly the elegant houses and hotels we passed on the way in confirmed this and the town supposedly attracts the 'beautiful people' and is on a par with places such as St Tropez, Mustique and Davos. Today it had attracted 300 bedraggled rallyists.

In the appalling rain however the going was difficult, even in our 4x4, as the main road was awash with water and the spray from other vehicles was colossal. We were glad to be in a 4x4 and not a classic.

Our hotel turned out to be a huge, modern Las Vegas style resort hotel with a large casino attached – the Conrad. We checked in and I parked the Colorado in the underground car park and as it was still raining I went and had a doze, while Pam went to investigate the hotel shopping arcade, but only after I insisted she leave her credit card behind.

Later we headed for the bar, where low and behold, the most wonderful sunset was laid out before us. The wide hotel entrance doors faced west and the weather had cleared for a while as the sun reached the western horizon and cast a yellowy orange glow across everything. Occasional clouds interfered with the view, but they threw their own colourful shadows across the water and were fringed with rays of orangey light. It all lasted about twenty minutes and it was beautiful.

Once more we joined David and Carole for dinner and as the hotel couldn't raise any taxis to take us into the town, one of the hotel drivers offered to take us to a local sea food restaurant, La Fragata, where we had a good meal.

Disaster strikes

Day 50 Saturday 24 November
Punta del Este - Porto Alegre (774 kms)

Today we had been on the road for fifty days and it seemed a lifetime. Everyone in the rally was in well established routines and this was life as we knew it. Our other lives, back home, seemed aeons ago, and although other people were beginning to talk about getting home, I had made up my mind not to think about that for a couple of days yet, not until we got to the last rest day at Florianopolis. In fact many people had been talking about what they considered to be the home run, Buenos Aires to Rio, for a long time and had started swapping notes about their flights home, how long they were staying in Rio afterwards and the like. This was all too early for me and I dismissed such thoughts to the back of my mind. They'd come soon enough.

After yesterday's rain, the sky was still overcast as we headed north out of Punta del Este and for the first time in what seemed weeks (eight days actually) we would have a proper Explorer Section to tackle, although only 50 kms long. Yesterday's affair didn't count!

It was approached across some nice sandy gravel roads that followed the folds in the gentle rolling landscape rather reminiscent of the Lincolnshire Wolds. The road book made reference to a series of 'Irish bridges' here - they were concrete causeways with drainage tunnels through them and many also had bends in them.

Paul Marsh, a South African who runs his own 4x4 vehicle preparation garage, and Dr Mark Human another South African, were the start marshals and stood in a light drizzle to sign our time cards.

Paul is a delightful character with a soft accent and always concerned about how we should take things carefully on a forthcoming stage.

"Take it carefully," was his passing shot as we drove away from the

A High in the Andes

control following closely on the heels of the Angels, who in turn were following Sir Terence English.

Pam and I had made plans to video the whole of this stage which we reckoned would take about an hour. Following someone else made it easier to find our way, and in any case on most stages it was pretty obvious which way to go.

The Section, called Cerro Cathedral, was great fun. The track was narrower than most we'd been on, only single track, and had steep drop-offs bordered by hedges, beyond which was green farming land. The track followed the roll of the countryside and there were frequent water splashes, mostly not very wet despite all the rain.

We travelled on, the other two cars in front a few hundred metres away, when, as we were going down a hill towards yet another water splash which was hidden behind some bushes on the inside of a bend, we were forced to pull up behind the other two who had stopped in the road. Beside them on a steep bank leading down to the river was one of the course cars, well away from the road, and which looked like it had gone off.

In front of us, Carole had jumped down from her car to go and see whether any help was needed. She went off round the bushes to the water splash only to head back moments later laughing like mad to collect her camera. We got out of our car to see what was going on.

The rally cars were doing this Section as a regularity section where they had to travel at set average speeds with secret checks to monitor their progress. This was a secret check which was why the car was hidden so far off the road, and the marshals were also hidden at the water splash, itself hidden behind some bushes.

The marshals however were all but naked. To add some levity to the occasion Jingers, Dan and Greg had stripped off, hidden their vitals with a HERO direction arrow, a control board, and a clipboard – all they held were a pen and watch. And to add insult Jingers had the letters G and O marked on each buttock which he exposed when it was time for a car to leave the control. They must have been freezing because it was a wet and chilly day, but apparently they stayed the course till the last car was through. Full marks guys.

We took a photo for which they took delight in posing and headed on our way, only for me to go off on a ninety degree turning left! Pam and I were probably still discussing the last control and either I missed her instruction or was thinking about something else, but I had a moment.

The junction was marked in the road book as a 'turn left after crest' and even had two exclamation marks next to it. I missed the lot and drove straight on, off the 'main' track and onto a minor one where I immediately came to a stop.

"****!" I exclaimed.

Pam laughed, looking up from the video, "It's all recorded you know."

"Thanks a bunch."

I reversed back, now seeing that there were other wheel tracks here too, so I wasn't the only one, and we went back down the proper road.

We soon arrived at the finish control for the Section and the three Amazons that made up the Hooligans team were parked up.

"Everything alright?" I asked.

"Carol Flack has gashed her leg badly. She was getting out of the car and slipped in the mud and gashed it on the side rail. Nasty injury, but we've dressed it and she'll be OK."

"Anything we can do?"

"No, one of the medics has seen it and they're just waiting a while for one of the doctors to come through to give it the once over."

We headed on across Uruguay, the local police out in force manning every junction and waving us through. We felt like royalty, but soon we were on the main road north which was very busy with local traffic and long distance lorries. We started getting a bit bored again in the car so started pondering some new ideas for passing the time and came up with revising the currencies for the South American countries we'd visited.

Chile seemed a good one to kick off with.

"With a name like that the obvious standard unit of currency has to be the Ice Cube," I said.

"And it's 1,000 Cubes to the Tray," added Pam.

"And then it has to be another 1,000 Trays to the Fridge," came my second contribution.

"The trouble is this currency soon melts away," quipped Pam.

"Let's try another, how about Uruguay?" I said.

Initially we couldn't think of an easy basic unit to start with and opted for Urs.

"How about 10 Urs to the Argh?" I started us off.

"And then it will be 10 Arghs to the Um," Pam finished with.

We drove on a bit more and I was trying to think of something a bit better for Uruguayan currency.

"The trouble is it's Guay, not Gay," I said, "otherwise we could have ten Gays to a Condom, and ten Condoms to a Mince." We were in hoots of laughter in the car at this but then decided we couldn't use it as it would need to be Guays anyway, and it would cast a nasty slur on Uruguayan manhood.

"How about Argentina, then," said Pam.

"Argies has too many links with the Falklands War. Can't use that."

"Let's try Tinas then. Ten Tinas to the Tango, and then ten Tangos to the Samba."

"Sounds alright to me," I approved.

On we drove. At about midday we came to the final customs post of our trip, the crossing from Uruguay to Brazil. On the Uruguayan side, this was a set of single storey buildings on the right hand side of the road and there was a good crowd of people around to welcome us, all good humoured and keen to know how we were doing.

Inside we soon sorted out the routine, a series of offices for passports, one for the carnet and another to check everything was in order and we passed from one to another quite quickly getting all the right stamps.

Then it was back to the car and a few kilometres up the road to the Brazilian customs.

Here there was a very long queue of cars and lorries leading through the town of Jaguarao, but as we approached the end of the queue, someone signalled to us to go around the outside. So we drove about 500 metres on the wrong side of the road, jumping the queue and then up onto a bridge over the river that formed the actual border.

We'd done many border crossings in the weeks we'd been on the road and for all the Inca Trailers they had mainly been an inconvenient nuisance – fill in a form, get some rubber stamps in the passport and carnet, and then away. But for the bureaucrats this is all of the utmost importance and the data collected no doubt kept someone employed providing statistics that were never read.

But the bridge here between Uruguay and Brazil epitomised the bureaucratic ideal of border crossings. The span across the river had a single carriageway in each direction, with steep kerbs on either side, so there was no turning around or overtaking. In the middle of these was a single track railway line, but it didn't look like it had been used for some time.

The piece de resistance however were the twin towers at either end, where clearly the customs men had at one time carried out their administrative duties with aplomb and due diligence. Now the Uruguayans had moved theirs down the road, but the Brazilians still had their office in one of the towers on their side, and a quarter hour wait was needed to get close enough to take our carnet in and get it stamped. Officialdom was satisfied.

Back on the road again we started thinking about currencies once more.

"There's no obvious connection between Australia and Peru, but how about a basic unit of a Lima, then a hundred Limas to the Ru, and another hundred Rus to the Kanga." Pam thought this was acceptable.

"Now we're in Brazil we have to think of something for here. It has to be the Bra, doesn't it?" I suggested. "And you know far more about them than I do, so I'll leave this to you." Pam chuckled.

"OK then how about two Cups to the Bra," and then she thought for a moment, "and 10 Bras to the Strap …….. and 10 Straps to the MandS."

"And I suppose the notes are available in sizes A, B, C and D." We were in hoots again. Sad isn't it?

"Come on then, one last country to consider, Bolivia?" I said.

"Well the standard currency is the Bol anyway, short for boliviano," Pam commented.

"Right then. Its ten Snowballs to the Bol, another ten Bols to the Advocaat, and….. how about ten Advocaats to the Offy."

We'd had enough of this and were approaching Porto Alegre anyway so decided to concentrate on finding our way into town. It is southern Brazil's major city and a large sea port as well, as it boasts a natural harbour in the estuary of the Rio Guaiba. Our route in lay around this estuary on a fast dual carriageway and soon we were heading along the back of the docks till we reached the finish control for the day, at a sports centre on the site of a former gas works. There was a good crowd here, but mainly they were interested in the classics so we headed off to find the hotel.

The marshals had warned us not to leave the cars on the street overnight as they were at risk of being broken into and that we should use the specially arranged car park around the corner. Getting to the hotel was a nightmare. It was in the city centre, of a somewhat disreputable area of the port and all around us as we approached the right street were ladies of easy virtue standing on street corners. The buildings were drab and run down, and the whole place seemed seedy and squalid. We wondered what the hotel might be like, would we need to rent a room by the hour?

We eventually found the Hotel Sao Rafael which had a tiny loop road in front of the main doors, enough room for about three cars. We stopped and unloaded and I left Pam to check in while I went and parked. This was in a multi-storey car park around the corner where either the hotel or HERO had arranged for all the rally cars to be parked on the first upper level, approached by a steep and long ramp. We had no problem getting up, but I imagine some of the classics might have struggled. It surprised me that not too many cars were there, as the classics had been running ahead of us, and we weren't amongst the first of the 4x4s either.

There is a secret to parking in these places. If there are lots more cars to come, you need to find a spot that no one can park up too close to you so you can't open the doors, or park in front of you and block you in. You need to have room to manoeuvre to get out. Being early I thought I had a good spot, between two concrete pillars that didn't offer enough room for two cars and left plenty of room on either side of mine. To save walking back to the hotel a minibus had been laid on so it was straight to the bar to wind down. We were still there at 8.00pm when we finally decided to go for a meal in the hotel restaurant. However while in the bar we heard some bad news.

Paul Marsh and Mark Human who had been marshalling the start of the Explorer Section had been involved in a serious accident, and at the time, it seemed Paul's injuries were potentially very bad. They had been driving through the stage, gone off and rolled their Mitsi. Thankfully Mark had suffered no injuries at all, but Paul had injured his neck. As one of the event doctors, Mark knew exactly what needed to be done. He was able to help get Paul comfortable, make a preliminary diagnosis and then radioed for assistance. An air ambulance was called and Paul flown to the main hospital in Montevideo and we learned he was being treated in the spinal injuries unit and would have an operation later that night. There were worried faces all around as the news spread around the bar.

Other news doing the rounds was about Roland and Carol. Their Discovery, which had been giving trouble back in southern Argentina, couldn't be repaired in Buenos Aires so was being trailered back to Rio for onward shipment to the UK where a new engine would finally be fitted. Without their car they got a ferry to Uruguay, then buses as far as they could to Punte del Este and finally a taxi to the hotel with as many of their possessions as they could manage. They were now on the look out for lifts to get them back up to Rio and the end of the event.

As for Howard and Ann, they had waited at Colonia after we crossed on the ferry to keep Roy Sutch company while he waited for driver Derek Hunt in his Vauxhall Frontera, who missed the catamaran. They had left Colonia but hadn't been seen since.

We had no more news that night; we ate with Chris and Linda once more, but it took over an hour and a half to get served and we weren't in bed till gone midnight. We both said a quiet prayer for Paul.

World Cup Rally test

Day 51 Sunday 25 November
Porto Alegre - Florianópolis (608 kms)

Stage two of how not to get stuck in a rally car park paid off this morning. Part of our normal daily routine was that I was first up and showered and whilst Pam did so, I went down to the car to check it over or move it closer to the hotel. Today I would do the same. I took a couple of bags down to reception and then the minibus to the car park, although I had been prepared to walk. I was one of the first there and got my car out easily and drove back to the hotel and parked right outside – I thought the risk of a break-in now was fairly remote, and in any case there were some police about. Having parked up I then had the job of telephoning a couple of people to request them to get to the car park and move their cars so others could get out!

The trip out of Porto Alegre only confirmed our thoughts from yesterday about it being a dreary, grimy sort of place. On the main road out of the city we passed mile upon mile of barrios, the squalid, squatter dwellings built out of any scrap wood and corrugated iron – it wasn't very pleasant at all and stank to high heaven.

We turned inland off the main coastal highway and cut across country to one of Brazil's Germanic towns, Gremado. Like Campos de Jordeo - the town we'd stayed in at the beginning of the rally - Gremado looked like it had been transplanted from Bavaria. It had Alpine and Black Forest style buildings, well engineered and signed streets and it had that efficient teutonic feel about it that the rest of Brazil lacked.

We'd been climbing up through hills after we'd left the main road, and the higher we got, the damper and mistier it became. The approach roads to the town were lined with beautiful blue and lemon coloured hydrangeas and then we had the surprise of our lives!

We'd started the rally in the spring heat and humidity of Rio, passed through all manner of climates and weather and it was now nearly the end of November. Christmas was far from our minds and something we had forgotten about, and certainly seen no sign of since leaving the UK.

But here in the wet, misty main street of Gremado were row upon row of artificial, white Christmas trees with silver and blue decorations all along the central reservation. There were overhead decorations too, and at what appeared to be the central square, some much larger trees, all made from white plastic with the same blue and silver decorations. It was bizarre. Really weird after so long without seeing such trappings.

Just up the road we were due to start an Explorer Section, but first there was an opportunity to visit a car museum called Hollywood Dream Cars. In keeping with the area, the building was Alpine in style but with the front end of a 1950s American car mounted on the gable of the front. We parked outside adjacent to the main entrance and could hear Elvis Presley music blaring out from some speakers.

We put on our blue suede shoes and went in.

We knew our friend David was an American car nut, he owns several, and we could see immediately he would be right in his element. The museum had about thirty cars, all from the 1930s, 40s and 50s and in beautiful condition. There were Fords, Plymouths, Cadillacs, Pontiacs, Oldsmobiles and many more as well as the inevitable Harley Davidson motorbikes. All were lovingly prepared and in great condition and we spent ages looking round.

Later we heard that David had indeed enjoyed the visit and near enough bought out the souvenir shop of tee shirts, books and other memorabilia.

There was a chance to visit another museum just down the road where there was a collection of steam engines at Mundo o Vapour (World of Steam). The outside was spectacular, with a full size, bright red railway engine leaning against the front wall at about 45° with steam pouring out of it (probably frozen carbon dioxide). Reports on the content of this museum weren't too good so we gave it a miss.

Back in the car we would now renew our acquaintance with the London - Mexico Rally for the final time up the road at Canela. Back in 1970 the rally cars had left Rio de Janeiro, skirted around Sao Paulo and then headed this way towards Uruguay. Their second *prime* in South America had started at a town called Ituporanga and finished here at Canela. We would now retrace that *prime* in reverse direction, I suspect more or less as it was in 1970. It was called the Rio Grande Prime then, and John Brown had chosen the same name again and it was 185 kms long, whereas the 1970 rally *prime* was 190 kms long and they had 1 hour 40 mins to clean it.

In those days there was a wide selection of cars doing the event. Notable retirements on the *prime* were a Wagoneer Jeep, Prince Michael of Kent in a Maxi, a Peugeot 404, a BMC 1800 and a Vauxhall Victor Estate.

For us the section started on gravel in an area very reminiscent of mid Devon with deep river valleys and steep, tree-covered hillsides. The road was gravel and earth and was fairly rough by the standards we'd become used to. The countryside was green and lush with little farming villages every once in a while, and quite a bit of local traffic. It was a great drive though with lots of narrow bridges that one needed to line up for and approach straight on to avoid getting the wheels caught in the edges and the drop to a stream.

About 60 kms in, we joined a tarmac road for a while, passing through a couple more villages. In one we skirted round a couple of back roads and passed a church - the site was a strange one. A lorry with a load of headstones on the rear was backed up to the entrance of the church. The priest and a couple of dozen people all in their Sunday best were standing around and whilst we didn't stop to find out, we think the stones were being blessed before being taken to the cemetery.

Thirty kilometres further on we reverted to gravel again, the nature of the terrain becoming more like rural Surrey, very like home in Guildford, but the roads were rougher still. In the road book I'd seen an interesting feature – a long concrete ford, and sure enough when we got there we found it was about 100 metres and mostly covered in water. Beside it was a weir with a large body of water behind it. Fords make good video, so Pam filmed from the passenger seat as we went through, then I dropped her on the far side, returning to go through once more so she could film me approaching.

And there would be another interesting feature on the route a little way up the road. Reports of the 1970 Rally always show a long double plank bridge across the River Pelotas, again about 100 metres. The planks have now gone and been replaced by a single track concrete bridge with no guard rails, and a fast flowing river underneath. But even now the bridge is in poor repair and in the middle a collapsed section was bridged by two rows of planks.

The Section finished just short of Sao Joaquim and once we had negotiated some roadworks, we headed out the other side of the village towards Urbico. Christmas was coming here too, for as we left the village I noticed a huge plastic snowman about three metres high on the other side of the road.

A little further, on we came to a hillside restaurant and noticed that several other 4x4s had stopped. It was Sunday and nearly two o'clock so we decided we would look in and see what was on the menu. We found that Snow Hill Restaurant was owned by an elderly American couple who had come to Brazil many years ago as missionaries and settled. They ran the place with their relations, and besides a restaurant it offered accommodation, skiing, (although lack of snow prevented that for the last couple of years), walking etc. We were made very welcome and in all about a dozen of us stopped for some food, the cooked meats being served on a skewer and carved at the table.

The next half an hour was a terrific drive. We came to a newly surfaced and probably newly improved road that led through the hills through a long series of sweeping curves up and down the hills and around some villages and along valleys. The road had a flow to it that meant we always seemed to be in the right gear and had the right approach to corners and we flew along straightening the bends and seeing very little traffic.

The road brought us to Urbico a small country town, the main feature of which seemed to be a huge concrete structure that looked like a church. We were back to streets with awful cobbles and we bounced along these till we came to a petrol station and filled up. Pam popped into the office to pay, so while she did that I drove back to the church to take a closer look. It was ugly, and I mean ugly. It looked like an armadillo with an arched back, was orangey in colour and gigantic. I took a photo and went back to collect Pam.

There now remained a long, cross country drive back to the coast to Florianopolis where we were due to stay for two nights. Pam had been looking forward to getting here as, being a tennis nut, she was keen to visit the home town of Gustav Kuerten, at the time world number one player, and someone she'd seen play at Wimbledon.

Florianopolis is a large city and as we approached it, so the traffic grew in density and volume. Just off the coast is Ilha De Santa Catarina and two bridges take traffic to and from this island, about twice the size of the Isle of Wight. We would be staying at Costa do Santinho Resort, a self-contained complex on the east coast facing the Atlantic, and tomorrow would be the last rest day before the final few days of the rally leading up to the finish in Rio de Janeiro.

We checked in at the resort and settled into our room. It was raining lightly, but we had a walk round and found out the location of the main facilities. The beach was superb, and stretched away to the north for about two kilometres to a headland. Later in the evening, the Florianopolis Tourist Board held a reception for us and as there was free beer and nibbles there was a large turnout, and later we each received a small plaque to commemorate our visit.

The resort restaurant was full of Inca Trailers and we enjoyed a huge buffet with Dave and Carole, as well as Ted and Judy and caught up with their trials and tribulations since we'd last seen them.

Anyone for tennis?

Day 52 Monday 26 November
Rest Day, Florianópolis

We planned that this should be a nice lazy day, but we were woken at about 7.00am by builders working on the building opposite. However, we managed to stay in bed till 10.00am and once we were ready found we had missed breakfast so went and had a coffee. We were joined by Lady Pauline Harris, and then by journalist Genevieve Ord who competed in the Peking-Paris Rally and had flown down from the US with her mother to write some articles about the Inca Trail. She was particularly keen to interview Pauline so we left them to it.

We returned to our room and I sorted out the car for the final run, whilst Pam did some washing and sorted out some clothes. Later she achieved her ambition to play some tennis on the trip, and here in Florianopolis too, and had a couple of sets with Anna Pelly-Fry, Jill Wray and Angela Fenhalls. They played for an hour and a half, which in the heat and humidity was pretty good going, and she won in partnership with Angela.

Pam also had a swim, both in the large pool and the sea, whilst I took a walk over the southern headland where there was some rock art dating from many thousands of years ago, as well as some modern metal sculptures to look at.

We ate in the resort again, but didn't sleep too well. I was suffering from a sore throat and my coughing was not only keeping me awake, but Pam as well.

Sound of Music

Day 53 Tuesday 27 November
Florianópolis - Paranaguá (531 kms)

Today we would have the last lengthy Explorer Section of the rally, but first we had a tour of the southern part of Santa Catarina as the route took us past the pleasant lagoon and then up over the hills and back through Florianopolis onto the continent.

We then headed into the hills and once away from the main roads, passed through small farming villages, once more very reminiscent of Germany or Austria with Bavarian style houses and baroque churches. We passed a couple of school boys on the way, one with dark hair and skin as one might expect from a Brazilian, the other much more fair skinned and blond but almost certainly a Brazilian too.

We arrived at the start of the section at about 10.00am and the classics had been through before us. The roads were damp from the recent rain, and also the humidity that hung in the air like a wet palm tree leaf. The road was reddish sandy gravel and looped through hills and valleys passing still more alpine style buildings, tobacco drying sheds and plantations of bananas.

Early in the section we passed a house built in 1920. It was pure Germanic, with baroque paintings on the walls, now rather faded and cracked and wooden features straight from the Black Forest. Later in the village of Betania we drove by a school and all the children were out waving and cheering at us as we drove by, the majority of them with blond hair, just like the boy we'd seen earlier.

The Section, which was called Sao Pedro de Alcantara, wasn't very long, only 45 kms, but we renamed it Sound of Music, and we almost expected Julie Andrews and the von Trapp family to be at the end to cheer us on.

Just after the finish we headed into the village of Major Gercino and stopped along with a lot of other rally cars for fuel. Here Alexa Scott-Plummer, now navigated by Tony Humphrey, was in trouble. She had gone off on a downhill right bend near the end of the section (we saw the skid marks) and damaged a wing and, more importantly, the radiator. The delay in trying to get a repair done was putting her Gold Medal hopes in jeopardy, but there was little we could do. I had a bottle of Radweld in the back of our car and gave her that.

From here the classics turned east to do a section called Tobacco Road and I was very tempted to tackle it as well. Pam and I discussed whether or not to go, but decided to give it a miss; we'd come this far without major incident and our Gold Medal hopes were still strong, so we headed off on the 4x4 shorter route.

Initially we progressed along good gravel roads between farming towns as we headed back towards the coast again.

Somewhere along here we turned a sharp right hand corner to be faced with a coach being overtaken by a moped coming straight at us. I screeched to a stop: I couldn't go left at all because of the coach, and on our right was a ditch and a field. The coach came to a stop too, almost alongside us, but the look on the face of the moped rider was one of sheer horror. He had already committed to overtaking the coach, and couldn't slow, our car blocked his forward passage and I don't think he had brakes, because he just wasn't slowing down. Initially he came straight for us, and I thought, "Oh my God, he's going to hit us and fly over the bonnet." In the few seconds that all this took, he obviously thought the same, as at the last moment he headed to our right, bounced across the ditch and ended up in the bushes. Miraculously he was still on his bike and uninjured, but I'll bet his heart was pumping like mad.

Although he wasn't dead, or even injured, he got a look from me that might have killed him. The coach driver looked over to me, shrugged his shoulders and showed his palms to me as if to say, "There was nothing I could do." I acknowledged this and we drove on.

We were now heading north on the main north/south road in southern Brazil, Ruta 10, a busy dual carriageway with lots of traffic. Roadside stalls were now selling hands of bananas, and we also came on other stalls selling brightly coloured bath towels. We stopped here and bought a couple, one for each of our daughters with penguins and dolphins on, reflecting their passions.

At Garuva we turned east and as it was much warmer and more humid we were feeling the heat. For the first time in a long time we had the air conditioning on in the car and we stopped as I fancied an ice cream. Next door to the shop was a builders merchants and here I bought a length of chain and a small padlock. When we shipped the car home, I planned to run the chain through all the bags, spare wheels, tool box handles etc and padlock it to the dog guard to lessen the risk of theft.

Just down the road we came to a car ferry at Guaratuba, which was a gentle twenty minute sail across a pleasant estuary and bay, after which we had a short run to our hotel, Mata Atlantica Park. This is approached by a steep driveway with a couple of nice bends and the classics were due to have a timed hill climb run up here. When we arrived they were all queuing at the bottom, so we parked up with the aim of watching the fun for a while, until we could go up ourselves and check into the hotel. Along with all the 4x4s we were due to stay at this hotel and needed to drive up the hill.

However, it soon became clear that some sort of incident had occurred and the classics were being told to turn around and head for Paranagua, a town about another 30 kms along the road, where they were all staying for the night.

The reason for the delay soon became clear. When the test was due to start, marshals were sited at the top and bottom. It would seem there was some misunderstanding between them and a car was sent up the hill at speed only to meet another car coming down. They collided with damage to both and an injury to one of the hotel employees in the car descending the hill.

It didn't help that the rally car involved was that of Clay Regazzoni – one can just imagine the headlines. His Mercedes was seriously damaged on the front wing and the wheel had collapsed, whilst the other car, a Corsa, had similar damage to its offside. They were still parked halfway up the hill where the accident had occurred. What I couldn't work out was why Clay should be on the course as he was well down the running order and when we arrived at the hill, most of the cars were still waiting to go.

We also had an odd incident of our own here. I went to start the car, only for the ignition key to break up into four pieces in my hand. Fortunately we had a spare.

We checked in and heard that a Stewards Inquiry was to be held into the incident as it could have been very serious. The hotel wasn't up to much. It was surrounded by dense undergrowth, almost jungle, and didn't have any air conditioning. Just unloading the car with our overnight bags I was half bitten to death by some nasty little flies and when we went to sit by the pool with a beer it wasn't much better. Some 4x4 crews decided the hotel wasn't for them and checked out and made their own accommodation arrangements. However, Pam now had a taste for tennis and managed another game with some of the other ladies.

Tonight Don and Pat joined us and the Angels for a meal and we had a good chat, but sorting out the bill was a nightmare as the hotel tried to palm off a very expensive, but not very good, wine on us.

The night was hot and steamy, and without air conditioning we slept fitfully.

Motorway horses

Day 54 Wednesday 28 November
Paranaguá - Guarujá (499 kms)

Only two days to go and today we would do our last Explorer Section, a shortie of only 16 kms. But first we had to drive down to Paranaguá and join the other crews who had stayed at a hotel in the town. Many were glad to hear that their hotel hadn't been any better than ours and I think everyone was pleased to get going and leave town. The control was right down by the old port and it was drizzling lightly and if anything it was cold, unlike the humid heat we'd suffered the last few days.

Except by the old port, the town was awash with huge lorries delivering or collecting goods at the main port, and there were dozens of lorry parks with huge rigs waiting for loads. Our route took us down some side turnings and onto the old road out of town and the last Explorer Section.

We shared it with the classics who were doing a Regularity Section along it so there were plenty of marshals, but it was a bit of a nonsense Section, round the back of a poor housing estate, a couple of level crossings and then back onto the main road again. The main challenge was avoiding the locals who were all over the place going to school, work or whatever.

Another hazard was a swimming pool laying in the road! So far as we could judge a blue swimming pool moulding was being moved on the back of a flatbed truck and somehow had bounced off as the truck went over a severe speed hump and landed in the road. We arrived at the hazard and just about squeezed through, the guys trying to get it back on the truck being interrupted every few seconds by yet another rally car coming through. Moral: before moving a swimming pool, check there are no rallies on.

We'd completed all the Sections, all we had to do now was drive back to Rio de Janeiro safely and we were home and safe with a Gold medal. Pam and I gave each other a pair of high fives and a congratulatory kiss and then Peter Rushforth poked his head into the car to sign our time card.

"That's enough of that, you two. Well done."

"Thanks Peter. And thanks for supplying us with a great car. Like you said, the Toyotas are bullet proof," I said as I tapped the dashboard lovingly. "Do you want to buy it back?"

"What. Never raced, rallied or rolled? Not likely." We drove on and left him to his marshalling duties.

Just up the road, HERO had a Passage Control set up in the pretty village of Porto de Cima and there was an opportunity for a coffee stop. The rally was effectively over and all the classics were parked in the village as well as the 4x4s, and an air of euphoria was passing over everyone.

But farce was being acted out on the main road. There was little parking around the village green and cars were parked where they could on the fairly narrow main road, and a single policeman was doing his best to keep control of matters. The Inca Trailers were all diving into a Pousada for a cup of coffee and generally ignoring his requests for us not to stop.

However, today was the day the road was also being retarmaced, and at the far side of the green was a crew working its way towards all the rally cars putting down a new layer of tarmac, behind them were lorries feeding the tarmacing machine with asphalt. Add in other local traffic and some local people who'd come out to watch the rally cars – it was chaos. And even those cars who wanted to leave the scene couldn't, as the tarmacing machine was effectively blocking the road. Added to this the road workers were sweeping the road in advance of tarmacing, and their brushes were going around the rally cars parked half on and half off the road clearing the mud that was dropping off their cars.

It was bedlam, typical South American chaos. Another moral: before tarmacing, check there are no rallies on.

The rest of the day was on main roads but wasn't without incident. After leaving the coffee stop we headed up the Estrada Graciosa, a very steep cobbled road through tropical forestry that was both challenging to drive and beautiful to behold. The flowers and birds were very colourful and the road, which has been retained as a national monument, twisted and turned up through hairpin bends and steep curves.

We soon joined the BR116, the main road north, a fast dual carriageway that we would follow for nearly 240 kms, the bulk of the day's run. However soon after joining the road, we came upon Ted and Judy parked up at a Police Control point so stopped to see whether they needed any assistance. They had been pulled up because an earlier police point had noticed that their brake lights weren't working, so they'd signalled on to the next point who had pulled them over. Ted was on the case and we left him to it.

A bit further down the road, out of the corner of my eye I noticed Big Jim Taylor's Chevrolet going the other way on the dual carriageway in the company of a police car. Something serious had clearly happened for such a strange manoeuvre and potentially it was. As Jim explained later:

"We were heading down the road, minding our own business when we were waved down by a policewoman. We showed our passports and other documents but she wasn't satisfied so sent us over to a police control office. She waved down other cars too and asked them for documents as well." The office soon became crowded and as I thought I'd done what was requested gathered up my papers and left. However, the policewoman wasn't too happy about this, and although I didn't see it, got out her revolver and even cocked it as she pointed it at our car as I was driving away.

"Some way down the road we came to a roadblock and I was singled out to have to return to the first police post to satisfy the demands to see my documents. The tone of the conversation was that I was a criminal for driving off and faced serious trouble. We turned around and drove back the 50 kms to the first post where the woman police officer was really displeased that I had driven off without showing all our documents. After much more discussion, it seemed she wanted our drivers licences, which we hadn't shown previously and once she'd seen these her manner changed. "She still issued a ticket for disobeying a police officer, but when we offered a baseball cap and some Inca Trail bits and pieces the tone became more friendly and we parted friends. I still have the ticket though."

And as Jim said, "I've disobeyed a woman often enough, but this is the first time I've had a ticket for it!"

We headed on up this main road, which was effectively a motorway, towards Sao Paulo, the majority of traffic being big lorries. We were overtaking a group of lorries driving together when we came on a new type of hazard for us – a horse. It was being led across the road by a man holding its reigns, and another pushing it from behind. Like me, they were in the outside lane, but whereas I was doing 130 kms, they were walking across the road in front of me. I hit the brakes as they managed to reach the narrow central reservation, the rear end of the horse sticking out into my side of the road, the head and shoulders on the other. The two guys leading it, jumped for it. I kept going and left them to it, a few more grey hairs suddenly sprouting from my pate.

We skirted southern Sao Paulo and amid quite a bit of heavy industry, the first we'd seen for a very long time, drove out towards the coast again and the pleasant seaside resort of Guarujá. With the finish tomorrow we thought we should have the car washed, so found a garage where a couple of other Inca Trailers had also come up with the same idea, and then headed for the hotel on the promenade.

Everyone was staying in the Casa Grande and the underground car park was available to us to park the cars, there being very little parking in nearby streets. Once more there was chaos underground, and at first I could only park by blocking several others in.

The hotel was however a lovely place, and if I were to rank the hotels in order of preference it would certainly be near the top. There was nothing particularly special about it, just a very pleasant place with air conditioning. Being our last night on the road probably had something to do with it too.

Later we found a nice restaurant a few hundred metres up the road facing the sea and with the usual company of Dave and Carole, Linda and Chris as well as Ted and Judy, had a celebratory meal. We'd all but done the Inca Trail Rally.

Gold and sands beckon

Day 55 Thursday 29 November
Guarujá - Rio de Janeiro (561 kms)

So this was it. Fifty-five days on the road, six countries and 25,000 kms under our belts. Just a few more to get home to the finish and our gold medal in Rio de Janeiro. We felt good, but needed to be cautious as we didn't want to blow it on the last day. And rally organiser John Brown had a nice surprise in store for us today along the route too.

We were up promptly as I wanted to get on the road early and make sure we got to the finish in time to enjoy the moment and not arrive with a crowd of others and be rushed. What we hadn't reckoned on though was the intervention of the President of Brazil.

With the daily information sheet issued at the start, we had a note that the President of Brazil was due to be arriving at Fort Copacabana (the finish) at about 6.00pm and there may be some last minute alterations to arrangements. Some people thought he was coming to welcome us back to Rio de Janeiro, but even John Brown couldn't organise that. What it did mean though was that there would be security restrictions, more police than usual, but how that might affect the rally no one was sure. All the more reason to get there early.

We set off about 6.30am. The weather was better and soon we were driving along in glorious sunshine with blue skies. Initially the road was flat and boring, but soon it became more hilly as we drove along the coast and climbed over headlands, dropping down to beautiful sandy beaches. The road reminded me of some in Devon or Cornwall, only sunnier and warmer, as it twisted and turned between each cove or bay and its small village nestled behind the lovely sand. It was a stunning drive and anyone staying in Rio de Janeiro is recommended to try it.

We had, however, returned to the land of the vicious speed humps, and they were everywhere, especially in the little villages, and as before they hunted in packs with as many as a dozen to get over in a few hundred metres. Another hazard along this road was subsidence, and in many places the road had given way and cracks appeared. This also affected a few bridges too, and a couple of times the suspension bottomed out as we dropped off a concrete bridge onto a tarmac approach road that didn't meet up.

Subsidence had also caused problems with a block of flats we passed. There were actually two blocks beside the road, about seven storeys high and painted blue and white. They looked like holiday flats as they were close to the beach, perhaps too close, as one block was leaning over about 15° from vertical, empty of course and surrounded by scaffolding.

A lunch stop was organised at Paraty, a tropical bay with glassy smooth water surrounded by palm trees. The temperature was well into the thirties and as I parked up it looked like a desert island – I even thought about choosing some discs for Sue Lawley. The town was mainly whitewashed, single-storey cottages with cobbled streets and looked delightful, but in the heat we decided not to look round.

We headed on, seeing our first signpost for Rio de Janeiro and really felt we were nearly there. The road was much like before with lovely coves and bays, but as we got closer to Rio, the bays were more developed, often with yachting marinas, and there were offshore islands too. Soon we were on the outskirts of Rio de Janeiro, before long running alongside Leblon Beach and then Ipanema Beach.

We had decided earlier that we wouldn't go directly up to the Fort, but turned into the Sofitel Rio Palace Hotel opposite where we were all staying and unload the car first. So I pulled up on the forecourt and quickly we emptied everything out, including all the gear we were now carrying for classic crews. The hotel even laid out a red carpet for us, for as we walked into the entrance it was being put in place, not for us of course, but for the President. We walked up it anyway. We checked in, dumped everything in our room, and headed back out to the car once more.

At the entrance to the Fort much closer checks were being paid, presumably due to the impending visit by the President, but we were soon on the parade ground and down to the loop at the end where the finish banner was set up with a small crowd of people around.

And John Brown was there, to be fair not looking very well, but he couldn't resist the chance to be in at the finish of his baby. We pulled up to the finish line.

"Thank you John. We've had a wonderful time, an absolute ball. Can we go round again please."

"Well done Vic, there's nothing to stop you."

And a great surprise too was that Howard and Ann were there, as well as David and Patsie, the New Zealand couple who had crashed out in southern Peru. They'd been home, but now come back to Brazil to enjoy the end of the Inca Trail. It was nice to see them again, especially Patsie who was looking pretty fit and well. We enjoyed the moment and took some photographs.

When we set off, our odometer had read 57,375 kms, now it read 82,848 kms. We'd travelled 25,473 kms in seven weeks through six countries and all manner of road conditions and terrain.

We'd done it. We received our Gold Medal at the prize giving on the Sugar Loaf Mountain the next evening. We'd enjoyed every minute – the driving, the camaraderie, the scenery, the challenge.

We'd had our high in the Andes.

Reflections

The rest of the day was a blur. We parked up the car and spent an hour preparing it for shipping back to the United Kingdom. The chain I had bought a few days ago was looped through everything I could find and then padlocked, and the Brantz, which had been fitted to the car on the way out, was removed for the return journey – some had been stolen on the way out.

In the hotel there was a huge sense of euphoria and achievement with lots of hugging, kissing and hand shakes as we all congratulated each other on safe arrival back. This was much to the amusement of numerous 'suits' who were all over the hotel awaiting the arrival of the Brazilian President and who wanted to know what was going on.

Gradually everyone congregated in the pizza bar next door to the hotel that had been the meeting place before the rally, and was once more benefiting from its return. The place was full in no time and attracted so many street hawkers that a policeman, one of those probably on duty to protect his President, was stationed there to maintain control.

The President duly arrived at the hotel at about 6.30pm and although surrounded by aides and protection officers managed to give us all a wave. There was a small round of applause in return.

Later we went out for a meal with the Angels for the last time. They had won Gold too and as team mates we celebrated in muted but appropriate style, away from the rest of the rally crowd, at another restaurant along the sea front.

On the Friday, most people took their cars to the docks, but having missed out on sightseeing at the start of the Inca Trail, we were determined to use the day to see at least some of the beautiful city. We decided to start off with the huge statue to Christ the Redeemer, known locally as Corcovado and flagged down a taxi outside the hotel.

Initially the driver wanted to drive us to the top of Corcavado, but we insisted on him taking us to the railway station at the bottom where a cog railway begins its journey up the mountain. He didn't want this, but we explained as best we could that the train ride was part of what we wanted to experience. Despite two months in South America, our Spanish was still very limited! Anyway off we went, but Pam noticed he hadn't set the taximeter.

"Hey, you haven't set the meter," I pointed out to the driver.

He tapped it on the top and said, "No work."

"Well how much will the trip cost?"

"Not very much. I do good trip for you."

"No. No. Set the meter or we will get out."

"It's OK," he replied without doing anything with the meter.

"OK," I said, "No meter, we get out. Please stop."

"No. No. We do good trip," came his response.

"No, we want to get out," and as we were only going a few kilometres per hour approaching a set of traffic lights I opened my door as if to get out.

"You stay. No open door, " uttered our driver.

"You set the meter or we get out," my door was still open.

At this our driver saw the light and set the meter, which of course was fully functional, so I closed the car door and we set off in a stony silence.

He dropped us at the railway station for Corcovado and we paid him, but without a tip and he drove off rather angrily.

The trip up the mountain by the railway was very interesting and the views of the city from the statue were stunning. We returned to the bottom again and decided we would try a bus back to our hotel and after several attempts to find the right bus stop, were soon being whisked back towards Copacabana. We got off the bus about a mile from the hotel to do some shopping and later learned that David had been mugged not far away about the same time we were there. He was bitten on the hand in the ruckus, but had nothing stolen.

HERO had organised a formal prize giving in the evening and later we were coached, in proper luxury this time, to the base of the Sugar Loaf Mountain to be whisked by cable car to the top for a view of the city, (fabulous), before descending to the intermediate stage for the dinner in a function suite.

Buick, whose Rendezvous 4x4 hadn't faired very well in the rough conditions of the Inca Trail Rally, sponsored a champagne reception and while there I mentioned to John Brown that the officials needed a special mention and that I hoped one of the participants would say something. You guessed it, I was volunteered on the spot by John, who also asked if I would introduce each of the officials when they too would be receiving a medal marking their involvement in the rally.

The prize giving itself should have been a great evening, it had all the right ingredients, but somehow it failed to reach its potential. The food was good and there was plenty to drink, but there was still a lot of animosity amongst some participants towards HERO and John who was hosting the occasion.

In addition, there were simply too many awards and the whole affair dragged on and on. The classic car crews weren't too interested in the part of the evening devoted towards the 4x4s, and the reverse was true as well and there were problems maintaining interest in what was going on, especially when the main awards, the Gold Medals to the rally crews, were being handed out. John Bateson and Colin Francis in the Escort 2000 took the top award amongst the classics.

Everyone was glad it was over and rather than wait for the floor show that followed, most people ventured outside to get some fresh air or head back to the hotel. We stood and looked at the fabulous view for half an hour, watching the planes come in below us and sweep round to land at the city's smaller airport which is surrounded by the sea. It was windy, but it was a refreshingly warm breeze and it was difficult to drag ourselves away from the ambiance.

The following morning, Saturday, we took the car across town to the docks and checked it in, nearly getting stung again by the taxi driver that brought us back to the hotel. We left Rio de Janeiro later in the day and flew home overnight, and were in Guildford late Sunday afternoon.

The long flight home offered a chance to mull over what we had achieved. The Inca Trail Rally had been a terrific experience and something we wouldn't have missed for the world. For us, it had lived up to all our expectations and although there were various problems along the way, we hadn't been affected by them to any degree. Maybe it was a case of not letting them affect us.

But problems there were and clearly the event hadn't matched the expectations of other people, especially many of the classic rally crews. They had found it to be too rough for their aged vehicles and the trials and tribulations many of them suffered seemed endless. This justified my original decision not to get involved in the classic rally class in the first place and our problems were miniscule by comparison with some rally crews. We had time to sightsee, time to relax and time to enjoy the company of others. I nevertheless have the greatest admiration for many of them and their fortitude in overcoming innumerable problems to get to the finish.

Many small organisations reflect the dynamism, ego and character of the head of that organisation, and HERO is no different, so the lack of their figurehead meant, as someone said, that it was running around like a headless chicken. Being so satisfied with what we encountered over our eight weeks in South America, it is difficult to respond to such comments, but perhaps it is justified.

After the problems with the route, the situation with hotels only compounded any complaints participants may have had with the organisation. It seems that HERO only became aware of the potentially very damaging situation with their agents Hirca in Peru whilst we were all in Rio at the start.

The meeting that Joanna held in Lima with all the crews helped communicate their problems, but many felt that better communications along the way would have helped avoid some of the general air of dissatisfaction, frustration and disenchantment. Once more we don't subscribe to this view as we had no problems with hotels – we got more or less what we expected, a great mixture.

There was also great dissatisfaction about the quality of hotels used and the fairness by which they were allocated. There seem to be no easy answers to this. In Rio Grande for example, where the situation was at its worst, there are only a small number of hotels offering accommodation, and from what we saw they were mostly fairly modest establishments. As an organiser where do you put people up in such a town?

Some rallyists suggested we shouldn't have stopped in Rio Grande at all, but bypass it and head straight for Ushuaia and stay there for two nights. There is some merit in this angle, but then we would have missed out on some super rallying roads on Tierra del Fuego, where rallying is almost a national sport.

With so many people to accommodate and, in some towns at any rate, so few places in which to stay, it is inevitable that people have to suffer varying standards of accommodation. We had our share of top hotels, a goodly few medium range places and a couple of rather dingy dives as well, but we accepted this as part of the experience. All, without exception, were clean and offered what we needed – a bed and en suite facilities. We had the best and most personal welcomes in the bottom end establishments.

Perhaps HERO could have been more open with their allocation policies, if any, but I suspect that for some people it was below their dignity to stay anywhere else other than a five star establishment, even more so when their friends or team mates might be in one, and they were billeted elsewhere.

Many people, especially those in the unofficial touring class, would have been glad if the event had finished in Buenos Aires. They felt it had all been going on for too long and was becoming drawn out. Part of this view may have arisen as there had been no rallying for quite a few days, and to some extent we were suffering withdrawal symptoms there too. On two previous days we had stages cancelled, for two days before that we had transport or sight seeing days, and before that a treasure hunt around Trelew. We wanted some rallying again, but circumstances beyond the control of HERO prohibited it.

Perhaps a start and finish in Buenos Aires might have been more appropriate, but this is with the benefit of hindsight. Rio de Janeiro may have been chosen as the start and finish because of its links with the original London - Mexico Rally, but a base in Buenos Aires could have shortened the rally to six weeks, in most people's opinion long enough, and reduced the overall cost of participating.

Overall I believe HERO had it about right. The driving was a great challenge in marvellous terrain with so many interesting places to see. Plenty of advance notice had been given about the distances to be covered each day, as well as the need for a strong rally car or reliable 4x4. And many people seemed to forget that the 'E' in HERO stands for endurance and their motto is *Per ardua ad infinitum* – which if my schoolboy Latin serves me correctly roughly translates to *keep going for ever*!

Organising an event of this magnitude is a colossal enterprise and in reality very little went wrong. The HERO team are to be congratulated for keeping the show on the road for the whole 55 days and for finding accommodation for us all when things went awry in Peru.

Interestingly, HERO's next big event is the Great Silk Road Rally from London to Sydney, Australia in 2004 which will last a full three months with attended entry and participation costs to match. Originally I was keen to try and find a way to undertake this massive enterprise, perhaps continuing on from Australia to the USA and make it a round the world trip, but with the experience of the Inca Trail Rally under the belt, feel it is just too long. A decent lottery win may change my mind on this though! However, a repeat of the London - Capetown event in 2005 might well appeal.

Now we are home, many people ask whether we would do it again, or go to South America again. The answers to both questions are a qualified yes and no. We have seen most of the main tourist sites in the South American countries we visited, thanks to the Inca Trail Rally. More time at some of them would have been welcomed, but we saw plenty and are well satisfied. We also saw so much else that would never be possible on a routine package tour that we are now spoilt for anything else.

What the trip did prove is that with the right approach, the right vehicle and sufficient funds, one can drive around and visit these places under one's own steam, so to speak. We wouldn't want to do it ourselves, but the comfort factor and organisation provided by doing a trip with a body such as HERO make these trips very appealing, and as already stated, I would love to do one again. Pam admits she found the trip to be very long and might not try another, so I may need a navigator another time!

The other question we are asked is, do we have any regrets? Well, very few. The vehicle we chose was right, the approach to keeping it simple was right and we put some effort into being prepared for what might cause us problems. Greater enthusiasm at learning Spanish would have been beneficial, and a bit more planning for side trips to sites of interest might have been useful. But that's about it.

In closing this book I can only thank John and Joanna, and everyone else at HERO and elsewhere, who helped make the Inca Trail Rally happen, and also thank our sponsors and supporters too.

Pam too needs a thank you, as she was at first reluctant to join me on the trip, but now has no regrets.

We had a brilliant high in the Andes.

Postscript

At a reunion of some Inca Trailers in May 2002 we met up with Paul Marsh again and, thankfully, he was almost fully recovered from his horrific accident in Uruguay. He was in the spinal unit of a Montevideo hospital for some time before being flown home to the UK. He now has long scars down the back of his neck and upper spine and, having had plenty of physiotherapy, is virtually back to normal again.

On a sadder note, Spencer Flack was killed while motor racing in Australia in February 2002. He took part in the Inca Trail Rally with his wife Carol in a Toyota Amazon as one of the Hooligans Team.

On the charity front, we raised about £8,000 for our chosen organisations, split more or less evenly between each of them:

CEDAR Centre for Endocrinology and Diabetes Research

Being set up adjacent to the Royal Surrey County Hospital, the new research facility aims to become an international centre of excellence in this important area of medical research.

CHASE Children's Hospice Service

Construction of a new hospice for life-limited children was recently completed at Peasmarsh near Guildford where there will be residential and day care facilities for sick children. Guildford Lions have already raised £35,000 towards a hobbies room.

Imperial Cancer Research Fund

Probably needs little introduction. Their work is world renowned and they need all our help to fight cancer.

Lions Eye Health Programme

This international charity is administered by Lions Clubs International and supports eye health projects throughout the world, even in the UK sometimes. These include eyecamps where treatment is given in remote villages in the Third World to save or restore sight.

Water for Kids

This small charity supports the provision of water supplies in South American slums, particularly in Lima, Peru where they have several projects underway. A wholesome water supply is essential to ensure good sanitation and hygiene, and is frequently lacking in these very poor areas.

Our thanks to everyone who contributed.

Acknowledgements

There are many people to thank for their support, help and guidance before, during and after the event:

Sue and David Leah, Janet and Ian Garbutt, other friends, relations and the members of Guildford Lions Club for help in various ways.

The Lions Clubs of South America who received us with such generosity.

Mitsubishi Electrics for the loan of camera equipment and their generous donations to our charities.

Chris Bashall at Surrey Off-Road, Pete Malby at MVS Garage in Guildford, David Waghorn at Inchcape Toyota in Guildford for help with car preparation and spares, and also Hella Lighting and Guildford Tyre Services.

1st Merrow Scouts in Guildford for the loan of a tent.

The many companies, organisations and individuals who donated to our charities.

Ted and Judy Howles for permission to include extracts from their diary, and a photgraph of their car off the road

David Angel for permission to use the photograph of the lorry on its side.

Ford Motor Company for the photo of Hannu Mikkola, and to Hannu for agreeing to write a foreword.

To Pam, my wife and Pam Faithfull for editing and proof reading my manuscript.

HERO for permission to use their logos and extracts from the road book and the entry list.

And finally, to all the other participants and officials on the Inca Trail Rally, whether a classic or 4x4 crew, tourers or part of the organising team. Thanks for your companionship, humour and camaraderie. It was brilliant.

Appendices

Trials and tribulations of a classic car entrant
Entry list
Inca Trail 4x4 Adventure Drive - Major Award Winners
Inca Trail Classic Reliability Trial - Major Award Winners
Tools and spares list
First aid and medical supplies

A High in the Andes

Trials and tribulations of a classic car entrant

Reliant Scimitar GT
Ted and Judy Howles

Day 1: Lost a lot of time due to engine running on only five cylinders, running late so last section was in the dark. Only one headlight works so lose more time. Get to hotel to find boot lock jammed and have to borrow jemmy to break into car for luggage.

Day 3: Fuel started to siphon out of breather across garage forecourt, windscreen started to fall into car and we hit a speed bump so hard one of the rear side windows fell out.

Day 4: Problem with gearbox leaking too much oil, overdrive keeps slipping out so had to stop and get local garage to take gearbox apart and fit paper gasket. Arrived at hotel late and in dark again.

Day 5: Car wouldn't start in morning, flat battery as Kenlow thermostat did not cut fan out previous night. Judy went shopping to buy jump leads. After 100 miles overdrive started slipping again. Checked under the car to find oil coming out of gearbox again. Now we stop for both fuel and oil at garages.

Day 9: With temperatures up in the mid 30´s the car runs OK as long as you don't stop. But we have to stop for fuel and the temperature gauge immediately goes up into the red! It went right off the scale a couple of times! I kept topping it up with antifreeze so that it became almost a 100% mix. The gearbox trouble was eventually identified as a blocked breather but we had it in two garages before this was realised, at one time it was pushing out a litre of oil every 200 miles!

Day 14: We were confronted by a local 4x4 on the wrong side of the road on one hairpin and just managed to brake enough to only clip his rear wing, he didn't stop! We are OK. Car is reasonable I suppose. We had to have the lower rear shock mounting brackets welded back on, and the whole of the back suspension raised to stop the rear axle bashing the chassis cross member!

Day 16: After 3 hours of very rough gravel suddenly I have no brakes! Foot to the floor! The car smashed straight into a gully across the road and hit the biggest boulder in the road. The impact lifted the whole car into the air and we landed on the other side with broken rad. Closer inspection revealed that the vibrations had loosened the front brake pad retaining pins, one of the pads had come out, the main calliper was grinding into the disk and of course brake fluid was pouring out of the piston seal. Finally the impact had pushed the gearbox up into the tunnel so that I could not change gear! It took us 3 hours to make temporary repairs.

Day 17: Sump guard is doing its job but it was so mangled that it had to go on a steel press to be straightened! The reverse overdrive switch was damaged so I have pulled the wires up into the car and now we have to remember to disconnect them when we want to reverse.

Day 21: The socket for the speedo cable broke off, no speedo and no mileage. Found mechanic who took the gear drive out of the gearbox and soldered on a new socket for the cable end!

Day 23: The car nearly boiled! 110 degrees for the last 20 miles but we made it.

Day 28: The dust of the various deserts we have crossed has got in the starter motor and in the carb which makes the car run unevenly. It keeps stalling and the starter motor will not engage. I rewired the solenoid to use a spare but it only worked intermittently.

Day 31: This morning car would not start and I had to get a tow from a local to a garage. This was a one man outfit and I was not keen on him at first! But he eventually traced the fault to the ignition switch! He also re-tuned the carb and we are running well again.

Day 33: We had a lucky escape when the car slid off the edge of the road and stopped just short of a steep gully. It took both a local lorry and a 4x4 to pull the car back onto the road. Car and occupants unscathed, but we thought we'd better get new tyres quick! First we went to a gomeria (a tyre fitter) who then took us to the supermarket to buy the tyres - naturally we had insufficient cash so it was across the town square to the bank to acquire some money, then back to the supermarket to buy the tyres, then back to the gomeria to fit them. Of course they don't have tyres quite the right size, but never mind, they have a handy tool to cut away the bodywork!

Day 35: Had some welding done today.

Day 38: The car is being repaired again! The radiator has broken for a second time, coming off its brackets again on the rough gravel roads and we sprang a leak just as we were going well on a regularity. Bought and fitted a new ignition switch. Fault is now diagnosed as a "dead spot on the armature" when it happens (often) we have to rock the car in gear.

Day 43: Will the car make it? It's steadily falling to bits and now has a cracked windscreen courtesy of the gravel roads. It creaks and groans like an old woman but is still going - when it starts that is.

Day 48: Judy still has to push start the car and the suspension is down even lower but we still roll on.

Day 49: Rain! We were one mile from our overnight hotel Punta del Este when the coastal road we were on suddenly turned into a river! Too late to turn off many cars stopped and yes so did we. Paddling time and the water was warm! We ended up getting a tow right up to the steps of the hotel.

Day 53: I slowed down for a speed hump at some road works and one of the rally 4x4s did not! Rammed us up the rear!

Day 54: Brazilian police stop us for faulty brake lights! Our Portuguese was stretched to the limit!

Day 55: We have made it back to Rio!

Entry list

Inca Trail 2001
Entry list

Classic Reliability Trial

			Year	Nat
2	Richard Newman/Robert O'Hara	Chrysler Model 75	1929	USA/USA
3	Ruedi Mueller/Urban Faessler	Chrysler Imperial		
		Le Baron Roadster	1933	CH/CH
4	Paul Markland/Charles Markland	Buick Series 40 Convertible	1936	GB/GB
5	David Brayshaw/William Secrest	Ford Custom Convertible	1949	USA/USA
10	Do Meeus/Mrs Ans Meeus	Jaguar XK140	1955	NL/NL
12	Malcolm McKay/Nicholas Hall	Triumph TR2	1955	GB/GB
15	Chris Denham/Tom Hendy/			
	Ron Bendall	Alvis TC 21/100 DHC	1953	GB/GB
16	John Blanckley/Tony Davies/	Austin A90 Westminster	1955	GB/GB/GB
	Ms Anne Humphreys			
17	Ms Sue Shoosmith/	Austin A90 Westminster	1956	GB/GB
	Ms Alexa Scott Plummer			
21	Alastair Caldwell/Alastair Gibson	Ferrari 330 GT	1965	GB/GB
22	Ralph Jones/Mrs Dorothy Jones	Aston Martin DB4	1960	GB/GB
23	Simon Gaul/Ms Gae Exton	Ford Mustang	1965	GB/GB
24	Paul Kane/Ms Mary Kane	Ford Mustang Shelby GT350	1966	USA/USA
25	Lennox McNeely/Ms Reshelle Leia	Ford Mustang 2+2	1965	CDN/CDN
26	Jan van Geen/Ms Julienne Straatman	Ford Mustang Convertible	1967	NL/NL
30	Rick Dyke-Price/Mrs Diana Dyke-Price	Austin Healey 3000 MkI	1959	GB/GB
31	David Reville/Mrs Carolyn Ward/	Mercedes Benz 280 SL Coupé	1967	GB/GB/GB
	Anthony Ward			
32	Ms Rita Shelley/Mike Knox	MGC Roadster	1969	GB/GB
33	Ted Howles/Ms Judy Howles	Reliant Scimitar GT	1967	GB/GB
36	Paul Merryweather/Ms Sandra Deacon	Mercedes Benz 250 SL	1967	GB/GB
37	John Mathew/ Ms Laura Mathew/	Mercedes Benz 250 SL Sport	1967	GB/GB/GB/GB
	William Neill/Guy Mathew			
38	José Capristano/Inigo Paternina	Porsche 356B	1961	P/E
39	Malcolm Pickering/Derek McConnell	Sunbeam Alpine	1964	GB/GB
42	David Moffatt/MrsYvonne Moffatt	Bentley S2	1961	GB/GB
43	Tom Gatsonides/	Jaguar 420G	1967	NL/NL
	Ms Rosalie Gatsonides-Langenberg			
44	Rob Zwartendijk/Piet Knop/	Jaguar S Type	1968	NL/NL/NL/NL
	Arthur Brouwer/Jan Rosman			
45	William Caruana/Alan Smith	Jensen C-V8	1963	M/GB
46	Allart Constandse/Cees Bruin/	Rover P5B	1965	NL/NL/NL/NL
	Jaap Kroon/Richard de Nerée tot Babberich			

47	Clay Regazzoni/Claude Valion	Mercedes 300 Coupe	1967	CH/F
50	Thomas Noor/Maria Bouvier-Noor	Mercedes Benz 250 SEC	1966	D/F
51	Anton aan de Stegge/	Mercedes Benz 280 SE	1968	NL/NL
	Lammert van Keulen/Mrs Willemien aan de Stegge			
52	Ricardo Fox/Ms Silvia Calderwood	Mercedes Benz 220 SEB	1965	RA/RA
53	Renger Guliker/Ms Gerda Guliker	Mercedes Benz 300 SE	1964	NL/NL
56	Roberto Chiodi/	Lancia Flavia Coupé	1964	I/I
	Mrs Maria Rita Degli Esposti			
57	Bernard Legrand/Patrick Lance/	Mercedes Benz 190 C	1965	CH/USA
	Philip Perez/Jean-Phillipe Salzmann/Eric Bouvier			
58	Bart Rietbergen/Mrs Jolijn Rietbergen	Volvo PV544 Sport	1962	NL/NL
59	Paul Wignall/Mrs Jayne Wignall	Volvo PV544 Sport	1959	GB/GB
61	Leo Schildkamp/Cees Willemse	Volvo 123 GT Amazon	1967	NL/NL
62	David Inns/Miss Pamela Wallis	Volvo 144 S	1966	GB/GB
66	John Aspinall/Philip Jenkins	Ford Mustang	1971	GB/GB
67	Ms Jan Smith/Ian Brawn	Porsche 911	1965	GB/GB
68	Lady Pauline Harris/Mrs Ann Locks	Porsche 911	1967	GB/GB
69	Mike Barnes/Ms Jennifer Barnes	Porsche 2.7 RS	1973	GB/GB
70	Henri Guyonnet-Duperat/	Mercedes Coupe	1974	F/F
	Jean-Paul Decroix			
72	Tony Mather/Ms Pauline Mather/	Citroën DS23	1973	GB/GB/GB/GB
	Miss Ellen Mather/Dan Mather			
73	David Mitchell/Mrs Patricia Mitchell	Holden HQ Kingswood	1974	NZ/NZ
74	David Garrett/Tony Humphrey	Mercedes 250 SE	1973	GB/GB
75	Philippe Patenotte/Raynol Geoffroy	Mercedes Benz 280 SE	1972	F/F
77	Geoff Dorey/Mrs Jennie Dorey	Alfa Romeo Giulia Sprint GT Veloce	1967	GB/GB
78	John Catt/Mrs Judi Catt	Ford Cortina Mk1	1965	GB/GB
79	David Liddell/Mark I'Anson	Ford Escort RS1600	1971	GB/GB
80	John Bateson/Colin Francis	Ford Escort RS2000	1974	GB/GB

4x4 Adventure Drive

A1	David Angel/Mrs Carole Angel	Toyota Land Cruiser Colorado GX	1996	GB/GB
A2	Barry Aughey/Gerry McGuigan/	Hyundai Galloper	2001	GB/GB
	Eugene Courtney/Ms Deidre Aughey			
A4	Mr David Bishop/	Mitsubishi L200 4-life pickup	2000	GB/GB
	Ms Jennifer Bishop			
A5	Henk Born/Ms Sarah Born	Land Rover Discovery 300TDi	1977	NL/NL
A6	Peter Bornhauser/	Mitsubishi L200	2001	CH/CH
	Mrs Ann Bornhauser			
A7	Goos R Bos/Goos H Bos/	Nissan Patrol	2001	NL/NL/NL/NL
	Mrs Gerry Bos-Bollen/Ms Marissa Bos			
A8	Bert Daiberl/Joerg Mautz	Toyota Land Cruiser	1998	D/D
A9	Chris Elliott/Ms Linda Banks	Toyota Land Cruiser	1993	GB/GB
A10	Sir Terence English/	Toyota Land Cruiser	1992	GB/US
	Dr Chris McGregor/Dr Stuart Jamieson			

A12 Ahmad Fakhr/Reza Fakhr/ Bahram Fatemi/Michael Burton	Chevy Suburban	1999	USA/USA/ USA/GB
A14 Mrs Angela Fenhalls/ Richard Fenhalls/Mrs Heather Milne-Taylor	Mitsubishi L200 GLS	2001	GB/GB
A15 Spencer Flack/Mrs Carole Flack	Toyota Land Cruiser	2000	GB /GB
A16 Tim Franey/Ms Wendy Franey/ Colin Forster	Toyota Land Cruiser Amazon	2001	GB/GB/GB
A17 Trevor Green/Ms Barbara Smith/ Arthur (Gus) Gale/Ian Green	Land Rover Discovery	1995	GB/GB/ GB/GB
A18 Patrick Brooks/Kevin Clemens	Buick Rendezvous	2002	USA/USA
A19 Roland Guille/Mrs Carol Guille	Land Rover Discovery 200TDi	1990	GB/GB
A20 Edwin Hammond/ Mrs Carolyn Hammond	Land Rover Discovery 300 TDi	1997	GB/GB
A21 Colin Heathcote/Ian Read	Chrysler Jeep Grand Cherokee	1999	GB/GB
A22 Bob Howells/Mrs Thelma Howells/ Dr R Tanner	Land Rover Discovery	1995	GB/GB
A23 Derek Hunt/Roy Sutch	Vauxhall Frontera	1999	GB/GB
A24 Wilhelm Lambertz/ Ms Barbara Lambertz	Toyota Land Cruiser	2000	D/D
A25 Robert Lowe/Ryan Lowe	Land Rover Series IIA 109	1961	USA/USA
A26 Roger Lucas/Mrs Sarah Lucas	Toyota Land Cruiser	1994	GB/GB
A27 John May/Mrs Jill May	Toyota Land Cruiser Amazon	1998	GB/GB
A28 Arnold Meier/Mrs Melanie Meier	Toyota 4-Runner	1993	CH/CH
A29 Fred Nelan/Alan Crisp/ Mrs Ernie NelanMs Nina Nelan	Chevy Avalanche	2001	USA/GB/ USA/USA
A30 Huub Paymans/Bert Klaasens	Toyota Land Cruiser Turbo Diesel	2000	NL/NL
A31 Ms Anna Pelly-Fry/ Jonathan Pelly-Fry	Audi Allroad	2001	GB/GB
A32 Humberto Petersen/ Ms Michelle Denise Gjoerland/Anne-Melte Soerenson	Chrysler Cherokee Jeep	2000	D/
A33 Rolf Pritz/Mrs Ines Pritz	Land Rover Discovery	1999	D/RSA
A34 Georg Pollnow/Mrs Barbel Pollnow	Daimler – Chrysler G290 TDi	2000	D/D
A35 Vic Quayle/Mrs Pam Quayle	Toyota Land Cruiser Colorado	1999	GB/GB
A36 Paul Ranson/Roy Ranson/ Ms Jane Ranson/Mrs Alison Ranson	Land Rover Discovery TDS E	2001	GB/GB/ GB/GB
A37 Paul Rijkens/Ms Vanessa Rijkens	Toyota Land Cruiser	1983	NL/NL
A39 Peter Robinson/ Mrs Carolynn Robinson	Toyota Land Cruiser Colorado	1998	GB/GB
A40 Jochem van Rossenberg/ Co van Rossenberg	Toyota Land Cruiser CustomWagon	1997	NL/NL
A41 Ian Scott/Ms Glynis Scott	Hyundai Galloper	2001	USA/USA
A42 Ms Caroline Seed/	Toyota Colorado Ms Caroline Readings	1997	GB/GB
A43 Howard Seymour/Mrs Ann Bennett	Range Rover TDi	1994	GB/GB
A44 Dari Shalon/Ophir Nachum/ Rami Skaliter	Mitsubishi L200	2001	USA/
A45 Angus Stamper/Ian Rhodes Richard Beechner/Mrs Emma Stamper	Toyota Land Cruiser	1996	GB/GB/ GB/GB

A46	Greg Stanley/Tessa Bamford/Tracey Kenchington/Samantha Kenchington	Toyota Landcruiser Amazon GX	2001	GB/GB/ GB/GB
A47	Chris Cooper/David Tremain/ Richard Smith/Malcolm Stanley	Toyota HiLux	1998	GB/GB/GB/GB
A48	James Taylor/Eric Nesterenko/ Hubert Boger Jr/Dennis Flint/Kaitlin Taylor	Chevrolet Avalanche	2001	USA/CDN/ USA/USA
A49	Michael Waterhouse/ Ms Margaret Waterhouse	Toyota Land Cruiser Amazon	1998	GB/GB
A50	Christopher Wray/Ms Jill Wray	Hyundai Galloper	2001	GB/GB
A51	Len Wright/Dick Delo/ Mrs Tessa Wright/Paul Tappin/Adrian Pulleyn	Land Rover Discovery	1995	GB/GB/GB/ GB/+GB

Inca Trail 4x4 Adventure Drive

Major Award Winners

Gold Medal

A1	David Angel/Mrs Carole Angel	Toyota Land Cruiser Colorado
A15	Spencer Flack/Mrs Carole Flack Toyota	Land Cruiser Amazon
A26	Roger Lucas/Mrs Sarah Lucas	Toyota Land Cruiser Amazon
A27	John May/Mrs Jill May	Toyota Land Cruiser Amazon
A30	Huub Paymans/Bert Klaasens	Toyota Land Cruiser
A31	Ms Anna Pelly-Fry/Jonathan Pelly-Fry	Audi Allroad
A35	Vic Quayle/Mrs Pam Quayle	Toyota Land Cruiser Colorado
A36	Paul Ranson/Roy Ranson/Ms Jane Ranson/ Mrs Alison Ranson	Land Rover Discovery
A45	Angus Stamper/Ian Rhodes/ Richard Beechner/Mrs Emma Stamper	Toyota Land Cruiser Amazon
A48	James Taylor/Eric Nesterenko/ Hubert Boger Jr/Dennis Flint/Kaitlin Taylor	Chevrolet Avalanche
A49	Michael Waterhouse/Ms Margaret Waterhouse Toyota Land Cruiser Amazon	

Silver medals

A4	Mr David Bishop/Ms Jennifer Bishop	Mitsubishi 4 life Pickup
A18	Patrick Brooks/Kevin Clemens	Buick Rendezvous
A28	Arnold Meier/Mrs Melanie Meier	Toyota 4 Runner
A34	Georg Pollnow/Mrs Barbel Pollnow	Daimler-Chrysler G461
A50	Christopher Wray/Ms Jill Wray	Hyundai Galloper

No Bronze Medals were awarded

Inca Trail Classic Reliability Trial

Major Award winners

Gold Medal

2	Richard Newman/Robert O'Hara	Chrysler Model 75
17	Ms Sue Shoosmith/Ms Alexa Scott Plummer/Tony Humphrey	Austin A90 Westminster
24	Paul Kane/Ms Mary Kane	Ford Mustang Shelby GT350
58	Bart Rietbergen/Mrs Jolijn Rietbergen	Volvo PV544 Sport
80	John Bateson/Colin Francis	Ford Escort RS2000

Silver Medal

| 53 | Renger Guliker/Ms Gerda Guliker | Mercedes Benz 300SE |

Bronze Medal

12	Malcolm McKay/Nicholas Hall	Triumph TR2
31	David Reville/Mrs Carolyn Ward/ Anthony Ward/et al	Mercedes Benz 280 SL Coupé
33	Ted Howles/Ms Judy Howles	Reliant Scimitar GT
39	Malcolm Pickering/Derek McConnell	Sunbeam Alpine
59	Paul Wignall/Mrs Jayne Wignall	Volvo PV544 Sport
67	Ms Jan Smith/Ian Brawn	Porsche 911
74	David Garrett/Tony Humphrey/et al	Mercedes 250 SE
79	David Liddell/Mark I'Anson	Ford Escort RS1600

Tools and spares

2 x Spare wheels and tyres

1 x Fire extinguisher

1 x Towrope

1 x Toolbox (red) and assorted tools

1 x Workshop manual

1 x Fuel filler with filter

2 x Drinking water containers

1 x Tyre inflation cylinder

1 x WD40

1 x Damp start

1 x Brantz Odometer

1 x Navigator lamp

1 x Stationery box (pens, pencils, notebooks etc)

1 x Warning triangle

2 x Reflective tabards

1 x 3 ton trolley jack

1 x Spade

1 x Jump leads

1 x First aid kit

2 x Diesel filters

2 x Oil filters

2 x Air filters

2 x Alternator belts

2 x Air conditioning belts

2 x Supplementary belts

1 x Box of fixings, nuts, bolts etc

Assorted wire

Oils – various

First aid and medical supplies

First Aid Kit

2 pr Plastic gloves

Roll of tape

3 Triangular bandages

3 Sterile eye pads

2 Sterile dressings (med)

2 Sterile dressings (large)

2 Sterile dressings (xlarge)

8 Gause compresses

1 Tweezers

Safety pins – various

1 Scissors

2 Boxes Elastoplast

1 Pack of dressings

6 Moist cleansing tissues

2 Alcohol prep pads

1 Crepe bandage

1 Strip plaster

1 Sterile bandage (Large triangular)

1 Elastic bandage

1 pt Lint

Medical bag

2 Space blankets

100ml TCP Antiseptic

1 Thermometer

110ml Optrex

80 Bisodol tablets

20c Bisodol extra strong

26 Paracetamol tablets

16 Paracetamol caplets

12 Panodol, soluble

62 Imodium capsules

10 Stugeron travel tabs

10 Travel calm tablets

30 Strepsils

150g Andrews

180 Allergy relief tablets

43g Anusol cream

30g Betnovate cream

32 Co-codamol tablets

32 Nurofen tablets

8 Rehydration sachets

15g Daktarin cream

67g Deep Heat cream

30g Savlon

15g Sting relief

C000261118

CHINA⹁s
URBANIZATION
Migration by the Millions

Edited by Xie Chuntao

NEW WORLD PRESS

First Edition 2014

Edited by Xie Chuntao
Translated by Wang Chiying

Copyright by New World Press, Beijing, China
All rights reserved. No part of this book may be
reproduced in any form or by any means
without permission in writing from the publisher.

ISBN 978-7-5104-5213-0

Published by
NEW WORLD PRESS
24 Baiwanzhuang Street, Beijing 100037, China

Distributed by
NEW WORLD PRESS
24 Baiwanzhuang Street, Beijing 100037, China
Tel: 86-10-68995968
Fax: 86-10-68998705
Website: http://www.newworld-press.com
E-mail: frank@nwp.com.cn

Printed in the People's Republic of China

Foreword

The evolution of history is supposed to be a regular process absent governmental intervention. The issue we are faced with is a normal urban governance issue. However, polarized interest relationships built up over decades and solidified by the established system became a gap between urbanites with *hukou* and migrant workers without urban *hukou*. The central government is left with no choice but to try and break the bottleneck of development by overhauling the household registration system and the land administration system. Nevertheless, the reform is not as easy as we think. After all, the interests of urban citizens have become factors that inhibit such reform. Not to mention that these urbanites stand on a higher platform of policy making and they enjoy the right of elite discourse.

I am glad to see more and more people studying and paying attention to the urbanization issue. This book reveals, from the farmers' perspective, various complicated conflicts of interest and the kind of vim and vigor that urbanization has brought to rural areas and to the rural population.

Of course, what interests me most is that this book will help us readjust the subjective consciousness of numerous urban decision makers in order that they may put the focus of urbanization on the resettlement of farmers in the cities and that urbanization will go in the right direction, be less costly and improve resettlement (in cities) of the rural population.

Li Tie
October 2014

CONTENTS

Chapter One **The Long Process of Urbanization**   001

Prosperity and Civilization in Ancient Chinese Cities   002

The Rise of Modern Industrial and Commercial Cities   009

The Tortuous Path of the PRC's Urbanization Drive   017

Acceleration of the Urbanization Process in
     Post-reform China   021

Prospects of China's Urbanization   034

Chapter Two **Builders of Modernized Cities**   037

Sweat and Contribution   038

Bewilderment and Growth   046

Change and Vision   058

Chapter Three **Changes in the *Hukou* System**   073

Barriers That Need to Be Broken Through   074

No Return   085

Strengthening of Top-level Design   097

Chapter Four **Urbanization of Farmers**   111

Surging Tides of Migrant Workers   112

The Dream of Settling Down in the City   117

Improving the Quality of Life for Migrant Workers   127

Chapter Five **Distribution of Proceeds from Value-added Land** 139

Termination of the "Land for Development" Model 141

Land Empowerment–Seeking a Breakthrough in the Exploration Process 146

Comprehensive Land Management–from Regionalized to Centralized Approach 155

Distribution of the Proceeds of Value-added Land–Sharing the Benefits of Prosperity Through Competition 166

Land Reform and Urbanization 172

Chapter Six **Leaving Home for Jobs Close to Home** 177

The High Cost of Home Leaving 178

Recurrence of Leaving Home for Jobs Close to Home 185

Local Urbanization 191

Chapter Seven **Integration of Urban and Rural Development** 203

Let Farming Become a Decent Career Choice 204

Let the Farmers' Property Increase in Value 214

Equal Pay for Equal Work 222

Realize People-oriented Urbanization 229

Chapter One
The Long Process of Urbanization

A city is a child and symbol of human civilization. Cities have always been the cradle of human civilizations, both material and spiritual. As important icons of the Chinese civilization, cities have played prominent roles in its developmental process. The earliest Chinese city came into being more than 4,000 years ago. Thereafter, in the long-lasting agrarian society, China's urban development ranked among the frontrunners of the world, as a dazzling pearl of the civilized world of that era. After the Song Dynasty (960-1279), a reverse turn in urban development took place. Other than rushing into big cities, the population began to flow back into rural areas. As large cities went down in scale, new smaller cities and towns began to emerge in bulk in the south. After the five ports (Guangzhou, Xiamen, Fuzhou, Ningbo and Shanghai) were open for trade, modern cities began to develop along China's rivers and sea coasts, and cities began their metamorphosis from traditional forms into modern forms. After the founding of the People's Republic of China (PRC), under the planned economy, urban development took a sluggish and tortuous path. Only after the policy of reform and opening up was initiated did the country's urbanization process pick up the pace again. In today's China, urban development is faced with numerous bottleneck problems.

Prosperity and Civilization in Ancient Chinese Cities

Cities in China came about very early in history. If the lower threshold of a city is two thousand residents, the origin of Chinese cities can be traced back to the first dynasty of Xia (2070-1600 B.C.). The functions of Chinese cities during the Bronze Age were chiefly political, military and religious. The Spring and Autumn Period (770-221 B.C.) saw major development that came to change the very meaning and nature of cities in general. The prosperity of commerce and the handicraft industry made it possible for cities to take on economic functions in addition to political, military and religious functions. Many cities grew in population and economic prosperity. The well-known Linzi, capital of the State of Qi during the Warring States Period, was so crowded that "Chariots constantly bumped into one another, human shoulders brushed one another, and as people walked, and their sleeves looked as though connected into curtains. When people sweated and tried wiping away their perspiration, it looked as if it were raining."[1] Daliang, the capital of Wei, had "so many people, horses and chariots that the streets were bustling day and night. The huge multitudes

---

[1] Liu Xiang: *Strategies of the Warring States: Strategies of Qi*, Shanghai Classic Literature Press, 1993.

Along the River during the Qingming Festival (partial)

resembled a full-fledged army."[1] Some scholars estimate that there were more than 500 cities during the Warring States Period and that the urban population accounted for 15.9% of the total population then.[2] During the Qin and Han dynasties (221 B.C.-A.D. 220), the nature of the Chinese cities was pretty much set, and their number, size and population continued to increase against the Spring and Autumn and Warring States periods. The Qin Dynasty, with between 800 and 900 cities, established a political system composed of the capital, prefectures and counties. Chang'an (today's Xi'an), capital of the Western Han Dynasty (206 B.C.-A.D. 25), maintained a population of between 200,000 and 300,000 for a long time. A

1 *The Records of the Grand Historian: Biography of Su Qin*, Zhonghua Book Co., 1982.

2 Zhao Gang: *Collected Essays on the History of China's Urban Development*, New Star Press, 2006, pp. 57-58.

city known as the starting point of the Silk Road and the center of eastern culture then, Chang'an was so international that it even established a special agency to serve the needs of foreign merchants. By the Tang Dynasty (618-907), the same Chang'an (again made capital), became the first Chinese megacity with a population of more than one million. During the reign of Kaiyuan (713-742), its population went past 1.8 million. Luoyang, a city in today's Henan Province, was the world's largest city by size and had a population of more than 1.4 million during the latter half of the Tang Dynasty. Chinese cities during the Song Dynasty kept their momentum of rapid growth. Dongjing (today's Kaifeng in Henan Province), capital of the Northern Song Dynasty (960-1127), and Lin'an (in today's Zhejiang Province), capital of the Southern Song Dynasty (1127-1279), each had a population of close to two million. Both cities saw unprecedented development in urban economy and urban culture. *Along the River during the Qingming Festival* by famous painter Zhang Zeduan (1085-1145) was a vivid representation of the prosperity of Dongjing during the Northern Song Dynasty. A colossal change took place in the planning and design of Chinese cities during the Song Dynasty. The urban system of separation of residential area from commercial area gradually collapsed and the activities of urban residents were no longer restricted by time and space. A new, open pattern grew out of the old, closed pattern and became

Ancient City
Wall of Xi'an

established throughout the country. During Tang and
Song dynasties, the urban population in China was more
than 20% of its total. These two dynasties were both
peaks of ancient Chinese civilization marking the crown-
ing moment of urban development. It was a time when
China went far ahead of the rest of the world in urban
development. In the eyes of many Westerners, Chinese
cities were symbols of civilization and prosperity.

In 1271, a young man named Marco Polo came
all the way to China together with his father and uncle
and won the trust and promotion of the Yuan emperor
Kublai Khan. During 17 years of his stay in China, he
traveled all across the country before returning to his
home in Venice in 1295. Shocked by the prosperity and

civilization of the cities he had seen, he later recorded it all in the well-known *Travels of Marco Polo*. Marco Polo narrated that for 50 kilometers in the confines of Hangzhou, there were 12,000 bridges and 160 streets (each lined up with 10,000 houses). The streets were all paved with stones and bricks on each side, filled with small gravel in the intermediate part, and provided with arched drains for carrying off rainwater that fell so that they remained dry all the time. Because of that, people could travel to every part of the city without soiling their feet. The city had ten grand bazaars and numerous small street fairs. There were three market days every week, often visited by up to 50,000 people. A variety of fruits, vegetables, game, and seafood was available. The bazaars were surrounded with small shops and merchants dealing in spices, trinkets, jewelry and whatnot. The city also had 3,000 bathing units of various sizes, some of which were large enough to accommodate a hundred people at the same time. There were even residential streets designed specifically for prostitutes. People not only used gold and silver in trading, but also banknotes printed by the court, which were very convenient for carrying. Residents in the city carried a quiet demeanor, showed respect to women, and dealt with one another fairly and honestly in business, and neighbors treated one another like members of the same family. In the eyes of Marco Polo, Hangzhou was the world's most gorgeous and luxurious city, an unforgettable paradise. Months after the *Travels of Marco Polo* was published, it became a best-seller that swept Italy off its feet. People vied to copy it and spread it to all parts of the European continent. In the eyes of many Europeans, Chinese cities were heavenly places of beauty and abundance. It is none other than this fantasy that prompted European navigators to set sail for the East and unveil the curtain of exchange between Eastern and Western civilizations.

However, what Marco Polo had seen was far inferior to Hangzhou at its peak. During the long process of China's agrarian civilization, the Southern Song Dynasty was both a pitch moment and an important turning point of the country's urban development. In a long period from Qin, Han to Southern Song dynasties, growth rates of urban population had surpassed those of the total national population. Furthermore, increased concentration of the population in large cities quickly boosted the size of such cities. As urbanization fell into stagnation after the Southern Song Dynasty, however, the absolute value of the country's total urban population saw next to zero growth, and the proportion of total urban population in total national population dropped consecutively. This trend hit the bottom by the mid-19th century, when urban population went down to 6% from a high of 22% during the Southern Song

Dynasty. By contrast, boosted by the engines of the industrial revolution and international trade, urban development in Europe was running at full speed.

Why did urban development take a downturn after the Song Dynasty? The answer may lie in the country's per capita possession of grain. It is no coincidence that ancient China's per capita possession of grain peaked during the Southern Song Dynasty, at the climax of its urban development. Rather, the phenomenon agrees with the general law of urban development during the epoch of agrarian civilization. In the agrarian civilization, agriculture could either be the brakes or the revving engine of urban development. Agricultural labor and production of food crops directly affected the speed and scale of urban development. From the Qin, the Han to the Song Dynasty, the steady rise in China's per capita grain output laid the foundation for the continued expansion of cities and their population. After the Song Dynasty, population growth accelerated and went past 400 million by the mid-19th century. This produced a negative impact on China's urban development in at least two ways. On the one hand, due to the proliferation of population, the conflict between a huge population and limited farmland resulted in reduced per capita possession of grain. Consequently, agriculture could no longer sustain the prior trend of continuous urban expansion. With the downsizing of cities came the gradual decline of the proportion of the urban population. On the other hand, in order to absorb the excess population, individual small farmers had to strengthen their family handicraft production. This hindered the development of handicraft workshops and the invention and application of new technologies, thus making it hard for fundamental changes to occur in the cities. Agrarian revolution gave birth to cities, while industrial revolution made the cities dominate the world. As China kept lingering at the door of the Industrial Revolution, its urbanization stalled and started backsliding.

The Rise of Modern Industrial and Commercial Cities

In the mid-19th century, after the opening of the five ports, China's urbanization process entered a new stage. Even though agricultural production fell short of sustaining urban expansion, voluminous food imports made effective remedy. From the latter half of the 19th century to the early 20th century, due to the large-scale growth of foreign trade, China's imports increased more than 9 times while its exports grew more than 6.5 times. Foreign trade was carried out mainly through coastal cities or cities along rivers such as Shanghai, Tianjin, Guangzhou, Qingdao, Wuhan, Xiamen, and Chongqing.

These cities were not only both distribution centers and markets of foreign goods, but also export bases of Chinese raw materials. Consequently, commercial trading became the main substance of these cities. After the five ports were opened for foreign trade, foreign capitalists in Guangzhou, Ningbo, Shanghai and other places built modern factories that catered to the needs of commercial trade and transport services. By the 1860s, modern national industries began to appear in the treaty ports. In the aftermath of the Revolution of 1911, a boom of investment in modern industry was set off in all parts of the country. The decade from 1914 to 1923 was the golden era of modern China's industrial development. *The Herald* published the following report about construction in Shanghai on November 7, 1914:

"Many new industrial buildings are being built. This project marks a new stage in the development of the Shanghai concession into a great industrial center. In the West District, textile mills from the French Concession to the Suzhou River are adding a lot of facilities. On a large strip between Tokyo Road and Macao Road, a Japanese textile mill employing about 3,000 workers is being built. A nearby flour mill is being built as well. A candle factory of Price's (China), Ltd. is expanding too. Another large flour mill is being built opposite McHenry Road in the lower section of Suzhou River.... At the boundary on Seward Road, a new warehouse and a pharmaceutical plant are being built by Voelkel & Schroeder, Ltd. Huaxin Textile Mills is building workshops for three of its mills moved from Hong Kong to Shanghai. In addition, textile companies like Ewo, Laou Kung Mow and Ollerdessen, A. F. are engaged in large-scale expansion projects." [1]

If you pay no attention to the historical background, you might even think this was a description of what was happening in Shanghai in the late 1990s, but it was a true description of the rapidly developing modern Chinese industry along the coastal cities and cities along rivers. According to statistical data, the total amount of national capital in public transport enterprises reached 287.41 million yuan (about 46 million USD) in 1913. By 1920, the national capital of such enterprises grew to 579.77 million yuan (about 92.76 million USD). The average annual growth rate of industrial capital was 10.54%. In 1911, China had more than 40 flour mills, which had an output capacity of just over 4,300 bags of flour every 24 hours. By 1919, the number of flour mills grew to more than 120, which had an output capacity of more than 188,000 bags of flour every 24 hours. In 1913, the number of spindles in China's cotton mills totaled 515,783.

---

1 *Herald*, Nov. 7, 1914.

A Chinese city
in the early 20th
century

By 1921, that number had more than tripled to 1,713,992. Different levels of development were also seen in other industries. These included matches, cigarettes, cooking oil, knitting, papermaking, printing, glass, soap, canned food, tannery, sodium carbonate and so on.

With the opening of major coastal ports and the rise of modern commerce and industry, China's population began its shift into urban areas. By the early 1930s, Shanghai had a population of 3.5 million; Tianjin, 1.5 million; Guangzhou, 1.05 million; Wuhan, 1 million; and Nanjing, 750,000. In addition, urban development in Wuxi, Nantong, Ji'nan, Xuzhou, Chongqing was rapid as well. Due

to mining and industrial development, cities like Tang-
shan, Jingxing, Jiaozuo, Pingxiang, Fushun, Benxi, Daye,
Anshan and others generally reached a population of
between 200,000 and 300,000. Zhengzhou, Shijiazhuang,
Bengbu, Pukou and other cities thrived on the rise of
railways, while Zhenjiang, Anqing, Jiujiang, Huangshi,
Ezhou, Shashi, Yichang, Wanxian, Fuling, Luzhou, Yibin
and others rose due to the rapid development of water
transport.

The emerging coastal cities and cities along rivers
were radically different from traditional Chinese cities.
Starting from the 1860s, treaty port cities saw the gradual
appearance of modern municipal facilities such as elec-
tric light, tap water, gas, sanitary facilities, sewer systems,
waste water treatment, telephone, telegraph, trams, cars,
and new paved roads. The gradual emergence of public
services such as import and export companies, banks, exchanges, shops, department stores, large shopping malls,
restaurants, churches, hospitals, clubs, theaters and other
public facilities caused a lot of change to the living conditions of urban residents.

As Chinese and Western civilizations comingled
and collided with each other, Western culture and customs began to spread in Chinese cities. Many urban
residents became mad about Western cuisine, fashion

City of
Guangzhou,
1920s

and architectural styles. Some also took to Western dance, drama, film, folkways, and began to follow Western lifestyle. Changes in the secular behavior of urban residents inevitably led to changes in people's thinking and behavior.

Dramatic changes in modern Chinese ideology and culture took place primarily in the city. Western science and culture first made their headway into coastal cities, and some of the traditional Chinese intellectuals oriented themselves towards modernization and gradually realized their conversion. In the early 20th century, Western sciences and culture and Westerns schools of thought spread in more diverse ways into China. New institutions

Qianmen East
Train Station,
Beiping, 1930s

of learning replaced traditional private schools and acad-
emies, and studying overseas came into vogue. Out of the
emerging modern cities emerged a number of modern
intellectuals who would receive the new kind of education and be influenced by Western values. They translated Western books, ran newspapers and periodicals and
founded schools so that the Western science and technology, modern ideas and concepts, and moral ethics etc.
would first spread among the intelligentsia as well in industrial and commercial circles. As national and social crises deepened, out of these circles emerged ideas such as
nationalism, national salvation through industrialization,
science and technology, education and, finally, revolution.
Modern Chinese intellectuals were no longer reserves of

feudal bureaucracy; instead, they became chief drivers of social reform. Many of the earlier modernization leaders came out of this group. Within the modern cities, new social concepts like openness, reform, competition, efficiency, sense of time, democracy, and rule of law took shape and got accepted by more and more people. As a result, a change of mode of thinking, values and behavior patterns took place among urban Chinese and became a powerful dynamo of modernization.

After the five ports were opened to foreign trade, as Western civilization intermingled and collided with Chinese civilization along China's coastal cities and cities along rivers, the stagnation in urban development went on a course of change. New production patterns, new industrial and commercial systems, new municipal system and new culture and ideology emerged out of new cities to guide the country's future footsteps. However, the strength of the newly formed cities was miniscule in the context of a huge country. For more than a century, despite the heightened degree of urbanization, the level of urbanization remained extremely limited. In 1930, urban population accounted for about 6.24% of the national total. In 1949, it accounted for 10.6% of the national total. In the same year, the world's average level of urbanization was 28.8%. China remained a downright agricultural country.

The Tortuous Path of the PRC's Urbanization Drive

After the founding of the PRC, in attempts to eliminate poverty and backwardness, the Chinese government set its goal on industrializing the economy. In order to reach this goal, it adopted a system of planned economy and established a dual system of social management in which urban and rural areas were separated. In 1953, at the start of its First Five-year Plan, China began implementing a series of major urban industrial projects. Cities around the country opened their doors to rural areas to admit farmers for employment in downtown factories or remote mining areas. The newly built and expanded cities gave a great boost to the urbanization process. From 1949 to 1957, rural residents could freely migrate to the cities. In 1952, the state-owned industrial sector hired a total of 5.1 million employees, which was to increase to 23.16 million by 1958. A great majority of the increase came from rural areas. The number of cities in China grew from 135 to 176, and total urban population reached 99.49 million, which is 15.4% of the national total.

In 1958, China came up with a radical, steel-centered policy through which a national steel-tempering campaign was put on agenda. As a result, backyard furnaces were set up in every city and county almost

Downtown
Beijing, 1960s

overnight. In less than a year, ten million rural laborers migrated to the cities. The proportion of China's urban population rose from 15.4% in 1957 to 19.7% in 1960. In tandem with this radical industrialization, rural China went through a People's Commune movement that led to a sharp decline in agriculture. In consequence, rural economy could no longer sustain the rapid urbanization process. In the meantime, a dual management system that separated the cities from rural areas was being established. On January 9, 1958, the 91st Session of the First National People's Congress passed "Household Registration (*hukou*) Regulations of the People's Republic of China" stipulating that "Citizens migrating from rural to urban areas must hold proof of employment issued by the relevant city's labor department, proof of school admission, or approval for migration to the city issued by the city's household registration authorities. They must also apply for exit permission from their permanent residence registration office." Since then, the rural labor force lost the right of free entry into the cities to seek employment. Unless the government had any job vacancies, farmers would have no choice but to farm in rural areas. In April 1962, the Ministry of Public Security issued a "Circular on the Handling of *Hukou* Transfer Issues," which read, "People from villages and rural towns demanding to migrate to the cities shall be firmly discouraged from making such demands. Individuals who are too old, too young, too sick or disabled to take care of themselves and who have urban relatives to turn to may be entitled to special consideration depending on the case of the matter. Those who have already migrated to the city but have not completed urban household registration must be encouraged and persuaded to return to rural areas, when their conditions are fit for doing so." The People's Commune system established in rural areas during the late 1950s also played a special role in hampering the transfer and migration of rural labor to the cities. Changes were made consecutively to the systems of food supply, housing, health care and education in order to accommodate changes in the household registration system. As a result, transfer and migration of rural labor to the cities were put under strict and full governmental control. Farmers lost their free access to the cities. The result was a huge reflux of the urban population to rural areas. At the close of 1963, urban population went down 30 million and the proportion of urban population dropped to 16.8%. Due to the shrinking of commodity exchange and industry, many cities and towns went down the drain. By the end of 1964, 39 cities had been revoked. By the end of 1965, 1,527 townships had been shut down.

After 1966, China went through the Cultural Revolution, a period when all industrial and agricultural production stood still. In 1968, educated youths and numerous urban employees and officials settled down in rural areas. Within a decade, about 30 million people migrated from urban to rural areas. This movement seriously hampered the urbanization process. In 1978, urban population was 17.9% of the country's total, about the same proportion as that of 1966.

Before the policy of reform and opening up was initiated, due to the bumpy journey of industrialization, urbanization in China had to go through many dramatic twists and turns and inch slowly forward. The planned

Shenzhen in the 1970s, before it was made a special economic zone

economy and the policy of urban-rural isolation adopted after the founding of the PRC are products of special historical conditions. There is no gainsaying that urbanization prior to the reform in the 1980s was pretty much influenced by political movements and the will of the government. Economic development had little impact on the urbanization process.

Acceleration of the Urbanization Process in Post-reform China

China's economic reform started off in rural areas. Early in the summer of 1978, Anhui Province suffered from one of the worst droughts in 100 years. Xiaogang Village in Fengyang County reaped a bumper harvest

Downtown
Beijing, 1980s

one year after implementing a household contract agreement reached secretly among the villagers. The practice
became a huge role model. A variety of farmers' contract responsibility systems sprang up in other parts of
the country as well. Based on the experiences of these
largely spontaneous practices in different provinces, the
CPC Central Committee provided integrated guidelines
for systematic rural reform. In September 1980, the
committee issued the famous Document No. 75 to give
formal approval of the household contract responsibility system, which fundamentally broke up the egalitarian
operation in agricultural production and won wide-

spread support from farmers. By 1981, the system was being implemented in most parts of rural China. Farmers could now make their own decisions on the job they do, such as when and how to do it and how to distribute the fruits of their labor. Rural economic reform greatly stirred up farmers' enthusiasm for production. In 1984, China's grain output basically met the needs of urban and rural residents. Chinese people now had more than enough to eat and wear.

The household contract responsibility system greatly stirred up farmers' enthusiasm for production. However, continuous grain harvest was making the issues of surplus farm produce and surplus labor more and more patent. In October 1983, China replaced the people's communes and production brigades with township governments and village committees. The highly concentrated People's Commune system disintegrated. Transformation of the social management system in rural areas paved the way for the free flow of rural labor. As economic reforms were being unveiled in the city, a construction spree brought about substantial growth in the demand for labor. A free flow of labor was no longer just a necessity for farmers, but also became a real demand of economic development. In this backdrop, the state adjusted its policy of rural labor transfer. On January 1, 1984, "the CPC Central Committee Circular on Rural Work in 1984" proposed that "Farmers and their family members who are engaged in industrial work, business, or are working in the service sector shall be allowed to keep a fixed residence in town. Those who have business management abilities and those who work long-term in village and township enterprises or institutions shall be granted permanent resident status by departments of public security in a timely manner and shall be registered as having non-agricultural *hukou*." This meant that farmers who met certain conditions were now entitled by policy to transfer to urban non-agricultural industries and may even apply for urban *hukou*. The previous policy restricting the migration and flow of farmers was loosening up. From then on, having peeled off their identity as commune members, farmers were free to make their employment choices in both rural and urban areas. A huge number of farmers started making headways into the city and were en route to contributing to the development of urban economy. According to statistical data, from 1978 to 1987 alone, the population of transferred labor from the agricultural sector to non-agricultural sectors reached over 100 million. In 1992, the release of Deng Xiaoping's southern tour talks pushed forward a new round of reform and opening up. China's economy entered a new cycle of rapid growth, adding wings to rural labor migration to urban areas. In 1992, 35 million rural people flooded

Buildings of
sharp contrast,
Shanghai, 1992

into the cities. In 1993, up to 60 million got into the cities. By the 21st century, migration of rural labor into the cities became an irresistible trend in China.

A migrant worker
on a street in
Shenzhen, 1993

In tandem with domestic reforms, China also took
the initiative to merge into the tide of globalization.
After the Third Plenary Session of the 11th CPC Cen-

tral Committee, in order to open up the national gate, the CPC Central Committee decided in 1979 to set up special economic zones in Shenzhen, Zhuhai, Shantou, and Xiamen and to develop 14 coastal port cities[1] and Hainan Island in 1984. In 2001, China's accession to the WTO marked the full-scale opening of the Chinese market and the full integration of domestic and international markets. With the continued implementation of China's opening-up policy, a lot of foreign capital, advanced production technology and management systems entered China and powered up China's economic development. As the receiving forefront of the shifted international industries, China's east coast was developing at breathtaking pace, and a whole lot of the nation's manpower began migrating to the southeast coast. In the more developed eastern region, urban agglomerations came into being around the Bohai Sea, the Yangtze River Delta and the Pearl River Delta.

Due to the rapid growth of the Chinese economy and the massive transfer of rural labor to the cities, China's urbanization made great strides forward. The proportion of the total urban population grew from 17.9% in 1978 to 52.57% in 2012.

---

1 Dalian, Qinhuangdao, Tianjin, Yantai, Qingdao, Lianyungang, Nantong, Shanghai, Ningbo, Wenzhou, Fuzhou, Guangzhou, Zhanjiang, and Beihai.

Since the initiation of reform and opening up, transfer of rural labor to the cities sped up the process of urbanization. However, remnants of the old system still hindered the influx of rural population into urban areas. The household registration system and other associated systems were still barring farmers from making their entry into the cities. In the second half of the 1980s, as the government gradually loosened its grip on the growth of migration of rural labor, cities experienced another influx of rural labor. Many of the cities were ill prepared for the incoming pressure on urban transport, supply and public order. The call for reinforced management of the floating population grew louder and louder. In July 1985, the Ministry of Public Security issued "Interim Provisions on the Management of Urban Transient Population," which reaffirmed the registration requirement for temporary population as specified in the "Household Registration Ordinance" promulgated in 1958. Temporary residents of 16 or older who live more than three months in the city had to apply for a temporary residence permit, and rural people who engaged in various trades in the city on a relatively long-term basis would be registered as lodged *hukou*. Other departments, such as family planning, civil affairs, labor, urban construction, and education departments, also began formulating floating population management measures and regulations. Some large cities began to make comprehensive administrative rules too.

Under the restrictions of the existing household registration system and its associated institutional rules, many of the rural population in the city basically have no suffrage rights, social security, children's education rights and many other civic rights enjoyed by urban citizens. Not only do the city's original residents fail to recognize rural migrant workers as part of the city, the majority of the rural migrant workers themselves do not have a sense of belonging in the cities they live. As a result of the massive entry of rural migrant workers, the formerly enduring urban-rural dual structure is now being transformed into a new dual structure.

In more than 60 years' history, the PRC's concept of urbanization kept improving through the test of reality in line with economic development. In the early 1950s, in efforts to quickly change the legacy of poverty and backwardness from the past and to showcase the superiority of socialism, the government developed an economic development strategy geared toward catching up with and surpassing advanced industrialized countries. The country aimed at prioritizing development of heavy industry so that it could be quickly transformed from an agricultural country into an industrialized country. Under the planned economy, limited understanding of socialism shackled the development of social productive forces. Faced with the reality of extremely scarce material production, the country had a long-term pressing need to increase production capacity. As a material gathering center confronting villages that provide rations for basic subsistence, the city was subjectively inhibited in its development.

Prior to the reform and opening-up initiative, the basic driving force of urbanization was the government. The ups and downs and twists and turns of urbanization were largely triggered and manipulated by political movements. During the era of reform and opening up, with the restructuring of the rural and urban economic system, the gradual establishment of a market economy and the rapid development of a non-public sector economy, the maladies of an urbanization model arranged by the government, excluding the role of markets and ignoring civil power, became increasingly obvious. In order to meet the new requirements of the market economy and urban development, the government began to introduce market elements into the cities and apply them to urban construction, so that the market would play a fundamental role in the configuration of the economy. In the meantime, the government gradually loosened up systemic restraints, such as the household registration regulations that seriously shackle urbanization. Through governmental guidance and the role of the market, private capital became the main body of investment in urban construction. The driving force of urbanization turned from complete governmental control to a pluralistic mechanism combining governmental guidance with market role and civil participation.

Eye-opening achievement has been made in urbanization since China kicked off its program of reform and opening up. In just 30 years, China accomplished things that the Western world used 150 years to accomplish. However, many problems remain in the process of urbanization:

Insufficiency of urbanization. With an annual average growth rate of 1.39% in the past 15 years, urbanization in China has definitely maintained a high-speed momentum. A survey by the Chinese Academy of Social Sciences shows that China has an urbanization rate of about 51% and an industrialization rate of 47%. By comparison, in developed countries, the urbanization rate is about two to three times the rate of industrialization. What this tells us is that China's urbanization lags far behind its industrialization.

Past mode of urbanization unsustainable. This is first shown in the overexpansion of urban construction. In the past ten years or so, many cities were keen on widening their construction framework and kept their

Downtown
Jiujiang City,
Jiangxi Province,
September
24, 2014.
Urbanization rate
in China reached
53.73% by 2013.

focus on low-density development. From 2000 to 2010, China's urban built-up area increased by 78.5%, while its urban population over the same period grew by 46.1% only. Another set of data show that from 1995 to 2008, the rate of expansion of the urban built-up area reached an average of 7% per year, while the annual growth rate of the urban population was only slightly higher than 3%. In other words, the rate of urbanization of land more than doubled the rate of population urbanization. Another important indicator of the unsustainability of the development model is the excessive dependence of urban infrastructure construction on land financing. In 2010, national land transfer revenue reached 291.1 trillion yuan (about 46.58 trillion USD), equivalent to 71.7 % of the local general budget revenue. In addition, local fiscal tax revenues included taxes associated with real estate, such as deed tax, property tax, value-added land tax and urban land use tax. These tax revenues and the land transfer fees together constituted land financing. Due to the dwindling of transferrable land, overreliance on land development financing is not sustainable.

Big-city problems getting more and more serious. Overcrowding, traffic congestion, environmental pollution, housing shortages and other big-city problems are worsening. Downtown population density in Shanghai, Beijing, Guangzhou and other megacities each surpasses that of major cities in developed countries. In cities with a population of one million or more, 80 percent of the roads and 90% of the intersections have almost hit the limit of mobility. Economic losses caused by traffic congestion reach trillions of dollars each year. Air pollution, water pollution, noise pollution, garbage pollution and other environmental problems are hardened nuts to crack. Due to escalating housing prices and rent in large cities, the size of groups facing housing difficulties can hardly go down. The living conditions of the ever growing rural migrant workers are especially poor.

Prospects of China's Urbanization

A city is an important manifestation of human civilization, and the rise and fall of a city is often a symbol of the rise and fall of a civilization. In the long historical process of China's urban development, there have been dazzling brilliance, helpless stagnation, readjustment and contrived soaring at the stimulation of foreign civilizations. The rise and fall of Chinese cities prove that urban development must be based on a strong material and cultural civilization. There must be a spirit of openness that absorbs, accommodates and merges with the outstanding fruits of foreign civilizations. There must be willingness to learn how to allocate resources on a global scale to seek national development, and there must be a proactive attitude in welcoming the tides of the new age. Today, with the revival of the Chinese nation, urban development in China has entered a new stage. Urbanization in the future will be a billowy transformation. In the foreseeable future, hundreds of millions of Chinese farmers will be entering the cities. They will bid farewell to traditional modes of production and to their old ways of life. They will be dealing with new modes of production, and they will be living in ways different from those of their predecessors. In this transformation, the Chinese nation will walk out of a closed agrarian society into an open industrial and information society. People's mode of production, lifestyle, organizational style and moral ethics will all undergo great changes. In a word, it will be the greatest and most fundamental change ever. This change will not only deeply influence the lives of the Chinese people, it will also have a profound impact on the rest of the world. Joseph Stiglitz, Nobel Prize winner in economics in the year 2001, pointed out at the World Bank China Office: In addition to high technology, the most influential worldly events in the early 21st century will be China's urbanization. The process of urbanization is one in which the people develop a deeper understanding of their country's civilization as well as that of the world. It is also a process in which people will gain a deeper understanding of cities and of how best to develop them. It reflects the self-consciousness of a civilized nation. This process may not be that smooth. It may face obstacles of the system, obstacles of self-interests, obstacles of emotion, and even obstacles of wisdom. There could be hope and optimism or great disappointment; there could also be painful disillusionment and infinite regret. As the lyrics of a pop song goes: "Here I laugh, here I cry; here I live, here I die; here I pray, here I confuse; here I look, here I get lost." However, the dreams, hopes and the great creativity of the Chinese people will never cease.

Chapter Two
Builders of Modernized Cities

For the last three decades or more, an important external manifestation of China's development has been its breathtaking changes in urban construction. The level of modernization in the country's urban construction has been affirmed and praised by international friends. In November 2013, China International Talent Exchange and Development Research Association and the *International Talent Exchange Journal* co-sponsored a campaign electing the top ten most attractive cities in China. The winner cities, decided by foreign talents, were Shanghai, Beijing, Tianjin, Guangzhou, Shenzhen, Xiamen, Nanjing, Suzhou, Hangzhou, and Qingdao. We have to say that these foreign talents' judgment is sharp and penetrating, because these cities are also among the favorites of Chinese nationals. One might as well ask: How on earth could so many modern metropolitan cities have emerged in China in a matter of 30 years? The answers can be all different if given from different perspectives. But there can be at least one consensus: These fascinating modern cities are the products of hard work by tens of millions of builders. As we enjoy the amenities of these modern cities, we should not forget them, nor should we shut them out of the city gates. Instead, we should gradually let them in so they could become part of the cities as "new citizens."

Sweat and Contribution

When speaking of the breathtaking changes in urban construction, we cannot skip the phrase "Shenzhen
Speed." After the policy of reform and opening up made
Shenzhen the first special economic zone, the city was
pushed into a full swing of construction. In a period of
37 months from November 1982 to December 1985, the
First Branch of China Construction Third Engineering
Bureau Co. Ltd set the national record of building one
floor in three days. From then on, "Shenzhen Speed" and
"a floor in three days" became a legacy and legend of
Shenzhen's builders. Behind "Shenzhen Speed" lay the
sweat and the contribution of countless urban builders.

Professor Ge Jianxiong of Fudan University analyzed
the term "city builders" in its broad and narrow senses.
In the broad sense, he thinks "city builders" refers to all
those who have made contributions to the development,
operation and maintenance of the cities. In other words,
all city residents and external labor (including managers)
are builders, except those who do not have the ability to
work, those who are retired, and a small minority of social welfare recipients. "City builders" in the narrow sense
refers to those who are engaged in urban infrastructure
construction, including both local residents and non-local
workers. External workers often account for a large pro-

portion of the city builders. During the phase of urban development or urban expansion, they may even be the mainstay of such builders. This is because a lot of external labor is needed to make up for the shortage of builders when a city is developing at an extraordinary pace. When construction projects involve special requirements or go in different stages, the need to maintain a large number of builders or trained professionals dies out. Under such circumstances, it is more economical and reasonable to hire external labor. Besides, some of the jobs that local people feel reluctant to take, jobs that involve a lot of physical strength or exposure to filth and squalor will have to be done by external labor. These city builders we are talking about here refer to the narrow sense and are known as migrant workers.

In tempo with the footsteps of reform and opening up, the tide of rural workers migrating into urban areas has been surging for more than three decades. The well-known "Chinese New Year Rush" is the best footnote to this tide. During every Spring Festival (known as Chinese New Year in the West), a holiday season when families gather together, a mighty torrent of home-going migrant workers gather themselves in railway stations and water docks patiently waiting for a ticket to get them back to their remote homes. When the holidays are over, they flow back to the cities to pursue their various dreams. We must point out that it is totally inappropriate to compare the tens of millions of farmers unbound from land to take urban construction jobs in the cities to any drifters or refugees in history. Human migration in feudal China, often caused by loss of land or other calamities, was subject to governmental control to avert any potential threat to social order due to the refugee status of the migrants. As the offspring of reform and builders of a new brand of industrialization and urbanization, migrant workers today are important pushers of further reform and opening up. These are the people who take up low-pay and labor-intensive urban jobs in dangerous and/or unhealthy environments. Migrant workers have become indispensable players in the urban economy, covering a wide range of fields, including construction, transportation, agribusiness, service and industry. In every city across the country, we find countless cases where migrant workers have boosted urban construction.

For example, subways and skyscrapers, which are symbols of modern cities, are undeniably built with the sweat of their labor.

In July 2012, at a subway construction site in Nanchang, Jiangxi Province, journalists interviewed a couple of laborers working on a broiling day at a temperature exceeding 35°C. Fang Tongrong, who was busy sprinkling

water to help cool the workplace, said: "I have been working in subway construction sites for eight years. I was in
Shanghai and Hangzhou before. It's so hot in Nanchang
that you would be sweating all over just standing here
doing nothing." The 55-year-old is a native of Dazhou,
Sichuan Province, who joined the team of subway builders in Nanchang this March. Fang is in charge of building
the continuous walls on the subway construction site. A
glare of the bright sun beat on the tanned face of Wang
Yachao and the drilling machine he was operating. From
his appearance and calloused hands, it was hard to tell
he was only 19 years old but had been working for years
on various construction sites. At the Causeway Bay Plaza
construction site, Zhou Shiming, an excavator driver from
Guangfeng County in Shangrao Prefecture, was skillfully
operating his excavator from the steamer-like driver's
cabin. "These are tough, hot days! But the thought that
I would be able to help my family out by sending them
money gets me energized." Zhou said that he would bring
his family members here shopping when the large shopping mall is completed. "By then I will be able to tell
them that I have dug the foundations of those big buildings. That'll be great!" Zhou said.[1]

Migrant workers are not just in the inland big cities.

---

1 Jin Luyao, Li Lu and Yang Wenlu: "Salute the City Builders," *Jiangnan City Press*, July 5, 2012.

They can be seen in small and medium cities in frontier areas too. In the Bortala Mongolian Autonomous Prefecture of Xinjiang, which is called the first entrance to Western China, Miao Liyang from Jiangsu Province begins his day's work in the first rays of the sun as his construction machine roars into action. Now in the fifth year working away from home as a construction worker, he was in turn a reinforced steel man, a concrete mixer, a painter, a whitewasher and a loader. The only thing he did not do was building an external wall. He was currently doing interior ceiling and glass panels. He said that he had been working 10 hours a day for four months, making about 200 yuan (32 USD) per day. Jiang Hui from Anhui Province is a reinforced steel worker. He said while working: "This is a very dirty and exhausting job. When working on vertical bars, I stay on the steel frame for the whole day. Squatting on the template, I become dizzy in the blazing sun. In hot weather, the steel feels as if it's been roasted and I dare not touch it. I have to drink a large bottle of water every hour. I basically don't have to go to the toilet. The sweating does it all. When I return to my plank room by the end of the day, I have sores and aches all over me — hands, feet, neck, you name it. The most rewarding part of the job is the income I make, which is at least 150 yuan (24 USD) a day. The company provides board and lodging. We usually start working at 6 a.m., so we have to get up right after five." Fu Weigang, who does concrete mixing, has to face the concrete mixer all day long. Though he does not have to shuttle back and forth in mid-air as others do, his constant exposure to noise is not doing any good to him either. Big Sister Zhang, a scaffolder, routinely sets up scaffolds in the heat of the sun. The iron scaffolds baked by the sun scalds easy. She gets blisters even with her gloves on. Zhang is from Qinghai. She came to Xinjiang together with her husband. "All we have is some low-yielding farmland and two kids who need to go to school. I forget about all the hardship whenever I think of my kids at home. The kids mean everything to me and my husband. We are out here because we want them to receive better education so that they would have an easier way of life," Zhang said. The great, hard work done by the migrant workers is recognized and appreciated by urban citizens like Ms. Ma. Ma has witnessed how migrant workers remodel the new apartment she was buying downtown. "They keep doing painting for whole days, as a daily routine. They don't even have a lunch break. I see them start working again right after eating the lunch they have prepared for themselves," Ma said. Liu Ya'nan, another citizen of the city, says that he admires the construction workers. "It takes a lot of courage to go back and forth on the high steel frame. This is a risky job, and you have to keep working in defiance of the scalding sun. They are such great people!" He said. Xu Zhijian, a sophomore at Xinjiang Normal University said,

Two migrant workers working on a construction site in Huai'an, Jiangsu Province, September 14, 2014. Data show that more than 60% of China's migrant workers work in the eastern region.

"While on vacation at home this summer, I saw a lot of construction workers working in different spots in town. They are taking some of the toughest and riskiest jobs, either for the purpose of making a living or of changing the financial status of their families. They are the most beautiful images of the summer and they are builders of the city deserving al lot of praise," Xu said.[1]

The cases cited above are an epitome of the daily life of urban construction workers in China. A beautiful and prosperous city would be unthinkable without the hard

1 Gao Xiaoping and Luo Li: "Top City Builders," *Bortala Daily*, July 29, 2013.

work of city builders represented by migrant workers. A poem entitled "You Are the Best–To City Builders" expresses praise for migrant workers:

I

Steel bars, however hard,

become soft in your hands

Passionate, you draw countless three-dimensional geometric shapes

Scattered silt gather together

and arise as walls of iron and bronze

to protect the spine of the city

And you, so many of you (I never get to see your face),

shown as the colors over your heads: red, yellow, blue and white

Blink continually into every sunrise and sunset

and the midday sun bright

and shine in every corner

of the diamond city

II

It's quiet now

Take time to rest your fatigued eyes

and stop the machines that keep roaring day and night

Rest

or squat like a mountain, on the dirt floor

But then you raise your head to look

Are you homesick

The blue sky is mute

Only the smoldering cigarette butt

set against your languid but bright eyes

beam stronger than the rays of a diamond

I know this is not your home

but a place where you toil day and night

and call it home

III

When I look back

at the bricks, tiles and mud that I so love

you have turned into a work of art, ere my footsteps

were to depart

Let the surging river waters

send over waves of reverence

and blessing

The city abounds in beauty

but in my eyes, you alone are the best

Bewilderment and Growth

It's no exaggeration to say that migrant workers are the greatest creditors to the fast advance of urbanization in China. The term "migrant workers" refers to agricultural *hukou* holders who take non-agricultural jobs in the cities. This customary term may sound vague and simplistic, but we have no way of avoiding its use.

Migrant workers, as key contributors to urban construction,
fail to benefit from urban civilization and prosperity.

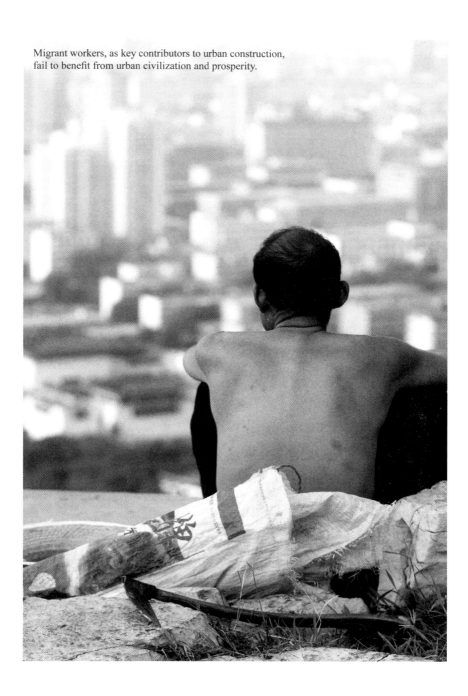

In contrast to the great contribution they have made to urbanization, their social position is deplorable. They are frequently neglected, despised and even maltreated. Cases of this nature are far too common: a migrant worker offering his seat to a fellow passenger on a public transit vehicle gets rebuffed for making the seat dirty; a city hosting grand sports events clear out up to 100,000 so-called "high risks to public order;" more seriously, some cities would even block roads to keep migrant workers from passing through.... This is none other than a social paradox and irony: Migrant workers build high-rises in the cities on the one hand but get rejected by cities on the other. However, admit it or not, urban development would be unthinkable without the involvement of migrant workers because they have infiltrated every part and parcel of the city. On an average day, you may not feel their presence; but during holidays, especially during the Spring Festival, you will suddenly realize how deserted or empty the usually bustling city has become. The omnipresent breakfast stalls are all gone and nannies and temp workers are nowhere to be found.... All of a sudden, the pace of the city seems to have slowed down. Without them, life is just not that convenient for the urban citizens. Though much needed in the city, migrant workers have not been treated quite right. No equal pay for equal work, no pension or health insurance, no access to school enrollment in the city for their children…. In one word, they can hardly share the same rights and interests with urban citizens. It is said that in a quickly urbanizing country, the relationship between city-dwelling farmers and urban citizens is the most self-contradictory parable of our time. They are interdependent but strictly incompatible. They live together, but enjoy different treatments. They are inseparable but separated. They are involved in each other's lives, but fail to see each other clearly.

Bewilderment can cause helplessness, sense of loss and lamentations, but it cannot prevent migrant workers from growing. Compared to their parents, migrant workers of the new generation are earning a niche of their own through their unique skill and capabilities.

Standing in front of the searing steel-tempering furnace, by just looking at the colors of the flames, 37-year-old Zhu Zhisheng can tell the exact temperature and chemical substances of the liquid steel. More startlingly, his visual estimation of furnace temperature has a margin of error of less than 5°C. This is just one of Zhu's "miracles." The ladle furnace three-dimensional deoxidization method invented by him can greatly improve the purity of the tempered steel. A new operating method of his that shortens the tempering cycle in the converter can reduce the average tempering time of

Zhu Zhisheng
monitoring the
steel tempering
process

each furnace of steel by five minutes and five seconds, which boils down to 2,000 more tons of steel per furnace per month…. A migrant worker having worked at Hangzhou Iron and Steel Group Company for 14 years, Zhu has made his name through studious research and bold innovation. He was twice elected model worker of the company and worker of the year multiple times. He was also honored as one of the "top ten external workers of Hangzhou City." In April 2006, Zhu and 17 other migrant worker delegates attended a national conference in which they were honored as winners of the May 1 Labor Medal. "I have never dreamed of being honored like this. I owe it all to my country and the era of reform

Xu Longjie
checking the
quality of a
welding process

and opening!" He said excitedly.

Thirty-year-old Xu Longjie, with similar experiences, shares the same feeling. Twelve years ago, when he started out as a welder apprentice at the Chemical Engineering and Construction Company of Jihua Group Corporation, Xu had but one goal in his mind: make money as quickly as possible to relieve the financial burden of his family. "My home village is Weiguang Village, Huangsongdian Township in Jiaohe City, Jilin Province. My father died a premature death, and my mother is in poor health. My younger brother is at school. Being a regular worker in the city has always been my dream," Xu said. Xu made up his mind to become a skilled welder after witnessing magnificent working scenes at some petrochemical enterprises. Xu's efforts more than paid off. Not only did he become an industrial worker, he has become a welding expert as well. He invented methods for the automatic welding of pressure vessel cylinders to ellipsoidal heads and for the automatic welding of cylinders to conical heads. Such techniques improved efficiency, reduced labor intensity and guaranteed quality. Today, Xu still holds the record of a one-time pass rate of 100% in tube plate welding for heat exchangers. In 2001, Xu's company provided him with a scholarship to study welding at Xi'an Jiaotong University. He was the first migrant worker who went to college under the company's sponsorship. Because of his outstanding performance, Xu was awarded honors such as Top Ten Accomplished Young Talents and May 1 Labor Medal. "Since I am a migrant worker myself, I fully understand my co-workers' desire to make progress, and I am very willing to share what I have learned with them. By learning the skills as quickly as possible, we will be better equipped to make contributions to society and better control our own future," Xu said. Xu is now Jihua Group's designated training engineer. He is also the company's first technical manager, who has been granted a special subsidy by the State Council in recognition of his expertise. In order to better train young workers, he bought training textbooks for 13 job categories with his prize money won in contests. The books became part of a mobile library he set up in the workshop. Under his training, two became technicians and more than 60 became senior technicians.

Accelerated urbanization made it possible for more and more migrant workers to move into the cities and become vital forces in all walks of life. Not many of them would become technical experts like Zhu Zhisheng and Xu Longjie. Most of them are unknown to the public, but have earned heartfelt understanding and respect from the public through their hard work. "Good Man Xiao Dong," whose real name is Dong Xuefa, is one of them. Eighteen years ago, he came to Beijing from Wuwei, Anhui Province, with dreamful excitement. Rows upon rows of high rises and continuous flows of vehicles got on his nerves. As an elementary school graduate with no special working skills, would he be able to blend with the city and get accepted? Through an act of providence, Dong became a maintenance worker in the fifth sub-district of Jinsong, Chaoyang District. He devoted all his efforts to the job and volunteered to patrol around the community to keep order. In the past 13 years, he had 36 life-and-death fights with gangsters; he was injured 15 times trying to protect the property of residents; he caught more than 100 criminal suspects and confiscated more than 500 stolen items. In 2005, he was honored as one of the Ten Outstanding

Youths of Beijing, the first migrant worker ever to receive this crown of glory. "Residents of the community treat me like one of their own. I wish to do my bit to improve the social order and environment here," he said. Dong proved with his action that, on an average post, migrant workers can also do extraordinary things and be integrated into the city.

The CPC Central Committee and the State Council are working hard to solve a multitude of problems brought about by a massive group of migrant workers. In March 2006, the State Council published Proposals on Dealing with the Issues of Migrant Workers, highly praising the great contribution they have made to urban prosperity, rural development and national modernization. The proposals state that the issue of migrant workers is in essence the issue of employment transfer. It demands that all localities and departments concerned amend and revoke all discriminatory regulations and unreasonable restrictions on farmers who migrate to the cities for employment and comb through administrative approval procedures and administrative charges on enterprises that hire migrant workers. No migrant workers shall be repelled or shunned on the pretext of solving the employment problem of urban labor force. The proposals argue for providing workers' compensation insurance for migrant workers according to law, prioritizing medi-

Student volunteers give out watermelons to migrant workers at a campus construction site at Liaocheng University, Shandong Province, July 5, 2014.

cal assurance for critical illnesses and gradually solving the problem of pension for seniors. The release of the Proposals warmed up the hearts of a broad spectrum of migrant workers.

Some intellectuals are also appealing for the rights of migrant workers. In December 2008, Long Yongtu, general secretary of Bo'ao Asia Forum, said at the annual conference on Chinese economy in the 21st century: "We have developed our economy, but we have driven home our migrant workers. We all owe a lot to them. During the past 30 years of reform and opening up, migrant workers have worked wonders and made the greatest contribution to our country as they left the warmth of their homes to work in the cities. Ironically, we began to repel them from the cities on the pretext of 'preserving the qualities of the urban population' at a time when we were just beginning to see any signs of development. This is absurd!" Long said. At the end of 2011, Lu Zhangong, Party secretary of Henan Province, arguing that the term "rural migrant worker" is discriminatory, called for prudent use of the term. At the start of 2012, Wang Yang, Party secretary of Guangdong Province, said that Guangdong Province would speed up research and work out at the right time policies that would nullify the term "rural migrant worker" and seek to establish a system in which external workers would be entitled to basic public services corresponding to their occupation and employment history. Henan had a huge exodus of migrant workers, while Guangdong had a huge influx of them. Statements by the Party secretaries of these two provinces carried a lot of weight and caught the attention of the general public.

Actually, even before the two provinces proposed nullification of the term, many other provinces had already looked into the same issue. As early as February 2006, Qingdao City of Shandong Province started calling migrant workers "new urban citizens" and their sons and daughters "children of new urban citizens." This change was meant to upgrade their social status by providing them equal treatment with established urban citizens. Media outlets then said that Qingdao's measure was to "set an example" for the rest of the country. Six months later, the district Party branch and the government of Yanta, Xi'an City, jointly issued a Circular on Using the Standardized Title of "New Urban Citizens." The circular required that substandard titles of "external population," "external workers," "hirelings," and "migrant workers" all be replaced by "new urban citizens." After that, a "new urban citizen" heat was pushed up in many cities across the country. Shenyang and Changchun also advocated treating external labor as "new urban citizens." In national and regional congressional sessions every year, NPC deputies and/or CPPCC members spared no efforts appealing for the rights of migrant workers. In January 2012, the Ministry of Civil Affairs issued proposals concerning the integration of migrant workers into urban communities. This provided important systemic protection for the integration of migrant workers into the cities. In the same month, eight lawyers and scholars in Henan Province submitted the Citizen Suggestions to the State Council. They argued that the term "rural migrant worker" has a discriminatory note in it, which is bad for *hukou* system reform. They suggested to the State Council that the term "rural migrant worker" used in all administrative rules and regulations, departmental rules and official government

documents be modified. On the basis of that, the lawyers and scholars further suggested a push for equality
of rights between rural and urban citizens. [1]

Today, promoting integration of migrant workers
into the cities and thereby removing the wall between rural and urban citizens has become a rallying call of the era
and a consensus among all the people.

Change and Vision

Song Dynasty poet Zhang Yu wrote a poem entitled
the *Silkworm Woman* which goes: "Yesterday I went to
town in high spirits, I returned sad with tears; Of those
clad in fine silk, not one is a silkworm woman." If migrant workers were not merged into the cities, they would
inevitably fall into the sad state of the "silkworm woman," a situation that will seriously jeopardize efforts to
build a harmonious society and complete the building of
a moderately prosperous society.

Easier said than done. Analysis of a problem is the
start of a possible solution.

Changing the title of migrant workers may be one
of the ways to get started because it is a positive sign that

---

1 Gao Jiatao: "City Builders Are Being Rejected by the Cities They
Build," *Shangdong Business Press*, January 13, 2012.

local governments are making conscious efforts to eliminate discrimination against migrant workers, help them
merge into relevant local societies, and convert them into
"new urban citizens." Under these circumstances, the
design of social security and social management systems
that migrant workers are most concerned about becomes
imminently important. The Party and the government are
now actively taking measures to deal with such issues.

A place to live in. High housing prices in large and
medium cities like Beijing, Shanghai, and Guangzhou give
a "mountain of pressure" to average wage-earners, let
alone migrant workers. A good sign is that they now have
opportunities to apply for public rental housing. In 2009,
Zhongshan City in Guangdong Province took the lead in
implementing an accumulated point system for floating
population administration. External migrants can obtain
urban *hukou* and seek school enrollment for their children
through accumulated points. In November 2012, Zhongshan City kicked off the application process of the 2013
accumulated points system. The threshold of the system
was further lowered to allow for more applications. External migrants who do not have lawful real property but do
have lawful employment for three full years may apply for
hukou in their places of employment. Applying for public
rental housing is another option for external migrants. In
December 2012, a national conference on housing and

Children of migrant workers doing art work with recycled objects in an elementary school for migrant children at Yaohai District, Hefei City, Anhui Province, April 21, 2014

urban-rural construction work required that cities above the prefecture level must cover external migrants in providing housing security.

A place to learn. Because of the dramatic rise in the number of rural people migrating to the cities, policy makers are faced with the issue of migrant children's education and school enrollment issues. On December 30, 2012, after years of cautious probe, the cities of Beijing and Guangzhou released national entrance exam measures for migrant children. Allowing examinees to take the national entrance exams in their places of residence instead of places of *hukou* is now seen as an important measure for providing close to 300 million migrant workers and their families with equal opportunities to education.

Right of expression. The biggest dream of migrant workers is probably to enjoy the right of political expression and to make sure that their political rights are recognized and respected. Progress is being made in that direction as the government is paying more and more attention to this issue. In 2007, one migrant worker was elected delegate to the Party's 17th National Congress. By 2008, three migrant workers were elected deputies to the 11th National People's Congress. This small step in political reform was in actuality a big step forward in political thinking.

On March 3, 2008, Zhu Xueqin, Kang Houming and Hu Xiaoyan came into the limelight as freshmen NPC deputies. They come from Shanghai, Chongqing and Guangdong Province, respectively. Zhu Xueqin said that more and more migrant workers today want a decent income, a stable job, and sustainable health care and pension protection. More importantly, they all have deep spiritual and emotional needs. At the least, there is that yearning for respect, understanding, and recognition. Kang Houming's motions at all congressional sessions involve migrant worker issues, such as children's schooling, social security, minimum wage, and job skill training. Each motion has got attention from departments concerned, as reflected in their letters of response. Kang says that the result has been satisfactory. Proposals Concerning Workers' Compensation Rights for Migrant Workers, a motion he submitted in 2012, was based on his real-life experience while helping migrant workers claim their rights. He says from his own perspective in the industry that work-related injuries in the construction industry are quite common and that rights claims in this industry are plagued by tough issues. For example, employers could deny the existence of a labor contract, or they simply cannot afford the costs of medical treatment. Labor relations confirmation takes a few months, work injuries appraisal several months, and then claim for compensation a few more months. Thus, two to three years can go by before any compensation is made. In most cases, employers won't budge even when the workers are already burnt out. Kang's proposals are meant to help shorten the journey of rights claims for migrant workers.

Hu Xiaoyan thinks of herself as "a lucky dog of the times." At her first press conference in 2008, Hu was "ill at ease" as she stood there on the rostrum. She dared not even greet experts and officials in the Guangzhou delegation, and she gave simplistic answers to reporters' questions. When an American reporter asked her what

Hu Xiaoyan
arriving in
Beijing to attend
the first session
of the 11th NPC,
March 2, 2008.
Three of the 2980
NPC delegates
were migrant
workers.

she would do next as a delegate, she thought about it and said, "I don't quite know yet, please bear with me." But she has attained maturity after just a few years. In 2009, Hu changed her *hukou* status from rural to urban. Subsequently, she quit her job as a deputy workshop manager at New Pearl Building Ceramics Inc. in Sanshui District, Foshan City. She switched to sales and became a "white collar." "I haven't changed much even though my rural household has changed," Hu said. She still lives among migrant workers and her own family members remain migrant workers. She works and communicates with them, cares for them and voices their claims. In her blog, she updates her work process and her contact information, including phone numbers and email addresses. She handles a large volume of messages and mail, and often has to take various phone calls. In June 2010, Hu set up a special mailbox representing the voice of migrant workers in collaboration with *Nanfang Workers Daily*. In August 2011, she advocated the opening of "Xiaoyan Summer Vacation Camp" catering to the needs of the children of migrant workers. During the "two sessions" period, she made motions that education of migrant children be included in the country's education development plan and education budget. She further suggested that migrant workers subscribe to pension insurance based on different categories. "Whoever speaks on behalf of migrant workers is their real representative," Hu said. [1]

Showing concern and care for migrant workers so that they may enjoy the fruits of reform has gradually become a consensus of Chinese society. The 18th National Congress of the Communist Party and the Third Plenary Session of the 18th CPC Central Committee put on their agendas the orderly conversion of the rural transfer population into new urban citizens. This is a new target and requirement for migrant worker affairs. In 2013, China had a total migrant worker population of 269 million, including 166 million who work far away from their home-

---

1 Kong Pu: "Hu Xiaoyan, Migrant Worker Delegate, Has the Same Mentality Despite Her New Identity," *The Beijing News*, February 28, 2012.

towns. More than 70% of the migrant workers belong to the new generation. Compared with the older generation, the new generation of migrant workers demonstrates some changes in their quest of life. The former returned home for further development after making money in town, while the latter heads to the city for employment and merges into the city for further development. The former mainly requested full payment of wages, while the latter requests participation in social security. The former mainly requested improvement of labor conditions, while the latter calls for the sharing of the fruits of business and urban development.

In view of the reality that the new generation of migrant workers has a deep desire to merge into the city, Yang Zhiming, vice-minister of Human Resources and Social Security, said that problems of skill upgrading, housing improvement, *hukou* registration, and rights protection that the new generation of migrant workers are faced with all need to be solved through systemic restructuring. He pointed out that, during the process of new urbanization, the central government has a general plan to actively push for migrant workers' entitlement to basic urban public services and to provide them with decent working conditions and a host of other good things that cause them to stand on an equal footing with urban citizens. These would include jobs in the city, training in

Taiyuan, Shanxi Province. A newlywed couple posing for a photograph at a construction site where they have worked together

the workplace, contracts of employment, insurance benefits, guaranteed pay checks, channels of rights claims, improvement in housing conditions, children's enrollment in school, spare time recreational activities, and objectives of development. The goal is that the majority of migrant workers may grow into skilled labor through job training and that eligible migrant workers may gradually turn into urban citizens. Conversion of migrant workers into urban citizens on a conditional and voluntary basis will be gradually realized through the inclusion of their children into urban schools, integration of migrant workers and their families into urban communities and into the city as a whole.[1]

In order to provide better service to migrant workers and orderly convert the agricultural transfer population into urban citizens, on July 30, 2014, Premier Li Keqiang presided over a State Council executive meeting in which he put forward four requirements:

1) Create job and business opportunities for migrant workers. A number of concrete measures were proposed at the meeting, including: a) implementation of professional skill upgrading plans, b) rebuilding and expanding professional schools and polytechnic colleges geared toward enrollment of rural students, c) providing vocational education to all recent junior or high school graduates in the countryside who fail to make it to high school or college, d) developing the service sector and medium, small and miniature enterprises, f) creating jobs fit for migrant workers, g) helping migrant workers set up businesses through provision of financial support, business and investment guidance, small secured loans and interest subsidies, as well as production or operating premises. Encouraging migrant workers in their business endeavors and providing them with high quality jobs are

---

1 "70% of China's Migrant Workers Are Part of the New Generation with Strong Desire to Merge into the Cities," Chinanews.com, February 20, 2014.

some of the best ways to help migrant workers improve their quality of life.

2) Safeguard migrant workers' labor rights protection. The meeting produced a series of systemic labor rights protection measures, including measures to solve the problem of default in wage payment typical of the construction industry. Such measures include establishment of a guaranteed wage payment plan and/or a revolving wage-default fund, imposition of project general contractor liability in wage payment to migrant workers, combination of labor protection supervision with law enforcement in dealing with malicious wage default, and imposition of general liability on local governments in solving the problem of wage default. Other measures proposed include implementing the policy of equal pay for equal work between migrant workers and urban citizen workers, opening up the "green channel" for arbitration over labor disputes concerning migrant workers and improving the efficiency of arbitration.

3) Further the reform of the supply system of basic public services and, on conditional and voluntary basis, promote the orderly resettlement of migrant workers and their families in towns and provide them with equal access to basic public services. Premier Li Keqiang is particularly concerned

Premier Li
Keqiang talking
with migrant
workers on a
scaffold at a
waste water
treatment plant
construction site
in Chifeng, Inner
Mongolia, May
22, 2014

about how best to let those who have made contributions to urban development share the fruits of development on a footing with established urban citizens. Premier Li emphasized that migrant workers with relatively
permanent jobs who live long-term in the cities should
be allowed to gradually convert to "new urban citizens"
entitled to full civic services and rights. As he put it, they
should not be seen as "second-class citizens." Furthermore, the meeting provided a list of specific answers to
questions such as how to convert migrant workers into
new urban citizens and how to provide their children
with equal access to public education. The list includes:
a) public schools providing compulsory public education

must be open for all migrated children, b) provide community health and family planning services to migrant workers, c) gradually provide migrant workers with basic old-age pension and basic health insurance that regular urban employees are entitled to, d) gradually expand the scope of the housing security and pension fund system to cover migrant workers.

4) Reinforce public cultural services to migrant workers and provide them with free and equal access to sports and cultural facilities. Because mere material security will not give them a true sense of "home," migrant workers must be spiritually merged into city life through sports, recreational activities and other public cultural services. The meeting stressed that migrant worker services concern the overall interests of the country as a whole. Focus should be put on helping those with relatively permanent jobs and long-term residency in the cities merge thereunto. On the other hand, care and assistance must be given to freewill migrant workers as well. The ultimate goal of such efforts is that hundreds of millions of migrant workers will be entitled to job security, a basic means of subsistence and spiritual well-being. A mind of peace begets a home of peace, and a home of peace begets a country of peace. Premier Li said, "We must come to grips with this reality: Migrant workers were, are and will always be an accomplished economic force of major importance, a driving force that supports China's stride toward a moderately prosperous society." Migrant workers are an important part of China's industrial workforce that has made great contributions to the country's economic and social development. Consistent and quality service to migrant workers is conducive to forging a new, quality labor force that supports industrial transition and upgrading. It will also promote social equality and justice and help bring about a new colony of consumers that put the economy on a healthy track of sustainable development.

From a global perspective, transfer to non-agricultural industries is a general trend of industrialization and urbanization all across the world. Migrant workers' integration into the cities is a historical process. Solution to current problems necessitates the strengthening of top-level design, the courage to reform and explore and a step-by-step approach. We are pleased to see that a top-level design is already on the go and that the prospect of having the builders of modern cities merge into the cities is looming larger and larger on the horizon.

Chapter Three
Changes in the *Hukou* System

The household registration system, also referred to as the *hukou* system, was established when China was practicing a planned economy. This uniquely Chinese system divides the *hukou* into agricultural *hukou* and non-agricultural *hukou* based on geographic location and family relationship. It administers citizens as family units. Through the division of *hukou*, the Chinese government was able to use the "scissors differential" between industrial and agricultural products to help the country take its first step toward industrialization at a time of poverty. Meanwhile, the system puts population flow at a standstill for a long time to come, chocked social vitality and stalled the urbanization process. Economic reform programs that began in 1978 and accelerated in 1992 revealed that the *hukou* system was actually becoming a barrier or inhibitor to the modernization process. Removing the wall of rural-urban divide has become an imperative for promoting urbanization and comprehensive social development.

Barriers That Need to Be
Broken Through

Establishment of a modern *hukou* system that secures civic rights is an important indicator of systemic civilization in the transition from a traditional society to a modern one. Regrettably, China's *hukou* system bore a deep stamp of the planned economy from day one.

In March 1949, at the Second Plenary Session of the Seventh CPC Central Committee, the Party made it clear that the future focus of its work would be shifted from the countryside to cities. The Party would immediately proceed with construction and learn urban management step by step and would set as its central task the restoration and development of production in the city.

At its founding, the PRC set household management as a foundational priority for building the new country. The *hukou* system was first established in the cities before moving on to the countryside. During the early days of the People's Republic, due to a policy of free migration that imposed few restrictions, about 15 million rural people moved into cities. While copying the experience of the former Soviet Union in building a highly centralized planned economy, in efforts to reduce the pressures of population and employment and to secure urban economic

development, the state began to curb the blind flow of
farmers into cities. As the *hukou* system began to materialize, the government began to impose more controlling
measures on population migration. In August 1955, the
State Council promulgated provisional measures on state
monopoly of grain purchase and marketing in the countryside and provisional measures on food supply in urban
areas, which directly linked food supply with household
registration. Subsequently, the State Council promulgated
the Provisions on Standards of Urban-Rural Division,
which set "agricultural population" and "non-agricultural
population" as different demographic indicators. Thus,
a dual household registration management system that
separated "agricultural population" from "non-agricultural
population" began to take shape.

The Household Registration Ordinance of the
People's Republic of China enacted in January 1958
imposed restrictions on *hukou* transfer through clearly
defined migration application and certified *hukou* registration procedures. From then on, migration, whether
from countryside to cities or from small cities to large
cities, was placed under severe restrictions. In compliance with the planned economy model, a *hukou* policy
that divided urban and rural households and a *hukou*
management model featuring one *hukou* booklet per
household came into being. These institutional arrange-

ments also fit in with the strategic needs of industrialization in the planned economy model. As is commonly
known, China's primitive accumulation of capital for industrialization was achieved through the policy of "state
monopoly of purchase and sale" using the "scissors differential" between industrial and agricultural products.
To ensure the implementation of the industrialization
strategy, the government used a high-level social welfare
system in the city to keep low-paid urbanites fully employed. In the countryside, farmers were tied to the land
to ensure the relative stability of agricultural production.
Therefore, under the prevailing historical conditions of
the time, the *hukou* system had a historical rationality of
its own. The problem was, because of farmers' bondage to land, industrialization and urbanization had to be
separate as well.

During the 1960s and 1970s, China attached to the
hukou system over a dozen sub-systems, including housing, grain supply, foodstuff and fuel supply, employment,
health care, pension, labor protection, and marriage and
birth, which together constituted a systemic barrier guard-
ing the exclusively Chinese urban-rural dual structure.
Urbanites could access relatively high-level welfare and
forcefully administered employment opportunities while
farmers tied to the farmland were barred from such civic
benefits. Thus, two different identities were created and

two unequal social groups were formed. Coupled with co-ercive control through the rural people's commune system and the urban work units system, population migration from the countryside into urban areas became well-nigh impossible. What followed were the cut-off of urbaniza-tion from industrialization and the protracted trailing of urbanization behind industrial development. For a period of 30 years, between 1949 and 1978, China's gross indus-trial output increased nearly 30 times. The proportion of urban population in the total population rose from 10% to 12.9%, while its urbanization rate grew only eight per-centage points.[1] To put it in numbers, urban population increased by 100 million, while rural population grew by 300 million. Ultimately, 80% of China's population took root in the vast countryside, became alienated from the urbanization process and lived in relative poverty.

The country's modernization would not resume until after the Cultural Revolution. In view of fundamental change in national development strategies, to adapt to the shift of focus to economic construction, the ruling Communist Party now found it necessary to orchestrate the rational flow of talents and began to deal with the vital issue of "spousal separation because of work." To

---

1 *Social Statistical Data in China*, compiled by the Department of Social Sta-tistics, National Bureau of Statistics of the People's Republic of China, China Statistics Press, 1985, p. 15.

this end, the government introduced a number of policies that made partial readjustments to the *hukou* system. After some limited readjustments were made, policies concerning personnel and *hukou* transfer became somewhat relaxed.

As economic and political reforms went ahead neck and neck during the 1980s, major changes began to take place in China's social structure. In the countryside, the demise of the people's commune and the rise of the household contract responsibility system freed up the labor force, boosted productivity and brought about increased grain output. The flip side of the coin was that the long-existing latent problem of surplus rural labor began to unravel. In reaction, the government loosened up its migration policy toward farmers who work or do business in the city. Rural enterprises began to thrive and huge masses of rural surplus labor poured into the cities to make a better living. Subsequently, the downsizing of agricultural population paved the way for further urbanization.

To meet the new challenge, the government issued a guideline in 1982, providing "strict control over large cities, moderate development of medium cities and active development of small towns." This urbanization model was summarized as "leaving home without leaving the home village and entering the factory without entering the city." Wan Li, then vice premier of the State Council, said: "Except for those who work in a few mines, the bulk of our 800 million farmers can only 'leave their farmland without leaving their home villages.' Farmers who engage in commercial production outside the cities in lieu of working their farm fields are the ones who 'leave their farmland but not their home villages.' This is our national policy." Despite continued strict control over farmers' migration to cities, the policy of "transferring from agricultural *hukou* into non-agricultural *hukou*" began to be implemented around the 1980s. Unfortunately, this policy was too narrowly tailored to benefit average farmers. Farmers would obtain urban *hukou* only in the following exceptional cases: those whose land have been acquired by the government, those admitted to college, those who join the army and become officers, and those who benefit from some special policies. The quota was so small that it only equaled 2% of the country's non-agricultural population. In 1984, the Party issued another document that would allow farmers to obtain urban *hukou* when certain conditions were met. The new policy was tailored to farmers and their family members who had jobs in towns or townships, those who ran an urban business or service, those who had long-term dwellings, those who had business management skills, and those who worked long-term in village and township enterprises. That was like a

On May 13, 2013, a migrant family got their *hukou* booklet in Yinchuan, Ningxia Hui Autonomous Region, after five years of life and work in the city

crack in the urban-rural dividing wall that had been built at the start of the planned economy. According to statistical data, in less than three years (by the end of 1986), the government approved up to 16,338 new urban households (benefiting 4,542,988 people). [1]

The next step was to widen that crack by introducing compatible supporting policy measures related to the issue. In September 1985, the NPC promulgated and began to implement the Regulations of the PRC Concerning Resi-

1 Yin Zhijing and Yu Qihong: *Household Registration Reform in China*, China University of Political Science and Law Press, 1996, p. 14.

dent Identity Cards, requiring all citizens over the age of 16 to apply for resident ID cards. Implementation of the ID card system marked the transition from a household-based management model to an individual-based management model. These preliminary reform measures made it possible for talents and people in general to navigate in a wider sphere and gave more room to farmers to access employment opportunities in cities.

By the late 1980s, in what has been referred to as a "migrant worker tide," farmers from all corners of the country swept into the major cities to seek employment and business opportunities. In 1988, the total migrant worker population reached more than 120 million. This included about 90 million township enterprise employees, about 30 million rural migrant workers who worked outside their hometowns, and about 5 million who worked outside their home provinces. The "migrant worker tide" that ebbs and flows with the farming seasons boosted national economic development and spurred on the urbanization drive. On the other hand, the "tide" dashed against the dividing wall of the *hukou* system and loosened up the hardened urban-rural dual *hukou* structure.

However, we cannot ignore the fact that these changes were taking place in the framework of the planned economy. The controlling nature of the planned economy caused considerable confusion to *hukou* administration. The most serious problem was the case of residents living away from their registered place of *hukou*. This was a common phenomenon that came with large-scale migration of people. The crux of the problem was that, on the one hand, authorities overseeing the *hukou* of the rural migrant population lost track of the "missing" residents and had no way of caring for them even if they had wanted to and, on the other hand, authorities in the urban areas did not have the wherewithal to properly manage them. The result was a series of social problems, including problems of public security and family planning. In the meantime, while implementing the policy of *hukou* transfer from agriculture to non-agriculture, the practice of *hukou* selling in the disguise of urban resettlement fees began to appear in different parts of the country. The rippling effect soon made *hukou* transaction an open, national phenomenon. However, the population absorption capacity in urban areas was still under the financial constraints of a planned economy. Limitations in the allocation of resources and services, including rationed food supply, health care, employment, housing, retirement benefits, etc., made it impossible for the cities to indefinitely absorb incoming farmers and provide them with non-agricultural *hukou*.

In view of the above problems, the government reasserted the importance of imposing stricter control over the "transfer of rural *hukou* to non-agricultural *hukou*." In 1989, the State Council issued a circular on the strict control over excessive growth in "agriculture to non-agriculture *hukou* transfer." The circular requested that "Each administrative region must keep the *hukou* transfer quota strictly within the stipulated standard. No over-the-limit quotas will be allowed. Any over-the-limit *hukou* transfers that have already been done must be deducted from next year's quota plan." In compliance with this circular, all local governments unanimously strengthened control of the rural to non-rural *hukou* transfer. Between 1989 and 1991, some large cities cleared up non-local residents, and rural migrant workers in the cities had to return home because they were identified as holders of "agricultural *hukou*."

This "one size fits all" approach is a tested and highly effective administrative measure under the planned economy, but it was a blow to lots of farmers who were wishing to break through the barriers of *hukou* and become urbanites. No wonder people would have mixed feelings about the *hukou* issue for a long time to come. Those who loved it, mainly urbanites with an inherent sense of superiority, saw the "non-agricultural" urban *hukou* as a natural shield that unabashedly protected their status and benefits. Those who hated it, mostly rural residents, saw it almost as an icon and sought it as though it were the goal of a lifetime. What was a shield for those who love it was a barrier for the ones who hated it. This may seem agreeable with the laws of life, but it is not consistent with the values of equality and justice that match the objective of social development. Some of the maladies of the *hukou* regulations are obvious. For example, without urban *hukou*, a rural maiden and an urban young man would balk at getting married because the *hukou* of their future children would have to stay with the future mom. If the husband was an urbanite and the wife a rural resident, their children would have to be "farmers," just like the mom. Since urban *hukou* is so precious, very few males would want to consider marrying rural girls. For this reason, urbanites and rural residents were pretty much segregated from marrying one another. The road to urban *hukou* through marriage was almost completely blocked as well.

In 1992, endorsement of a socialist market economy shifted China to the fast track of industrialization. The pace of urbanization accelerated and the flow of population rose to unprecedented scale. All other sub-systems attached to the *hukou* system gradually lost their original functions and the negative effects of the entire system were now fully exposed. The wall of *hukou* began to collapse.

No Return

In the 1990s, with the establishment of the socialist market economy, reform continued to advance into deep waters. Especially after 1992, the prices of grain and oil were liberalized, and food coupons and oil vouchers became history. Farmers were further let loose from their bondage to land, and they were able to migrate into cities with greater freedom. In 1992, the country's total floating population reached nearly 100 million, the majority of it being farmers. The outpouring of a huge floating population broke through the constraints of "leaving land without leaving the home village." A perimeter barrier between urban and rural households was finally opened up by the drive of market economy, and the pace of household registration reform quickened.

In March 1992, Chang Guiming and Wan Shouheng from Shanxi Province and other NPC deputies submitted to the NPC a proposal on reforming the decision-making process for "agricultural to non-agricultural *hukou* transfer." The motion mentioned that the then-existing policy of "agricultural to non-agricultural *hukou* transfer" had maladies that were not good for breaking the urban-rural dual structure. "The current *hukou* system is no longer able to control labor allocation or the scale of urban population. In cities and towns, especially in large cities, people actually living outside the *hukou* system have come to a considerable scale and have become an important part of the stably settled resident population," the motion pointed out. The deputies further suggested that "There should be planned guidance in revamping the existing *hukou* system and the *hukou* transfer policy. Farmers should be allowed to enter cities, and urbanites should be allowed to settle down in the countryside. Agricultural *hukou* should be permitted to convert to non-agricultural *hukou* and vice versa. Meanwhile, the Ministry of Public Security and other state departments should enact household registration laws." The motion also said that "The time for reforming the household registration system and for revamping the agricultural to non-agricultural *hukou* transfer has come. After more than a decade's reform, people are now mentally better prepared than ever before."[1]

Local authorities started acting by selling *hukou*. As far back as 1986, Qinlan Township in Anhui's Tianchang County (now Tianchang City) made it a rule that farmers who engaged in business or worked as skilled labor would have the right to settle down and live in Qinlan Town

1 Yin Zhijing and Yu Qihong: *China's Hukou Reform*, China University of Political Science and Law Press, 1996, p. 20.

On September 1, 2014, Guiyang City in Guizhou Province lifts the housing purchase ban on non-local *hukou* residents.

after paying an urban construction fee of 5,000 yuan per person. The effect was phenomenal. In two years, Qinlan Town's population grew from a thousand plus to nearly ten thousand. Later, researchers unanimously agreed that Qinlan Town was the pioneer of *hukou* reform centered on the commercialization of non-agricultural *hukou* in urban areas.

In 1992, with the change of the macro-environment, non-agricultural *hukou* transactions in urban areas became more heated and farmers developed a greater urge to make their way into cities for a better life, while local governments were motivated to handle such transactions because of the financial benefits involved. That year, *Jiangsu Economic Daily* carried a story on how farmers in a township were spending money to buy urban *hukou*. In August 1992, a total of 1,006 people in this township bought urban *hukou* at the cost of 12,000 yuan per person. A self-employed woman said when asked why she would want to buy *hukou*: "I ran a clothing store in town ever since I was a little girl. That year, I fell in love with Xiao Zhang, an urbanite who was being very nice to me even though his mom had a picky eye for me. I married Xiao Zhang any way, but troubles kept coming. The saddest part was when my son went to school, he got bullied. Some of his classmates called him 'little country pumpkin.' Slowly, I began to resent my rural *hukou* too. Ever since I bought this *hukou*, my home seems to have changed for the better, and my son never got bullied again. And, believe it or not, my mother-in-law started treating me like a friend too."[1]

According to estimates by departments of public security and finance, in 1992, total proceeds from *hukou* transactions in all parts of the country might have reached as much as RMB 24 billion (about 391.8 million USD today). Since the country's total fiscal revenue in

---

1 Yu Depeng: *Urban-Rural Society: From Separation to Opening*, Shandong People's Publishing House, 2001, p. 53.

1992 was RMB 418.897 billion (about 68.386 billion USD
today), the proceeds from *hukou* transactions accounted
for about 5.9 percent of the gross national revenue in the
same year.[1]

In October 1992, the Ministry of Public Security
issued a circular on adopting the locally valid urban
residency system. More than ten provinces, including
Guangdong, Zhejiang, Shandong, Shanxi and Hebei,
started using the "blue seal *hukou*" system one after another. The locally valid urban residency system provides:
"For urban *hukou* transferred from rural *hukou* on a payment basis, if such *hukou* holders meet the standards
for blue seal *hukou* and have all the needed paperwork,
they shall be granted blue seal *hukou*." This was de facto
legalization of *hukou* transactions. Today, there are different comments on this type of *hukou* transaction, but
it did play the role of breaking through the high-walled
hukou system. Further down the road, the blue seal *hukou*
practice found its way into some vanguard cities of reform, such as Shanghai, Tianjin, Shenzhen, Guangzhou,
Xiamen and Hainan. In February 1994, Shanghai issued
the Interim Rules Regarding Blue Seal *Hukou* Administration. The Rules provide that anyone who invests
RMB one million (about 163,252 USD today) or above

---

1 Yin Zhijing and Yu Qihong: *Household Registration Reform in China*, China
University of Political Science and Law Press, 1996, p. 14.

in Shanghai, or purchases real estate of a certain area, or has a fixed residence or lawful and stable employment, may all apply for blue seal *hukou* in Shanghai. After living for a certain period, such blue seal *hukou* holders may be converted to permanent residents. In August 1994, the Office of the Tianjin Municipal Government released the Interim Rules for Blue Seal *Hukou* Administration enacted by the city. The Rules provide that non-Tianjin residents who purchase commodity housing of specifically required value, those who make business investment of the required scale, and those who are special-talent employees in Tianjin may apply for blue seal *hukou*. Blue seal *hukou* holders are entitled to the same benefits as permanent Tianjin residents in terms of children's enrollment in school, higher education opportunities, etc. As one of China's municipalities, Tianjin has rich educational resources and high college admission rates, which is something many parents find attractive. This official document marked the unveiling of Tianjin's "new deal" of blue seal *hukou* in 20 years. This shows that a person's identity restrictions have been gradually replaced by market factors. Factors such as assets, technology, housing, and normal and steady income have become main elements of *hukou* migration. The essence of this policy is the use of money to fill up the gap of the urban and rural divide.

Wang Daiming (front left) and his family members in a subsidized rental apartment in Chongqing. Wang became a Chongqing citizen in April 2011, after working more than a decade in the city. He is working on buying the rental apartment the family is living in.

Developments of the situation also forced the central government to come up with ways to reform the *hukou* system. At the end of 1992, the State Council set up a *hukou* system reform document-drafting team under the Ministry of Public Security to go about researching and drafting plans for reforming the *hukou* system. The following year, the document-drafting team headed consecutively to different provinces for research and investigation. These provinces include Heilongjiang, Liaoning, Hebei, Anhui, Hubei, Hunan, Henan, Jiangsu, Zhejiang, Fujian, Sichuan, Guangdong, etc. In June 1993, the drafting team drafted a *hukou* system reform general plan, namely, a draft of the Decision of the State Council to Reform the *Hukou* System. The decision detailed the principles, objectives, and procedures of reform and set the goal of the reform as follows: "Abolish the dual system of agricultural and non-agricultural *hukou*, set up a uniform *hukou* system, follow the principle of *hukou* registration at residential place, list fixed lawful residential place, stable employment and/or sources of income as basic conditions for granting *hukou* status, and overhaul the current *hukou* migration policy." On the procedures of the *hukou* system reform, the decision stated as follows: "Household management is a large and complex system project. Overhaul of the *hukou* system must be coordinated with compatible, corresponding reform measures. A huge volume of work needs to be done in a well-planned, step-by-step manner." The decision specified that the overhaul will go in two phases. During the first phase of about three years, professional management structures will be established to administer rural *hukou* in the same way that urban *hukou* is being administered. All registration will be done using the uniform standard of the "People's Republic of China Residency." During the second phase, which ends at the end of this century, full integration of urban and rural *hukou* management will be realized through a legal management system consisting of laws and regulations governing household registration, migration, birth certificate and identity certificate management. Such a legal management system will be set up on the framework of the Household Registration Law of the People's Republic of China.[1]

Now it looks clear that the general plan for *hukou* system reform was overly optimistic in its grasp of the status quo and future circumstances. However, the way it responded to social concerns was commendable. Faced with the claim that "a bed in the city is better off than a house in a village," the government had nothing to offer except proactive reaction. As the saying goes, "No shot arrow is going to return." Each step of reform thereafter is going to be a catalyst for demolishing the urban-rural dual *hukou* structure.

In 1994, the government canceled the dual structure of agricultural and non-agricultural *hukou* based on the food rationing standard. A new standard based on residential place and occupation was used to differentiate agricultural *hukou* from non-agricultural *hukou*. Based on that, a new registration system based on permanent residency, temporary residency, and lodging residency was established. The main idea of the reform was the gradual adoption of an ID management system. In July 1996, a new *hukou* registration form and a new *hukou* booklet

---

1 Yin Zhijing and Yu Qihong: *Household Registration Reform in China*, China University of Political Science and Law Press, 1996, pp. 96-98.

were officially released for use. The new booklet reclassified "household types" into "family household" and "collective household," thus abolishing the former "agricultural" and "non-agricultural" classification. Since then, household registration has been in a position to truly reflect the actual residence status and identity status of citizens. In June 1997, the State Council further approved the Tentative Measures on the Reform of the Household Registration Management System in Small Cities and Towns and the Proposals for Improving the Rural Household Registration Management System prepared by the Ministry of Public Security. According to the new policy, rural *hukou* holders in small cities and towns who meet certain conditions may apply for long-term urban *hukou*. Such conditions include: lawful and stable non-agricultural employment and/or stable sources of income, plus a minimum of two years living in a fixed legal residence. Farmers granted approvals to settle down in small towns are entitled to the same treatment and benefits as original urbanites. This effectively paved the way for the practices of distinguishing urban and rural population by geographic region and distinguishing agricultural and non-agricultural population by occupation. In July 1998, the State Council approved the Ministry of Public Security's Proposals on Solving Some Ongoing Major Issues in *Hukou* Management. The proposals introduced up to four new *hukou* policies, including a voluntary approach to the choice of a newborn's *hukou*, a loosened policy in favor of spousal consortium, a policy providing flexibility for retired seniors to either return to their original place of employment or to their domiciles to join their spouses or children, and a policy granting *hukou* status to non-urban citizens and their immediate family members who invest in the host city. Meanwhile, the proposals emphasized that strict control would be imposed on Beijing, Shanghai and other megacities or large cities through specific policy measures. In July 1999, the Ministry of Personnel Affairs and the Ministry of Public Security once again issued a circular requiring that the problem of "special talent" married couples who live separately because of work be solved in a timely manner regardless of age, duration of separation or *hukou* quotas. Meanwhile, for megacities, emphasis was laid on relaxation on the basis of strict control. These household registration reform measures reflected the basic principles of humanitarianism and human rights by giving priority to societal migration. In June 2000, the State Council issued the Several Suggestions on Promoting the Healthy Development of Small Towns, proposing that farmers who have legal and fixed residence, stable gainful employment or sources of income in downtown county-level cities, county seats, and small towns and townships at or below county level can all transfer to urban *hukou*. In March 2001, the State Council approved the Ministry of Public Security's Proposal on

Promoting Reform of the Household Registration Management System in Small Cities and Towns. The Proposal clearly stated that quotas of *"hukou* transfer from agricultural to non-agricultural *hukou"* will be abolished in all of the country's towns and in the urban areas of county-level cities, and that all planned quota management would cease to exist. All non-local people who have legal permanent residence, stable gainful employment or sources of income may apply for permanent urban *hukou*. In May 2001, the state abolished the Certificate of Transfer of Rationed Food Supply for Urban Residents, marking the end of the food and oil rationing system that had accompanied *hukou* registration since August 1955.

In August 2001, the city of Shijiazhuang began to implement seven new provisions of household management, which would grant *hukou* status to the non-local citizens who: a) have worked a year or more as managers or professionals with special expertise, b) are contract workers who have worked for at least two years, c) have bought housing property in the urban area, invest in industrial enterprises and do business, d) college graduates and other graduates with advanced degrees who have been recruited by employers. In the same month, a new policy encouraging development in the west China region was put into practice in Urumqi. All people who have lawful fixed residence and stable income in Urumqi may apply for urban *hukou* upon payment of city maintenance fees.

The above-mentioned household registration reform measures were all part of a paced reform program geared toward establishing a market economy. It favored the fair, orderly and free flow of labor so as to push forward the urbanization process. From 1978 to 2000, the number of cities grew from 193 to 663, while designated towns rose from 2,173 to 20,312. Total urban population increased from 170 million to 456 million, or from 17.9% of the total population to 36.1%.[1]

This indicates that, as it marched into the 21st century, China had entered the stage of accelerated urbanization development and that the conditions of urbanization were gradually being met.

Strengthening of Top-level Design

In many ways, reform of the *hukou* system was cornered into acceleration by the urbanization process. However, the *hukou* system is a system of integrated nature whose reform involves redistribution of a broad and complex range of rights and interests. A revamp of the system necessitated gradual stripping of all other supple-

1 Fei Weiwei: "Urbanization's Focus on Small Cities and Towns," *Peoples' Daily*, August 7, 2001.

mentary systems, gradual elimination of the money-oriented factors of *hukou*, and restoration of its actual function of demographic management during the process of pushing for urbanization in the framework of a market economy. This is a gradual, step by step process in which the gaps in the dual social structure are filled. It involves an active but cautious approach toward *hukou* reform, and it means that all related planning and design have to be scientifically demonstrated to avert reversals. In many cities, household registration reform had to halt for lack of associated reform measures to withstand numerous benefits attached to *hukou*. The household registration reform undertaken in the city of Zhengzhou from 2001 to 2004 was a typical case of radical attempt.

Zhengzhou was not one of the early starters of the *hukou* system reform among large and medium cities in China, but the city was recognized for its thorough approach. On November 1, 2001, the Zhengzhou Municipal People's Government issued its Circular No. 13. The circular provided that from that day forth, family dependents, newborn babies, home buyers, investors and taxpayers, certain categories of employees, college graduates, etc. may all apply for Zhengzhou urban *hukou*. According to *Dahe Daily*, "During the first week after the new policy took effect, more than 10,000 people were registered as urban *hukou* holders."

Analysts believed that the backdrop of this policy had a lot to do with Zhengzhou's ambition to grow big. According to its plan, Zhengzhou had a population goal of reaching five million by 2020 so that it would be "on an equal footing" with Wuhan, Xi'an and other surrounding cities. At that time, Zhengzhou's urban population was less than two million. Relaxation of household registration so that outsiders could move in was a strategy adopted by Zhengzhou to "enlarge the contours of the city." According to a survey by the city's Public Security Bureau, from November 2001 to July 2003, Zhengzhou had an addition of 105,075 people, including 64,542 relatives of existing families.

Obviously not content with this pace, the city came up with a more liberal policy. In August 2003, the municipal government issued Circular No.19, providing that starting from August 22 that year, Zhengzhou would cancel the existing "agricultural *hukou*," "temporary *hukou*," "small-town *hukou*" and "non-agricultural *hukou*" and implement a uniform "Zhengzhou resident *hukou*."

"At the hotel where I work, we had a maximum of 16 service workers who applied for urban *hukou* in one day. We felt that everything was coming so abruptly, as if life would change completely by tomorrow." Swan Hotel waitress Zhang Juan said, "Before long, I suddenly realized Zhengzhou had a huge increase in population, especially during rush hours. February 7 Square would become so crowded that no vehicle could budge at all." She blamed the traffic jam on the new household registration policy.

Zheng Mingzhu, principal of Weiwu Road No. 1 Elementary School in Jinshui District, Zhengzhou City, apparently has a deeper understanding of the population boom. "We planned to enroll 300 students in six classes this year, but ended up enrolling 664. We had to add two more classes. Right now, each class has more than 80 students, and the largest class has 90 students. This is far too many!" The principal believes that the main reason for such pressure is the huge influx of school-age children after the *hukou* liberalization policy was put in place. "Our survey shows that after September 1 last year, when a more liberalized *hukou* policy took effect, 215 more students were enrolled as urban family dependents in the school district," Principal Zheng said.

The same school population "explosion" also occurred in 25 other elementary schools in the Jinshui School District. According to Wu Xuejun, director of the School District, more than 7,000 schoolchildren of migrant workers were enrolled all at once in Jinshui District last year. Those who came as "friends and relatives" were no less numerous than children of migrant workers, Wu said.

Guo Jinhan, deputy director of Zhengzhou Education Bureau, said that the influx of a large number of students into the urban area was a big toll on the city. Due to
lack of investment in education, the city has built no new
elementary schools at all in recent years, Guo said. As reported in *Zhengzhou Daily* on August 25, 2004, problems
of "small schools, crowded classroom and shortage of
funds" were prevalent.[1] Data from Zhengzhou's Public
Security Bureau show that after August 2003, the total
newly registered population reached 150,104. Among
these, 92,203 new urbanites obtained their *hukou* by joining their urban relatives, and 65% of them are schoolchildren at or below 18.

Meanwhile, public transport and social security failed
to keep pace with population growth. Take the public
transport card as an example. The city's original plan was
to issue 200,000 cards in three years. In reality, more than
800,000 cards were issued in just two years. Civil administration departments saw the impact too. Clerks in charge
of low-income insurance at the emergency and disaster
relief department of Zhengzhou's Bureau of Civil Affairs
say that more than 40,000 people in the city now enjoy

---

1 Liu Binglu and Tao Jianjie: "Vicissitudes in Zhengzhou's Three-year '*Hukou*
New Deal,'" *The Beijing News*, October 9, 2004.

low-income insurance benefits, as compared to just over 30,000 the year before. "After further *hukou* liberalization in August 2003, we felt the pinch and sought help from the municipal government, but we did not receive any reply. So right now we have temporarily suspended all applications for low-income insurance from all new urbanites."

So, in 2004, a year after declaring full liberalization of *hukou* registration, Zhengzhou City called a halt to the "*hukou* registration measure for friends and relatives of original urbanites" in order to "release pressure brought about by a sharp rise in population." The rationale was multi-faceted. With the accelerated pace of industrialization and urbanization, the city grew a lot both in geographic area and urban population, while social services like schools, hospitals and other public facilities fell behind. In short, there was a lack of forward-looking top-level design.

Regardless of all that, Zhengzhou's experiments made a lot of sense. In many cities, farmers who had obtained urban *hukou* would find that their status in term of children's education, health care, employment, etc. did not get upgraded. Keys to the city did not open the doors of urban citizenship benefits for them. On the other hand, original urbanites complained about the huge influx of farmers who were here to share their "cake" of welfare benefits. Other local governments who had taken larger strides in reform also found themselves in a dilemma: Relax urban *hukou* restrictions and you have a great inflow of rural population into the city, which increases the difficulty level of urban population management and taxes the city's capacity. Full liberalization of *hukou* would certainly bring about "overwhelming burdens" to the city.

Therefore, some experts pointed out that the very complexity of the issue was the reason why the reform of the *hukou* system made little progress or even reversed over the years. *Hukou* system reform involves redistribution of a very wide range of rights and interests. Technicalities from municipal governments and *hukou* administrative departments alone would not lead to the right path and program of reform. During NPC and CPPCC sessions in 2007, CPPCC member Yang Chunxing gave a speech titled "Speed up Reform of the *Hukou* System to Eliminate Institutional Barriers That Shackle Coordinated Development of Urban and Rural Areas." He believed that household registration reform had to be coupled with supporting policies befitting an economic society. Lack of cohesion between the two would void the *hukou* system reform, he said. The state should accelerate its pace of *hukou* system reform and explore and develop appropriate supporting policy measures. Public resources need to be enjoyed by all citizens, regardless of geographic location, identity or occupation. There should be equal share of rights and interests and responsibilities and obligations. Many people of insight also suggested that stipulation of the *hukou* system reform plan should involve the NPC and its standing committee because the *hukou* system concerns very important issues of civic rights. As a public policy, the *Hukou* system should be revamped on the basis of broad consensus of the general public and not carried out by the relevant departments "behind closed doors."[1]

Just as the experts have said, technicalities from municipal governments and *hukou* administrative departments alone would not lead to the right path and program of reform. The knot has to be untied by the one who tied it. The Chinese *hukou* system has been a top-level national design from day one. Today, as we push for *hukou* system reform, the government's top-level design clearly cannot be found missing. On the contrary, it has to be reinforced.

The 2010 Shanghai World Expo, with the theme of "Better City, Better Life," showcased humanity's dream and expectations for future urban life. As the world's largest urbanizer, China has a clear urbanization goal. Since the convening of the 16th CPC National Congress in

---

1 Shi Guosheng: "Icebreakers in China's *Hukou* System Reform," *People's Daily,* May 9, 2007.

A kindergarten at Nanjie Village, Linying County, Henan Province, January 12, 2012. By the end of 2011, Henan's urban population has surpassed 40 million.

2002, for the first time, the ruling party set "acceleration of the urbanization process" as its priority task. By 2007, the 17th CPC National Congress further set its goal of realizing "industrialization, IT application, urbanization, marketization and globalization." However, neither of the congresses made any mention of *hukou* system reform. Under the guidance of the "urbanization" strategy, China's urbanization during the "11th Five-year Plan" (2006-2010) saw rapid development. As of 2009, its urban population reached 620 million or an urbanization rate of 46.6%. Whether in terms of annual net increase or total urban population, China's urbanization scale has long been in the world's leading position. China's total urban population is twice that of the United States, and 25% higher than the population of all EU-27 put together.

Fast-track urbanization served as a spearhead of household registration reform. In 2011, the General Office of the State Council issued a Circular on the Active and Steady Promotion of the *Hukou* Management System. The National Development and Reform Commission, the Ministry of Human Resources and Social Security and other relevant departments issued supporting policies, 18 provinces (including autonomous regions and municipalities) gave specific proposals for implementation and 14 provinces (including autonomous regions and municipalities) established uniform *hukou* registration systems. Thus, a preliminary channel was opened up for agricultural population to settle down in urban areas. According to a survey by the Ministry of Public Security, from 2010 to 2012, 25.05 million of the country's total rural population was resettled in urban areas, which meant an average of 8.35 million per year.[1]

The 18th CPC National Congress held in 2012 proposed that the country would "adhere to the new path of industrialization, IT application, urbanization and agricultural modernization with Chinese characteristics." For

1 Xu Shaoshi: "State Council Report on Urbanization Construction During the Third Session of the Standing Committee of the 12th National People's Congress" on June 26, 2013, www.npc.gov.cn, June 27, 2013.

the first time in the Party's history, the issue of household registration reform was directly put on agenda. The Congress requested accelerated reform of the *hukou* system, gradual urbanization of rural population and provision of basic urban social services to all permanent residents. Thus, *hukou* system reform has become part of a systemic top-level design. The will of the central government is clear and firm. In November 2013, the Third Plenary Session of the 18th CPC Central Committee issued a Decision on Some Major Issues Concerning Comprehensively Continuing the Reform, which called for improving the system and mechanism for the healthy development of urbanization. The decision gave clear instructions on household registration reform: "Accelerate reform of the *hukou* system, completely lift registration restrictions in towns and small cities, gradually relax restrictions in medium cities, decide the criteria for resettlement in large cities in a reasonable way and strictly control the population size of megacities."

Underneath this top-level design, local authorities also readjusted the direction of *hukou* system reform. On May 31, 2014, the city of Tianjin put an end to the "blue seal *hukou*" through which non-local residents obtained *hukou* by buying commodity housing, establishing or investing in businesses, or through stable employment. Thus, the "blue seal *hukou*" policy that had been in practice in Tianjin for about two decades was replaced by a new, more equitable accumulated points system.

On June 30, 2014, a CPC Political Bureau meeting approved the Proposal for Further Promoting *Hukou* System Reform. The meeting noted that accelerating reform of the *hukou* system is an important measure involving hundreds of millions of migrant agricultural population. Emphasis was put on adhering to the guideline of an active, steady, orderly and normalized approach, respecting the will of the people, and abstaining from quota allocation or having strings attached to policies. According to the proposal, priority will be given to those who have had long-term employment in the city, those with strong job skills, and those who can adapt to a competitive life in urban areas so that they and their family members can settle down permanently in town. The end of the measures is orderly distribution of population. Chen Xiwen, Deputy Director of the Central Rural Work Leading Group, said that the proposal was approved in principle after being examined and discussed in four sessions and that it would be publicized pending further revision. Chen further said that the proposal laid out three principles: 1) priority will be given to clearing up the "inventory" of urban *hukou* applicants who have lived in town for longer time. Next, take a steady approach towards cases of newly added applicants; 2) implement the policy of differentiated resettlement for different types of cities; 3) urbanization does not mean everyone will settle down in town. The resident ID system will continue to exist for a long time to come. The right to free migration will be given to the masses in a step-by-step manner. Chen Xiwen argues that the reform of the *hukou* system cannot be done overnight and that it's not just a matter of changing the *hukou* booklet either. Four problems have to be solved in order to attract agricultural transfer population into urban areas, namely, constant provision of employment opportunities and solution of migrant workers' problems of housing, social security, and children's education.[1]

Police working on *Hukou* booklets, Yuncheng City, Shanxi Province, July 30, 2014. The day marked the beginning of the phase-out of the urban-rural dual household registration system which had been in existence for more than half a century.

1 Lin Yuan: "Chen Xiwen Says *Hukou* System Reform Proposal Will Be Released Soon," *Economic Information*, July 7, 2014.

As can be seen, the top-level design for household registration reform after the 18th CPC National Congress focused on a household registration policy that features differentiation and classification. Because there are major differences between cities of different size, China has to take different approaches in *hukou* system reform. Megacities like Beijing, Shanghai and Guangzhou have limited loading capacity and are already overloaded. So, strict population control has to be exercised over them. For large cities, *hukou* access policies with some sort of threshold can be adopted for selective *hukou* system reform. A typical example would be to convert rural migrant population into urban citizens through the resident ID system. For medium cities, the policy can be orderly lifting of resettlement restrictions. Small cities and designated towns can provide full *hukou* access.

This is the direction of China's current *hukou* system reform. The effect of this program is still to be tested, and the test result is something we look forward to seeing.

Chapter Four
Urbanization of Farmers

After its founding in 1949, the PRC put in place a highly centralized planned economy that nailed a multitude of farmers to their farmland. At some points of time, they had to obtain letters of recommendation from the production brigades they belonged to before they went to visit cities. Since the economic reform that began in 1978, Chinese farmers have started flowing into cities with relative freedom, pushing up wave after wave of migrant workers. Some of these migrant workers chose to settle down in the city to lead a decent life just like the urbanites. Others chose to return to the root of their home. In order to achieve modernization, China has to move a considerable size of its rural population into cities and convert them into urban citizens. This means that in the process of social economic development, through the work of industrialization and urbanization, traditional farmers complete their conversion to urban citizenry in terms of occupation, identity, thinking, lifestyle, etc.[1] Urbanization of farmers is first and foremost urbanization of migrant workers.

---

1 Shan Jingjing: *Studies on the Urbanization of Migrant Workers*, Social Sciences Academic Press, 2012, p. 25.

Surging Tides of Migrant Workers

The large-scale population migration and urbanization that began in the 1980s is one of the events that has made a far-reaching impact on China's economy and society ever since the initiation of the policy of reform and opening up. According to a 2013 national survey on migrant workers released by the National Bureau of Statistics, China had a total of 268.94 million migrant workers in 2013, representing an increase of 6.33 million (or 2.4%) over the previous year. Most of these people were in the age range between 20 and 40. On the one hand, migrant workers are injecting tremendous vim and vigor into the urban economy; on the other hand, they are making a huge impact on urban life with their mixed sense of bewilderment, disorderliness and agitation. Their unstoppable power is evidently changing the outlook of the Chinese society and economy and writing new chapters of the country's future.

All this started with the reform policy that was adopted more than three decades ago. At the Third Plenary Session of the 11th CPC Central Committee held in December 1978, China decided to shift the focus of its work to building socialist modernization and paved the way for the economic reform that first took place in rural areas. The rural reform was so successful that the country became self-sufficient in food supply and basically solved the nation's problem of food and clothing in a matter of five years. Backed by a government policy that encouraged entrepreneurship, newly rich farmers began exploring different ways of doing business. Because grain production was growing too fast, grain became a hard sell for the first time in history, and the industrial structure in rural areas had to be readjusted. One of the measures taken was to use 70 million hectares of land to produce economic crops. This kind of readjustment stimulated the growth of the rural processing industry. Village and township enterprises began to mushroom, and tens of millions of freed-up rural laborers flooded to them, pushing up the first "tidal wave of migrant workers" across the country. According to statistical data, village and township enterprises absorbed a total of over 100 million migrant workers in the 1980s. The first "wave of migrant workers" rolling toward village and township enterprises can be summarized as "leaving the farmland but not the village and entering factories but not cities." As vital competitors, rural enterprises caused a lot of stir to the planning departments. In 1988, a panic buying spree and bank run occurred. When the state adopted a policy of currency tightening, village and township enterprises bore the brunt of the shock. By the early 1990s, after losing financial backing from the government, such enterprises

Jinan Railway Station in Shandong Province during the first day of the Spring Festival Rush on January 7, 2004. About 40,000 passengers departed from the station that day, marking the growth of more than 10,000 people over previous days. Most of these passengers are migrant workers returning to their home city.

went downhill, and their ability to absorb labor was significantly compromised. The first tide of migrant workers ebbed away.

In 1992, Deng Xiaoping gave important speeches known as the "southern tour talk" as he took a southern inspection tour of Shenzhen, Zhuhai and other cities, encouraging local officials to keep their commitment to deepened reform. The published speeches heightened the national morale, and the central leadership was in for a new and faster round of reform and development.

Local governments responded by establishing economic development zones that generated numerous manufacturing jobs. A second wave of 40 million migrant workers swept across the country. In contrast to the first wave of migrant workers, who were targeting neighboring villages and townships, the majority of the second wave was now heading into opportunity-laden medium and large cities. The transit system was so overloaded with people that special trains for migrant workers had to be arranged. Inside such special trains, you would see people everywhere: in the luggage racks, down under the seats, any corners or crevices available. In order to avoid serious accidents, some provinces simply blocked migrant workers from entry. Swamped by this unstoppable tide of dream seeking and shackled by the restrictions of the *hukou* system, the cities typically resorted to a policy of "economic absorption but social exclusion." Migrant workers remained marginalized in the city. Consequently, urbanization of migrant workers did not materialize in the 1990s.

Later in the 1990s, with the return of Hong Kong to Chinese sovereignty, a great many manufacturing enterprises in Hong Kong, Macao, and Taiwan moved into Guangdong Province. Cheap labor, quality infrastructure and huge consumption potential also turned China's coastal areas into new bases of international manufacturing businesses. These factors contributed to the rise of the third "wave of migrant workers." Every year, right after the Spring Festival, southbound migrant workers converged at Guangzhou Railway Station before heading to factories in different parts of Guangdong Province. It was common for passengers to line up and wait for up to an hour for a chance to get into the restrooms. From then on, the number of migrant workers in the cities began to rise steadily and continuously. In 1992, the cities had a migrant worker population of 46 million; by 1994, it grew to 60 million. Thereafter, that number began to increase at the rate of eight to ten million on annual basis.

Transfer of surplus rural labor in the 21st century is continuing in tempo with the pace of economic development. In recent years, new characteristics emerged in the pattern of total growth. One trend is that the growth rate and growth speed of local rural workers are surpassing those of outgoing migrant workers. In 2013, for example, the population of local migrant workers grew by 3.59 million, or 3.6%, which is 850,000 or 1.9% more than outgoing migrant workers. This means more and more rural transfer labor is being employed locally. The other trend is that the growth rate in the total number of rural workers is continually falling. Growth rates in 2011, 2012 and 2013 went down 1.0, 0.5 and 1.5 percentage points, respectively, over the previous year. These two trends show that, on the one hand, the government's reinforced support for the development of the central and western regions, plus inter-regional transfer of industries aimed at upgrading during economic restructuring, gave a formidable impetus to economic growth in central and western regions and effectively alleviated the shortage of employment opportunities for surplus agricultural labor in those regions. On the other hand, the two phenomena show that, with the peaking of the work-age population in China and with the increased resettlement of transferred agricultural population in cities and towns, rural surplus labor supply will soon witness a turning point.

The "tidal waves of migrant workers" are major events in the history of contemporary social development in China. Born with industrialization and urbanization, it broke through decades of a watertight urban-rural split and brought about a revolutionary impact on the entire social structure. It involves the choice of paths to China's modernization drive and, in a sense, it is impacting the country's future development. The "tidal waves of migrant workers" were small steps toward urbanization through the farmers' change of identity.

The Dream of Settling Down in the City

It's now dark, but I don't want to leave
Seated atop the skyscraping scaffold looking

I fancy how the urbanites in this metropolis

are walking, hastening homebound

I count the streets and lanes recalling

every spring, summer, fall, and winter I've been through

As I ponder in the darkness all by myself

A dream began budding in the bottom of my heart

It's the dream of a home in the city

Don't you mock at me, I mean what I say

even though in your eyes, my dream seems crazy

Nothing in my mind is blocking

that dream of a home in this city

for her and me, so that we may quit wandering

I will fight for it, for that is my dream

I trust that shore of happiness

I will certainly reach

This is a song expressing migrant workers' common wish of "settling down in the city."

"Never think those arriving with trolley suitcases are the same type of people as those who arrived carrying PVC bags on their shoulders in the old days. They would rather starve to death than leave the coastal cities," Tang Renjian, a scholar who has been tracking rural issues, said. A survey done by the China Youth Research Center confirmed what Tang was saying: Some new features began to appear among the third wave of migrant workers. They

December 1,
2010, rural
migrant band Xu
Ri Yang Gang in
performance

are more poised to long-term stay in the cities rather than short-term. In fact, they try to stay as long as possible, and they want to have their whole family migrated there. This "new generation of migrant workers," with next to zero farming experience, is more identified with the city than with the countryside. As their consciousness of upholding their rights awakens, they began to resort to law

Human resources market, Yiwu, Zhejiang Province, February 16, 2013. Huang Yusong and his two friends did not go home for the Chinese New Year holidays. They stayed in order to get a better job.

and public opinion to protect their rights and interests. Meanwhile, migrant workers of new generation are living in a social environment where their tremendous contribu-

Jia Xiangfeng, a
new generation
migrant worker,
from Zhaotong,
Yunnan Province,
working on a
shoe assembly
line in Hangzhou,
Zhejiang
Province, on
February 17,
2013

tion to economic development is being recognized. They
are seen as "relevant interests" of modernization, rather
than mere bystanders. According to survey data, half of
these people want to settle in the cities.

Yang Xutian from Linyi, Shandong Province, has
been working in the Zhejiang city of Fuyang for six
years. He wants to "have a home" in Fuyang not just
because he can afford it, but also because he is not used
to living in his home village any more. Conditions in
the village can't compare to those of Fuyang, Yang said.
The village roads are all dirt roads that would turn his
leather shoes gray within hours. The only restroom, lo-

cated in the backyard, is not easily accessible at night because it's so dark out there he'd have to use a flashlight. Furthermore, there are even gaps in communication. He and his friends and relatives can hardly find common topics of conversation. He is surprised so many of his former classmates would feel bad about having a baby girl instead of a baby son. When Yang talked about the financial crisis and financial bottlenecks for private enterprises, his friends showed no interest at all. Yang is currently looking for an apartment with a floor space of about 90 square meters. "Once I get that, I would have a real home here in Fuyang," he said.

A lot of the migrant workers in town are easily satisfied. They often say, "We'll be fine as long as we have a place to sleep in." West Dawang Road, a central business area between East Third Ring Road and the East Fourth Ring Road in Beijing, is lined up with numerous landmarks of high-end shopping centers, apartments and office buildings. People bustling through here are all well-dressed. They would hardly know that just 500 meters from the city's most luxurious commercial district is a "village within the city." Trash cans at the intersection are reeking. Potholes of waste water and grease make the roads wet and slippery. Low bungalows crammed on the sides of a one-meter-wide path host dozens of households. Doors with faded paint, brick walls with cracked and bubbled plaster ready to peel off, windows all covered up in dust – a perfect picture of decrepitude. Behind the bungalows stand a public latrine shared by dozens of households. Liu Hongyan from Xiantao, Hubei Province, has been living here since she came to work in Beijing in 2003. She and her husband plus two children live in a room of about 20 square meters. Liu said that her house with an outer and inner room "can be counted as relatively big." The outer room (the kitchen) has a cooking stand, a sink and a small dinner table; while the inner room (bedroom) contains two beds placed side by side and a small clothes cabinet in a corner. No other furniture. Such a tiny, shabby house costs her a monthly rent of 1,000 yuan (about 160 USD). Surveys reveal that, except for construction workers who work on building sites, most of the migrant workers in town choose to rent housing as close as possible to their workplaces. The houses they rent are often located in nooks and crannies of prosperous downtown areas. The cabins they live in are often less than 20 square meters. In "villages of the city" of this type, houses or apartments rented by migrant workers commonly lack basic sanitation facilities. Some don't even have water supply and sewage systems. They typically share public water taps, public baths and public latrines. As a matter of fact, "villages of the city" inhabited by low-income migrant workers are now turning into "quasi-slums." Chen Qiang, a construction worker from

Shaoxing, Zhejiang Province, August 14, 2014. Migrant workers taking a break outside a mobile plank house they rent at a daily fee of about one dollar

Anyang, Henan Province, told a reporter that it is impossible to find stable housing without a stable job. He could not afford being too picky about housing. "Though I am working here today, I have no idea where I will be after this. I could leave Beijing at any time," he said.[1]

In fact, during multiple tides of urbanization in more than three decades, through efforts of their own, some migrant workers have already set roots in the city. Though they do not have urban *hukou*, they have become home and car owners living a decent life in the city. The kinds

1 Wang Wei and Wang Zhiyi: "Migrant Workers' Dream of a Home in Town," *People's Daily*, October 27, 2011.

Nanning City, Guangxi, August 21, 2014. A migrant worker takes a break in a makeshift residence under a bridge. Average monthly income per capita of China's 269 million migrant workers is estimated to be around 417 US dollars.

of worries they have are utterly different from those of the newcomers. Their top concern is their children's education because a lot of the existing policies are keeping children of migrant workers out of the urban school system. Secondarily, they are faced with the problem of cultural integration. They need acceptance from their neighbors, and they need to follow the code of conduct befitting their citizenship. These are problems encountered by migrant workers on a daily basis – problems that beg of being solved as quickly as possible.

Of course, there is a small number of migrant workers who do not wish to stay in the city, especially small and medium cities far away from their home villages. In 2003, Huai'an City of Jiangsu Province introduced a policy that hardly set any limits on migrant workers who want to settle down in town. However, so far, the city has not yet received any *hukou* applications from any migrant workers. One main reason is that they simply cannot accept the rule that they have to forfeit the land in their home villages once they get the urban *hukou*. Sun Zhiguo, an interior decorator in Beijing, said: "I am now doing decoration in Beijing. The money I make can be used to buy a house in my hometown. My parents can take care of the fields while I provide for their daily needs. Owning a house in my hometown does not put me to any inconvenience. The *hukou* papers are of no use to me." He said that even if he had no way of taking care of the land, he could still rent it to someone else and earn an income of about a thousand yuan per *mu* per year. Qu Quanfu from Henan Province says that it only costs him between 80 and 100 yuan (13-16 USD) to participate in the new rural cooperative health care system in his hometown. If he were to settle down in town, he would have to spend three to four hundred yuan (about 48 to 64 USD) a month just to pay for his pension plans. School enrollment for his children is another big headache. "City life is too much stress. We come to town mainly to make money to buy a house or start a small business in our hometown. *Hukou* in a large city like Beijing is attractive, but we wouldn't want to lose the land in our hometown just for *hukou* in a small city," Qu Quanfu said. Qu added that older migrant workers like him feel that they are not accustomed to city life. He doesn't like taking off his shoes right before entering a room. Other inconveniences include lack of a sense of neighborhood and having no one to talk to. He sees no point getting a *hukou* in town because he wouldn't be entitled to low-income insurance or free health care any way. He feels that he is a better fit for the countryside.[1] This in fact reflects the absence of urban public service functionality. Cities should not just focus on their own need for migrant workers to contribute to GDP growth. In order to retain migrant workers in the city, authorities need to do more to improve public services and provide workers with adequate benefits and protection.

Improving the Quality of Life for Migrant Workers

In November 2012, the Report to the 18th CPC National Congress made it clear that China would "push for citizenship for the agricultural transfer population in an orderly manner." Urbanization of migrant workers has become a basic public policy. Local governments at all

---

1 Che Hui: "Loosened *Hukou* Shackle in Second and Third Tier Cities Unlikely to Retain Migrant Workers," *Workers Daily*, Dec. 1, 2011.

levels are actively exploring ways to absorb migrant workers so that urbanization would become a reality.

Guangdong Province started the "Accumulated
Point System for *Hukou* Registration" as early as June
2010. The province's Zhongshan City used this system
very well. In Zhongshan, migrant workers accumulate
points through academic credentials, social security
payments, real estate purchases, investment, and contributions to social services to compete for urban *hukou*
quotas. On December 10, 2012, Qiu Baoxin from Zao-
zhuang, Shandong Province, accumulated 189.5 points
in three years, which is 59.5 points more than what is required to become a citizen in the city where he has been
working for 13 years. "It's a surreal surprise," Qiu said.
In 1999, Qiu started working in a Taiwanese company
located in the Torch Development Zone in Zhongshan.
In 2004, he bought an apartment in the zone with borrowed money. He and his wife had a baby son in the
same year. "As a double income couple with a place of
our own, we could send our son to a private kindergarten and live a comfortable life," Qiu said. Qiu and his
wife did not see the value of *hukou* until it was about
time for his son to go to school. He had learned that
a co-worker of his who had no Zhongshan *hukou* had
no choice but to send his two kids to a very expensive
private school. "He has to pay 10,000 yuan (about 1,600

On January 18, 2012, Li Huicheng became a documented Guangdong citizen through the accumulated point system, after working about 20 years in Guangzhou.

USD) per child per year," Qiu said. Fortunately, in 2010, Zhongshan City initiated the accumulated point system for public school enrollment and *hukou* registration. Qiu decided to apply. Qiu had made a total score of 67 then, which was higher than the 50 point threshold for his son's school enrollment, but was about 40 points short for *hukou* registration (the threshold was 103 points). Although he failed to get his *hukou* at first try, his son's qualification for public school enrollment through the accumulated point system gave him a lot of hope. So he made a commitment to donate blood every year and even joined his company's voluntary fire-fighting service team. Through these social services he earned 40 additional points. By 2012, his wish was finally fulfilled. In fact, every year after that, Zhongshan City would amend its policy by increasing the basic points for each standard so that the threshold for *hukou* registration would be lowered. In 2012 alone, 2,540 people were found qualified for *hukou* registration.

Tianjin adopted the Residence Permit System. On September 23, 2013, the Tianjin Municipal Government issued the Interim Measures for Residence Permit Management in Tianjin City and the Table of Standards for Accumulated Points Governing Issuance of Tianjin Residence Permits and the Associated Score Value. The Measures provides that January 1, 2014 to December 31, 2015 will be the trial period for implementing a new residence permit management policy governing non-local population. The existing temporary residence permit system will be abolished. The new system will follow the principle of "residence permit + accumulated points access + total quota," namely, the residence permit system will be used to manage the incoming non-local population, while the accumulated point system will be used to select those non-locals who wish to settle down as Tianjin citizens. A total quota will be set to put a lid on the annual number of new households. Residence permit holders will be entitled to housing, education, social security, health care and other public services. The Interim Measures encourage young, educated, highly skilled and established personnel to work, set up businesses and

On September 5, 2014, Taihe District Junior Vocational College in Jinzhou, Liaoning Province. A few new generation migrant workers are receiving skill training in automobile repairs and maintenance.

permanently settle down in Tianjin. Shen Jian, a migrant worker from Jiangsu Province, said: "The accumulated point *hukou* system made it possible for us to settle down in a large city. We have a greater sense of home now because our temporary residence permits have been replaced by residence permits." In 2014, the total quota of residence permits for migrant workers was within the 20,000 range. The "accumulated point residence permit system" pried open long-term restrictions on the access of migrant workers to *hukou* status in the megacity. It will effectively attract to Tianjin younger and better talents in more diversified industries.

Chongqing maintains that farmers may have urban

hukou while retaining their farmland. In August 2010, Chongqing kicked off its household registration system reform, focusing on obtaining *hukou* for migrant workers and their younger generation. What's new about this reform is that it is clearly specified that farmers may retain their land rights and interests in their hometown while applying for *hukou* in the city. Such rights and interests include contracted land, homestead, woodlands, titles attached to land and various agricultural policy benefits. Prior to the household registration reform, Chongqing's urbanization rate among its permanent resident population was 53%, while its urbanization rate in registered household population was only 20-plus percentage points, which does not reflect the actual level of urbanization. A large number of migrant farmers have been doing business in town for many years. They have lived, worked and acted as part of the city for years, and many of them do not intend to return to farming in the countryside. If they do not transfer to urban *hukou*, they will not be entitled to pension, health care, housing, education and other benefits in the city and, compared with urban residents, they will end up paying more for their children's schooling, medical care, pension, and other things closely connected to the quality of life. The purpose of Chongqing's household registration system reform is to let migrant workers who have housing and income in the city keep living there with greater peace of mind. The city of Chongqing made it clear that as farmers transfer their *hukou* into the city, they may keep their land in the countryside. They will not have to trade land for *hukou* or social security. Will their land left behind be abandoned or laid waste after *hukou* transfer? The answer is no because the city has made corresponding policy changes. Farmers who have had *Hukou* transfer are not allowed to have their land go to waste. They may either let professional land cooperatives manage their land and share the proceeds by mutual agreement or they may rent it to larger contractors for rental income. Those who voluntarily give up their contracted land have two ways of exit: 1) transfer once for all to other village members or any other farmers willing to join the relevant villages or communities. The price of transfer will be determined by the law of supply and demand. 2) give back to the relevant collective economic organization. The city further provides that farmers may retain their homestead and farm houses after *hukou* transfer. For farmers who transfer their entire family's *hukou* into the city and who willingly quit their homesteads, the city would dispose of them using the "land ticket" method. In 2008, Chongqing started establishing the first land exchange in China. After reclamation of rural collective land used for construction, a "land ticket" tradable in the rural land exchange will be issued to the relevant farmer. Proceeds from such "land tickets" will be fully used to benefit farmers, farming, and rural areas. Currently, a one-*mu* "land ticket" in Chongqing can sell for more than 100,000 yuan (about 16,000 USD), which can be used by the relevant farmer as capital for migrating to the city.

At the entrance-end of the *hukou* system reform in the city, through budget increase and consolidation of social resources, Chongqing put its emphasis on the integrated reform of guaranteed housing, pension insurance, health insurance, minimum living standard, and training of rural migrants who have just obtained urban *hukou*. After farmers are transferred into "new urban citizens," they will be endowed with "civic rights" entitling them to pension plans, health care, affordable housing, employment and other benefits and services that regular urbanites enjoy. Take affordable housing system as an example. As the focus of Chongqing's transfer population, migrant workers with favorable conditions will be incorporated into the city's affordable housing system the moment they arrive in the city. As for public rental housing, in the next decade, Chongqing will build public rental housing with a total floor space of up to 40 million square meters. Such housing will be mainly for the "new urban citizens" and new college graduates who have not yet settled down in the city. In order to provide for school enrollment of the children of "new urban citizens," Chongqing will build

115 elementary and high schools. Newly converted urban citizens whose children are entitled to free public education will be admitted as near their primary residence as possible. They will not have to follow the old practice of going to designated schools. Liu Jian, whose home village is Xuxi Village, Changyuan Street in Rongchang County, works with his wife at a motorcycle assembly plant in the county seat. In 2010, the whole family transferred into the city and bought an apartment in the county seat. Their daughter could attend the nearest public school for free. The couple could also enjoy higher standard employee pension plans and health insurance than employees of urban enterprises enjoy. After *hukou* transfer, Liu Jian voluntarily let go of his old house and homestead in his home village and received 66,700 yuan (about 10,672 USD) in compensation. After paying his mother's pension premium of 41,000 yuan (about 6,560 USD), he still had a balance of 25,700 yuan (about 4,112 USD). Now, Liu's mother is receiving a monthly pension of more than 500 yuan. "Reform is not to deprive farmers of their basic rights and interests, nor is it to let them go homeless and fall into 'slums' that emerge in the cities. The government's wholesale large budget for social security and public services is meant to let farmers march into the city with dignity and wealth. This is not just meant to affirm their identity and status, but also to respect and protect the basic rights of these new urban citizens." Since the

implementation of reform of the household registration system, Chongqing has taken the lead in forming a sound and integrated policy system for the reform and has issued more than 30 policy documents in areas of social security, education and health care. Through systematic regulations, the migrated farmers can enjoy the same treatment as other urban citizens. Their employment, social security, housing, children's education and health care are all incorporated into the urban security network. As a result, their quality of life in terms of school enrollment, employment, health care, pension and housing is significantly improved.

Lauded by the media as the "most pro-migrant-worker city," Hangzhou has done a lot of work to promote the urbanization of migrant workers. In 2005, the city issued Several Proposals on Providing Favorable Living and Working Conditions for Migrant Workers, which specifies that within five years migrant workers and local residents shall have the "same treatment." All migrant workers will be called "incoming workers." On the streets of Hangzhou, you can easily see billboards saying "People from Lishui, Quzhou, Jiangxi and Guangdong are all part of Hangzhou," which express warm and friendly feelings toward migrant workers from across the country. The city's administrators say that the new title of "incoming workers" denotes respect for and recognition of the value of migrant workers. On the other hand, it implies that migrant workers are future masters of the city.[1]

Although China's urbanization level has surpassed 50%, numerous problems remain to be solved. Most strikingly, with a relatively low citizenship conversion rate, migrant workers in general are still in a "semi-urbanized" state. This is mainly reflected in two ways. First of all, there is little room for optimism about the overall living conditions of migrant workers. Typical problems include unstable employment, low-income that barely makes ends meet, spending which is limited to daily necessities and rental housing and lack of social security. Second, current migrant workers are scarcely merged into the city, and their rate of conversion to citizenship is low. Third, there are still serious flaws in the design of the current system that affect migrant workers' conversion to citizenry. Fourth, although the *hukou* threshold for migrant workers is gradually lowering, the cost threshold is going up on a daily basis. In the coming decades, if China were to continue to promote urbanization of farmers, we would first and foremost need to accelerate reform of the household registration system and build an integrated urban and rural labor market. Next, we would need to

---

1 Shan Jingjing: *Studies on the Urbanization of Migrant Workers*, Social Sciences Academic Press, 2012, p. 159.

promote full employment of migrant workers and lay the economic foundation for the urbanization of migrant workers. Thirdly, we would need to improve our social security system and relieve migrant workers of their burden of worries about an uncertain future. Finally, we would need to create new ways of managing incoming migrant population and reconstruct the social network of migrant workers. Urbanization of migrant workers still has a long way to go!

Chapter Five
Distribution of Proceeds from Value-added Land

Land is a farmer's sanctuary, the source of his livelihood and the base from which he expands his horizon. The land issue is an extremely complicated one, a sticking point of which is distribution of proceeds from value-added land. Upon its founding in 1949, the PRC, in efforts to convert China from an agricultural country into an industrial one in an expedited manner so as to complete the process of modernization smoothly, borrowed the Soviet model of development and established a dual system of urban-rural economy and adopted a development strategy in which agriculture served industry and the countryside supported cities. In this model of development, the government monopolized the primary land market and made land an instrument of the drive for development. The result was the formation of a distribution system of value-added land proceeds centered in cities.

Under the traditional planned economy, the land system established through rural reform supported the fast advance of industrialization and urbanization as well as the continuous expansion of the national economy. However, a land-based economic development model evolved out of this growth. And this model was soon to manifest, in an increasingly serious manner, incoordination, irregularity, and unsustainability. Apart from providing administrative and municipal services, local governments must also promote economic development and create employment opportunities in their jurisdictions. On the spur of local governments, a low-efficiency land transfer model emerged in China. As extra-budgetary revenue from land transfers gradually became a major part of the local governments' gross fiscal revenue, farmers paid the price of losing their land and becoming victims of social injustice.[1]

Fortunately, in recent years, the Chinese government gradually recognized the drawbacks of the "land for development" model, and as a remedy, took an important measure of reform through empowerment of land rights and redistribution of value-added land proceeds. The Decision on Certain Major Issues Concerning Comprehensively Continuing the Reform, passed at the Third Plenary Session of the 18th CPC Central Committee, requested the establishment of a mechanism for distribution of proceeds from value-added land on condition that it complied with planning and usage control regulations. Such a mechanism must take into account a combination of national, collective and individual interests, bring about a reasonable increase in personal income, and optimize the secondary market of land leasing, land transfer and land mortgages. These provisions are meant to deal with the key issues of China's current land system. At present, the government's urbanization plan for the next decade is providing a new window of opportunity for deepening land management system reform.

---

1 Development Research Center of the State Council and World Bank: *China: Promotion of Efficient, Inclusive and Sustainable Urbanization*, China Development Press, 2014, Beijing.

Termination of the
"Land for Development" Model

During its last decade of strategic opportunities, China managed to propel high economic growth and rapid industrialization and urbanization. Such achievement can be attributed to a number of factors. The first factor was ample supply of land that served to guarantee economic growth. Between 2003 and 2012, the country's total annual supply of state-owned land for construction grew from 286,400 to 690,400 hectares, at an annual average growth rate of 10.27%. The second factor was the low cost of land for industrial use that served to guarantee the rapid advance of industrialization. Between 2000 and 2012, comprehensive land prices, commercial land prices and residential land prices grew by an annual average rate of 10.04%, 11.40% and 14.42%, respectively, while annual average growth rate of industrial land prices stopped at 3.35%, which is far below that of commercial and residential land. Thirdly, land expansion and land capitalization promoted urbanization. Between 2000 and 2012, the urban built area more than doubled, and revenue from land transfer increased by 45 times. By 2012, loans through land mortgage financing in 84 major cities reached RMB 5.95 trillion (about USD 0.95 trillion), becoming an important source of funding for urban infrastructure construction.[1]

However, the "land for development" model also caused numerous problems that not only restricted the healthy development of urbanization but also brought about latent woes to the next round of economic growth. For example, two salient problems are occurring in east China: the decline in revenue from land transfer and the slowing of growth in transferred land area. In 2012, land transfer revenues of the four first-tier cities of Beijing, Shanghai, Guangzhou and Shenzhen fell by 38.60%, 23.10%, 22.02% and 50.13%, respectively. Between 2000 and 2007 the average annual growth rate of the transferred land area in east China was 25.2%. Between 2008 and 2012, however, the average annual growth rate in the same region dropped to 9.06%. The third problem is the rigid rise of land prices. Between 2010 and 2012, industrial land prices in the Yangtze River Delta, the Bohai Rim and the Pearl River Delta rose at an annual average rate of 8.75%, 7.19% and 10.53%, respectively. Industrialization based on governmental land price subsidies to maintain low cost is no longer sustainable.

---

1 Liu Shouying: *Facing the Land Issue in China*, China Development Press, 2014, Beijing.

Meanwhile, under the existing land acquisition system, expropriation of rural land and the scale of such expropriation have led to intensified conflicts between rural residents and the local governments concerned. Land disputes have been multiplying and, as farmers grow more and more conscious of their rights and interests, legal disputes involving land grew as well.

The Tough Deal of Relocation

Acreage defined, the big headache of demolition talks begin

Forces gathered, small groups of attackers are off to the fray

Employees gathered and tasks given, small groups crack the nut one by one

Some find your friends and relatives, and all of your relations

Sweet tongues of persuasion, urging you to give in.

If carrots doesn't work, then comes charges of "illegal construction."

Fearless Maozhuang Village defends itself with relevant laws.

One bad trick deserves another, now try the nails of birth control.

Thus locked in a stalemate, a breakpoint has to be found.

Hidden worries translated into harassing phone calls

Till one idea popped out of many heads: find a soft nut to crack!

You are done if your attitude reveals a weakness

With feasts, gifts and phone calls, they haunt you and your home like ghosts

All yeas and amen if you sign the contract, all vows melt when the job is done.

This doggerel truly reflects the multi-fold difficulties, conflicts and disputes that arise during the process of land acquisition and resettlement. These problems cannot be ignored because they are jeopardizing rural economic development and social stability. A study by the State Council Development Research Center in 2011 show that group incidents related to land acquisition happened in 137 districts/counties both in economically developed and underdeveloped areas. The farmers' protests were chiefly against unfair compensation and non-access to the benefits of urbanization. A majority of such protests were directed at improper state action during the land acquisition process. More than half of the protests were related to the gap between what is owed by law and what is actually paid. Forty-two percent of the incidents were related to land acquisition without lawful approval. A lot of the conflicts rose out of a multitude of factors, including unfair distribution of compensation, non-disclosure in the selection of land for acquisition, non-disclosure in actual use of land, and governmental mishandling of the land acquisition process.[1] Increased default risk of local governments, the rising costs of land acquisition on an annual basis and the recurrence of conflicts in land acquisition are all indicators of the fact that the "land for

1 Development Research Center of the State Council and World Bank: *China: Promotion of Efficient, Inclusive and Sustainable Urbanization,* China Development Press, 2014, Beijing.

development" model of economic growth has been unsustainable.

Under the present institution, farmers' rights to labor
are not well protected in certain scope, nor are their property rights to the land. "The media said that in some place
there was a piece of land bided at an extremely high price,
then the farmers asked how much did you pay us for that
originally?" said Chen Xiwen, deputy leader of the Central Agricultural Work Leading Group and director of its
general office. According to a survey by the State Council
Development Research Center, the compensation fee the
farmers got only accounted for 5-10% of the proceeds
from value-added land.

As industrialization and urbanization accelerate, the
pinpoint of the current "three rural issues" (referring to
agriculture, rural areas and farmers) is how to correctly
handle the relationship between farmers and land, which
is, in effect, distribution of proceeds from value-added
land. Land reform incorporating distribution of proceeds
from value-added land is a core issue determining the success or failure of a new type of urban-rural and agrarian-
industrial relationship, a core issue determining whether
farmers can participate in the modernization process and
have a fair share of the fruits of modernization. At present, China on the whole has entered a developmental

stage in which industry lifts up agriculture and cities bring along villages. Moreover, our national economy is now in a position to feed agriculture and support rural areas. The new urbanization strategy also provided opportunity for reforming "the land for development" model. With the ongoing advancement of comprehensive, urban-rural integrated reform, the country has made many useful inroads into areas of land empowerment and distribution of proceeds from value-added land. Such exploration, which represents the future direction of land reform in China, provides valuable input for efficient, inclusive and sustainable urbanization.

Land Empowerment–Seeking a Breakthrough in the Exploration Process

Farmers' access to more land property rights is the premise and foundation for raising the distribution proportion of revenue from value-added land. Farmers' paucity of land property rights is one of the roots of the dualistic urban-rural structure. It is also a major factor affecting social stability in rural areas. Since the late 1970s, the state has taken a series of policy measures to provide farmers with land property rights in a gradual, piecemeal manner. The rural reform of 1978, characterized by the household contract responsibility that gave farmers land use rights and usufruct, not only enlivened

June 25, 2004, Pingshan Village, Yushan District, Ma'anshan City, Anhui Province. About 560 villagers are resettled in a commercial residential district of high-standard housing.

the rural economy, but also laid the foundation for the growth of the national economy as a whole. Farmers' land property rights mainly include land contract and management rights, homestead rights, and distribution rights of collective proceeds. The household contract responsibility was established to provide farmers with land contract and management rights. The government reinforced the farmers' land use rights and usufruct through policy measures and legislation. For example, Article XVI of the Rural Land Contracting Law of the People's Republic of China promulgated in 2002 provides: The land contractor "shall be entitled to the use and proceeds of the contracted land and to the circulation of the rights of contracted land management." This provision defined the land use rights in the Law of Land Management as three specific rights: land use right, right to receive proceeds, and circulation of land contracting and management rights. However, for now, farmers still do not enjoy full rights of land contracting and management; specifically, they do not possess the rights of disposal, mortgage, security and inheritance.

Homestead in China is acquired for free through lawful application. It is a special arrangement in the land system. Ever since its founding, the PRC has improved its rural homestead management and approval mechanism through a series of systemic reforms. After the enactment of the "Property Law of 2007," the system of rural homestead rights became gradually standardized. Currently, the main features of China's rural homestead is as follows: collective ownership of homestead ownership, farmers' homestead use rights, and farmers' home ownership rights. Farmers' homestead use rights belong to membership rights. In order to protect farmers' homestead use rights and interests, the central government issued circulars in 2010 and 2013 requesting definition, registration and certification of homestead use rights. To further increase farmers' property rights, the Decision

February 19, 2014, farmers' residential quarters in suburban Junshan, Wuhan City. Wuhan is making plans to help farmers turn their homesteads into "hens that lay golden eggs."

of the Third Plenary Session of the 18th CPC Central Committee made the following requirements: "Protect the usufructuary right of farmers concerning homesteads, revamp and improve the rural homestead system, select several localities for pilot projects, and carefully and steadily push forward farmers' exercise of rights concerning the mortgage, security and transfer of their property rights so that they would have more channels to increase their property revenue. However, during the process of industrialization and urbanization, the large flow of rural labor into urban areas gave rise to the marketing needs for farmers' homesteads, especially those located in suburban areas. A lot of "limited deeded homes" exist in suburban areas, even though homesteads are not entitled to rental, transfer and transaction rights.

Collective income distribution rights refer to farmers' rights to participate in the distribution of various natural resources and capital gains as members of collective economic organizations.[1]

For a long time, due to ill-defined property rights of rural land, village officials become de facto grantors and beneficiaries of collective land for construction use, thus jeopardizing the interests of the farmers. "Property Law" provides that "collectively owned property is protected by law. Any unit or individual is prohibited from encroachment, grabbing, looting, partitioning, or destruction." In order to give collective members more property rights, the decision requested protection of the rights of members of farmers' collective economic organizations, active development of joint-stock cooperation among farmers, and gave farmers shares of possession of collective assets, proceeds, compensated exit, mortgage, security and inheritance rights and interests.

Compared with land contract and management rights, rural collective land for construction use is char-

---

1 Kong Xiangzhi and Liu Tongshan: "Give Farmers More Property Rights: Necessity, Meaning and Strategy," *Teaching and Research*, No. 1, 2014.

acterized by its large scale, broad scope and great complexity. By improving the system of rural collective land for construction use, farmers will be motivated to produce more and make more out of their assets. On the other hand, collective revenue will significantly increase, and urban and rural layout will be optimized. Industrialization and urbanization on collective land for construction use created, in effect, a mechanism of interest distribution different from the current land acquisition model dominated by the government. Once farmers retain ownership of collective land for construction use, they will be entitled to long-term income from the incremental value of land.

Beginning in 1999, major systemic adjustment has been made in rural collective land for construction use. Rural collective land for construction use has been made part of a system of annual land use plan management. Based on this system, rural collective land can only be used as premises for village and town enterprises, homesteads for farmers and establishment of village public services. Only state-owned construction land will be used for any other purposes. Therefore, land use rights owned by farmers collectively shall not be let, transferred or leased for non-agricultural construction. However, the truth of the matter is, violations of this rule are quite common. Plus, society now has mixed views on this issue. Supporters tend to emphasize equality between collective land ownership and state land ownership. They think that the Land Management Law should be amended for the establishment of a unified land market. Under the efforts of all parties, the decision made the following provision: "On condition that planning and usage control rules are met, allow rural collective land for business construction use to be transferred, leased and held in shares so that it can enter the market on the same terms, at the same price and with the same rights as state-owned land."

In fact, pilot work for the circulation of rural collective land for construction use made its debut in Fujian, Zhejiang and other provinces as early as the 1990s. During the same period, a village in Beijing blazed its own trail of urbanization on collective rural land for construction use. Zhenggezhuang Village, with a land area of 4,432 *mu* (295 hectares), has 1,502 villagers, including 1,106 farmers. As of 2012, the village set up on the collective land 96 enterprises that provided about 13,000 jobs. In 2012, the village created on the collective land an output value of RMB 9.5 billion (USD 1.52 billion). Back in 1998, Zhenggezhuang Village mapped out an ecologically friendly "21st-century Eco-ranch," which divided the village's land into four sections: residential section, culture and education section, techno-

July 6, 2014,
Daoshi
Village, Daoshi
Township, Lin'an
City, Zhejiang
Province.
Retirement
certificates
entitling retirees
to monthly
pension funds
are being handed
out to the
village's retired
employees.

logical and industrial section, and tourism and leisure section. In 1999, the village first allocated the farmland to each villager, then guided the villagers to entrust their contracted land to the collective enterprises in the village for the development of secondary and tertiary industries. That same year, Zhenggezhuang Village carried out property rights system reform and reasonably defined the relationship between the village and its enterprises. In 2000, through replacement, payment of reclamation fees and other measures, the village collective converted 1,600 *mu* (about 107 hectares) of its total of 2,200 *mu* (about 147 hectares) farmland into land for construction use.

Subsequently, Zhenggezhuang Village acquired development and management rights over 2,400 *mu* (about 160 hectares) of collective land for construction use. Currently, using collective land, Zhenggezhuang Village has built an industrial chain consisting of construction, culture and tourism, high technology and industry, education and scientific research, creative cultural projects and real estate development. In addition, because farmers in Zhenggezhuang Village practiced self-urbanization, the village paid all infrastructure expenses, including water, utilities, heating, etc. By 2012, accumulated investment in various municipal infrastructure facilities amounted to RMB 500 million (USD 80 million). Villagers' sources of income consist of wages, welfare, shareholder returns, land revenue and housing rental income. In 2012, farmers' net per capita income reached RMB 59,800 (USD 9,568).[1]

Cases similar to the Zhenggezhuang Village development model abound in China. Compared with the governmental land acquisition model, the farmers' autonomous urbanization model manifests some unique advantages. On the one hand, the farmers' independent urbanization model gives full consideration to the villagers' employment and prioritizes industrial support to urbanization,

---

1 Liu Shouying: *Facing the Land Issue in China*, China Development Press, 2014, Beijing.

thus effectively protecting farmers' interests. Under the premise of collective ownership of land, as shareholders of collective assets, farmers can earn continual dividends from appreciated assets and value-added land proceeds. On the other hand, farmers' autonomous urbanization goes by way of villagers' autonomy. Compensation for village renovation is allocated through internal negotiation. Out of personal interests, farmers are in the habit of checking on one another to prevent corruption practices like mooching and cheating. Because of that, the cost of urbanization can significantly go down and social conflicts can be reduced.

Comprehensive Land Management– from Regionalized to Centralized Approach

The State Council Guidelines for Supporting Accelerated Construction of the Central Plains Economic Zone in Henan Province provided some guidelines for comprehensive land management: "Follow the principle of fore-planning, employment-based development, acting within capacity and free choice by the people. Actively and steadily establish pilot areas of new rural community construction, and promote more concentrated use of land, large-scale agricultural operations, farmers' employment close to home, and improvement of rural environment." In recent years, based on local experiences, comprehensive land management has become an effective means of coordinated development of urbanization and construction of new rural communities. Comprehensive land management features concentrated living quarters for farmers, reclamation of their original homesteads, and use of saved land use right quota of collective land for construction purposes to maintain the balance between increase and decrease. Funds will be mainly used for project planning, housing subsidies, homestead reclamation and public facilities and infrastructure facilities construction in the newly built concentrated residential areas. Comprehensive land management is an important means of maintaining the balance between increase and decrease. The objectives of the balancing policy are as follows: "Convert rural land for construction use (demolition of buildings on old lots) back into arable land. After priority allocation of construction land for various rural developments, use a small part of the saved quota for building new residential quarters in towns and townships. Thus, the original rural land for construction is converted into urban land for construction. Sound implementation of this policy not only can raise the value of rural land and provide sufficient land for urban development and expansion, but also provide sources of funding for rural development so that the goal of coordinated urban-rural development could be reached. In some areas, implementation of balancing projects served the dual purposes of providing cities with land use quota and of realizing urbanization of rural population. Xinxiang of Henan, Pixian County of Sichuan, and Suzhou of Jiangsu have experimented proactively in these areas.

Xinxiang's approach is to combine comprehensive land management with urban planning and industrial development. Construction of new rural communities is being carried out following the pattern of "farmers moving to community centers" and "industries moving to industrial parks." Based on a whole-picture perspective, Xinxiang implemented integrated planning of industry, new countryside, land, public services and ecological environment. Improved planning can be seen in the following plans: "Modern Urban System Plan of the Entire Administrative Region of Xinxiang," "Plan of a Pastoral City on the Central Plains," "Research Plan for the Cluster-style Development of Central Cities and Towns in Xinxiang" and "Village and Town System and Layout Plan of Xinxiang." As a result, a full administrative region urban-rural planning system covering the central city, the county seats, towns and new rural communities came into being.

To promote healthy and orderly construction, following the principle of "acceptability by the people, affordability by the government and sustainability of development," Xinxiang worked out a classification

June 7, 2014, farmers at a new rural community in Huaxian County, Henan Province are sowing corn in the harvested wheat field. In the background are a group of tall buildings at their second phase of construction. The new town of Jinhe, enveloping 33 administrative villages with a total of 12,747 farming households, has a planned construction area of 2.097 million square meters. The project with 3.304 billion yuan investment will accommodate 54,000 residents. Once completed, the new town will be the largest new rural community in Henan Province.

guide to the construction of new rural communities in the city. With a focus on a first-class community, the city takes a comprehensive approach to community building through demolition and reclamation, capital consolidation, policy implementation and farmer entrepreneurship and employment, etc. During the first half of 2014, Xinxiang completed new housing construction projects totaling 3.239 million square meters in floor space, providing housing for 6,231 farmer households. In the meantime, 3,299 *mu* (about 220 hectares) of homesteads were demolished to create 955 *mu* (about 64 hectares) of arable or ecologically friendly land. Meanwhile, efforts were made to achieve local industrialization and urbanization. For example, the Xinxiang Municipal Government set up an annual special fund of RMB 20 million (about USD 3.2 million) to develop and construct an industrial cluster area. The money is mainly used to award the introduction of major projects into the industrial parks, construction of research and development platforms and promotion and upgrading. In 2014, 197 mega projects with an average value of more than RMB 100 million (about USD 16 million) were implemented in the city's 12 industrial parks. The total investment was RMB 96 billion (about USD 15.4 billion). More than 100 kilometers of fast-track transportation links were built in the industrial center. Five wastewater treatment plants, four electrical substations and a central heating project extending to Weihui Industrial Center went into construction. In places not covered by the industrial zone, great efforts will be devoted to the development of farmers' entrepreneurial parks. By now, all of the 24 farmers' entrepreneurial parks are open for construction. Twenty-two of them have completed written planning and revision and been approved by planning commissions at county level. A total of RMB 873.25 million (USD 139.72 million) has been invested in infrastructure facilities. A land area of 51,588 *mu* (3,439.2 hectares) has been planned for. The parks' built-up area has reached 14,489 *mu* (966 hectares), 110 kilometers of highways have been built, 283 enterprises have established corporate presence in the parks, and 49,000 farmers have been employed. Workshops built in the parks totaled 1.253 million square meters, while total investment reached RMB 3.98 billion (about USD 636.8 million) and total corporate output value reached RMB 6.71 billion (about USD 1.07 billion).

In the process of building new rural communities, Suzhou City vigorously promoted environmental renovation projects. Efforts have been made to improve villages' environmental conditions through planning guidance and designs of form, architecture, color, elevations etc. and through increased budget. Currently, the city has more than 100 reservation villages that are speeding up construction of compatible infrastructure facilities and creating more unique, ecologically friendly and more beautiful and livable villages. In addition, Suzhou City has also established sample construction areas of "beautiful towns and villages." Based on the general standards of "excellent ecological environment, reasonable spatial layout, sound supporting services, solid financial foundation, and harmonious social mores," the city has accelerated the making and revision of town and village layout plans, giving full respect to differences in rural industrial structure, functional status, spatial landscape and social culture, etc. Great attention has been paid to the tapping of natural scenery, local culture, and architectural tradition. Efforts have been made to mold 71 "beautiful village" samples that carry distinctive Suzhou features characterized by waterside southern landscapes with painted walls and dark tiles and villages of rice and fish. By the end of 2013, the target of basically completing the construction of beautiful villages would have been met.

In terms of the building of concentrated residential areas, Suzhou City has emphasized coordination, policy implementation, and hard-nut cracking as part of its efforts to speed up construction of farmers' concentrated residential areas. Under the guidance of the government, relevant departments are providing quality services in a series of links, including planning, project establishment, approval, start-off, inspection, acceptance and replacement so that the related quota can be used as new construction land as soon as possible. To raise the level of land use with high efficiency and to make full use of the balancing between lands for urban and rural construction and the policy of flexible land use, Suzhou City established a diversified guarantee mechanism to properly monitor the balance between project construction funds, land use and the interests of the village collective and individual farmers, to speed up housing allocation for completed projects and ensure that farmers' share holdings, housing exchange, employment, and to have public services enter into cities and towns in an equalitarian manner. Meanwhile, the city continues to promote the gathering of "small and scattered" industrial enterprises into industrial parks of township level and above and actively revitalize efficient use of land and optimize allocation of resources.

Pixian County in Sichuan Province is one of the first counties across the country to carry out comprehensive land management and explore ways of balancing the increase or decrease of land used for urban and rural construction. Hengshan Village, for example, had 453 households, or 70% of the village total, that applied for residence in the concentrated residential area. The main reason why farmers made this choice is that their current residence was located in a poor environment with poor infrastructure facilities. Through transfer of use rights of saved collective land, Huapai Village made RMB 380,000 per *mu* (about USD 60,800 per 0.67 hectare), of which RMB 320,000 (about USD 51,200) was used as compensation for farmers who chose to live in the concentrated residential area. Farmer households that chose to live in apartment buildings would get a subsidy apart from living in there for free. The remain-

June 8, 2007, Beigan Street, Xiaoshan District, Hangzhou City. Farmers who have lost their land are receiving employment skills training. Due to urbanization, more than 6,000 people are resettled in Beigan.

ing RMB 60,000 (about USD 9,600) will be used for the construction of supporting infrastructure facilities and for payment of water, utilities, gas and broadband Internet fees. In terms of balancing of rural and urban land, Pixian County's 16 comprehensive land management projects, which have been implemented, have added 3,670 *mu* (about 245 hectares) of arable land to the county and have transferred 2,569 *mu* (about 171 hectares) of land for construction use in the urban planning zone, thus easing the problem of lack of land for urban use. In addition, in accordance with relevant provisions of Chengdu City, 5% of the collective land saved through comprehensive management is to be used for the future development of the collective economic organization.

Of course, the pros and cons of concentrated residence should be analyzed objectively. In economically developed areas or suburban areas, farmers are entitled to many non-agricultural employment opportunities. They therefore are less dependent on land and have a stronger desire for external transfer. Concentrated residence can save land, offer better living conditions, and bring about some additional earnings. However, for farmers still engaged in agricultural production, concentrated residence means not just changes in the layout of housing, but also more travel and commuting time. According to the survey, concentrated residence has a lot of negative impact on large specialized animal husbandry professionals, even more so for family livestock or aquaculture farmers. Such negative impact can be devastating. Small-scale, part-time farming households will be around for a long time to come. The bulk of them may be women and seniors. For these marginalized farmers, concentrated residence in tall buildings will undoubtedly increase their living costs and reduce their income, resulting in a lower standard of living and compromised welfare. After the village renovation, a considerable number of new communities did not arrange spaces for placement of farm tools and grain drying fields. As reflected in the survey, this further undermined the convenience for farmers to engage in agricultural production and resulted in non-refined management of agricultural production.[1]

In other areas, there have been cases where some local governments have, during the process of comprehensive land management, infringed upon farmers' land rights and interests by forcing them to live in tall buildings. Faced with this phenomenon, the central government issued Circular No. 1 in 2013, which said: "Relocation of rural settlements and merger of villages must be approved by the villagers' committee after due consideration of the farmers' will. [The government] does not advocate or encourage the demolition or merger of villages, or the building of large-scale concentrated rural residential areas. No farmer shall be forced to move or live in apartment buildings." Therefore, the following principles must be upheld in carrying out comprehensive land management in rural areas: 1) The centralized way of living must suit local conditions. Villages in which the majority of the farmers engage in agricultural production are not fit for large-scale centralized residency. 2) Housing designs must be in agreement with the unique conditions

---

1 See Comprehensive Land Management Research Group of the Rural Development Institute Under the Chinese Academy of Social Sciences: *General Report on Land Management Research*.

and characteristics of the countryside. Uniformity and stereotypes must be discouraged, while full consideration to the farmers' needs in agricultural production must be given. 3) Long-term plans must be made to avoid duplicate construction and short-term major demolition and construction. Let those who have true needs gradually move into concentrated residences but provide for the diverse needs of different farmer households.

Distribution of the Proceeds of Value-added Land–Sharing the Benefits of Prosperity Through Competition

With the rapid advancement of industrialization, urbanization and agricultural modernization, competition for land between agricultural and non-agricultural industries, rural and urban areas is becoming more and more heated. On the one hand, arable land area has been sharply decreasing. According to the *Statistical Data of 60 Years of Chinese Agriculture*, total arable land area across the country at the end of 1978 was 1.491 billion *mu* (about 99.4 million hectares). After renovation and reclamation, total arable land area reached 1.951 billion *mu* (about 130.67 million hectares) in 1996, which is the largest since 1949. Along with the growth of marketization of the Chinese economy and urbanization construction, a lot of farmland has been acquired as land for urban construction. China's arable land at the end of 2008 was 1.826 billion *mu* (about 121.73 million hectares), down 125 million *mu* (about 8.33 million hectares) net from that in 1996. On the other hand, urban areas have been quickly expanding. From 1995 to 2010, the urban built-up area across the country increased by 20,793.8 square kilometers, or an annual average growth of 1,386.3 square kilometers.

With the dramatic decrease of arable land, the issue of profit allocation during the farmland acquisition process became a focus of public attention as well. The land acquisition process is also the process of continuous growth of land revenue. Under the state-led land acquisition model, the lion's share of profits goes to the government while little goes to the farmers. Not only does the government monopolize the primary market of farmland conversion, it well-nigh dominates all stages of the land acquisition process. Strictly restricted from participating in decisions on farmland conversion, farmers can only passively accept compensation standards and allocation plans devised by the government. For example, China's land transfer revenue in 2011 surpassed RMB 3.15 trillion (about USD 0.5 trillion), including RMB 2.7 trillion (about USD 0.43 trillion) in revenue from land transfer for real estate development. By contrast, by November 2011, only about RMB 123.4 billion (about USD 19.74

The Land Administration Act provides that farmers will be exclusively compensated for the removal of their houses.

billion) in land transfer revenue was spent on agriculture, rural areas and farmers.[1] Besides, in order to cut the cost of business invitation, local governments expanded the scope of land acquisition at will and lowered the standard of compensation. What's worse, there were frequent cases of embezzlement, corruption and theft of compensation funds. The result was constant land disputes that intensified social conflicts.[2] Obviously, the imperfect profit sharing mechanism in the land acquisition process

1 Han Jun: "Let Farmers Have a Direct Share of the Proceeds from Value-added Land," *China Economic Herald*, February 21, 2012.

1 Liu Shouying: "Reform the Land for Development Model," *China Reform*, No. 1, 2012.

will directly affect the stability of rural China as well as the entire society. Therefore, reform of the land acquisition system will be one of the main items of China's rural land system reform.

According to data released by the Ministry of Finance, in 2012 the expenditures from land transfer revenue amounted to RMB 2.8418 trillion (about USD 0.45 trillion). Of this, cost-related expenditures such as land acquisition compensation accounted for 79.6% of the total of local expenditures from land transfer revenue. Although the current land acquisition system is playing an important supportive and protective role in ensuring the country's economic development and speeding up the process of industrialization and urbanization, the traditional pattern of low-cost and coercive land acquisition has seriously affected social stability. To overcome the maladies of government-dominated land acquisition, Shenzhen's Bao'an District has created a new model for land acquisition and resettlement based on its own experience. This model can be summarized as "governmental guidance, collective coordination in the village, farmers' participation and sharing of proceeds."

On December 20, 2013, Shenzhen's first collective-owned rural lot was successfully put up for sale. Owned by the Phoenix Community on Fuyong sub-district,

Bao'an District, the lot covers an area of 14,500 square meters. The lot was sold to Shenzhen Forge Precision Components Co. Ltd at an upset price of RMB 116 million (about USD 18.56 million). Seventy percent of the land revenue went to the government, while 30% went to Phoenix Community Co., Ltd, a village stockholding enterprise. The government provided two ways of allocating rural collective land revenue: the government and the village each having half, or the government get 70% and the village get 30% plus 20% of the real estate. The Phoenix Community chose the latter. Wen Yongchang, director of the Phoenix Community, holds that the second way can ensure long-term development of the community. When the project is completed, Phoenix Community Co., Ltd will have 20% of the gross floor area from Shenzhen Forge Precision Components Co., Ltd for free.[1]

According to the Bao'an allocation scheme, land revenue distribution between the local government and the rural collective is basically 50/50. The local government's net proceeds did not shrink while its costs in dealing with the farmers were able to drop significantly. As a result, farmers' income rose sharply, and the community enterprise received property proceeds needed for sustainable development.

---

1 Zhang Xiaoshan: "Distribution of Proceeds Is the Kernel of Land Reform," *China Report*, No. 2, 2014.

Apparently, this is a mild, gradual and win-win reform format. It tells us that by having farmers directly engage in land acquisition and resettlement and by empowering collective-owned land with the same pricing mechanism and the same rights and interests as those of state-owned land, the government can serve the dual purpose of lowering land acquisition costs and truly protecting the farmers' long-term subsistence. Therefore, on condition of compliance with state land use rules and the general plan of land use, efforts should be made to leave more non-rural construction land to farmers for collective development so that farmers can directly share the proceeds of value-added land.

The government should borrow the (Shenzhen) Bao'an experience, acquire all rural collective land by law, raise farmers' share of proceeds from value-added land and establish a profit-sharing system in which farmers whose land have been acquired are guaranteed to enjoy improved standard of living for years to come. First, speed up reform of the land acquisition system. Further improve the land acquisition compensation and relocation apparatus, broaden the means of resettlement and seek alternative models like settlement on reserved land and land shareholdings. Practice "preservation of rights for benefits" or "transfer of rights for benefits" to ensure farmers' long-term subsistence. Build up a sound coordination and arbitration system for land compensation disputes, widen the channels for relief and protect the legitimate land rights and interests of farmers. Second, make a clear distinction between "incremental value of land as common property" and "incremental value of land as government property." Prevent the "common property" in the form of incremental value of land from becoming extra-system income of local governments or even of some local officials. Make sure that the proceeds of value-added land will be used to benefit society as a whole. Third, set up a land fund system. Gather together an appropriate proportion of land revenue for the purpose of balancing financial surplus and deficit, and alleviate the impact of market fluctuations on local finance so as to realize a reasonable annual distribution of land revenue.[1]

Land Reform and Urbanization

A land system is a basic rural system, something that determines the whole picture of the economy and society. As proven by decades of economic reform, apart from expediting urbanization, land has also brought about fast economic growth and long-term social stability in China. In a period of more than 60 years since the founding

---

1 Liu Shouying: *Facing the Land Issue in China*, China Development Press, 2014, Beijing.

of the PRC, a land rights system featuring separation of ownership rights from usage rights and a land management model centered around planning and usage control have been essentially established. In the next 20 years, land will remain an important resource for the urbanization drive and a key factor for guaranteed, efficient, tolerant and sustainable urbanization. By now, China has converted its formerly monistic and overconcentrated public ownership into a pluralistic land rights system. Continued endowment of land rights is effectuated through separation of ownership rights and land use rights under the precondition of public ownership of land. This systematic arrangement not only preserved the stability of the land system, but also solved the problem of systemic incentives to investors, thus achieving significant economic results. The fundamental goal of land reform lies in the supply of land resources and guaranteed long-term and efficient supply of funds needed for urbanization. Furthermore, the ultimate purpose of such urbanization should be the guaranteed fair share of the benefits of urbanization by all citizens.[1]

During the past several decades, China achieved fast economic growth through the help of a special land

---

1 Development Research Center of the State Council and World Bank: *China: Promotion of Efficient, Inclusive and Sustainable Urbanization*, China Development Press, 2014, Beijing.

Liutuan Village,
Xianggong
Township,
Hedong District,
Linyi City,
first village
in Shandong
Province
facilitated with
utilities and gas
services

ownership system. However, the "land for development" economic model has also brought about problems of imbalance, incoordination and unsustainability. By now, the Chinese government has developed a sober understanding of the maladies of the current land system and has started comprehensive reform in many important realms and key links. Based on the Decision on Some Major Issues Concerning Comprehensively Continuing the Reform reached at the Third Plenary Session of the 18th CPC Central Committee, the current land system reform in China is an overall, integral and systematic measure. The reform proposal involves a wide range of issues during the process of transition from rural society to urban society, including systematic arrangement of farmers' land rights, reform of the land acquisition system, fair distribution of proceeds from value-added land among all parties of interest (a pivotal interest issue in the urbanization process), structural conversion of land use in the non-agricultural land market, and design of the framework of future land management system.

In specific terms, the decision not only brought up the point of endowing farmers with land rights of occupation, use, profit generation, transfer, hypothecation and security of contract management rights, but also clearly defined the scope, manner and means of market entry of collective land for construction use. The decision further proposed the broadening of the scope of compensated use of state-owned land as well as reduced allocation of land for non-public use. It also suggested reform of the land acquisition process and reduction of the scope of land acquisition and the building of a pluralistic, standardized and reasonable protection system. These series of regulations clarified the direction, focus and means of continuing land system reform.

To implement the spirit of the Third Plenary Session of the 18th CPC Central Committee, the Ministry of Land and Resources has already started its "new deal" of land reform, consisting of land acquisition reform, market entry of rural collective land for construction use and rural homestead reform. In October 2013, the Ministry of Land and Resources put forward Policy Proposals on Continuing Reform of the Land Management System, covering multiple aspects of the land management system, including land ownership rights, land acquisition, etc. However, no order of priorities in the relevant fields of reform has been listed. By August 2014, the Ministry of Land and Resources had, according to relevant rules of the State Council, made the above-mentioned three fields the overall target of land management system reform. Based on this "new order," the Ministry of Land and Resources will consecutively issue Guiding Proposals on the Market Entry of Rural Collective Land for Construction Use and Rural Homestead Management Measures and establish in a timely manner pilot areas for land acquisition system reform. Predictably, sometime in the future, a property rights system composed of urban state-owned land and rural collective land, complete with equal rights on the same market, will further mature. The market will be playing a predominant role in the allocation of resources. Reform of the land acquisition system will quicken in pace, and a fair and equal system for distribution of value-added land proceeds will be gradually established. All these measures will surely further boost the realization of efficient, tolerant and sustainable urbanization.

Chapter Six

Leaving Home for Jobs Close to Home

Every year, hordes of migrant workers hurrying home to celebrate Chinese New Year set off a spring travel rush without exception. Dubbed the largest annual human migration in the world, the rush puts tremendous strain on the already fragile transport system in China. In recent years, however, things began to change. More and more migrant workers are moving their eyes away from developed cities such as Beijing, Shanghai, Guangzhou, Shenzhen, and Wuhan to their own home cities or cities near their home. Thus, the pressure on the public transport sector eased a little bit. It looks as if the phenomenon of "leaving home for jobs not too far away from home" has reoccurred, even though it's quite different from what it was in the 1980s.

The High Cost of Home Leaving

When able-bodied people leave home for jobs in the city, the ones left behind farming are mostly the elderly, the tender-aged, the sick and the handicapped. This left-behind population is vividly nicknamed "386199 unit." "38" is the code for women, "61" for children, and "99" for seniors. These numbers all have something to do with holidays for women, children and different age groups. March 8 is the International Women's Day; June 1 is Children's Day and September 9 is the Double Ninth Festival honoring seniors. As young and middle-aged adults head out to cities, villages literally begin to "hollow out." Currently, China has more than 150 million migrant workers. In the future, as urbanization grows, more farmers will spill into cities. The children, women and seniors left behind will gradually develop into social problems with Chinese characteristics.

Let's first look at the children of the migrant workers who are left behind. In the winter of 2012, five left-behind children died of carbon monoxide poisoning while trying to keep warm by burning trash in a trash trunk. A few got drowned while swimming on hot summer days. Such cases, which resulted from lack of custody, inflicted irreparable pain on the families concerned. It is also a task on our social conscience and sense of ac-

A family picture without mom, dad and elder brother at Xinghuliu Village, Jiazhai Township, Shiping County, Shandong Province, March 26, 2014

countability. Moreover, these children at a crucial stage of their development often fail to benefit from the guidance and help their parents are supposed to provide, whether in terms of cognizance and ways of thinking, or in terms of value concepts. Because they lack the love and care of their parents, they are prone to deviating in their cognizance and value systems and psychological development.

According to an authoritative survey, rural China has now 58 million "left-behind children." Among them, 57.2% have only one parent taking care of them, while 42.8% have both parents working in the cities. Of all the

A "left-behind" senior at a secluded village in southern Shandong Province, January 5, 2008

left-behind children, 79.7% are in the custody of grandparents, 13% in the custody of relatives and friends, and 7.3% either have no custody at all or are undefined. Because left-behind children are mostly in the care of grandparents, their lack of parental guardianship and education has produced adverse effects on the overall health of their development. The most serious problem among these children is a "generational gap in education."

According to the survey, as parents of left-behind children typically work in the cities far away from home and spend very little time even communicating with their

July 13, 2014. Xiao Ronghui is helping her grandma do the dishes at their home in Gangwei, Dapo Administrative Village, Rong'an County, Liuzhou City, Guangxi. More than one fourth of the elementary and middle school students in the county are "left-behind" children.

children, they are actually far from exercising their roles as guardians. In addition, the overwhelming large proportion of intergenerational education received by the kids is hardly satisfactory. Such a situation can easily lead to a "thirst for parental love" among left-behind children, which causes deviation in mental health, personality and other aspects of well-being. Consequentially, their academic performance can also be affected. Because of a lack of parental affection and compromised mental health, a large section of left-behind children demonstrated closed minds, apathy, low self-esteem and cowardice, withdrawn behavior, lack of love for others, and passivity in interaction. Some of them are hot-tempered, impulsive, irritable, and tend to pick up a fight over trifles.

Another group of left-behind people are women. A senior researcher on the left-behind population says that China today has a huge number of left-behind women who are bearing burdens that are rare not just in the country's history, but also in the history of world modernization. Let's look at some of the main problems these women are faced with. First and foremost is spousal separation because of work, which often leads to loss of consortium and marital crises. Living in separated worlds, these women often find their marriages hard to maintain because they have little face-to-face communication or intimate emotional exchange with their spouses. As the husband grows more accustomed to life in the city, he may gradually develop thoughts and mentality very different from those of his wife living in an isolated village. The lack of spiritual common ground becomes a hurdle in keeping the marriage continuing. Next comes the burden of spousal infidelity. Some migrant workers who have become rich tend to get involved in extramarital affairs in the city. Either for the sake of their children, or as an attempt to evade moral condemnation by the general public, such husbands sometimes try to work out a deal through which the spouses receive property or monetary compensation in return for accepting the status quo, without going through divorce. The third burden left-behind women bear is heavy farm work and household chores. When the husband is gone, the wife at home not only becomes the chief labor for agricultural production, but also has to do housework and take care of the kids and the elderly. Because agricultural production in many rural areas has not yet been mechanized, these women have no choice but to conduct heavy manual labor. Moreover, house chores such as caring for the old and young, washing clothes, cooking, and livestock feeding take a huge toll on the women's health as well. The fourth burden is heavy psychological pressure and a strong sense of loneliness. Left-behind women's top worries are health of the elderly and truancy of their children. Next up is their "three worries" about their husbands: low income, personal safety and potential extramarital affairs. Because of these fears, a lot of them become anxious, fragile, and exhausted. They seldom have physical checkups, and many are reluctant to seek medical treatment even when they are sick. One difference that separates average rural women from left-behind women is the latter's loneliness. Loneliness that rises to a certain level typically leads to loss of emotional control and other related problems. The fifth burden is lack of safety. When the men are out working in the cities, the women left behind are easy victims of robbery and sexual harassment. To make things worse, because of the relatively closed and conservative nature of rural life, women subjected to sexual harassment would usually stay quiet.[1]

The main problems left-behind seniors are faced with are low income, poor living conditions, the stress of having to take care of their grandchildren, lack of family atmosphere, a monotonous spiritual life, lack of love and care, security loopholes, lack of health care and medical treatment, financial insecurity and absence of any pension plans. Although most young people in rural areas would do their best to financially support their elderly parents, the problem comes when they themselves are hard up. Couples with child-support burdens find it even harder. A lot of migrant workers in cities are not making good money because of a lack of job skills and a strong educational background. As consumer prices go up, the young people earning five hundred U.S. dollars or so in the city could hardly make ends meet for themselves. Moreover, in cases where the elderly have several children earning different incomes, support for the elderly could become a thorny issue of ugly infighting. The offspring could play a game of buck-passing or squabbling to shuffle responsibility. The end result is that the issue of senior support remains unsolved, thus inflicting a chilling sense of stress and pessimism that weighs heavily on the seniors' mind.

---

1 "Old Problems and Developments of the Phenomenon of Left-behind Women," *China Women's News*, July 1, 2014.

With its operational mechanism still in the making, the recently established rural social pension system remains immature and can only be applied in a very limited scope and geographic area. Consequently, the majority of seniors left behind in the countryside would suffer from lack of basic financial security and health care.

Recurrence of Leaving Home for Jobs Close to Home

In line with industrial upgrading in the eastern regions and accelerated development in the central and western regions, many of the farmers in the western regions are now able to find jobs in their hometowns because some of the labor-intensive industries have been transferred there. This is a phenomenon referred to by some as "finding non-farm jobs without having to leave the hometown." And because jobs are now available in the hometown, the "left-behind problem" is solved automatically. This is in actuality a thorough approach for solving the problem, and it is an important reason why China is so committed to the new type of urbanization.

In the rural areas of Xinjiang Uygur Autonomous Region, scenes of farmers hibernating during the fallow season of winter are getting rarer and rarer today. Under the guidance of the government, more and more farmers are choosing to work or start their own businesses near their homes. A number of ethnic local cooperatives are providing money-making opportunities for farmers who make such choices. Winter is no longer a leisurely season for these people.

Since 2005, Xinjiang proactively guided rural surplus labor toward non-agricultural employment while supporting the development of rural cooperatives. The process of rural surplus labor transfer took big strides, resulting in an annual average of 1.6 million farmers getting employed. During the first three quarters of 2012, Xinjiang provided 2.2 million transfer jobs for its rural surplus labor, raking in revenue of RMB 7.1 billion (about USD 1.14 billion). Take Midong District in Urumqi, a national-level labor transfer demonstration zone, as an example. Under the guidance and financial support of the government, a large number of farmers and herdsmen released from the bondage of farmland began to take jobs in the industrial and service sectors which are main channels through which rural people in the district increase their income. Located in northern Urumqi, Midong District has a population of 298,000, including 110,000 in rural areas. Its arable land area is limited to about 200,000 *mu* (about 13,333 hectares). Under these circumstances, farming alone will hardly meet the basic needs of a farmer household. On the other hand, the existence of a plethora of

October 4, 2014. Mingguang City, Anhui Province. "Left-behind" women working at Aifu Electronics Company Ltd. The local human resources department is arranging 6-hour work shifts for "left-behind" women at 76 businesses in the city so that they may have time to transport their kids to and from school and to care for the elderly.

labor makes transfer of rural labor inevitable. To advance the process of rural labor transfer, local employment and re-employment offices worked hard on job skill training of the workforce and set up various entrepreneurship training bases so that more and more rural labor would be employed. In 2012, Midong District's budget for rural labor force training went past RMB 8 million (about USD 1.28 million), which is RMB 1,200 (about USD 192) per farmer/herdsman. Economic development in Midong District made the regional economy a major carrier of expanded urban-rural employment and local farmers' employment, providing employment to more than 60% of the transferred rural labor force. Eight years ago, Zhang

Yunxiu of Changshanzi Township in Midong District joined the town's Edible Fungi Cultivation Association in cultivating bisporus mushrooms. She contracted a three-leveled greenhouse with an area of 600 square meters, earning an annual net income of about RMB 30,000 (about USD 4,800).

Some cities committed to developing a variety of enterprises would help farmers get employed as close to their home as possible so that they could work both as employees and as independent farmers. Shi Fengxia, a woman in Henan Province, chose to work in a greenhouse less than half a mile away from where she lives. She works eight hours a day taking care of vegetables and harvesting them. She tends to her farm crops when her shift is over. She says that the job at the greenhouses is undemanding and that she could make more than RMB 1,000 (about USD 160) a month. Many of her fellow villagers make the same choice. Greenhouses like these were not the result of individual efforts. Rather, they were set up by Kangda High-tech New Agricultural Development Co., Ltd, a company that combines R&D, production, marketing and sales all into one. The company plans to enlarge its vegetable base to 5,000 *mu* (about 333 hectares) in area. Because many factories and residential areas will be set near the vegetable base, this tract of land will soon become as prosperous as the urban area. Henan Zhongpin Company, Yuanhua Biotech Company, Xuchang Tianhe Company, Shijixiang Edible Fungi Company…are all topnotch agricultural companies of Xuchang known throughout the country. These companies have hired lots of rural surplus labor, providing for them abundantly so that they would not have to leave their homeland for jobs elsewhere.

The "Third Summit on New Urbanization in China" held in Beijing on July 5, 2014 discussed in depth the issue of local urbanization. Among the participants, Ma Junyun, Party secretary of Lingxian County, Dezhou Prefecture in Shandong Province, gave a report with the title "Building Idyllic Towns: Lingxian County's Endeavors in Realizing Urbanization Close to the Villages," which was highly commended on by all experts present. Ma said in his speech, "Urbanization close to the villages necessitates following the laws of economy, respecting the people's will, readjusting production relations, meeting the requirements for developing rural productivity, developing beautiful towns of historic, cultural, geographical and national connotations, and creating urbanization development models that are both realistic and variegated." Since 2011, in order to adapt to the new trend of urban-rural integrated development, Lingxian County has been vigorously promoting the building of residential quarters in sync with industrial parks. It is now en route to a new urbanization model marked by synchronic transformation in the production mode and lifestyle of farmers and the synchronic growth of rural industrialization, urbanization and agricultural modernization. Based on the development concept of "urbanization and industrialization," the county vigorously built residential and industrial areas at the same time and systematically solved a series of harassing problems, including readjustment of rural industrial structure, public services, the hollowing out of the collective economy, and grassroots organization building.

For purposes of scientific planning, Lingxian County commissioned the Planning and Design Institute of Shandong Architecture University to work out a modern urban system plan for the county. The plan features a downtown area in the county seat, two "subcenters" at Mizhen and Bianlinzhen, nine specialty towns including Huiwangzhuang and Qiansun and 30 large communities, including Zhangxiqiao Community and a Muslim community. Each community has full-fledged infrastructure facilities, including water, electricity, heating, waste water treatment facilities; community services including kindergartens, supermarkets, etc.; public spaces such as plazas, storage areas, and fish and livestock areas. The communities are designed in a way that creates an environment in which residents could work and live without undue worries. So far, they have been in the process of building 20 rural communities. Some 32,000 farmers have moved out of low-lying ranch houses into bright and spacious new buildings. By now, the county has built 25 rural industrial parks and absorbed more than 30,000 employees. In 2013, the county's farmers had a per capita net income of RMB 11,199 (about USD 1,792), reaching a historic growth rate of 16.8%.

The experiments and practices mentioned above have proved so successful that they even caused labor shortages in the eastern coastal regions.

Local Urbanization

The recurrence of the phenomenon of "leaving home for jobs close to home" is a direct manifestation of a national effort to reinforce urbanization construction and to bring about urban-rural integration. It is this very effort that has created jobs and given farmers the option of working close to their homes in lieu of working as migrants in remote coastal cities.

The city of Chongqing is the testing ground of China's comprehensive and integrated urban-rural reform. In 2007, as the vanguard pilot area of Chongqing's reform, Jiulongpo District trailblazed the Jiulongpo model characterized by "using social security in the city to trade for land contracts in the countryside and using urban residential housing to trade for rural homestead." This was a new road of urbanization by converting farmers into urban citizens and providing jobs close to the farmers' homes.

Beginning in 2007, Jiulongpo has been implementing a series of reforms concerning circulation and transfer of land management rights. The first measure is leasing of land contract rights. The rent is about RMB 1,000 (USD 160) per *mu* (0.67 hectare). Transfer of rights is on a voluntary basis. The aim is to liberate farmers from land so that they may choose to work in an agricultural park or urban enterprise. The company they work for provides them with social security insurance. Meanwhile, they will be entitled to fixed proceeds from the land and their revenue will keep rising. The second measure is "land for social security." Jiulongpo District promulgated a policy that anyone with stable non-agricultural income who is willing to give up homestead land use rights and contracted land management rights may apply for urban *hukou* and enjoy equal treatment with urban residents in terms of children's enrollment in school, employment support, pension insurance, medical insurance and other benefits. Currently, Jiulongpo set up land transfer stations in three pilot towns at township and village levels through which farmers lease their land to the village, which then further transfers it to the township or industrial park. Further

August 20,
2014, migrant
workers working
at an electronics
assembly line
in Luocheng
County, Guangxi

down the road, the government will lease these vacated lands to companies and individuals of financial strength to develop sizable modern agriculture and specialty industries. That way, farmers would be able to work close to their homes without having to leave their villages.

On the other hand, in order to crack the bottleneck of urban construction land, pilot towns in Chongqing would trade urban housing for rural homesteads. In Baishiyi, the pilot town in Jiulongpo, the local government used about 20% of the former rural homestead to build new rural communities and turned about 80% of the rural homestead into urban construction land. The profit margin from the land transfer was used to subsidize the purchase of housing for farmers. The first pilot area of three villages, namely Qinghe, Gaotiankan and Gaofengshi, has a total of 740 *mu* (49.3 hectares) of rural construction land. Based on the density of urban residential buildings, just 20% of the original construction land will be enough to meet the housing construction needs of all the farmers. So the remaining 80% of the construction land can be allocated for urban construction. The cost per square meter of the newly built housing is about RMB 900 (about USD 144) per square meter. If sold to a resettled farmer at RMB 580 (about USD 93) per square meter, assuming that the price difference be paid with revenue from the land used for urban construction and with the compensation fund for demolition of the farmer's original house, the farmer would basically be able to get an urban apartment of 80 square meters for free. In other words, by trading homestead land for residential housing, farmers can basically move into high standard urban housing units. The greatest breakthrough about it is that residential housing can be freely marketed, rented or sold for proceeds.

Chongqing Zongsheng Fruit Company was founded in 2006 to grow citrus fruits on a large scale. It was a stockholding company established by 508 households of farmers in Qilin Village, Shiyan Township, Changshou

District, on the principle of equality and mutual benefit. The farmers invested with their land management rights. Part of the company's registered capital was the assessed value of rural land contract and management rights in the amount of RMB 2.5342 million (about USD 405,472). Since every household is a shareholder in this joint-stock cooperative, all personal interests are closely linked to the rise and fall of the company itself, making it possible for the farmers to overcome the drawbacks of traditional peasant economy operation. Meanwhile, the shareholding farmers can work in the orchards as staff of the company. As a result, the farmers' revenue from land is now a combination of equity, salary and profits.

In addition, Chongqing has made many experiments in the realm of *hukou* reform, seeking a balance in rights and interests. Based on the reform program designed by its Municipal Development and Reform Commission, the city revised its population management system and gradually disrobed urban residency of its social equity and made inroads into a dynamic resident population and floating population management system through social security accounts. That is, household registration reform is no longer simply a change of *hukou*. It must reflect equality of rights and interests. At present, social welfare distribution among Chongqing residents is based on urban *hukou* alone. Low-income insurance, medical insurance and other social benefits are all based on the kind of *hukou* you have. In the future, *hukou* reform will start with the establishment of social security accounts, and the distribution of social benefits will be based thereon. The end of the reform is to gradually eliminate the gap between urban and rural households. For example, rural migrant workers working at Shangqingsi will pay their social security taxes at Shangqingsi. Because their social security accounts are local, their children will naturally attend local schools. Besides, Chongqing Municipal Public Security Bureau issued a regulation in 2013, providing that all migrant workers who work or do business in town and have bought housing units to live in or have been renting from public housing authorities and have lived therein for three or more years, may apply for urban residency status together with family members they are living with, including spouse and children.[3]

These measures taken by Chongqing befitting its local conditions removed the cost barriers for providing migrant workers in town with equal access to urban housing, education, health care, pension, social security and other social welfare. Step by step, an integrated urban-rural *hukou* management system is established to guide and encourage qualified rural migrant workers from two-way flow to permanent urban residency. This is a typical case of turning farmers into local urban residents.

The unique path taken by Guiding County in Guizhou Province is that farmers will be converted to industrial workers right where they are, without having to move into town.

Development of village tourism is an important measure taken by Guiding County to integrate urban and rural development and to realize localized urbanization. Development of village tourism can bring to the countryside a huge influx of people, goods, capital, and information. Through development of tourism, part of the urban consumer fund can be transferred to the countryside to increase rural economic capacity and farmer income. Furthermore, urban-rural interchanges and communication through village tourism help increase investment in and policy support to rural areas, tilt various resources and capital toward the countryside and boost rural economic development in general.

In 2005 and 2006, relying on the unique landscape of Yinzhai Village, Guiding County successfully hosted the "Jinhai Snow Mountain Tourism and Culture Festival" and "Jinhai Snow Mountain Panjiang Plum Festival," which unveiled the scenic beauty of Yinzhai of Bouyei ethnic group and successfully branded the "Jinhai Snow

Mountain" tourism program. The Jinhai Snow Mountain Tourism and Culture Festival quickly led the local people in their transfer to the tertiary industry centered on tourism and service. Typically, 70% of Yinzhai Village's young and middle-aged people are engaged in farming during farming seasons and in tourist services during non-farming seasons. Here, village tourism converted many farmers into tourist service workers. Records show that, since the kick-off of the festival, the number of farmers who took local service jobs reached thousands. Such jobs include catering, tour guiding, tourist commodity manufacturing, small commodities trading, and transportation. A number of surplus labors who were planning to work away from home stayed to engage in tourist services. Up to 120 farmers who were previously working long-term in faraway cities returned home for jobs in tourism and service-oriented industries. Farmers in Yunwu Township became tea industry workers engaged in the production, processing, marketing and sales of tea. Close to 1,000 farmers in Yanxia Village became workers in the fishing industry by raising giant salamanders. Farmers in Luobei-he Village became permanent boatmen through the Luobei River rafting program. In villages and townships like Dingnan and Duliu, farmers formed associations to grow pollution-free, organic vegetables for sale, thus becoming permanent vegetable growers and dealers.

Plum and rape
blossoms at Yinzhai
Village, Panjiang
Township, Guiding,
Guizhou Province

Yinzhai Village's honest and pure folkways and natural landscape are the best tourism resources that people can access for relaxation and creation. Currently, Yinzhai Village is building a Jinhai Qigu Project, seniors' apartments, a country club, and a leisure and holiday zone around the downtown area. Centered on Yinzhai Village, Guiding County is remaking itself by turning its county seat into a tourist resort incorporating full services in catering, hotel accommodation, travel, sight-seeing, shopping, and entertainment, etc. Village tourism brought a lot of new information and new ideas from the city into the countryside. Farmers began to make efforts to learn new things and technologies. Many managed to learn standard Chinese and improve other skills. With tourism as its engine of development, Guiding will have an effective bridge that links urban and rural development. Yinzhai Village became a valuable reference for the quiet turn from infrastructure building to "soft power" in new rural construction.

Urbanization in Guiding focuses on unified and coordinated urban and rural development, so that all citizens of the county may share the fruits of development. Hailuo Group's new cement factory with a production capacity of four million tons, which is located in the village of Xinchang in Dexin Township, had this demand from the county government during the negotiating process: Solve the problem of local employment and guarantee that at least one person from each household is hired by the factory. The cement factory would eventually hire more than 90% of the local labor force. It is estimated that by the time the first production line goes into operation, more than 500 people would be hired. When the second line goes into production, 1,000 people would get hired. Since 2002, many industrial companies have set up projects in Panjiang of Guiding, invested more than RMB 200 million (about USD 33 million) and hired over 1,000 local laborers. Corporate employment for migrant workers absorbed surplus rural labor and entitled them to conversion to urban citizenry at the same time. The measure is a natural boost to the growth of urbanization.

To change the farmers' status, efforts must be made to effect change in their mentality. Otherwise, there would ⸱ no fundamental change in their lives. The Guiding Co⸱ ⸱ty government gave full consideration to the farmers' relocation needs. Farmers having moved out of their land were all able to move into brand new residential buildings. Here they have access to tap water, electricity, public transit, and cultural and fitness facilities. They are to doff their bad habits and to suit their new lifestyle as agricultural workers. They don't have to leave their home or village to become workers. Though not much different in appearance, they have in essence taken on a new identity and a new inner reality.

For those who enter into the city, the city government keeps their homestead on their behalf; for those who have already settled down in the city, the county government provides them with an environment in which they could live in peace. Thus, the city government has created a nice and fair environment in which companies could generate wealth. Under the same blue sky, people live and work in peace, order and equality. Guiding County held on to such good ideas and achieved positive results.

The phenomenon of localized urbanization in some parts of China is both a true picture of urbanization development and a true reflection of coordinated regional development in China. The recurrence of localized urbanization has a lot to do with the local government's efforts in developing local economy and with the growing opportunities of employment in local areas. Urbanization or urban-rural integration is the general direction of future development. In practicing these things, government leaders need to keep improving their governance capacity in order to adapt to this new trend.

Chapter Seven

Integration of Urban and Rural Development

More than three decades ago, in a move widely seen as the unveiling of rural economic reform in China, 18 farmers at Xiaogang Village in Fengyang County, Anhui Province, ran an enormous political risk, signing a land contract document that laid down the framework for parceling out collective land to all villagers. Three decades later, the Third Plenary Session of the 18th CPC Central Committee passed the Decision on Several Major Issues Concerning Comprehensively Continuing the Reform. The loud trumpet call of reform is heard once more. Just like its predecessor, this new round of reform will begin in rural areas. The only difference is that the newer version is no longer geared toward solving the problem of food and clothes for the farmers. It's more about having farmers participate in the modernization process and giving them a fair share of the fruits of modernization. As Chen Xiwen put it, "Let the farmers judge whether they are enjoying a comparatively well-off life or not." Chen is the deputy director of the CPC Agricultural Work Leadership Group and director of its general office. The best path to have the farmers lead a decent and comfortable life enjoyed by the urbanites is to establish a sound mechanism for integrating urban and rural development and put it into effective use.

Let Farming Become a Decent
Career Choice

Since the initiation of reform and opening up, a basic and broadly promoted agricultural economic system "combining unity with division and double-tiered management" gave a lot of vim and vigor to agricultural production in China. As a result, eye-opening accomplishments have been made in agricultural production. However, with the deepened reform and opening up and the continued development of agricultural production, problems like the lack of land resources, large-scale migration of rural labor and the hollowing out of villages began to loom large. Statistical data show that by the end of 2012, a rural labor force of 262.61 million was transferred to the urban or non-agricultural sector, comprising 48.76% of the total number of agricultural employees of the year. A direct consequence of such migration is that middle-aged men and women and seniors now comprise the majority of China's agricultural population. Besides, the proportion of farmers' net income from agriculture is patently decreasing. For a great many farmers, agriculture has become a "sideline" for income growth. Questions of "who is going to farm" and "how to farm" have become issues that are directly related to the rise and fall of the country's agricultural future. Therefore, promotion of creative ways of agricultural management and construction of a new

September 18, 2014, rich villager Zheng Zucheng (2nd from left) is teaching chicken raising technology to fellow villagers at Wudoujiang Village in Shuichuan County, Jiangxi Province. In 2013, Zheng gave up his job in Hangzhou in order to lead the village and help the villagers become rich.

agricultural management system have become priorities of imminent importance.

Bengbu, Anhui Province, has made proactive contributions to the establishment of a new agricultural management system. Zhao Qirui is a farmer at Macheng Township in Bengbu's Huanyuan County, the largest glutinous rice production base in China. As far back as 2004, when more and more villagers were flowing out of the village to work in cities across the country, Zhao began to farm the deserted land left behind. Today, he is farming a land area of 10,200 *mu* (about 680 hectares), growing rice

and wheat by turns. In 2012, a bumper harvest of glutinous rice was reaped in Huaiyuan County, and Zhao had
a gross income of more than RMB 2,000 (about USD
320) per *mu* (0.67 hectare). With a handsome income,
Zhao became a big boss just by growing rice and wheat.

Zhao Qirui's road to wealth was typical of the road
followed by many of Bengbu's main grain producers. Statistical data show that a great majority of the 564 new enterprises are engaged in grain production, processing and
high-efficiency agriculture. By 2013, Bengbu has worked
out a regional planting industry plan through large-scale
production and industrialized management of 2 million

Big grain producer
Zhao Qirui loading
up dried wheat for
warehousing in
Huaiyuan, Anhui
Province, June 1,
2011

mu (about 133,333 hectares) of high-quality wheat, 1.2 million *mu* (about 80,000 hectares) of high-quality rice, 1 million *mu* (about 66,667 hectares) of high-quality corn and 870, 000 *mu* (about 58,000 hectares) of high-quality peanuts.

Apart from big producers like Zhao, a new body of entrepreneurs based on processing of agricultural products has appeared in Bengbu as well. The most typical is Modern Dairy Farming. Modern Dairy Farming invested RMB 2.4 billion (about USD 3.84 million) in Wuhe County, Bengbu City, in the construction of 100,000 *mu* (about 6,667 hectares) of pasture, a dairy farm of 40,000 heads of milk cows with a production capacity of 600 tons of liquid milk. On the premises of guaranteed basic land revenue, a labor force of about 30,000 can be liberated. By conservative estimates, the farmers' gross proceeds per year will increase to about RMB 500 million (about USD 80 million).

Bengbu's successful practices in the exploration of new types of business entities attracted a large number of leading national-level agricultural enterprises to set up bases in the city. Companies that came to invest or set up factories include Chinatex Grains and Oils, Dacheng (Taiwan), Zhejiang Senhe, Dalian Chengda, and Nanjing Yurun. By 2011, Bengbu had a total of 162 leading agricultural enterprises. Large agro-processing enterprises had an annual output value of RMB 36.68 billion (about USD 5.87 billion), an increase of 73.7%. Bengbu's total output value and total growth rate ranked, respectively, fifth and first in Anhui Province.

If you could make money and get rich by farming, and if you could become a big boss through such attractive ways of farming, why would there still be a shortage of farming professionals?

Zhang Xiaohong, 31 years old, is a tractor driver at Qiushi Grass Company in Wuhe County. For a long time in the past, she was a migrant worker in Zhejiang Province. She did little farming because revenue from agricultural production was too low. What has changed her mind? Why is she now willing to be a tractor driver in her home village? The reason is that the new way of management made it possible for her to earn a good income without having to go far away from home.

In 2012, after transferring about a dozen *mu* of land to a grass company, Zhang Xiaohong became a full-time tractor driver through technical training, earning three sources of guaranteed income every month: a land transfer fee of RMB 750 (about USD 120) per *mu*, a grain production subsidy of about RMB 200 (about USD 32) per *mu* and a salary from her job as a tractor driver, which

September 24, 2014, Yiling District, Yichang City, Hubei Province. Tangerine growers picking fruit at a farm. The district has 60,000 households of tangerine growers working an area of 335,000 *mu*. With an annual harvest of 606,000 tons, tangerine farming has become a leading industry for income and wealth growth for local farmers.

is RMB 3,800 (about USD 608) per month. "I can live a very good life without having to get out of the village. Why should I go work in the cities?" Zhang asked.

As agriculture grew more efficient and farming became more profitable, new professional farmers will naturally continue to grow. Some may even quit their original jobs to become farmers. A case in point is Wang Han, president of Hongtongtong Agricultural Production Cooperative at Renqiao Township, Guzhen County, Bengbu City. A former construction worker, he made money the hard way, going through thick and thin. Because he was optimistic about the prospects of agriculture, he abandoned his original expertise and resolutely returned home, bought 3,000 *mu* (about 200 hectares) of land and started large-scale cultivation. Today, the former building expert has turned into a downright professional farmer, thus completing a revolution from an "outsider" in farming to "an expert in farming."

New professional farmers like Zhang Xiaohong and Wang Han are bound to become the main force of the new business entities. The training of new professional farmers is a key issue for establishing a new model of agricultural management system. It is also a key to solving the problem of "who will be farming" and "how to farm."

Another question is: Will the circulation and transfer of land management rights lead to the loss of land contracting right?

The Third Plenary Session of the 18th CPC Central Committee has clearly defined regulations on this issue. The rural land contracting system will remain intact and unchanged for years to come. On condition that the most stringent farmland protection policies are being adhered to and improved, farmers will be entitled to the rights to possess, use and gain proceeds from the contracted land, the rights to transfer, mortgage and hypothecate the management right of the contracted land. They will be allowed to invest in industrialized operation of agriculture through contract and management right shares. Because China's rural land is collectively owned, the land use rights enjoyed by farmers are mainly divided into two parts: land contracting and management rights, including the rights to contract and manage farmland, woodland and grassland. According to relevant laws and regulations, a farmland contract has a period of 30 years, a grassland contract 30 to 50 years, and a woodland contract can range between 30 and 70 years. The other part is the right to the use of a homestead. According to relevant law provisions, land contract and management rights are usufructuary rights, including the contracting right to possess, use, generate proceeds, contract management, subcontract, lease, exchange and transfer, etc. Therefore, the worries and concerns of some farmers are utterly unnecessary.

In accordance with the provisions of the Property Law prior to this, farmers' land contract management rights cannot be secured or used as a guarantee. The Third Plenary Session of the 18th CPC Central Committee gave farmers more land use power so that they would have the right to hypothecate and secure land and can carry out transactions in those categories.

Soon after the 2014 Chinese New Year, Guo Zhaojian, a 41-year-old plant seedlings provider from Wenjiang

District in Chengdu, acquired a loan of RMB 620,000 (about USD 99,200) from the bank. Compared with previous loans, this is not a big one, but it has a special meaning for Guo because it came from the collateral of his rural land use rights for 122 *mu* (about 8.13 hectares) of land. It was also the first loan of its kind from a state-owned bank in Chengdu.

Initiated by Sichuan Standard Real Estate Appraisal Company, Ltd, this loan was the result of collaboration among relevant departments in Wenjiang District, a banking institution, a guarantee company and a farmer representative. Together they gave appraisal of the management rights of the 122 *mu* of land contracted by Guo Zhaojian for a period of five years. The appraisal showed that these rights were worth RMB 881,100 (USD 140,976), and based on that the bank in Chengdu provided him a loan of RMB 620,000.

Guo Zhaojian said: "In the past, the bank only accepted a mortgage on what grows on land, and the procedure was also very complicated. Because of the fluctuation of market prices, the bank saw that the risk was big. Usually with plants and seedlings worth RMB 40 million (USD 6.4 million), we would get a loan of RMB 10 million (about USD 1.6 million). This RMB 620,000 loan came not from secured plants and seedlings, but from land use rights. The procedures are simple, and the loan will cover the production and management expenses of the following three years." Adding hypothecation and guarantee functions to land contracting and management rights will not change the collective ownership of rural land, because the rights hypothecated is the right of land use rather than rights of land ownership. Hypothecation of the right of land use will not change the nature of collective ownership of rural land.

Construction of a new farming management system is a systematic and long-term project faced with many new issues and problems. The Third Plenary Session of the 18th CPC Central Committee stressed the foundational role of family business in agricultural development and the predominant role that agricultural households play in agribusinesses. The committee also emphasized the fostering and expansion of new models of agricultural production and management organizations. Meanwhile, innovation in agricultural management models is encouraged through the joint development of family operation, collective management, co-ops and entrepreneurial management. New ideas for rural land management and modes of agricultural operation have been proposed as well. We believe that in the near future, with the improvement of the new farming systems, more and more people will regard farming as a decent, lifelong career.

Let the Farmers' Property
Increase in Value

A weird phenomenon has existed in China for a long time. Houses bought by urban residents have full titles and can be used for hypothecation, security, and transaction, while houses built by farmers on their own premises are denied the same, and they cannot be sold to a non-member of the collective. It is the same with land. State-owned land use rights acquired by enterprises can be used for hypothecation and security interests, while collective land use rights owned by farmers cannot be used for the same purpose. Farmers have ownership over collective assets in the countryside, but their interests cannot be effectively realized in terms of economic benefits.

At the bottom of the unworthiness of farmers' property lies the inequality of property rights between rural and urban residents. Insufficiency of property rights seriously restricts the building up, accumulation and expansion of farmers' wealth. It also undermines the entry of farmers' property into the social asset incremental system, credit system and circulation system. It also restricts farmers' equality with urban residents in economic rights, and ultimately, it undermines the integration of urban and rural development. In order to effectively increase farmers' income, it is necessary to give them more property rights. Greater property rights and full actualization of such rights in terms of economic benefits will bring farmers more property income so that it becomes a new income growth point that effectively drives their income to faster and more sustainable growth and gradually minimizes the income gap between urban and rural residents.

The Third Plenary Session of the 18th CPC Central Committee proposed giving farmers more property rights, which means that farmers' property would gain in value. Chen Xiwen, deputy chief of the Central Rural Work Leading Group and its office director, who participated in drafting the Decision of the CPC Central Committee, sees this in two ways: First, property rights of farmers provided for by law have not been adequately protected. A series of policy measures have yet to be worked out to fully protect the fundamental legal property rights of farmers. Reform of the collective forest rights system in rural areas and initiatives such as rural collective land ownership registration and certification are laying an important foundation in protecting the property rights of farmers. Second, create a better system in which farmers' property rights are better utilized. To this end, the plenary session decided to create a series of rights for farmers, including the right to possess shares of collective assets and to generate proceeds, the right to paid exit, hypothecation, security, surety, transfer, and the setting-up of rural property rights transfer markets, etc. These are all important measures in efforts to protect farmers' property rights. It should be noted that, during this process, we can neither harm the rural collective land ownership nor let farmers become displaced.

Suzhou City in Jiangsu Province has a well-developed rural collective economy. In 2013, the total assets of Suzhou's rural collective economy exceeded RMB 135 billion (about USD 21.6 billion). Average village income exceeded RMB 6.5 million (about USD 1.04). New cooperative economic organizations reached 4,168, and more than 96% of farmer households were shareholders. In 2013, the farmers' net income per capita was RMB 21,600 (about USD 3,456). At the beginning of the 2014 Chinese Year, news was spread among the farmers of Suzhou that collective shares held by farmers could be passed on as legacy to their heirs.

The benefit comes from a reform measure taken by Suzhou Municipal Government to promote urban-rural integration. The city's Proposals for Implementing Deepened Reform towards Urban and Rural Integration suggested the following reform measures: 1) implement equity cure reform to accelerate the capitalization of resources and assets and the stockholding of capital,

2) deepen reform of the property rights system with an emphasis on curing the equity of rural cooperative economic organizations, 3) promote the quantification of collective assets into individual or household shares so that farmers will be provided with ownership rights of collective capital shares, rights to generate proceeds from such shares, rights of paid exit, rights of hypothecation, guarantee, and inheritance; 4) ensure that farmers' income growth rate would surpass urban citizens' income growth rate. This also means that farmers holding shares of collective assets will be able to pass such shares to their heirs.

Another way to increase farmers' property income is to make use of their homesteads. In accordance with China's current homestead regulations, each household can only have one homestead, and the area of such homestead cannot exceed the standards set by the relevant provinces, autonomous regions and municipalities. The monistic homestead use right has restricted the attributes and functions of the homestead as part of the farmers' property. Because the houses farmers build on their homestead do not carry title, the ownership rights and the ensuing economic functions of these houses, including hypothecation and security interests, are circumscribed. As a result, farmers' housing property rights cannot be fully monetized or increased in value or circulate in the market. This situation jeopardizes farmers' property rights and interests and detriments protection of farmers' property rights and interests. This is why farmers' property carries little value, just as we have mentioned earlier.

Hence, the current homestead system needs to be overhauled. The first step in that direction should be title registration and certification of rural homesteads by giving rural households legally binding title certificates and establishing a sound and uniform registration system of homestead use rights. The next step is to expand the scope of the homestead use rights. This can start with some pilot projects in selected areas, where farmers' housing property rights can be hypothecated, secured and/or transferred so that homestead use rights can convey full title functions, thus paving the way for farmers' real property to enter into the social asset increment system, credit system and circulation system. That way, farmers' property will increase in value, and in the near future farmers' houses will be just as valuable as houses of urban residents.

In this regard, certain cities and towns in Guangdong Province have made some very good probes. News reports show that some villagers in Guangdong Province are gaining long-term and stable income by renting out houses built on their homesteads. Other villagers are letting or renting out their homestead use rights and the buildings attached to the homesteads and then using the gain to buy houses and cars and settle down in the cities, thus effectively protecting their homesteads' usufruct.

While fully protecting farmers' homestead usufruct, proactive reform measures must be taken against maladies existing in the current homestead system. At present, rural homesteads are faced with two issues.

The first issue is excessive occupation of homestead, which constitutes encroachment of farmland resources. Such encroachment goes in two ways: one household with multiple homesteads and one household with one homestead whose area is patently above par. According to a sampling survey by the land resources department of a central province, about 15% of households in the surveyed province have multiple homesteads, while more than 40% of the urban villages and suburban villages have multiple homesteads. Even among farmers with one homestead, the phenomenon of over-occupancy of a housing area is very common. Although most local government authorities restrict such housing areas to between 120 and 200 square meters, an overwhelming majority of the farmers consider this standard to be the base area of the main building only, thus excluding auxiliary buildings, haystack areas, threshing floors and courtyards. As a result, an ill trend of over-occupancy of land, illegal and superfluous construction, and jealous competition in land encroachment took place. Such phenomena are even more common on the flat plains, and the exceeded area is also larger. According to a survey by Beijing authorities, farmers in a suburban town in Beijing have an average of 1.2 *mu* (0.08 hectare) of homestead per household, an average of 1.15 courtyards per household. Based on the standard of "one courtyard per household," their total area of over-occupancy accounts for 59% of the total homestead area. According to a survey by an eastern province, the province's rural residential area increased by an average of 34% per capita, from 122 square meters in 1996 to 164 square meters in 2004.

Second, a lot of homestead land is staying idle or being wasted. This can go in two main ways: building a new home without tearing down the old one and long-term idling of a homestead. In many rural areas, farmers do not remove their existing old house even after moving into their newly built homestead. Nor would they return their old homestead to the local authorities concerned. According to a survey by a provincial land resources department on one of the counties composed of 9,792 villages, more than half of these villages build new homes without tearing down their existing ones. Another survey done by the Ministry of Land and Resources show that rural idle and wasted homestead and unfarmed land account for 9% of rural residential area. Apart from serious loss of land resources, the waste has also affected the landscape and the outlook of the villages and has led to many "empty villages." According to a survey done by the Institute of Geographical Resources under the Chinese Academy of Sciences, rural homesteads and idle housing have triggered a conspicuously serious "empty village" problem. The institute estimates that comprehensive treatment of the "empty village illness" on a national scale would yield a farmland increase of up to 114 million *mu* (7.6 million hectares). Data from the Ministry of Land and Resources also show that such a measure would bring about an arable land increase of between 10% and 15%.

To solve the above-listed problems, measures must be taken to reinforce homestead management by sticking to the policy of "one homestead per household," strictly restricting homestead area, and putting an end to the phenomena of "multiple homesteads per household," and "over-the-limit homestead." Furthermore, we must strengthen homestead reclamation, eliminate idle homesteads by turning all idle homesteads into arable land so as to prevent waste.

"One path to urbanization, which is also an important part of promoting fairness and justice, is reformation of the bifurcated urban-rural system and promotion of the integration of urban and rural economic and social development. By providing farmers with more property rights, we are also showcasing the next step of rural reform and sending an important message about our drive to raise farmers' standard of living and to further stimulate their enthusiasm in pursuing a better life," Chi Fulin, president of China (Hainan) Institute of Reform and Development, said in an interview.

Equal Pay for Equal Work

A survey on the payment of new-generation migrant workers in Guangzhou showed that, in 2010, the year of a pay increase, 16% of the respondents were earning an average wage of less than RMB 1,030 (about USD 164.8) per month; 34.6% of them between RMB 1,500 and 2,000 (between USD 240 and 320), and 17% of them between RMB 2,000 and 3,000 (between USD 320 and 480). That means 80% of the new-generation migrant workers in Guangzhou were earning a monthly income of less than RMB 2,000. Nearly half of the respondents say that unequal pay for the same work was the greatest injustice they had experienced. They said that the city had a variety of restrictions and unreasonable charges on migrant workers. "Equal pay for equal work" is a cry from the bottom of their heart.

Fortunately, rural migrant workers are seeing a new light of hope as reform and opening up continues in China, especially after the Third Plenary Session of the 18th CPC Central Committee. "The government work report talked about seeking the right of equal pay for equal work for migrant workers, temporary employees and contract workers. This means hope and opportunity for these people," said He Zhongju, a deputy to the Shandong provincial people's congress. She told the writer about how she has personally benefited from the policy of equal pay for equal work. "Last year, our company had a pay rise for every employee. We, contract employees, were paid same as regular employees. This makes us feel something hopeful in the future." She also said that in some hospitals contract nurses do the same kind of work as others and even work harder, but they earn six or seven hundred yuan less than regular employees, and they have no corresponding benefits. He suggested that the government should increase monitoring of its own organs and departments over their employment practices. Departments concerned should introduce measures to allow certain excellent contract workers to convert into regular workers so that they would see hopes in the future. Such measures can also stabilize the workforce, she said.

The amended Labor Contract Act of July 1, 2013, provides that temporary employees are entitled to equal pay for equal work that full-time employees enjoy.

The Linyi Municipal Government issued "A Proposal on Further Improving Work on Migrant Workers under Current Circumstances." According to the proposal, by 2015, the city of Linyi will include all migrant workers who have stable employment relations with their employers in its social security system. A policy of equal pay for equal work will be basically followed. Wage arrears will be reduced to the minimum, and the work contract signing rate is expected to reach 85%. In addition, the tuition-free policy will extend to middle-level vocational education. By 2020, the contracting rate for migrant workers will exceed 95%, their average income will double that of 2010, and a long-term mechanism to protect the interests of migrant workers will be established.

The Decision on Some Major Issues Concerning Comprehensively Continuing the Reform issued at the Third Plenary Session of the 18th CPC Central Committee said: "[We will] protect farmers' rights and interests concerning the factors of production, ensure migrant workers receive equal pay for equal work, ensure farmers share equally the gains from added value of land, and ensure financial institutions' rural deposits are allocated mainly for agricultural and rural use." To guarantee equal pay for equal work for farmers is to change the unequal employment and labor remuneration system so that migrant workers may enjoy equal labor remuneration rights and interests as urban employees do. To ensure that farmers have a fair share of value-added land proceeds is to allow rural collectively owned profit-oriented construction land to be sold, leased and appraised as shares, make sure that it can enter the market with the same rights and at the same rates as state-owned land. In the meantime, measures must be taken to reform the land acquisition system, reduce the land acquisition scope, standardize land acquisition procedures, establish a mechanism for the distribution of incremental benefits from land that takes into account the interests of the state, the collective and the individual, and appropriately raise farmers' income share ratio in such benefits. To guarantee that rural deposits are mainly used for agriculture and in the countryside, we must improve rural financial service channels and systems so that deposits absorbed by financial institutions from the countryside are mainly used for agriculture and rural development.

In addition to safeguarding farmers' rights and interests in the essential factors of production, we must also establish a better agricultural support and protection system, reform our agricultural subsidy system, and improve the interest compensation mechanism in grain producing areas. These are all important aspects for promoting equal exchange of urban and rural factors and balanced allocation of public resources.

Generally speaking, China's agricultural production, which is deeply affected by its natural conditions, remains a kind of natural reproduction. Because of the relative fragility of the industry, Mother Nature can pretty much determine the abundance or deficiency in China's agricultural harvest. In addition, due to inadequate market demand elasticity and income elasticity, and due to the lack of market price advantage relative to industrial and other products, proceeds from grain and other agricultural production based on the same capital and the same piece of land are far less than those from other industries. For example, in 2011, of the 70 major grain-producing counties (including state-owned farms) in Heilongjiang Province, 43 had a fiscal revenue of less than RMB 100 million (about USD 16 million), 21 remained under the poverty line, and more than 60 still depended on fiscal subsidies. Economic development and residents' social welfare within these counties were greatly hampered. This situation directly affects food production and national food reserve security, and it has a negative impact on sustained and healthy development of China's agriculture.

Implementation of the agricultural subsidy program brought farmers tangible benefits and gave them the incentive to engage in farming. Fu Zhenbing is a villager in Kalunshan Village, Sijiazi Township, Heihe City, Heilongjiang Province. In recent years, due to large-scale increase in the price of agricultural materials and labor costs, half of the 1,200 villagers became migrant workers in large cities. Obviously, farming was not a financially attractive profession. However, he saw hope from the agricultural subsidy program. His family has 75 *mu* (5 hectares) of land, and they rented more than 900 *mu* (60 hectares) of land from other people. In 2012, he reaped a harvest of corn and soybeans totaling more than 50,000 kilograms. His net income per *mu* was more than RMB 130 yuan (USD 20.8). "When grain subsidies, farm tool subsidies, and seeds subsidies are added together, total subsidy per *mu* would exceed RMB 100 (USD 16). Usually paid in March or April, the subsidies help solve the problem of tight cash flow in the spring," Fu Zhenbing said. Fu added that such favorable policies gave him a lot of incentive to engage in farming.

The fly in the ointment for Fu is that the subsidies were mainly given to big grain producers with a planting area of more than 1,000 *mu* (about 66.7 hectares) or those with a single block of contiguous fields with an area of no less than 500 *mu* (about 33.3 hectares). So, in fact, very few farm households can benefit from the subsidies. Fu said that most local large grain producers like him do not have "a single block of contiguous fields with an area of no less than 500 *mu*." Because of the piecemeal nature of their farmland, they could hardly get any subsidy for renting farm machinery, plowing, and harvesting. According to relevant regulations, currently, most agricultural subsidies are paid to the contractor. Fu can only get subsidies for 5 hectares of his own land. The remaining 60 hectares have to be fully funded by himself. Fu said the subsidies should be adjusted according to actual circumstances so that they may benefit grain producers more.

The newly issued CPC Central Committee circular calls for an overhaul of the agricultural subsidy system so that it may play an active role in promoting agricultural production capacity and grain production capacity in particular.

Efforts will be made to change the present practice of subsidies that are based only on contracted area, regardless of how much grain is produced and of whether or not grain is produced at all. Use of direct subsidies to grain production, seed subsidies, farm machinery purchase subsidy, comprehensive agricultural subsidies, etc. will be mainly for grain producers. In particular, newly added subsidies will be geared toward main grain producing areas, large grain producers, family farms, and farmers' cooperatives so that agricultural subsidies will be hooked up with grain production. The ultimate goal is to have agricultural subsidies support grain production in a real and practical way by giving grain producers more subsidies.

Realize People-oriented Urbanization

Joseph Eugene Stiglitz, an American Nobel Prize winner in economics, lists China's urbanization and America's high technology as two key factors influencing the developmental process of humanity in the 21st century. He thinks that urbanization is the No. 1 challenge that the new century demands of China. After more than 30 years of reform and opening up, China has made great progress in urbanization. As of 2012, China's urbanization rate based on the permanent urban resident population reached 52.6%. On the other hand, the urbanization rate based on the registered urban household population is only 35.3%, which is 17% less than the former. From 2000 to 2012, the difference between the urbanization rate based on permanent urban resident population and the urbanization rate based on registered urban household population grew from 10.5 percentage points to 17.3 percentage points. Research by the Chinese Academy of Social Sciences shows that the composite index of China's migratory agricultural population that has obtained urban *hukou* is only about 40%. Although counted as urban population in statistical surveys, the migratory agricultural population has never obtained urban *hukou* for real. Because of that, they are never entitled to the same treatment as urban residents. Nor can they enjoy stable employment or live long-term in the city. They are at best in a semi-urbanized status, which affects not just the legal rights and interests of the migratory agricultural population, but also affects the harmony between different strata of society and the quality of urbanization.

Thus, a new dual structure is formed in urban areas. These phenomena and problems are most prominent in developed coastal areas and large cities. The good environment, development opportunities and the advanced culture of large cities make them more attractive to outsiders than small and moderate cities. According to the sixth census data in 2010, 35.9% of Beijing's 19,612,000 permanent residents are from outside the city; 39% of

Shanghai's 23,019,100 permanent residents are from outside the city; and 37.48% of Guangzhou's 12,700,800 permanent residents are from outside the city.

In Guangzhou, Shenzhen, Foshan, Dongguan and other manufacturing-based cities in the Pearl River Delta and the Yangtze River Delta, workers born in the 1980s and 1990s are becoming the main labor force on the assembly line. They are called "a new generation of migrant workers." According to a survey by the All China Federation of Trade Unions in 2010, when asked about their purpose of seeking employment outside their home turf, only 18.2% of those born in the 1980s chose "making money" as the answer, as opposed to 34.9% of those born in the 1970s and 76.2% of those born in the 1960s. Obviously, the younger generation is a generation of dreamers. They have become accustomed to city life, but find it hard to "merge into" it. They belong to the countryside, but have no way of "turning back." The household registration system (*hukou*) is like an iron gate that the ambitious "migrant workers of the new generation" have worn themselves out trying to kick it open.

Over the past two decades, urbanization of land went in a much faster pace than urbanization of population. Between 2000 and 2010, the national urban built-up area increased by 78.5%, while national urban population grew by just 45.9%. Such intensive urbanization of land is simply beyond the capacity of our land resources. Human-centered urbanization means to reverse the wrong direction of land urbanization through which lots of land is enclosed to build cities while inhabitants of the land are driven out. The focus is coordination between urbanization of land and urbanization of people. Institutionalized promotion of human-centered urbanization necessitates accelerated reform of the household registration system, total removal of restraints on resettlement in designated towns and smaller cities, orderly loosening of restraints on resettlement in medium cities, and the setting of rational standards for resettlement in large cities so that qualified agricultural migratory population may be converted into urban citizens. To that end, efforts must be made to steadily push for full essential public service coverage of all permanent urban residents so that agricultural migratory population may enter, resettle and merge in cities and towns and find employment or career therein. The key of urbanization is urbanization of the people or conversion of farmers into urban citizens.

"Take the road of new urbanization with Chinese characteristics, and promote people-oriented urbanization, promote coordinated development of large, medium and small cities and towns, integrated industrial and urban development, promote coordinated advancement of urbanization and new countryside construction, be innovative in population management, accelerate reform of the *hukou* system...." This is not only a solemn commitment from the new top leadership elected at the 18th CPC National Congress, but also a major initiative of the Party to further reform in a wider scope. For those "outsiders" in the cities who have been baffled by the household registration system, this is nothing less than a kind of gospel.

The good news is that with the continuous progress of reform and opening up, many cities have already looked into and initiated reform of the household registration system. Reform of the household registration system will, to the greatest extent, create conditions for the optimal use of people's knowledge, intellect and wisdom so that talents will find their best niches. This is the inevitable requirement of social development and an important symbol of social progress. It will play a significant, landmark role in the country's economic development and the amelioration of people's livelihood. Vigorous promotion of coordinated development of large, medium and small cities and towns is both an important feature of the new urbanization with Chinese characteristics and an important prerequisite for perfecting the healthy growth of the system and mechanisms of urbanization.

In this regard, two important measures must be

taken. One is strict control of population in megacities. Due to various reasons, it is becoming increasingly clear that China's population is overly concentrated in a few megacities. This is bound to cause traffic jams, air pollution, shortage of resources, ecological pressure on the environment, high cost of living, and other "urban diseases." Take Beijing as an example. Downtown Beijing has six traffic loops, a number of subways, plus many other public transport systems, constituting a sound and complete transport infrastructure. However, despite restrictions on the use of private cars in the city, traffic congestion remains a grave problem. According to an IBM Global "Commuter Pain" survey, 69% of Beijingers sometimes give up driving home, 84% of them say traffic conditions affect their job and academic performance because they have to spend on average an hour per day on the road. Therefore, in order to exercise strict control of population size in megacities, new and innovative ways must be sought to reinforce population control, prevent excessive concentration of population in megacities, and maintain rational distribution of population in different urban spaces.

The other important measure is to increase the capacity of small and medium cities to absorb population. Since small and medium cities are the mainstay for absorbing population, we need to optimize the structure and management of urban space, mightily develop small and medium cities and small towns by prioritizing industrial development. Industrial development is the key to the rise and prosperity of a city because it plays a major role in job creation. By proactively guiding population flow into small and medium cities, population will find a way of forming a benign pattern of reasonable distribution in all kinds of cities and towns. We must also set sound standards for city building, stipulate strict examination and approval procedures, and convert counties into cities when they meet conditions for administrative upgrading. Towns of considerable population and economic clout should be endowed with administrative powers commensurate with their population and economic scale.

People-oriented urbanization is comprehensive and coordinated urbanization. It means economic growth is no longer the one and only goal. It means comprehensive development based on multi-faceted needs of the people in all aspects of life, whether economic, political, cultural, social, or ecological. People-oriented urbanization should be unified and efficient, not just focused on economic benefits, but also on social and ecological benefits and the coordinated development of people, cities and the environment. People-oriented urbanization should be full of human vitality. As cities and towns belong to the people, they should be carriers of humanitarianism and human values. They should reflect culture and individuality. People-oriented urbanization should be fair and equal for all. The purpose of urbanization is to build harmonious and livable modern cities and towns so that the rural migratory population may truly merge into the cities and towns and that a broad spectrum of residents may have a fair share of the fruits of development. Only urbanization of this nature can "have cities merge with nature, have residents see mountains and waters and know clearly where they belong." This is what new urbanization with Chinese characteristics means and what makes integration of urban and rural development possible.

Afterword

The issues of rural areas, agriculture and farmers are some of the largest and hardest issues in China. Urbanization is the only way to go toward solving these problems. Since the kick-off of the policy of reform and opening up, the CPC and the Chinese Government have made intense efforts to promote urbanization and have made salient achievement in this regard. However, many problems remain. This book is meant to help readers gain a fuller and deeper understanding of China's urbanization initiative by doing two things: 1) describing and explaining the efforts of the Chinese Communist Party and the Chinese government devoted to urbanization and the efficacy thereof, and 2) describing the difficulties of China's urbanization drive and the reasons thereof.

The book was planned, outlined and edited by Xie Chuntao. The writing was done by a multitude of writers: Chapter One by Qi Xiaolin; Chapters Two & Three by Li Qinggang, Chapter Four & Six by Shen Chuanliang, Chapter Five by Gao Qiang and Chapter Seven by Han Xiaoqing. During the course of conceptualization, writing and editing of this book, editors from the New World Press, including Editor-in-Chief Zhang Hai'ou, and senior editors Li Shujuan and Qiao Tianbi have provided a lot of assistance. We sincerely acknowledge them over here.

Xie Chuntao
November 2014

图书在版编目（CIP）数据

中国城镇化：亿万农民进城的故事：英文/谢春涛主编；
王池英译. ——北京：新世界出版社，2014.11
ISBN 978-7-5104-5213-0

Ⅰ.①中… Ⅱ.①谢… ②王…Ⅲ.①城市化-研究
-中国-英文 Ⅳ.①F299.21

中国版本图书馆CIP数据核字(2014)第257871号

China's Urbanization: Migration by the Millions
中国城镇化：亿万农民进城的故事

主　　编：谢春涛
翻　　译：王池英
策　　划：谢春涛　张海鸥
责任编辑：李淑娟　闫传海
英文审定：徐明强
封面设计：贺玉婷
版式设计：北京维诺传媒文化有限公司
责任印制：李一鸣　黄厚清
出版发行：新世界出版社有限责任公司
社　　址：北京市西城区百万庄大街24号（100037）
总编室电话：+86 10 6899 5424 68326679（传真）
发行部电话：+86 10 6899 5968 68998705（传真）
本社中文网址：http://www.nwp.cn
本社英文网址：http://www.newworld-press.com
版权部电子信箱：frank@nwp.com.cn
版权部电话：+ 86 10 6899 6306
印　　刷：北京中印联印务有限公司
经　　销：新华书店
开　　本：640×960 1/16
字　　数：100千字 印张：15.25
版　　次：2014年11月第1版 2014年11月北京第1次印刷
书　　号：ISBN 978-7-5104-5213-0
定　　价：78.00元

the gut-loving
COOKBOOK

First published in the United Kingdom in 2022 by
Pavilion
43 Great Ormond Street
London
WC1N 3HZ

ISBN 978-1-91168-214-1

A CIP catalogue record for this book is available from the British Library.
10 9 8 7 6 5 4 3 2 1

Reproduction by Rival Colour Ltd
Printed and bound by Toppan Leefung Printing Ltd, China

www.pavilionbooks.com

Editorial Director: Sophie Allen
Editor: Cara Armstrong
Infographics design: Scarlett Chetwin, Harry Lee and Myron Darlington at Revolt
Logos and branding: Jones Knowles Ritchie
Book design: Maeve Bargman and Nathan Grace
Food stylist: Kitty Coles
Prop stylist: Rachel Vere
Photography: Haraala Hamilton
Production manager: Phil Brown

DISCLAIMER: The information in this book is provided as an information resource only and is not to be used or relied on for any diagnostic, treatment or medical purpose. All health issues should be discussed with your GP and/or other qualified medical professional.

the gut-loving
COOKBOOK

Over 60 deliciously simple gut-friendly recipes

—

from Alana & Lisa Macfarlane

of

the gut stuff

PAVILION

contents

1 Introduction

where's the science at? p.8

    the gut tips p.18

    top trio of gut-loving food p.19

    it ain't just about food p.24

    supercharge your storecupboard p.28

2 breakfasts & brunch p.39

3 a gut lunch p.57

4 the classics p.79

5 sides 'n' sauces p.117

6 just desserts p.137

7 ferments p.153

8 index p.174

introduction

Between 2015 and 2020, Google searches for gut health increased by over 400%. Far from being a flying fad, the microbiome market is skyrocketing, so why is everyone still so bloomin' confused? And, more importantly, why are 'gut health' conversations still only happening in health food stores and hot yoga queues? Why hasn't the message reached the wider population, and especially the people who suffer the most?

We interviewed scientists across the world – we even wrote a book with them! – to try and squeeze out some lifestyle tips for us to share with people until the science and industry caught up. We were expecting futuristic toilets seats that scan our poos, a pill filled with all our digestive hopes and dreams and maybe even a miracle cure. But what did they tell us? Simple stuff, like eat more fibre, cut down on ultra-processed foods, look at how you're sleeping and managing your stress levels. Drink water, for goodness' sake! Everything our granny used to tell us! Gut health is brilliantly complex – because it's so brilliantly important – but how we speak about it doesn't have to be. Everyone deserves to know their gut – they've got it for life, after all.

Disclaimer: This book isn't going to make you a gourmet chef with impeccable culinary prowess. It isn't going to have you scouring the supermarkets for the newest, most unusual ingredients to impress your dinner guests, nor is it going to transform your plates into the envy of the Instagram #foodie. It goes way deeper than that – to explore what is there inside you, literally.

Alana

Lisa

Welcome to The Gut Stuff dinner table, COME sit with us. We're laying out the table of misconceptions, pouring a smooth glass of 'why' and serving a plentiful helping of 'how'.

Think of this as snacking at the back of a biology lesson; dip in and out, try and read the juicy bits and make sure you pass along your favourite parts to your classmates. We peer into the wonderful world of food through the magnificent lens of gut health, but we'd like you to add on 'your health' at the end of the telescope – this is your toolkit, not a rulebook.

We were both kinda fed up of cookbooks that needed ingredients we couldn't find, so we've made sure there is absolutely something in here for everyone – if Alana can do it, anyone can! Lisa, on the other hand, really enjoys cooking and is the hostess with the mostest at dinner parties. Whichever camp you fall into, or somewhere in between, we hope you get a lot of use out of this book and it gets suitably marked with stains and your own little notes.

So, let's gut started…

Alana and Lisa
x

where's the science at?

Your gut is a bit like an avocado – you can't tell what it's like just from looking at it from the outside.

Don't be put off by the word 'science'. We used to think it was all high-school chemistry classes and Bunsen burners, but it really just means the study of nature and how natural things behave and the knowledge we gain from this.

 Nutrition is actually the science of nourishment.

Before we jump into the recipes, we want to take you on a date – a date with your gut – so you can get to know each other better. Light the candles, get comfortable and pay attention; you're about to get up close and personal with your insides. For starters, we are going to talk you through how your gut works, where our knowledge is at right now (and this changes quickly – so always keep an open mind) and learn how to use food (and other tactics, see pp. 26–29) to keep your new relationship with your gut blossoming and thriving.

We say 'gut'

you say 'what'

'Gut health' is a vague term and isn't as clear-cut as other areas of health, such as heart health, as there is still so much we are discovering.

When we talk about gut health, we are referring to the health of two different things:

'gut'

1 **The gastrointestinal tract (your gut), which is nearly 5 metres (over 16 feet) long!** When people hear the term gut, they often just think of their stomachs. However, the stomach is part of your upper digestive tract, along with your mouth and oesophagus, and your lower digestive tract contains your small and large intestines – upstairs and downstairs.

'what'

....stay with us...

2 **Gut microbiota (the trillions of microbes living [mostly] in your large intestine).**

These both work in harmony with the rest of your body and have a profound impact on your health. This book will focus mostly on your gut microbes and the recipes included are not a 'fix', 'cure' or magic pill, but aim to nurture these microbes with some simple, easy and affordable ideas.

what is the gut?

starts here

hold up
I thought
this was a
cookbook?

Cells lining your gut secrete enzymes and juices into the lumen (the hollow bit) and hormones into the blood.

Pharynx

Pushes food into your oesophagus (food pipe).

Oesophagus

Quick ride straight to your stomach.

Stomach

Strong muscles mix up your food with stomach acid (hydrochloric acid) and enzymes to both mechanically and chemically break down your food into something called chyme (pronounced kaim).

Gallbladder

Like your liver's sidekick, it stores bile ready for when it's needed.

Liver

Produces bile to help you digest fats (and has many more other functions – it's a clever beast).

Pancreas

Produces and releases pancreatic juice, including enzymes, which neutralize chyme and support the breakdown of carbohydrates, proteins and fats.

Large intestine

If food isn't digested in the small intestine, it passes into your large intestine for further digestion and this is where the majority of your gut microbes live (more on this on p.18).

rectum

ends here

Small intestine

Here is where a lot of enzymes get to work digesting your food further and where the majority of nutrients are absorbed.

Your gastrointestinal tract (or GI tract)

This is actually a flexible hollow tube made up of lots of layers, including a mucosa, which is home to some interesting species of bacteria. Your mucosa is a physical barrier that separates you from your microbes, it works hard to defend you, can change the make-up of microbes in your gut and some bacteria even feast on it!

digestion:
a tale of two parts

We talk about this ALL the time, but what do we actually mean?

Part 1 – Chemical

We know you want to get to the making bit, but we think it's important to understand how your body digests and absorbs food and the role of your gut microbes as this is the 'why' that helps you fundamentally change your behaviour – it was the light-bulb moment for us!

First of all, why are we bothered? Well, food contains important nutrients and digestion breaks food down into smaller pieces so the nutrients can be absorbed for use in your body and for your microbes to ferment.

So, where do chemicals break down the food in the body then? It turns out – lots of places!

Step 1: The mouth – Enzymes in your saliva break down carbohydrates.

SNACK FACT: *Enzymes in saliva (salivary amylase) primarily help break down starch. Another enzyme (lingual lipase if you're curious) supports the digestion of fat (this enzyme can decrease as we get older).*

SNACK FACT: *An enzyme is just a fancy word for a protein that can change something into another thing or speeds up a reaction.*

Step 2: The stomach – Stomach acid (hydrochloric acid – not the stuff you put on your face!) and bile work to supercharge the enzymes (and those in the small intestine) to break down proteins.

Step 3: The pancreas – Enzymes break down carbohydrates, proteins and fats.

Step 4: The small intestine – The membrane of the small intestine releases enzymes to further break down fats. Proteins and carbohydrates are mostly broken down in the small intestine.

Deep down in the small intestine is something called a brush border, which is made up of microvilli – tiny wave-like structures to maximize the surface area for absorption.

you want to impress your pals!). This is where your body secretes digestive fluids in response to a thought (like looking at a menu), sight (imagine a colourful platter of fruit), smell (your favourite meal) or taste (a lick of your cooking spoon).

Your vagus nerve (the physical connection between your gut and brain, not a restaurant in Las Vegas) controls this process.

How long does all this take? Sounds like a lot to be done. Well, digestion typically takes 24–72 hours.

Part 2 – Mechnical (happening alongside the above – busy body!)

Step 1: Before food even reaches your mouth, digestion can kick in. This is called cephalic digestion (a bit of lingo there if

SNACK FACT: *Around 25% of the enzymes and other substances produced by your pancreas happen in this phase.*

If you think about it, if you are mindlessly eating as you work, walk or scroll on your phone, this important part of digestion might not be kicking in as well as it could be.

Step 2: The Mouth Next up, your mouth, which has its own ecosystem of bacteria (oral microbiota) living within it. Your pearly whites aren't just for selfies and Instagram smiles, they serve a very important role in the process of digestion: chewing. Teeth mechanically break down your food into smaller pieces, creating a larger surface area for saliva (containing enzymes, like we've just learned) to work upon, plus the time spent chewing allows those enzymes to get to work.

Don't eat standing up – you digest food more efficiently when sitting. If you are standing, you might not be giving your food the focus it needs to optimize digestion.

Treat each meal as a date with your gut and its microbes Tools down, screens away and focus on what you are about to eat. Importantly, look forward to it and don't force yourself to eat something you don't enjoy. You wouldn't be scrolling the Gram while looking at the menu on a date, would you?! (Don't answer that!) So, we suggest that you:

- Put your knife and fork down between mouthfuls.

- Put away distractions.

- Chew, chew and chew again – you need to chew your food much more than you think. If you are guilty of a couple of chomps and swallowing (we used to be vacuums!), chances are you need to think more about how much you chew your food. It should be semi-liquid before swallowing.

Your saliva is 99.5% water!

Where does it travel to next?

FOOD PIPE (OESOPHAGUS) – Food mixed with saliva in your mouth forms a ball called a bolus, which travels past the pharynx down into the food pipe, a 25cm- (10 in-) long fast-track to your stomach (wheeeee!). It takes around ten seconds for a wave-like movement to propel food to your stomach, technically called peristalsis. Your stomach produces gastric juices and holds the food that you swallow and acts as a mixer (up, down, around and around) to combine food with gastric juices and enzymes to form a runny liquid called chyme.

The pH of gastric juice is the same as lemon juice (pH 2). Water, alcohol, some medication and a few minerals are absorbed in the stomach.

'Motility' is the ability of your GI tract to move by itself – like a wave (moving and shaking in your stomach isn't necessarily a bad thing). Contractions in your stomach happen around 3 times per minute, 8–12 per minute in your small intestine and around 7 times per minute in your large intestine. These wave-like movements help move food along to the next stage of digestion... and on we go.

Your stomach's volume is around 50ml (2 fl oz) when empty and can expand to around 1–1.5 litres (1¾–2½ pints) !

Takeaway

The rate at which food leaves your stomach (in the form of chyme) depends on what you've eaten. Fibre, fats and proteins slow down how quickly food leaves your stomach – it takes around 2–6 hours for it to empty.

SMALL INTESTINE – Into the small intestine we go; cue chyme entering from the stomach. Here is where the magic of nutrient digestion and absorption happens. It's split into three parts:

1. Duodenum
2. Jejunum
3. Ileum

It has a HUGE surface area of around 300m² (think three football pitches in length and nearly 1m-/3 feet-wide). How? The small intestine is full of folds of mucosa, villi (like fingers protruding into the lumen – the middle bit – and microvilli, similar to the villi but much smaller, like hairs). Enzymes are produced here to help digest food further. Antimicrobial substances are also secreted here to fight the unwanted guys – it's like an organizing, clearing out and getting rid of junk operation all at once. Clever guts.

SNACK FACT: *Fats and carbohydrates are typically absorbed within 30 minutes of reaching the small intestine.*

The small intestine receives bile from the gallbladder and pancreatic juices to neutralize hydrochloric acid coming from the stomach. Think of your pancreas, liver and gallbladder as the best pals to your gut. For more info on what they do, check out our first book.

LARGE INTESTINE – This is where the microbe magic happens. What doesn't get absorbed in the small intestine gets passed through to the large intestine, which is called 'large' not because it is longer but because the middle bit (lumen) is bigger.

 Salts and water get absorbed here (around 90–95%).

You have a lovely mucus lining in your large intestine, which is protective, lubricating and provides a damp environment for your microbes to thrive (they love it!). Bicarbonate, a by-product of metabolism, helps keep an alkaline environment and neutralizes acidic by-products produced by anaerobic bacteria (without air) in your large intestine.

TAKEAWAY: The absorption process takes 12–70 hours from the moment chyme enters until it plops into the toilet bowl. To give you an idea of the amount absorbed, for 1 litre (1¾ pints) of chyme at the start, it ends up as around 200g (7 oz – the weight of 2 small bananas), including dead cells, water, undigested food (including fibre) and bacteria.

GUT MICROBES – We cannot forget our dear microbes. If you're on a date with your gut, your microbes are the team of friends or family that stand behind you, making you who you are. OK, maybe that's a bit too conceptual. Let's try another analogy…

CLOSE YOUR EYES – you've got your wellies on in a field, you're filled with happiness, surrounded by music tents blaring various different tunes. There's a waft of food in the air and there's a helluva lot of people. You've guessed it, you're at a festival. We want you to liken all the different people at the festival to your gut microbes – some love a chip van, others prefer a veggie buddha bowl, some like heavy-metal mosh pits, others prefer a singalong to 90s pop and some might be there to cause trouble if given the right opportunity. Everyone's there together, but there's lots going on. How do we keep them all happy at the festival? (The technical term being ferment.) What do they like to eat?

Carbohydrates (mostly fibre, the bits of plants we can't digest) but they'll also munch on undigested protein (and broken-down protein in the form of amino acids). Some bacteria help to break down alcohol (thanks pals!) and lactose from dairy. All this fermentation produces acids (yep, really), the key ones being lactic acid (similar to what happens with kefir, which we'll get on to later) and short-chain fatty acids.

An example of a type of short-chain fatty acid, butyrate, is used as fuel for your gut cells (super clever right?!). Our gut microbes also produce different gasses, like methane, hydrogen, hydrogen sulphide and carbon dioxide (they have different or no smells) – hello farts!

the gut tips

As we touched upon before, unfortunately there isn't a magic ingredient for good gut health... we've asked scientists, doctors, dietitians and nutritionists and the three simple tips that come up time and time again are...

A message from your gut:

G ive me variety

U p my fibre

T ry ferments

If you keep all the different microbes happy, they can do incredible things like help to control your blood sugar, produce vitamins, manage cholesterol and hormonal balance, prevent you from getting infections, control the calories that you absorb and store, communicate with your nervous system and brain, influence your bone strength and so much more. Therefore, for each recipe we've supplied a key (see below) so you can keep track of all the variety, fibre and ferments in every meal, which leads us very nicely on to the next section of gut tips...

recipe key

variety   fibre   ferments   add ons

top trio of gut-loving foods

Variety – the spice of gut life

OK, what does the science say? Well, a study found that people who ate thirty-plus different plant-based foods a week were found to have a more diverse mix of gut microbes than those who ate less than ten. Remember our festival analogy from before? (See p. 19 for a reminder.) Think about thirty different types of music lovers at the festival; the more bands (plant-based foods) there are, the more people will be enjoying the festival as everyone will have something they like! We've also added in a 'quick tips' section to show you exactly where you can get that variety from (see pp. 30–37).

'Polyphenol' is one of those buzzwords that is often thrown around, but what does it mean? A polyphenol is a natural chemical found in some plant-based foods, from fruits and vegetables to coffee, chocolate and even red wine! Polyphenols are mini superheroes – they fight against damage caused by free radicals (a lot of this damage is an essential part of your body's processes). Polyphenols are like your microbes' cheerleaders – they help your microbes be their best selves by making them more efficient and feed those responsible for producing short-chain fatty acids.

Takeaway

Thirty plants a week may seem like a high number to hit but the recipes in this book

have 'gut' you covered, with extra additions to try in the recipes and 7 ways to up

your variety, coming up in just a few flicks…

Fibre

Fibre is the unsung hero of nutrition, like the bassist in the band whose name nobody knows. Adults need 30g (1 oz) of fibre a day, but 90% of us simply aren't getting enough. (The amount children need varies by age: 2–3 years = 15g/½ oz; 5–11 years = 20g/¾ oz; 11–16 = 25g/1 oz. Like adults, children in the UK aren't eating enough either.) With the increased consumption of processed foods, lack of fruit and vegetables in our diets and popularity of low-carbohydrate diets and/or fasting, fibre has been somewhat cast aside and we're here to bring it BACK.

Great, so we've got to up it, but where do we get it? Getting fibre from vegetables and fruit alone is tricky, so you need whole grains, nuts and seeds and pulses to add to the mix. Also, do your gut bugs a favour and don't cut carbs. This is where our easy peasy recipes come in; each meal being high in fibre (at least 6g per 100g fibre in each portion). Skip to p. 30 for our fibre table and quick fibre boosters.

You may have heard of soluble and insoluble fibres but we now know (thanks science) that there are many different types of fibre and it's this variety that's the key. Your microbes each enjoy different foods and so focusing on just one type of food (even a 'superfood') won't give you the gut benefits of eating a variety of different plants.

The plant wall contains around 95% of all fibre (need a reason to keep the skins on your tatties?) and the type of plant and the part (root, leaf or stem) you are eating will make a difference to the type of fibre and quantity it contains.

Takeaway

What is fibre?
The non-digestible carbohydrates found in plants that we can't digest but our gut microbes can.

Where can you get it?
It's either naturally found in plants that we ingest or fibres can also be isolated or manufactured and added to foods.

Providing you've not been medically advised otherwise, we want you to ditch the restriction and diet mentality and think about what you can ADD for your gut, not take away.

Ferments:
the tangtastic addition

Variety, tick. Fibre, tick – what else is there?

Fermented foods have been around since Neolithic times. They're often associated with a hefty price tag, making them something a lot of us wouldn't even think to put in our shopping baskets. However, they don't need to be expensive and, once you've learned the basic principles, you can make fermented foods really easily at home (see pp. 157–175).

tip!

A note about shop-bought ferments: always check that they contain live bacteria and aren't pasteurized or that they contain 'live cultures' (often added back in after pasteurization), otherwise you may lose the potential benefits that the community of microbes bring.

Why ferment food?

Historically, food was fermented to simply make it last longer and preserve it for consumption later (often by just making a brine with salt). Due to the bacteria and yeasts, fermented food is also tasty and may, in some ferments, increase the food's nutritional value. When bacteria and yeasts ferment food, they produce something called metabolites. These metabolites include lactic acid, vitamins and exopolysaccharides (sugar molecules) and may support our health and wellbeing (we are still trying to understand how and why).

Lots of different foods can be fermented, such as dairy, fish (yes really!), vegetables, cereals and fruits. The key bacteria found in fermented foods include Lactococcus, Lactobacillus, Streptococcus and Leuconostoc but yeasts and other bacteria also feature, depending on the ferment. The number of microbes (and their by-products) present will depend on how and where the ferment is made, how it's stored and what it's made from.

The sourdough bakers in San Francisco say their bread has a unique taste because of the unique microbes that inhabit their mothers (the sourdough starter kind).

Why do some ferments say ' probiotic' on the packet? Well, 'pro' means 'life' in Greek, so when food contains live bacteria, cultures and/or yeasts it is often termed a probiotic. However, you are not legally allowed to call a food a probiotic in the UK so you may see ' live cultures' instead. If done right (this is key!), fermented food can be a great source of bacteria and their by-products.

myth bust

Don't get ferments confused with pickles (like we did!) – they are a totally different thing.

Different ferments will contain different bacteria, cultures and by-products (variety is also key when it comes to ferments; two principles in one!). We're going to be speed-dating different types of ferments later, then showing you how to make your own to add into all our recipes.

it ain't just about food

We agree this feels slightly counter-intuitive for a cookbook – but sometimes it is about more than just WHAT we eat...

The science of habit forming

It is all well and good knowing WHAT to eat but how do you put that into practice? How many times have you said you're going to take up a new habit only for it to last a week? Both hands up for us!

Before we delve into the HOW, let's explain the WHAT.

A habit is a behaviour that you repeat regularly – it could be an action (like planning your meals or writing a diary), a routine (like shopping on a Sunday) or a lifestyle (like making sure you're active). Eventually, these behaviour patterns become subconscious and part of your day-to-day life – this is great news if the habit is a positive one, and even better if it's going to support you living that gut life!

Takin' the easy way outtt...

When given the choice, us humans often pick the easiest, quickest or most enjoyable option (we know that's the case for us!). Now, there's nothing wrong with this but when it comes to choosing an action that supports your gut, creating simple habits that become part of your routine may be better than the perceived easiest option. For example, if you always find yourself not knowing what to cook and reaching for the simplest and quickest option (like a ready meal or takeaway), planning your meals ahead and making a weekly habit of it may help you to eat a more gut-friendly diet.

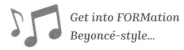 *Get into FORMation Beyoncé-style...*

The formation of a habit isn't as complex as you might think, but there are steps (and a little effort) required up front to make that habit stick. For an action to become a habit, it needs to be repeated and is often triggered by a cue (e.g. washing your hands after going to the loo).

Gotcha. OK, gimme the HOW.

- Decide on what goal you want to achieve (we've got some ideas for you below).

- Choose a simple action that you will do at a set time (e.g. making breakfast the night before).

- Plan when and where you will do this (e.g. 7 p.m. when cooking dinner in the kitchen) and your cue (e.g. planner on the fridge).

- Do the action (e.g. making breakfast).

- Keep doing it at the same time. You might find it useful to keep track of it by writing it down in a diary – you may find our gut diary helpful here (available from our website).

- Once it becomes second nature = habit formed.

Great... so a couple of days and I'm all set?

Not quite. You may have heard that it takes twenty-one days to form a habit – we love facts and figures but the truth is, it depends on the habit you're trying to implement, who you are and a lot of other circumstances. One piece of research looked at how long it took adults to form healthy habits, from dietary changes to physical activity – on average, it took sixty-six days but there was quite a range, from 18–254 days! So keep that in mind.

It's also important to remember that you won't derail your efforts by not doing it every day (a common misconception).

Here is a little platter of gut habits to pick from...

One more plant

Plant-based variety is so important when it comes to gut health. Assess each meal you make and ask yourself: Is there one more plant I could add? It could be herbs, seeds or a different kind of vegetable. The cue is looking at your plate or ticking off your plant count in a diary or on a tally-mark table on the fridge. We can help you with that...our handy variety checklist magnet allows you to keep track of variety in your shopping list and help you reach thirty different plants a week.

Plan the meals you make at home in advance

Choose the same day each week to sit down and do this and stick a reminder on your fridge (or use our meal planner magnet).

Sit down to eat (and don't pick while making food)

Put away your phone, chew properly and be ready to digest. This is one of the easiest and most underrated things you can do, and it's free! Cues: If you're standing, don't eat.

Make your own fermented food

Start slow, set time aside once a month to make your ferment or sourdough. Cues: Put your ferment schedule somewhere visible, regularly check on your ferment, care for it like a pet and, when it's done, have it in sight in your fridge so you remember to add it to dishes. There are loads of ferments coming up later, see p. 155–173.

Fibre-fuelled breakfast

Make your breakfast the night before so it's ready to grab and go. Our overnight oats (see p. 40) are super simple and we have lots of toppings to tickle your fancy.

Use a diary

If you're experiencing gut symptoms, try a notebook or diary to record what you're eating and the symptoms you're experiencing. This will help you tune in to your body and spot patterns that might be helpful.

Mindful eating

Enjoy the foods you eat, not because they are 'good' for you but because they are nourishing and you enjoy them.

Take a seat, turn off distractions and focus on what you are about to eat.

Rest your knife and fork on your plate between mouthfuls and chew your food. Savour the taste before swallowing.

Ask yourself the following questions:

Are you responding to an emotional want, thirst or your body's needs?

Is your stomach gurgling?

Do you feel hungry or do your energy levels feel low?

Are you reaching for food due to stress or for comfort?

Could you eat nourishing foods to support how you feel instead?

Are you focused on your food or is your mind distracted?

How does your food taste, smell and feel? During your meal, check in with yourself and ask how full you are feeling? Despite what your mamma told you, you don't need to finish your plate if you are full.

Living, working or even just eating alone can mean we fall into habits that aren't doing our guts any favours (think slumped in front of the TV, mindlessly chowing down). Having the radio or a podcast on can bring a feeling of company while still allowing you to focus on your date with your gut.

myth bust

'Don't drink liquids with food' is a myth. There's no robust evidence to support this or to say that liquids impair the digestion of food. There's some research that alcohol and caffeine may have an effect but it depends on the type and quantity.

supercharge your storecupboard

Here are tips for utilizing the stuff in your cupboards, plus easy swaps to get your gut on the right track.

7 ways to up your fibre

1 Don't let veg and fruit skins go to waste, just give them a good scrub. Grate carrots with the skin on, roast potatoes without peeling (we promise they're just as crispy) and save yourself a load of mess by keeping the skin on beetroot.

2 Go for wholegrain over refined white versions of the same food. Try and swap white rice, pasta and bread for wholegrain varieties.

3 Add nuts and/or seeds to breakfasts, soups, salads or stir-fries, or snack on them with a piece of fruit. We've always got a bag of nuts in our handbag or a jar in the house for snacking during the day.

4 Understand what's on a label: 6g or more per 100g = high fibre, 3–5.9g per 100g = source of fibre.

5 Add beans, like butter beans or chickpeas or lentils to meals, like adding red lentils to Bolognese sauce (see p. 82). These are great to bulk out and add extra nutrients to soups, stews and salads.

6 Start the day right. Enjoy oats or bran for breakfast and you avoid all those ultra-processed, sugar-laden cereals.

7 Get to know your numbers – check out our fibre table to see which foods give you the most fibre for your buck. We think you'll be surprised how much fibre is in certain foods – we know we were!

7 ways to up your variety

1 Tuning in to what you eat can help you spot patterns and see how much variety you are really getting. Note down what you've eaten and tally up the number of different plants you've consumed over the week. Did you make it to thirty?

2 Research shows us that, if we plan meals ahead and use shopping lists, we are more likely to eat more vegetables and healthier meals. Set aside 30 minutes at the end of the week to plan the week ahead or keep a notepad to jot down your shopping needs. We've got some handy shopping lists in this book (see pp. 36–37)!

3 Use mixed bags of salad as they usually contain over three different types of leaves – win!

4 Use all the colours of peppers (each counts separately!) – different colours mean more points and points mean prizes!

5 Buy a bag of mixed frozen veg – the freezer is your friend (see p. 32).

6 Make your own nut and seed mixes to sprinkle on salads or soups for a bit of crunch. You can get up to five or six cheeky points here! (See recipe, p. 135.)

7 Switch up your pasta and include lentil, pea and chickpea pasta with your favourite sauce (yes, really!).

spice up your life

Cupboards full of spices and don't know which spice girls to put in the band? Here's a handy guide to get them singing harmoniously together.

coriander

- + ginger
- + garlic
- + chilli
- + fennel
- + cinnamon
- + turmeric

- ♥ curries
- ♥ salsa

mint

- + basil
- + cumin
- + ginger
- + oregano
- + parsley
- + thyme

- ♥ aubergine
- ♥ fruits

sage

- + garlic
- + paprika
- + parsley
- + thyme

- ♥ stuffing
- ♥ tomatoes

basil

- + paprika
- + garlic
- + oregano
- + rosemary
- + thyme

- ♥ tomatoes
- ♥ soups

parsley

+ basil
+ garlic
+ paprika
+ mint

♥ fish
♥ salads

thyme

+ basil
+ garlic
+ nutmeg
+ oregano
+ rosemary

♥ chicken
♥ stews
♥ veg

chives

+ fennel
+ mint
+ parsley
+ sage
+ thyme

♥ avocado
♥ salads
♥ cold plates

rosemary

+ garlic
+ mint
+ parsley
+ sage
+ thyme

♥ root veg
♥ stews

oregano

+ basil
+ cumin
+ garlic
+ rosemary
+ sage
+ thyme

♥ pasta
♥ tomatoes

dill

+ basil
+ garlic
+ cumin
+ ginger
+ turmeric

♥ cabbage
♥ potatoes
♥ fish

freezer friendship 101

While we're at it, let's spring clean the food cupboard too. This section is the gllllloowwwwww upppppppp....

Frozen food shouldn't be shunned – it's a great way of having nourishing food at hand, avoiding food waste and making cooking cheaper and more efficient.

These are our freezer staples to help get variety:

SPINACH – Great for smoothies and to add to hot meals for an extra portion of plants.

PEAS – not just for fishfingers but a great addition to stir-fries, curries and even pasta!

FRUIT (RHUBARB, BANANAS AND BERRIES) – Top on porridge, add to kefir (not the water kind) or have as a snack.

RATATOUILLE MIX – Perfect for last-minute meals: top with fish, lentils or make a pasta sauce.

HERBS – Chop and freeze in little pouches; ready to go. This was a game changer for us!

READY-CHOPPED ONIONS AND GARLIC – Super-easy to add to the base of most dishes to increase fibre and variety and save on time when you're busy during the week.

what: chilli
when: 17.03.21
portion: two

use clear containers

freeze in portion sizes

freezer glow up

sort it, so you don't have to chuck it

meat/fish

fresh vegetables

dairy

turmeric
oregano
smoked paprike

herbs & spices

use by:
17.03.22

use by

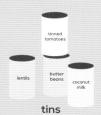
tinned tomatoes
lentils
butter beans
coconut milk

tins

food cupboard glow up

sort it, so you don't have to chuck it

Shopping List

shopping list

spring clean

dry goods

your simple weekly gut-loving shopping list

Food Cupboard – having a well-stocked cupboard doesn't have to be expensive or require a foraging trip to find super-unfamiliar ingredients. Get these bits and bobs on your shopping list:

HERBS AND SPICES

Turmeric: great for colour and adding an earthy flavour to curries (but watch for the stains).

Cinnamon (not just for Christmas!) : add to smoothies, stewed fruits, banana bread and porridge for a warming feel.

Smoked paprika: great for Mexican or Spanish flavours, we like ours in baked eggs, on sweet potato chips and hummus.

Oregano: instant Mediterranean flavour. Mix it into salad dressings or on roast veg.

Chilli flakes: we love chilli on hummus or when we want to take a dish up a notch.

Ginger powder: saves you having to grate it (peeling the skin can be fiddly!), add to curries and stir-fries for extra flavour.

Garlic powder: like ginger, easy to add to dishes and saves the faff of crushing it (and no smelling hands = win!).

DRY GOODS

Dried pulses: a little goes a long way but you will need to soak them overnight in water – our favourites are dried beans, peas, chickpeas and lentils.

Quinoa: pronounce it however you like!

Wholegrain pasta, lentil pasta and chickpea pasta: great alternatives to regular pasta.

Soba noodles: we love these in ramen as they're great at soaking up broth.

Wholegrain couscous: makes a super-speedy lunch.

It ain't just about food

Oats: overnight oats, flapjacks, porridge or savoury oats.

Pearl barley: great to add to soups or instead of other grains.

Nuts and seeds: mixed bags to get those variety numbers up

Nutritional yeast: sounds random but a great cheese substitute! If you're vegan, look for added vitamin B12.

. . . .

OILS AND VINEGARS ETC.

Good-quality olive oil: packed full of polyphenols

Tahini: great for dressings and hummus

Tamari: for depth of flavour

Apple cider vinegar: with the mother

. . . .

TINS

Great for convenience and adding instant nutrition to foods:

Tinned tomatoes: for quick sauces

Coconut milk: for quick curries

Tinned pulses and beans: mixed ones will up those variety points

. . . .

FRIDGE

Hummus: (see p. 120)

Artisan cheese: these are the ones that typically contain plenty of bacteria (if unpasteurized).

Live yogurt: always read the label – look for 'live cultures' or 'live bacteria'.

Kefir: milk or water, see pp. 168–169

Kombucha: see p. 170

Ferments: or make your own; you get them here – see pp. 153–171

Veg / salad / fruit: Grab as many different types of fruit and veg as you can. If you're making some of our recipes, be sure to put the ingredients for them on your list. Aim for as much variety and as many colours as possible.

. . . .

FREEZER

Fruits: berries of any kind, avocado, sliced bananas, mango, pineapple, pomegranate

Veg: spinach, mixed veg, peas, sweetcorn, onion, garlic, mixed peppers, green beans

And now on to the main event – we've learned some stuff, we've sorted some stuff, now it's time to MAKE some GUT STUFF.

On your marks, get steady... COOK!

a note on dietary requirements

Before we get started, a little word on how you can change these recipes to suit your dietary needs or allergy requirements.

Gluten: All the recipes in this book can be made gluten-free, using the following alternatives:

- Gluten-free flour, rice flour, gram flour
- Tamari *(gluten-free)* instead of soy sauce
- Gluten-free stock cubes
- Oats *(while they don't contain gluten themselves, they are often processed in a factory that may have handled gluten – always check the label.)*
- Flavoured tofu and some plant-based alternative products.

Gluten comes in many forms, from white flour to a spelt sourdough – if you don't need to remove it from your diet, think about variety; make sure you mix it up with different grains, like rye or spelt.

Dairy-free: Where we use dairy kefir or yogurt, you can swap for a dairy-free alternative *(such as coconut kefir)*. Swap cheese for nutritional yeast or vegan cheese *(or you can omit altogether)*

Swap dairy milks for plant-based milks – the choice is endless *(coconut, oat, almond, soya and cashew)*. Look for ones that don't have lots of thickeners and stabilizers in.

Eggs: In baking, you can use a 'flax' egg – a tablespoon of flaxseed and a tablespoon of water. Add to recipes as you would an egg. Note – this doesn't make a poached egg substitute!

FODMAPS: *What are they and what's that got to do with this book? Some types of carbohydrates can go unabsorbed in the small intestine and make it to the large intestine where they get fermented by our microbes. If you have IBS, it can spark the onset of gut symptoms, like gas, pain and change in stools.*

Researchers at Monash University Australia found that by avoiding high FODMAP *(Fermentable Oligosaccharides, Disaccharides, Monosaccharides and Polyols)* foods – essentially types of carbohydrates – some IBS sufferers had fewer symptoms. Foods high in FODMAPs include starchy foods made from wheat, like bread, pasta and biscuits, specific fruit (like apples), vegetables (onion, garlic and beans) and certain types of dairy. This resulted in them creating a type of elimination diet, which focuses on avoiding foods high in FODMAPs, which is split into three phases:

1. Elimination,
2. Reintroduction
3. Personalisation.

Not everyone with IBS will benefit from following a low-FODMAP diet and there is no evidence to suggest those without IBS will benefit, plus it also comes with its risks. If you think high FODMAP foods trigger symptoms for you, always consult with a FODMAP dietitian to see if this diet is right for you and to get the support you need. The recipes in this book do not follow a low-FODMAP approach.

food hygiene

How to prep, store and use in a safe way

It's all well and good knowing how to cook but we also want to help you with some practical tips to minimize food waste, reduce the risk of food poisoning *(always a win)*, and encourage good habits when it comes to storing food.

AND before you get going... a bit of food hygiene *(very important where microbes are involved)*.

Before you start: Before prepping and eating, ensure you wash your hands with soap and water *(including any little people involved)*. It may sound simple but many of us forget. Make sure you've got a clear surface wiped down with soapy water before you start. We always find it handy to get everything out of the cupboard/fridge-freezer before we start and have our equipment primed and ready *(and wash this too before fermenting)*.

Wash: Wash all vegetables and fruit under cold water and, if they are particularly muddy, give them a good scrub.

Contamination: Minimize cross-contamination of raw and cooked meat and fish as these may contain potentially harmful microbes.

chapter

2

breakfasts & brunch

overnight oats

This brekkie is truly for EVERYONE, couldn't be easier to make and can add all your favourite toppings to suit your tastes! What's not to love – a great start to your day! Alana x

10 minutes | Serves 1

9.3g per portion

minimum 4

milk kefir

allergens: *gluten, milk, nuts (make gluten- and dairy-free using alternatives and omit the nuts if needed)*

40g (1½ oz) oats

150ml (5 fl oz) milk kefir *(see p. 168)*, yogurt or milk *(dairy, plant, nut or other milk)*

1 apple, grated *(skin on)*

1–2 tsp nut butter *(such as peanut, almond or cashew) or mixed seeds (pumpkin, sunflower, seame, flaxseed or linseed)*

1 tsp ground cinnamon

1. Place all the ingredients into a 500ml (18-fl oz) jar, stir well, cover with a screw-top lid and place in the fridge for a minimum of 2 hours or ideally overnight.

2. When the oats have hydrated and thickened the mixture, pour the contents of the jar into your bowl. Add the toppings of your choice just before serving.

Store in the fridge for up to 4 days.

FLAVOUR COMBOS

Fibre – 8.5g
carrot cake – Swap the grated apple for a grated carrot (skin on) and add 1 teaspoon honey or maple syrup and swap the ground cinnamon for 1 teaspoon allspice. Swap the nut butter or mixed seeds for a handful of chopped walnuts to top.

Fibre – 9g
blueberry cobbler – Swap the grated apple for a handful of blueberries and add 1 tablespoon chia seeds.

Fibre – 9g
spiced pear – Swap the grated apple with a chopped pear (skin on). Swap the ground cinnamon for 1 teaspoon allspice and swap the nut butter or mixed seeds for a handful of chopped walnuts to top.

Fibre – 7.5g

strawberries and cream – Swap the grated apple with a handful of chopped strawberries and top with a spoonful of milk kefir yogurt.

Fibre – 12g

cherry chocolate – Swap the grated apple with 80g (3 oz) cherry chia jam (see below). Swap the cinnamon for 1 tablespoon cacao powder.

Fibre – 10.3g

peanut butter and strawberry chia jam – Top with 2 tablespoons strawberry chia jam (see below) and 1 tablespoon peanut butter (see below).

FRUIT CHIA JAM

15 minutes | Servings 4

strawberries
4.8g per 80g
cherries
2.9g per 80g
mixed berries
3.9g 80g
raspberries
7g per 80g

300g (10½ oz) fresh or frozen fruit, such as strawberries, cherries, mixed berries or raspberries

2 tbsp chia seeds

1. Place the fruit in a small saucepan over a low heat, stirring occasionally, until it begins to break down. Use a spoon to mash the fruit to your desired consistency, adding a splash of water to loosen if required. Stir in the chia seeds until combined. Remove from the heat and leave to cool for 5 minutes.

Once cool, store fruit chia jam in the fridge in an airtight container for up to 4 days.

NUT BUTTER

25 minutes | Servings 10-12

peanuts
1.5g per tbsp
almonds
3.3g per tbsp
cashews
1g per tbsp

250g (9 oz) nuts, such as peanuts, almonds or cashews

pinch of sea salt

1. Preheat the oven to 180°C fan/200°C/ 400°F/gas mark 6. Scatter the nuts over a large baking tray and toast in the oven for 10–15 minutes until golden. Remove from the oven and leave to cool. Transfer the nuts to a blender with the salt. Blend for 5–10 minutes until you're left with a smooth nut butter.

Store nut butter at room temperature in an airtight container for up to 2 weeks.

spiced green pancakes

Who said pancakes gotta be sweet? I love these for a weekend brunch or a lazy late lunch. Excellent with a spicy Bloody Mary ;) Lisa x

50 minutes | Serves 4
(including 20
minutes resting)

7.7g per portion

11

milk kefir

allergens: *gluten, cow's milk (if using), eggs*

PANCAKES

1 garlic clove, peeled

handful of fresh coriander

handful of spinach

½ tsp ground cumin

½ tsp ground cardamom

100ml (3½ fl oz) milk or oat milk, plus extra if needed

125g (4½ oz) spelt flour

2 large eggs

1–2 tbsp butter

salt and pepper

TOPPING

1 avocado, cut into chunks

2 spring onions, finely sliced

2 handfuls of spinach

2 tbsp milk kefir *(home-made, see p.168, or shop-bought)*

1 x 200g (7 oz) can of sweetcorn, drained

½ tbsp chilli flakes

squeeze of lemon juice

1. Put the garlic, coriander, spinach, cumin and cardamom in a blender and blitz to a smooth green paste. Add a splash of the milk or oat milk to loosen if needed.

2. Add the flour to a large mixing bowl and create a well, then add the eggs, slowly whisking them into the flour. Add a pinch of salt and stir, then gradually add the milk, followed by the green paste and whisk to combine. Leave to rest for 20 minutes at room temperature.

3. Put all the topping ingredients in a mixing bowl, season with salt and pepper and stir to combine.

4. Melt the butter in a 20cm (8 in) non-stick frying pan over a medium heat. Once hot, whisk the batter, then ladle 60ml (4 tbsp) into the pan. Cook for 2 minutes, then flip and cook for a further minute. Transfer to a plate and repeat, serve with the mixed topping.

Store any leftover pancakes in an airtight container in the fridge for 3–4 days. The topping is best prepared and served immediately.

sourdough french toast with mixed berry compote

This is a tooty fruity but not-too-sweet twist on traditional French toast (or eggy bread!) using sourdough. Frozen berries are a quick way to add variety and great for the winter months when berries tend to be out of season. Lisa x

20 minutes | Serves 2

6g per portion

minimum 4

sourdough and milk kefir yogurt

allergens: *gluten, cow's milk (if using), egg*

1 egg

50ml (2 fl oz) milk *(dairy, plant, nut or other milk)*

1 tsp ground cinnamon or allspice

zest and juice of ½ lemon

2 slices of sourdough *(homemade, see p.156, or shop-bought)*

200g (7 oz) frozen mixed berries

20ml (4 tsp) water

1 tbsp butter

2 tbsp mixed seeds *(pumpkin, sunflower, sesame, flaxseed or linseed)*

2 tbsp honey or maple syrup *(optional)*

1 tsp coconut flakes *(optional)*

milk kefir yogurt *(homemade, see p.168, or shop-bought),* to serve *(optional)*

1. Whisk the egg, milk and cinnamon or allspice together in a shallow bowl. Stir in the lemon zest. Add the sourdough slices to the mixture and leave to soak for 2 minutes, then turn over and soak for a further 2 minutes.

 Fibre and Variety – add a side of chocolate hummus *(see p.121)*
Ferments – add a spoonful of milk kefir yogurt *(see p.168)*

2. Place a small saucepan over a low heat, add the mixed berries and the lemon juice and water. Cook for 5 minutes until the berries have softened.

3. Heat the butter in a non-stick frying pan over a medium heat. Add the soaked sourdough, cook for 2 minutes until golden brown and then flip to cook the other side for a further 2 minutes.

4. Serve the sourdough toast topped with the mixed berry compote, mixed seeds, honey or maple syrup, coconut flakes and a dollop of milk kefir yogurt (if using).

Store any leftover compote in an airtight container in the fridge for up to 4 days.

bubble and squeak

A classic, PLUS if you leave your mash to cool completely, the potato starch becomes magic resistant starch with prebiotic properties for your good ole gut bugs. Lisa x

40 minutes | Serves 2
(including 20 minutes resting time)

 minimum 7g per portion without toppings

 minimum 4

 see topping suggestions

allergens: *cow's milk, if using milk kefir yogurt; fish, if using smoked salmon*

2 large handfuls of mixed vegetables, such as Brussels sprouts, cabbage *(any colour)*, kale or cavolo nero

1 parsnip *(skin on)*, roughly grated

4 spring onions, sliced

500g (14 oz) leftover mashed potato or grated potato *(skin on)*

1 tbsp olive oil

salt and pepper

TOPPINGS

milk kefir yogurt, smoked salmon and fresh chives

4 tbsp milk kefir yogurt *(homemade, see p.168, or shop-bought)*

120g (4¼ oz) smoked salmon handful of fresh chives, roughly chopped

hummus, sauerkraut and fresh parsley

50g (1¾ oz) hummus *(homemade, see p.120, or shop-bought)*

50g (1¾ oz) sauerkraut *(homemade, see p.160, or shop-bought)*

handful of fresh flat-leaf parsley, roughly chopped

avocado, kimchi and fresh coriander

1 ripe avocado, sliced

50g (1¾ oz) kimchi *(homemade, see p.164, or shop-bought)*

handful of fresh coriander, roughly chopped

Mashed potato

1. Roughly chop the potato (skin on) into cubes. Bring a medium saucepan of salted water to the boil. Add the potatoes and cook for 20–25 minutes until tender. Remove from the heat, drain and steam-dry for 5 minutes. Roughly mash using a potato masher, then rest for 20 minutes to cool completely for magic resistant starch.

2. Wash and finely shred the mixed vegetables. If using kale or cavolo nero, remove the woody stalks first. If using grated potato, squeeze out any excess liquid from the potatoes.

3. Add 1 tsp of the olive oil to a medium non-stick frying pan over a medium heat. Add the shredded veg and cook for 2–4 minutes until it begins to wilt. Remove from the heat and set aside. In a mixing bowl, combine the mashed potato, grated parsnip, spring onions and vegetables. Season well.

4. Add the remaining olive oil to the medium non-stick frying pan and return to a medium heat. Add the potato mixture and press down, using a wooden spoon or spatula, so it covers the base of the pan. Cook for 4 minutes, then fold the crispy bottom back into the mixture. Press the mixture back down and cook for a further 5–7 minutes until golden brown, then flip and cook the other side until golden brown. If the mixture breaks when flipping, press it down again. Top with one of our topping suggestions.

Store any leftovers in the fridge for up to 2 days.

creamy mushrooms on sourdough

I used to think the cashew soaking was a FAFF but it's well worth it to pimp up that toast. Lisa x

20 minutes | Serves 4
*+ 15 minutes
to pre-soak cashews*

8g per portion

minimum 6

sourdough

allergens: *nuts (cashews), gluten, cow's milk*

50g (1¾ oz) cashews

200g (7 oz) shredded kale

1 tbsp olive oil

1 x 400g (14 oz) can of cannellini or butter beans, drained and rinsed

50ml (2 fl oz) water

1 tbsp salted butter

1 shallot, finely diced

1 garlic clove, crushed
handful of fresh flat-leaf parsley, stalks finely chopped and leaves kept whole

400g (14 oz) mushrooms, such as button, chestnut, portobello finely sliced

4 slices of sourdough

salt and pepper

1. Place the cashews in a bowl and soak in boiling water for 15 minutes, then drain.

2. Preheat the oven to 180°C fan/200°C/400°F/gas mark 6. Spread the kale over a baking tray and drizzle with the oil, scrunching to ensure it's evenly coated. Season and cook for 10–15 minutes.

3. Place the soaked cashews, beans and water in a food processor and purée until smooth. Thin out with more water if required. Season with salt and pepper.

4. In a medium frying pan, heat the butter and cook the shallot for 3–5 minutes until softened. Add the garlic and parsley stalks and cook together for 1 minute. Add the mushrooms and cook for a further 3–5 minutes . Add the cashew and bean sauce and heat through.

5. Serve the mushrooms on toasted sourdough, topped with the crispy kale and parsley leaves.

Best eaten straight away.

veggie brunch

I love doing this if I'm feeling a bit swanky on a Saturday – and such a great way to use up my greens. We stuck with veggie here, but I also like to add a couple of sausages. Lisa x

20 minutes | Serves 2
with the TGS baked beans (make in advance)

 8.4g with TGS baked beans per portion

 minimum 9

 sourdough

allergens: *cow's milk, gluten (if using sourdough), eggs (if using)*

1 tsp butter
150g (7 oz) mushrooms *(any variety)*, roughly chopped
400g (7 oz) baked beans *(homemade, see p.52 or shop-bought)*
2 handfuls of greens *(such as spinach, cavolo nero or kale)*, shredded
120g (5¾ oz) halloumi, cut into 1cm (½ in) slices
salt and pepper

TO SERVE (OPTIONAL)
2 eggs *(the fresher the better)*
1 tbsp white wine vinegar
2 slices of toasted sourdough *(homemade, see p.156, or shop-bought)*

 Fibre – a handful of mixed seeds
Variety – use a mixed variety of mushrooms
Ferments – add a side of sourdough toast or olives

1. Add the butter to a large non-stick pan over a medium-high heat, add the mushrooms and brown for 3–5 minutes.

2. Meanwhile, add the baked beans to a small saucepan and heat through over a medium-low heat. Add the greens to the mushrooms, reduce the heat and cook for a further 3 minutes, stirring occasionally. Add a splash of water, if required. Season, then push the mixture to the edge of the pan and add the halloumi. Cook for 2 minutes on each side until golden brown.

3. If you're having eggs; while the halloumi is frying, fill a small saucepan with water and bring to a rolling boil. Add the vinegar and crack the eggs carefully into the water. Cook for 2–3 minutes, then remove with a slotted spoon. Serve with the veggie brunch on toasted sourdough.

Store any leftovers in an airtight container in the fridge for up to 3 days.

'gut' baked beans

Our mum used to always sing the 'beans beans, good for your heart, the more you eat...' etc. etc. whilst serving us baked beans and now we've got our own rootin tootin version. Alana x

40 minutes | Serves 4

 5.4g per portion

 minimum 7

 sourdough

1 tbsp olive oil

1 onion *(white or red)*, roughly chopped

2 peppers *(red or yellow)*, deseeded and roughly chopped

2 garlic cloves, roughly chopped

1 heaped tsp paprika or smoked paprika *(for a smoky twist)*

pinch of chilli flakes *(optional)*

1 x 400g (14 oz) can of tomatoes *(any type)*

1 x 400g (14 oz) can of white beans, such as butter beans or haricot, drained and rinsed

salt and pepper

toasted sourdough *(homemade, see p.156, or shop-bought)*

a baked potato or veggie brunch *(see p.51)*, to serve

 Fibre – add 2 handfuls of frozen spinach for the final 5 minutes of cooking
Variety – use a mixed variety can of beans

1. Heat the olive oil in a saucepan over a medium-high heat. Add the onion and a pinch of salt and cook for 5 minutes until softened, stirring occasionally.

2. Add the peppers and cook for 2 minutes. Add the garlic, paprika and chilli flakes (if using) and cook for 2 minutes.

3. Add the tomatoes, then swill a splash of water around the can and add this to the pan too. Bring to the boil, then reduce the heat and simmer for 15 minutes.

4. Remove from the heat and use a stick blender to create a smooth sauce. Season to taste. Return to the heat, stir in the beans and cook until warmed through.

5. Serve on top of toasted sourdough, a baked potato or with our veggie brunch.

Store in an airtight container in the fridge for up to 3 days.

chapter

3

a gut lunch

chicken goujon caesar salad with fibre cracker croutons

Love this if I've got pals round and want to make a wee alfresco dining effort without just shoving packets of goujons in the oven... My cheeky twist is to use almonds to make a crunchy coating. I usually make a full batch of fibre crackers to keep, but they're usually all munched as I'm cooking ha! Lisa x

1 hour 10 minutes | Serves 2
(including fibre crackers)

8.6g with fibre cracker per portion

minimum 9 *(based on 3 different types in the mixed leaf bag)*

milk kefir yogurt

allergens: *nuts (almonds), egg, fish, cow's milk*

½ fibre crackers mixture
(*see p.61*)

2 skinless chicken breasts

30g (1¾ oz) ground almonds

1 tsp paprika

1 egg

2 romaine lettuces

2 handfuls of mixed leaves

salt and pepper

DRESSING

20g (1¾ oz) Parmesan cheese

1 small garlic clove, grated

2 canned anchovy fillets, finely chopped

squeeze of lemon juice

4 tbsp milk kefir yogurt (homemade, see p.168, or shop-bought)

1 tbsp extra virgin olive oil

1. Preheat the oven to 180°C fan/ 200°C/400°F/gas mark 6 and line two baking trays with baking paper.

2. Begin by mixing all the ingredients for the fibre crackers together.

Recipe continued overleaf

Fibre – top with 100g (3½ oz) jarred artichoke, roughly chopped
Variety – a handful of sliced cherry tomatoes
Ferments – top with a handful of olives

3. While the fibre cracker mixture is soaking, prepare the chicken goujons. Using a sharp knife, cut the chicken into strips. Mix the ground almonds and paprika in a shallow bowl and season well. In another shallow bowl, whisk the egg. Coat the chicken goujons one by one in the beaten egg and then the almond-paprika mixture. Arrange on one of the lined baking trays.

4. Once the fibre cracker mixture has thickened, spread it thinly over the second lined baking tray until it's around 5mm (¼-in) thick. Bake for 25 minutes, then add the tray of chicken to the oven too and bake both for a further 25 minutes, turning the chicken halfway through cooking.

5. To make the dressing, finely grate half the Parmesan and add to the milk kefir yogurt in a jug with the anchovies, garlic, lemon juice and olive oil. Stir well to combine and season to taste.

6. Shred the lettuce and add to a large mixing bowl with the mixed leaves and coat in the dressing.

7. Crumble the fibre cracker and use a peeler to cut the remaining Parmesan into shavings.

8. To serve, top the leaves with the chicken goujons, sprinkle over the crumbled fibre cracker and Parmesan shavings.

Best served immediately.

fibre crackers

I buy huge bags of nuts and seeds and prep loads on a Sunday to make crackers for dipping and crumbling onto soups 'n' salads...moreish beyond belief... Lisa x

20 mins prep | Makes 10
+ 50 minutes   crackers
cooking   5 portions

5.8g per portion

5

65g (2¼ oz) sunflower seeds

50g (1¾ oz) pumpkin seeds

35g (1¼ oz) chia seeds

35g (1¼ oz) sesame seeds

20g (¾ oz) whole flaxseeds

½ tsp salt

180ml (6 fl oz) water

1. Preheat the oven to 180°C fan/ 200°C/400°F/gas mark 6 and line a medium baking tray with baking paper.

2. Mix all the ingredients together and leave for 15 minutes for the chia seeds to soak up the water. Once the mixture has thickened, spread thinly over the lined baking tray until around 5mm (¼-in) thick. Bake for 50 minutes. If the cracker doesn't feel crisp after 50 minutes, return to the oven for a further 5–10 minutes.

3. Remove from the oven and leave to cool before breaking into crackers.

Store in an airtight container for up to a week.

Fibre – top with hummus *(see p.120)*

Variety – top with a handful of rocket

Ferments – top with sauerkraut or kimchi *(see pp.160 and 164).*

oMEGA salad

Tuna Salad is my Go-To if grabbing lunch on the move, so this is a homemade better-version-of (in my opinion!). Genuinely so fill(et!)ing too... bring on the Omega 3! Alana x

30 minutes | Serves 4

10g per portion

minimum 9

olives

allergens: *fish, eggs*

4 eggs
200g (7 oz) baby new potatoes, halved
2 handfuls of green beans, trimmed
2 Little Gem lettuces
200g (7 oz) cherry or plum tomatoes
50g (1¾ oz) stoned olives
1 small red onion
handful of fresh flat-leaf parsley

1 x 400g (14 oz) can of chickpeas, drained and rinsed
2 handfuls of mixed leaves
2–3 tbsp extra virgin olive oil
100g (3½ oz) marinated white or canned anchovy fillets
squeeze of lemon juice
salt and pepper

1. To soft-boil the eggs, ensure the eggs are room temperature. Bring a medium saucepan of water to a rolling boil, add the eggs and set a timer for 6–7 minutes.

Fibre – top with 2 tsp mixed seeds
Variety – add 2 handfuls of spinach leaves
Ferments – toss the salad in milk kefir yogurt (see p.168)

Transfer the eggs to cold water to cool before peeling and cutting into quarters.

2. Heat a large saucepan of salted water over a high heat. Once the water is boiling, add the potatoes, reduce the heat and simmer for 15–20 minutes until tender. Add the green beans for the final 2 minutes. Drain and leave to steam-dry while you prepare the rest of the salad.

3. Remove the end of each lettuce and cut into quarters lengthways, halve the tomatoes and the olives, thinly slice

the onion and roughly chop the parsley. Add to a large mixing bowl (except the olives) along with the chickpeas, cooked potatoes and green beans. Drizzle over the extra virgin olive oil, combine and season to taste.

4. To serve, top the dressed salad with the quartered eggs, olives and anchovies. Finish with a squeeze of lemon juice.

Store any leftovers in an airtight container in the fridge for up to a day.

shredded brussels sprouts salad

I am FOREVER thinking up what to do with sprouts – my go-to was always pan-fried with pancetta and walnuts, but here's a cheeky non-Christmas alternative. Got a newfound love for them. Lisa x

20 minutes | Serves 4

8.1g per portion

 8

allergens: *milk (if using feta), nuts (walnuts)*

60g (2¼ oz) walnuts

100g (3½ oz) kale

1 fennel bulb

200g (7 oz) Brussels sprouts

handful of fresh flat-leaf parsley

2-3 tbsp extra virgin olive oil

400g (7 oz) cooked quinoa

zest and juice of ½ lemon

120g (2¾ oz) crumbled feta cheese *(optional)*

seeds of 1 pomegranate

salt and pepper

 Fibre – top with crumbled fibre crackers *(see p.61)*
Variety – a side of hummus *(see p.120)*
Ferments – top with sauerkraut *(see p.160)*

1. Preheat the oven to 180°C fan/200°C/400°F/gas mark 6.

2. Scatter the walnuts over a baking tray and cook for 10 minutes until lightly toasted. Remove the woody stalks from the kale and roughly shred. Finely shred the fennel and Brussels sprouts. Roughly chop the parsley.

3. Add the kale to a mixing bowl along with 1 tablespoon of the olive oil and half the lemon juice. Season well and massage the kale leaves for 2–5 minutes until softened. Add the Brussels sprouts, fennel, quinoa and parsley. Gradually add the remaining lemon juice (checking the flavour as you add!) and the zest, remaining olive oil and season to taste.

4. Roughly chop the toasted walnuts. Top the mixed salad with the crumbled feta (if using), chopped walnuts and pomegranate seeds.

Store any leftovers in an airtight container in the fridge for up to 3 days. Leftover walnuts will keep better stored at room temperature in an airtight container.

sunshine bowl

Colourful, quick summer in a bowl. Pre-cooked packet grains are great for this. Enough said. Lisa x

10 minutes | Serves 2

 minimum 11g per portion

 minimum 9

 milk kefir yogurt

allergens: *nuts (dependant on nut used in crunchy nut and seed topping), cow's milk*

250g (5½ oz) pre-cooked grains *(freekeh, buckwheat, bulgur or brown rice)**

1 carrot *(skin on)*

1 pepper *(any colour)*, deseeded and sliced handful of cherry tomatoes, halved

2 handfuls of baby spinach

4 tbsp milk kefir yogurt *(homemade, see p.168, or shop-bought)*

4 tbsp crunchy nut and seed mix *(see p.133)*

salt and pepper

1. Use a vegetable peeler to slice the carrot into ribbons lengthways.

2. Place the carrot, pepper and tomatoes in a mixing bowl along with the spinach and grains, stir in the milk kefir yogurt and season.

3. To serve, divide the grains and vegetable mixture between two shallow bowls and sprinkle with the crunchy nut and seed mix.

Store any leftover salad in the fridge for up to a day. The crunchy nut and seed topping is best stored at room temperature in an airtight container for up to 2 weeks.

 Fibre – 1 sliced avocado
Variety – a side of green or black bean and lime hummus *(see p.121)*
Ferments – top with kimchi or sauerkraut *(see pp.164 and 160)*

*Heat the mixed grains according to the packet instructions.

build your own plant-based traybake

Like Tetris, for veg. You do you. Lisa and Alana x

30 minutes | Serves 2

Fibre – hummus
(see p.120)
Variety – mixed whole
grains or quinoa
Ferments – sauerkraut,
kimchi or fermented hot
sauce *(see pp.160, 164
and 131)*

BASE

choose 1 bean, pulse or veg
BEAN AND PULSES
1 packet or 400g (14-oz)
can of cooked lentils
1 x 400g (14-oz) can of
chickpeas
1 x 400g (14-oz) can of
beans *(butter, haricot,
black, cannellini, black-
eyed, aduki)*

BASE VEG
butternut squash *(skin on)*,
roughly chopped
sweet potato *(skin on)*,
roughly chopped
parsnip *(skin on)*, roughly
chopped
turnip, roughly chopped
swede, roughly chopped
carrot *(skin on)*, roughly
chopped

PLANTS

choose at least 2
handful of tomatoes, halved
1 onion, roughly chopped
(any colour)
1 pepper, roughly chopped
(any colour)
handful of broccoli, roughly
chopped
handful of radishes, halved
handful of asparagus,
woody ends removed

handful of green beans,
trimmed
1 aubergine, roughly
chopped
handful of baby corn
handful of mushrooms *(any
variety)*, halved
1 courgette, roughly
chopped
handful of grapes
handful of frozen broccoli,
peas or cauliflower

FLAVOUR

choose at least 1 *(see spice pairings infographic, pp.30–31)*

1–2 tsp dried spices *(ground cumin or coriander, sumac, paprika, smoked paprika)*

1 tbsp dried herbs *(oregano, thyme, rosemary, sage)*

citrus zest and juice *(lemon, lime or orange)*

garlic cloves, crushed or smashed

dried or fresh chilli

....

TOPPINGS

choose at least 1

2 tbsp crunchy seed and nut mix *(see p.133)*

2 tbsp mixed seeds *(pumpkin, sunflower, sesame, flaxseed or linseed)*

handful of stoned olives

2 tbsp mixed nuts *(walnuts, cashews, almonds,* hazelnuts or pistachios)

handful of mixed fresh herbs *(flat-leaf parsley, basil, coriander or chives)*

sliced avocado

60g (2¼ oz) crumbled feta

handful of leaves *(rocket, spinach, watercress or a mixture)*

extra virgin olive oil

2–3 tbsp olive oil, to cook

1. Preheat the oven to 200°C fan/ 220°C/425°F/gas mark 7. If using base veg, bring a pan of salted water to the boil, then parboil for 5–7 minutes, drain and steam-dry for 2 minutes.

2. Add the base beans, pulses or veg, your selection of plants and 2–3 tablespoons olive oil to a medium baking tray. Stir to coat the ingredients in the oil. Add the flavouring, if using spices or herbs or zest, scatter evenly and stir to combine. Finish with a squeeze of citrus, if using.

Cook for 15 minutes, then give everything a good stir. Return to the oven and cook for a further 10–15 minutes until everything is slightly golden and tender.

3. Once cooked, serve the traybake with your selection of toppings.

Store any leftovers in the fridge for up to 3 days.

one-pot chicken noodles

Every time I think about ordering a takeaway, I make this instead – so yum! Just make sure you don't spill all the peppercorns on the floor (like I did...) Alana x

1 hour | Serves 4

 minimum 7g per portion

 minimum 6

 miso paste

allergens: *sesame (if using sesame oil), soya, gluten (see miso paste), egg (check noodle packaging)*

 Fibre – use wholegrain noodles such as soba
Variety – top with crunchy nut and seed mix *(see p.133)*
Ferments – top with kimchi *(see p.164)*

250g (9 oz) dried soba noodles

1 tbsp sesame oil or light olive oil

4 shallots, roughly chopped

4 garlic cloves, smashed

7.5cm- (3 in-) piece of fresh ginger, unpeeled and roughly sliced

1 small chicken, weighing

1–1.2kg (2 lb 4 oz–2 lb 11 oz)

1.2 litres (2 pints) water

2 carrots *(skin on)*, roughly chopped

10 whole peppercorns

2–3 tbsp miso paste
(double check for wheat, barley or rye if need to avoid gluten)

120g baby or frozen spinach

salt

TOPPING

1 tbsp sesame oil or light olive oil

400g (14 oz) mixed vegetables, such as broccoli, green beans, frozen peas or sweetcorn, spring greens, kale, pak choi, asparagus, roughly chopped as necessary

1 red chilli, deseeded and finely sliced

1 garlic clove, finely sliced

handful of fresh coriander, roughly chopped

squeeze of lime juice

1. To make the stock, add 1 tablespoon of the oil to a large, lidded casserole pot over a medium-high heat. Add the shallot, smashed garlic cloves and ginger. Cook for 5 minutes until they are slightly golden. Add the chicken (breast down), water, carrots and whole peppercorns with a pinch of salt. Bring the water to the boil and reduce to a simmer, removing any scum that forms on the surface. After 25 minutes, carefully turn the chicken over and cover the pan with the lid.

Simmer gently for a further 20 minutes or until the juices of the chicken run clear when piercing the meat.

2. Once cooked, remove the chicken and leave it to rest for 10 minutes before shredding. To shred, tear the chicken off the bone (you can use your hands here!), removing any skin or fat, then use a fork to shred the meat.

3. Sieve the remaining liquid, discarding the vegetables, and return to the heat. Add the miso paste, spinach and chicken and stir through. Cook for 5 minutes on a low-medium heat. Season to taste.

4. Meanwhile, make the topping. Add the oil to a medium frying pan over a medium-high heat. Add the garlic and chilli and cook for 2 minutes. Add the vegetables and cook for a further 5–10 minutes until cooked through.

5. Cook the noodles according to the packet instructions and drain. Divide the noodles between four deep bowls and top with the chicken soup, mixed veg, coriander and a squeeze of lime juice.

Store any leftovers in the fridge for up to 3 days.

kimchi grain bowl

When you fancy a spice hit, plus a WHOPPER of a hit on the variety counter. Lisa x

20 minutes | Serves 4
(if using pre-cooked rice and quinoa)

7g per portion

15 *(if using TGS kimchi)*

kimchi

2 tbsp tamari or light soy sauce

250g (7 oz) firm tofu, sliced

1 tbsp sesame oil or light olive oil

2 garlic cloves, sliced

2.5cm- (1 in-) piece of fresh ginger, peeled and grated

160g (2¾ oz) kale

250g (5¾ oz) pre-cooked brown rice

250g (4¼ oz) pre-cooked quinoa

TOPPING

200g (5½ oz) kimchi *(homemade, see p.164, or shop-bought)*

½ bunch spring onions, sliced

1 tbsp sesame seeds

squeeze of lime juice

Fibre – add a small tin of canned sweetcorn to the kale

Variety – top with mixed beansprouts

Ferments – fermented hot sauce *(see p.131)*

1. Put half the tamari in a bowl, add the tofu and coat evenly.

2. Heat a frying pan over a medium-high heat and add the oil. Add the tofu slices and cook on each side for 2–3 minutes until golden. Reduce the heat to medium, add the garlic and ginger and cook for 1 minute. Remove the tofu from the pan and set aside.

3. Add the kale to the pan with the remaining tamari and cook for 2–4 minutes until the kale has wilted.

4. Heat the rice and quinoa according to the packet instructions and divide between two bowls.

5. Top the rice and quinoa with the tofu, kimchi, kale and spring onions and sprinkle over the sesame seeds. Add the lime juice and serve immediately.

kim-cheese

Quick, high-variety, extremely addictive! Double whammy on the ferment front! Alana x

5 minutes | Serves 2

6.7g per portion

11 with TGS kimchi

kimchi and sourdough

handful of fresh coriander

2 slices of sourdough
(*homemade, see p.158, or shop-bought*)

60g (2¼ oz) goat's cheese

40g (1½ oz) watercress

100g (3½ oz) kimchi (*home-made, see p.164, or shop-bought*)

1. Roughly chop the coriander and toast the sourdough.

2. Crumble the goat's cheese and roughly spread over the toast using the back of a fork. Top with the watercress, kimchi and coriander.

Best served and eaten immediately.

Fibre – top with 2 tbsp crunchy seed and nut topping (*see p.133*)
Variety – top with a handful of rocket

tomato and chickpea soup

There's something so comforting about a tomato soup. I like mine extra smookkeeey. Lisa x

1 hour | Serves 4

11g per portion

minimum 11

sourdough

allergens: *sesame (if adding fibre cracker), celery, gluten*

Fibre and variety – crumbled fibre crackers *(see p.61)*
Ferments – spoonful of milk kefir yogurt *(see p.168)*

200g (7 oz) cherry or plum tomatoes, halved

3 tbsp olive oil

1 tbsp balsamic vinegar

1 leek, sliced

1 carrot *(skin on)*, finely diced

2 celery sticks, sliced

2 garlic cloves, crushed or grated

1 tsp paprika

1 tsp chilli flakes

1 x **400g** (14-oz) can of chopped tomatoes

400ml (14 fl oz) vegetable stock

1 x **400g** (14-oz) can of chickpeas, drained and rinsed

2 bay leaves

squeeze of lemon juice

200g (7 oz) greens, such as Savoy cabbage, cavolo nero or kale, leaves roughly shredded

1 tsp smoked paprika

salt and pepper

toasted sourdough *(homemade, see p.156, or shop-bought)*, to serve

1. Preheat the oven to 180°C fan/200°C/400°F/gas mark 6.

2. Spread the tomatoes over a baking tray and drizzle with 1 tablespoon of the olive oil and balsamic vinegar. Season with salt and pepper and cook for 15–20 minutes.

3. Heat 1 tbsp of the olive oil in a large pan over a medium heat. Add the leek, carrot and celery and cook for 5–10 minutes until softened, stirring occasionally. Add the garlic and cook for 2 minutes. Stir in the paprika and chilli flakes and cook for 1 minute. Add the canned tomatoes, vegetable stock, chickpeas and bay leaves. Partially cover with a lid, reduce the heat to a simmer and cook for about

20 minutes until slightly thickened. Stir in the roasted balsamic tomatoes and lemon juice. Season to taste and remove the bay leaves.

4. In a separate pan, add the remaining 1 teaspoon of olive oil over a medium heat. Add the greens and smoked paprika and stir-fry for 5 minutes until tender.

5. Serve the soup topped with the paprika greens and a side of toasted sourdough.

Any leftover soup can be stored in the fridge for up to 4 days or frozen for up to 1 month.

chapter

4

the classics

spaghetti bolognese

Sometimes I take the additions in my bolognese a bit too far, ha! But always lentils for more fibre, then olives to jazz it up... Plus there's always the option to have mushrooms instead of beef?? Lisa x

1 hour | Serves 4+

11g with beef, 12g with mushrooms per portion

minimum 9

olives

allergens: *celery, cow's milk, gluten*

Fibre – use wholegrain spaghetti
Variety – top with a handful of rocket
Ferments – add a side of toasted sourdough bread

1-2 tbsp olive oil
1 onion, finely diced
2 carrots *(skin on)*, finely diced
2 celery sticks, finely diced
2 garlic cloves, crushed or grated
400g (14 oz) minced beef or mixed mushrooms, roughly chopped
1 x **400g** (14-oz) can of chopped tomatoes
1 tbsp dried oregano
1 tbsp dried thyme

90g (3¼ oz) stoned olives *(optional)*, roughly chopped
200ml (7 fl oz) beef or vegetable stock
1 x **400g** (14-oz) can of lentils green or puy, rinsed and drained
1 tbsp tomato purée
300g (10½ oz) spaghetti
handful of fresh basil leaves, torn
60g (2¼ oz) Parmesan cheese, grated
salt and pepper

1. Add the olive oil to a large non-stick pan over a medium-high heat. Add the onion, carrots and celery, season with salt and cook for 5–10 minutes until softened. Add the garlic, cook for a minute, then add the minced beef or mixed mushrooms and cook for 10 minutes, stirring, until browned.

2. Add the oregano, thyme and olives and cook for 2 minutes. Add the canned tomatoes, stock and lentils and tomato purée then bring to the boil. Reduce to a simmer and cook for 40–50 minutes or until the sauce has thickened. Season to taste.

3. Bring a medium saucepan of salted water to the boil and cook the spaghetti according to the packet instructions.

4. To serve, mix together the spaghetti and the bolognese sauce, divide between bowls and top with the torn basil leaves and grated Parmesan.

Store any leftovers in the fridge for up to 3 days or freeze the bolognese sauce for up to a month. Defrost thoroughly before reheating.

beetroot burgers with root vegetable chips

A wonderfully bright and light plant-based alternative. Alana x

1 hour | Serves 4+

 minimum 13g per portion

 minimum 8

 milk kefir yogurt, kimchi or sauerkraut

allergens: *gluten, egg, cow's milk, sesame*

BEETROOT BURGERS

1 tbsp olive oil, plus extra for brushing the burgers

1 red onion, finely chopped

2 tsp ground cumin

1 slice day-old sourdough

400g (14 oz) raw beetroot, coarsely grated

2 x 400g (14-oz) cans of chickpeas, drained and rinsed

2 heaped tbsp flaxseed

2 tbsp milk kefir yogurt *(homemade, see p.168, or shop-bought)*

1 egg

1 tbsp tahini

1 tbsp rice flour, plus extra if needed

salt and pepper

ROOT VEGETABLE CHIPS

1 large, sweet potato, *(skin on)* and sliced into chips

½ celeriac, peeled and sliced into chips

olive oil

TO SERVE *(optional)*

wholegrain buns

rocket

onion *(any variety)*, sliced

ferments, such as kimchi or sauerkraut *(homemade see pp. 164 and 160, or shop-bought)*

1. Preheat the oven to 220°C/200°C fan/425°F/gas mark 7 and line two medium baking trays with baking paper. Put the sweet potato and celeriac on one of the baking trays, drizzle with olive oil, season and set aside.

2. In a frying pan, heat 1 tablespoon of olive oil and fry the onion for 3–5 minutes until softened. Add the cumin and cook together for 1 minute.

Recipe continued overleaf

3. Put the sourdough in a food processor and pulse to breadcrumbs, then add the onion mixture along with the grated beetroot, chickpeas, flaxseed, milk kefir yogurt, egg, tahini and rice flour. Mix to a rough paste, then scrape into a bowl and season well. If the mixture is sticky, add a little more flour.

4. With damp hands, shape the mixture into about six burgers and space apart on the remaining baking tray. Brush the burgers with a little olive oil and bake in the oven alongside the root vegetable chips for 35–40 minutes until crisp and hot through.

5. Serve the burgers in wholegrain buns with rocket, onion and ferments as you wish.

Leftover beetroot burgers can be stored in an airtight container in the fridge for up to 4 days.

Fibre – serve with sliced tomatoes
Variety – *a handful of rocket*
Ferments – fermented tomato ketchup or fermented hot sauce *(see pp.130 and 131)*

chicken nuggets

Nuggets are my go-to hangover food - we've added some flaxseed for a fibre boost so your gut bugs can have a post-party munch too. Lisa x

30 minutes | 2 as a main or 4 as a side

5.6 g per portion

3

allergens: *nuts (almonds), eggs*

2 skinless chicken breasts

40g (1¾ oz) ground almonds

1 tsp paprika

2 tbsp ground flaxseed

1 egg

salt and pepper

1. Preheat the oven to 200°C/180°C fan/400°F/gas mark 6 and line a medium baking tray with baking paper.

2. Using a sharp knife, cut the chicken into chunks. Mix the almonds, flaxseed and paprika in a shallow bowl and season well. In another shallow bowl, whisk the egg.

3. Coat the chicken chunks in the beaten egg and then the almond mixture one by one. Transfer to the lined baking tray and bake for 15–25 minutes until cooked through and slightly golden, turning halfway through cooking.

Fibre and Variety – serve with a side of kefir tzatziki and sweet potato wedges *(see p.118)*

Ferments – fermented hot sauce or ketchup *(see p.131 and 130)*

Best served immediately but any leftovers can be stored in the fridge for up to a day.

aubergine and sweet potato katsu curry

Anything with Katsu Curry in the title... SOLD! Alana x

40 minutes | Serves 4

9.8g per portion

minimum 11

milk kefir yogurt

allergens: *nuts (almonds), eggs, soya (if using soy sauce),*

Fibre and variety –
corn salsa *(see p.129)*
Ferments – a side of
kimchi or fermented hot
sauce *(see pp.164
and 131)*

100g (3½ oz) ground almonds

1 egg or 20ml (4 tsp) almond milk

1 aubergine, cut into 1cm (½-in) pieces

1 medium sweet potato *(skin on)*, cut into 1cm (½-in) pieces

2 tbsp groundnut oil or a light olive oil

1 onion, diced

3 garlic cloves, crushed

2.5cm (1-in) piece of fresh ginger, peeled and grated

1 tbsp medium curry powder

1 tsp garam masala

½ tsp ground turmeric

2 carrots *(skin on)*, grated

1 apple *(skin on)*, grated

2 tbsp light soy sauce or tamari

1–2 tbsp tomato purée

500ml (18 fl oz) vegetable stock

salt and pepper

TO SERVE

240g wholegrain rice

handful fresh coriander

4 tbsp milk kefir yogurt

salt and pepper. In another shallow bowl, whisk the egg or add the almond milk.

1. Preheat the oven to 180°C fan/200°C/400°F/gas mark 6 and line two medium baking trays with baking paper. Put the ground almonds in a shallow bowl and season with

2. Coat the aubergine and sweet potato in the beaten egg or almond milk and then the almond mixture. Transfer to the lined baking trays and cook for 25–30 minutes until the vegetables are tender and the almond coating is golden.

3. Meanwhile, cook the rice as per the packet instructions and set aside.

4. Heat the oil in a large pan over a medium-high heat. Add the onion and cook for 5–7 minutes until softened. Reduce the heat, add the garlic and ginger and cook for 2 minutes. Add all the spices and stir through. Add the carrot and apple and stir to combine. Add the soy sauce or tamari, tomato purée and stock. Increase the heat and bring to the boil, then reduce the heat and simmer for

20 minutes. Remove from the heat and use a stick blender to blend to a smooth sauce. Season to taste.

5. To serve, divide the rice between four plates, add the sauce and top with the roast vegetables, fresh coriander and a dollop of milk kefir yogurt.

Store the sauce and vegetables in the fridge for up to 3 days. Rice should be stored for 1 day only and must be reheated until piping hot before eating.

sourdough pizza

WHAT A CROWD PLEASER. Get creative with toppings – I like to leave it to the guests if I'm entertaining as all sorts of tomfoolery and creativity ensues. Lisa x

30 minutes | Makes 2 pizzas

+ prep dough 1 day in advance

 see toppings

 see toppings

 sourdough

allergens: *gluten, milk, nuts (check per topping make dairy free using alternatives and*

PIZZA BASE
(MAKES TWO BASES)

1 tbsp olive oil, plus extra for greasing

275g (9¾ oz) strong white bread flour, plus extra for dusting

55g (2 oz) sourdough starter *(see p.154)*

185g (6½ oz) water

5g (¹/₈ oz) salt

TOPPINGS

Tomato sauce

1 x 200g can of chopped tomatoes

salt and pepper

60g mozzarella, feta, goat's cheese or **30g** Parmesan cheese

Plant-based toppings

¼ x 400-g (14-oz) can of chickpeas + 2g fibre

handful of broccoli + 2.8g fibre

5–6 asparagus spears + 1.4g fibre

80g (2¾ oz) jarred Jerusalem artichokes + 4g fibre

½ pepper *(any colour)* + 1.8g fibre

handful of chopped cooked aubergine + 2.5 g fibre

80g (2¾ oz) tomatoes + 0.9g fibre

80g (2¾ oz) mushrooms + 0.8g fibre

Toppings to add once cooked

handful of rocket or spinach

1 tsp chilli flakes

50g jarred sun-dried tomatoes

1 tbsp crunchy seed and nut mix *(see p.133)*

50g sauerkraut *(homemade, see p.160, or shop-bought)*

drizzle of milk kefir yogurt *(homemade, see p.168, or shop-bought)*

drizzle of fermented hot sauce *(homemade, see p.131, or shop-bought)*

side of fermented tomato ketchup *(homemade, see p.130, or shop-bought)*

handful of fresh basil leaves, torn

2 tbsp walnut pesto *(homemade, see p.135)*

Jarred vegetables are great to have in the pantry to add on... think artichokes, peppers, sun-dried tomatoes and olives... Also we prep the dough the day before, so you can spend your time chattin, not rollin and kneadin.

1. To make the pizza bases, add all the ingredients to an oiled bowl and use your fingers to mix until you have a sticky dough ball. Cover with a tea towel and leave to sit for 30 minutes at room temperature. After 30 minutes turn the dough out onto a work surface and use the 'slap and fold' method to stretch and fold the dough until it feels stronger, smoother and more elastic. This can take around 10 minutes – keep going! Use a dough scraper to mould the dough into a ball. Return to the bowl, cover again and leave to sit at room temperature for 6 hours until the dough has begun to show signs of fermentation.

2. After 6 hours, turn the dough out onto a work surface, adding a dusting of flour if required, and use scales to portion into two equal balls. Place the dough balls on a lightly floured baking tray with high sides and cover with oiled clingfilm. Put in the fridge for 12–24 hours until ready to cook. (The dough will need to be brought to room temperature before cooking, so remove from the fridge for 30–60 minutes beforehand.)

3. Preheat the oven to 220°C fan/240°C/475°F/gas mark 9. Prep all your toppings. To prep the tomato sauce, add the chopped tomatoes to a bowl and season with salt and pepper.

4. To shape the dough, dust a work surface with flour and delicately work and stretch the dough into a round base roughly 25–27cm (10-12 in) in diameter.

5. Place a non-stick frying pan (the same size as your pizza base) over a high heat. Once the pan is hot, carefully add the dough. Next, add the tomato sauce, spreading it with the back of a spoon, then quickly arrange the toppings. Cook over a high heat for 2–4 minutes until the base has turned golden. Then use a spatula to remove from the pan and transfer to a baking tray. Bake in the oven for 8 minutes. Repeat with the second base. Finish by adding any of the extra toppings once cooked.

Leftovers will keep in the fridge for up to a day.

veggie chilli

Speaks for itself. We love to pour the leftovers onto baked sweet potatoes or our loaded fries, and would highly recommend with a dollop of kefir ;) Alana x

50 minutes | Serves 4-6

12g per portion

minimum 10

allergens: *check stock cubes for allergens*

2 tbsp olive oil

1 onion, diced

1 pepper *(any colour)*, cored, deseeded and sliced

2 garlic cloves, crushed

1 red chilli, deseeded and finely chopped

2 tsp paprika

2 tsp ground cumin

½–1 tsp hot chilli powder

1 medium butternut squash *(skin on)*, cut into 2.5cm (1-in) cubes

1 x 400g (14-oz) can of chopped tomatoes

300ml (10 fl oz) vegetable stock

1 x 400g (14-oz) can of red kidney beans, drained and rinsed

300g (10½ oz) wholegrain rice

1 lime, quartered

salt and pepper

Fibre – use wholegrain rice instead of white rice
Variety – top with a handful of chopped fresh coriander
Ferments – a spoonful of milk kefir yogurt *(homemade, see p.168)*

1. Add the olive oil to a large non-stick pan over a medium-high heat. Add the onion, season and cook for 5–10 minutes until softened. Add the pepper, garlic and chilli and cook for 2 minutes. Add the squash and stir to coat in the spices.

2. Pour in the tomatoes, swill a splash of water around the can and add this too along with the stock. Bring to the boil, reduce to a simmer, tip in the kidney beans and cook for 20–30 minutes until the squash is tender. Season to taste.

3. Meanwhile, cook the rice according to the packet instructions.

4. Serve the vegetable chilli with the rice and a squeeze of fresh lime juice.

Store any leftover chilli in the fridge for up to 4 days or freeze for up to a month.

one-pot butter bean, broccoli and leeks

A simple week-night dinner; fresh, quick and ooh so comforting. Lisa x

30 minutes | Serves 2

9.3g per portion

8

allergens: *cow's milk*

1 tbsp butter

1 leek

200g (7 oz) broccoli *(florets and stalks)*, roughly chopped

3 sprigs of thyme

2 garlic cloves, crushed

1 tbsp capers, finely chopped

1 x 400-g (14-oz) can of butter beans, drained and rinsed

1 bay leaf

handful of fresh flat-leaf parsley, finely chopped

½ mozzarella ball, torn

salt and pepper

1. Melt the butter in a medium pan over a medium-high heat. Add the leek, cut-side down, to soak up the butter. Season and cook for 2–4 minutes until golden, reducing the heat if the leeks begin to catch.

2. Add the broccoli and season with salt and pepper. Stir in the thyme sprigs, garlic and capers. Add 200ml (7 fl oz) water, followed by the butter beans, bay leaf and parsley.

3. Cover with a lid, reduce the heat and simmer gently for 20 minutes. When cooked, remove the bay leaf and thyme sprigs and season to taste.

4. To serve, divide between two bowls and top with the torn mozzarella and freshly ground black pepper.

Store any leftovers in the fridge for up to 2 days.

Fibre – top with a spoon of our walnut pesto *(see p.135)*

Variety – top with a handful of rocket

Ferments – a side of sauerkraut *(see p.160)*

baked salmon topped with sourdough crumbs

Fuss-free - great with a veg tray bake bonanza. Lisa x

30 minutes | Serves 2

6.1g

minimum 6

olives and sourdough

allergens: *gluten, fish, celery, nuts (walnuts, if adding walnut pesto)*

1 slice of day-old sourdough (*homemade, see p.156, or shop-bought*)

1½ tbsp olive oil

1 lemon, quartered

1 fennel bulb, finely sliced

1 red onion, sliced

2 handfuls of cherry tomatoes

100g jarred artichoke, drained

2 salmon fillets

2 garlic cloves, finely sliced

handful of stoned black olives

handful of fresh herbs, such as basil or flat-leaf parsley, roughly chopped

salt and pepper

Fibre – add 1 x 400g (14-oz) can of beans (*any kind*) to the vegetables

Variety – top with 2 tbsp of our walnut pesto (*see p.135*)

Ferments – sauerkraut (*see p.160*)

1. Preheat the oven to 180°C fan/200°C/400°F/gas mark 6 and line a baking tray with baking paper. Add the sourdough to a blender and pulse to breadcrumbs, then stir in the ½ tablespoon of olive oil. Season the salmon with salt and pepper and a squeeze of lemon juice.

2. Place the fennel, onion, tomatoes and jarred artichokes in a mixing bowl, season well and coat with the remaining olive oil. Spread out over a medium baking tray and cook for 15 minutes.

3. Remove the tray from the oven, stir in the garlic and olives, add the salmon and cover the salmon and vegetables with the sourdough breadcrumbs. Return to the oven and cook for a further 15–20 minutes until the salmon is cooked through.

4. Serve garnished with the chopped fresh herbs and an extra squeeze of lemon juice.

aubergine parmigiana with spicy courgettes

Homemade, bubbly, cheesy – all the good stuff. Lisa x

1 hour 10 minutes | Serves 4

9.8g per portion

minimum 9

allergens: *cow's milk*

 Fibre and variety –
corn salsa *(see p.129)*
Ferments – a side of
kimchi or fermented
hot sauce *(see pp.164
and 131)*

2 large aubergines, cut into
1cm- (½-in-) thick slices

1 tbsp olive oil

TOMATO SAUCE

1 tbsp olive oil

1 onion *(brown or red)*, diced

1 pepper *(red, yellow or
sweet pointed)*

2 garlic cloves, smashed

1 tsp dried oregano

1 tsp dried thyme

pinch of chilli flakes

1 x 400g (14-oz) can of
chopped tomatoes

1 x 250g (9-oz) packet
cooked lentils *(green, Puy
or beluga)*

125g (5½ oz) mozzarella

60g (2¼ oz) Parmesan
cheese, finely grated

salt and pepper

SPICY COURGETTES

1 tbsp olive oil

2 courgettes, sliced

1 garlic clove, finely sliced

1 red chilli, deseeded and
finely sliced

squeeze of lemon juice

1. Preheat the oven to 180°C fan/
200°C/400°F/gas mark 6. Arrange the
aubergine slices on one large or two
medium baking trays, drizzle with olive
oil and season. Cook for 15–20 minutes,
then remove from the oven and set aside.

2. To make the tomato sauce, place the oil
in a saucepan over a medium heat, add
the onion and cook for 5–7 minutes until
softened. Add the pepper, cook for
2 minutes, then add the garlic, oregano,
thyme, chilli flakes and a pinch of salt.
Add the canned tomatoes, swill a splash
of water around the can and add this too.
Bring the sauce to the boil, then reduce
to a simmer for 25–30 minutes, stirring
occasionally. Once reduced, use a stick
blender to blend to a smooth sauce. Add
the lentils, season and stir to combine.

3. Add one-third of the tomato and lentil sauce to a medium baking dish, and spread over the base, followed by a single layer of half the aubergines. Repeat with one-third of the sauce and the remaining aubergines before finishing with the remaining tomato sauce on top. Roughly tear the mozzarella and scatter over the top along with the Parmesan. Bake for 35–40 minutes until bubbling.

4. For the spicy courgettes, place the olive oil in a non-stick pan over a medium-high heat. Add the garlic and chilli and cook for a minute before adding the courgettes. Cook for 2–3 minutes on each side until slightly golden. Add a squeeze of lemon juice before serving.

Best served immediately, but it can also be stored in the fridge for up to 3 days.

spiced bean and jackfruit tacos

I'll be honest, I had to be convinced on jackfruit – I was like WAH? But now I'm a convert, and this is great for having the guys and gals round for a booch/mocktail/Margarita! Alana x

40 minutes | Serves 4

 17g

 minimum 12

 milk kefir yogurt

allergens: *gluten, cow's milk*

SPICED BEAN AND JACKFRUIT FILLING

1–2 tbsp olive oil

1 small red onion, sliced

1 pepper, cored, deseeded and sliced

1 large garlic clove, crushed

2 tsp ground cumin

2 tsp smoked paprika

1 tsp chilli flakes (*optional*)

1 x 400g (14-oz) can of jackfruit, drained

1 x 400g (14-oz) can of black beans, drained and rinsed

3 tbsp tomato purée

salt and pepper

squeeze of lime juice

SMASHED AVOCADO

1 avocado, peeled and stoned

1 shallot, diced

squeeze of lime juice

1 tsp chilli flakes (*optional*)

TO SERVE

milk kefir yogurt (*homemade, see p.168, or shop-bought*)

4–8 small wholemeal wraps

2 handfuls of fresh coriander, roughly chopped

1 lime, cut into wedges

1. Preheat the oven to 180°C fan/200°C/400°F/gas mark 6.

2. Place the oil in a medium saucepan, add the onion and cook for 5–7 minutes until softened. Add the pepper, cook for

2 minutes, then add the garlic, cumin, paprika, chilli flakes and a good pinch of salt. Add the canned jackfruit, black beans and tomato purée, together with 200ml (3½ fl oz) water. Bring the sauce to the boil, then reduce the heat and simmer for 25–30 minutes, stirring occasionally. Once the jackfruit has softened, use a fork to break it apart. Add a squeeze of lime juice and cook for a further 5 minutes. If the mixture looks a little dry, add a splash of water.

3. To make the smashed avocado, add the avocado to a bowl and mash with a fork to your desired consistency. Add the shallot, lime juice and chilli flakes, if using, and mix. Season to taste.

4. Add the wraps to the oven for the final 2 minutes of cooking to warm through.

5. To serve, spread a spoon of milk kefir yogurt over the warm wraps, top with some jackfruit and bean filling, smashed avocado and slaw or corn salsa, if you like.

Fibre and variety – a side of TGS slaw or corn salsa (see p.129)

TACO SALAD

Smashed avocado is best eaten fresh. Store any leftover corn salsa and jackfruit and black bean filling in the fridge for up to 3 days. Add to a bed of mixed leaves and fresh smashed avocado for a taco-style salad.

pantry fishcakes with celeriac slaw

Lauren on our team originally made this after a cupboard raid when it was snowing and she couldn't get to the shops! A budget week-night dinner when your food stores are running low; keep a couple of tins of fish in the pantry, in case you're caught short in extreme weather conditions like Lauren x

1 hour | Makes 6 fish cakes, serves 2-3

8.7g per portion

minimum 6

milk kefir yogurt

allergens: *fish, eggs,*

1 medium potato (*skin on*), cut into 2.5cm (1-in) chunks

1 medium sweet potato (*skin on*), cut into 2.5cm (1-in) chunks

2 x 100g (3½-oz) cans of salmon or mackerel, drained

4 spring onions, sliced into rounds

2 handfuls of fresh flat-leaf parsley, chopped

1 egg, beaten

zest and juice of ½ lemon

CELERIAC SLAW
½ celeriac, peeled

4 tbsp milk kefir yogurt (*homemade, see p.168, or shop-bought*)

salt and pepper

1. Preheat the oven to 180°C fan/200°C/400°F/gas mark 6 and line a baking tray with baking paper.

2. Bring a medium saucepan of salted water to the boil. Add both potatoes and cook for 20–25 minutes until tender. Remove from the heat, drain and steam-dry for 5 minutes. Roughly mash using a potato masher.

Fibre – a side of hummus (*see p.120*)
Variety – top the fish cakes with a handful of watercress
Ferments – a side of sauerkraut (*see p.160*)

3. Transfer the mashed potato to a medium mixing bowl, add the salmon or mackerel, spring onions, half the parsley and the beaten egg. Mix to combine and season well before stirring in the lemon zest and a squeeze of juice. Using your hands, mould the mixture into 6 fishcakes and transfer to the lined baking tray. Bake for 30–35 minutes until golden, turning halfway through cooking.

4. While the fishcakes are in the oven, grate the celeriac and add to a bowl. Mix in the milk kefir yogurt, remaining parsley and a squeeze of lemon juice. Season to taste.

5. Serve the fishcakes alongside the celeriac slaw.

Any leftover fishcakes and slaw can be stored in the fridge for up to 2 days.

loaded fries

Great for the members of the household who love a kebab/chippie, a crowd pleaser for all the family/roommates! Alana x

40 minutes | Serves 2+

13g per portion

minimum 11

milk kefir yogurt

allergens: *cow's milk*

FRIES

2–3 root vegetables (*skin on*), such as sweet potato, potato, parsnip, small celeriac, carrots, cut into chunky chips

1 tsp garlic powder

1 tsp smoked paprika

1–2 tbsp olive oil

TOPPINGS

2 portions of veggie chilli (*see p.92*)

60g (2¼ oz) feta cheese, crumbled

2 tbsp milk kefir yogurt (*homemade, see p.168, or shop-bought*) or kefir tzatziki (*see p.118*)

handful of fresh coriander, chopped

squeeze of lime juice

1. Preheat the oven to 180°C fan/200°C/400°F/gas mark 6 and line a medium baking tray with baking paper.

2. Bring a pan of salted water to the boil, add the root vegetables and parboil for 5–7 minutes. Drain and leave to steam-dry for 2 minutes.

3. Scatter the vegetables over the lined tray, add the garlic powder, smoked paprika and olive oil. Combine to coat and season well. Cook for 30 minutes until golden brown, stirring after 20 minutes.

4. Serve the fries topped with chilli, feta, a dollop of milk kefir yogurt, fresh coriander and a squeeze of lime juice.

Store veggie chilli in the fridge for up to 4 days. Serve the chips straight away.

Fibre – top with sliced avocado
Variety – top with 2 tbsp crunchy seed and nut mix (*see p.133*)
Ferments – top with kimchi or fermented hot sauce (*see pp.164 and 131*)

lentil shepherd's pie

You've got the family round on a Sunday – make this to please them and all your microbial relatives too. Trust us on the beetroot juice, but if you can't get hold of any, just use 200ml (7 fl oz) red wine. Alana x

1½ hours | Serves 4+

8.6g per portion

12

milk kefir yogurt

allergens: *cow's milk (if using milk kefir yogurt), gluten, fish (if using Worcestershire sauce), soya (if using Worcestershire sauce)*

1 large potato *(skin on)*, cut into cubes, cut into 2.5cm (1-in) chunks

1 medium sweet potato (skin on), cut into cubes

2 tbsp milk kefir yogurt *(homemade, see p.168, or shop-bought – optional)*

2 tbsp olive oil

1 leek, cut into rounds

2 carrots *(skin on)*, diced

2–3 garlic cloves, crushed

1 tbsp dried thyme

1 small swede, peeled and cubed, cut into 2.5cm (1-in) chunks

1 x 400g (14-oz) can of green lentils, drained and rinsed

200ml (7 fl oz) pressed beetroot juice

1 x 400g (14-oz) can of chopped tomatoes

200ml (7 fl oz) vegetable stock

1 tbsp tomato purée

1 tbsp Worcestershire sauce (optional)

salt and pepper

Fibre – a side of broccoli
Variety – 2 handfuls of frozen peas added to the pie mixture for the final 5 minutes of cooking
Ferments – side of fermented ketchup or hot sauce *(see pp.132 and 133)*

1. Preheat the oven to 200°C fan/220°C/425°F/gas mark 7.

2. Bring a large pan of salted water to the boil. Add the potatoes and cook for 20–25 minutes until tender. Once cooked, drain and use a potato masher to mash by hand. Once cool, add the kefir (if using) and season.

3. Add the olive oil to a large pan over a medium-high heat. Add the leek and carrots and season. Cook for 5–10 minutes, stirring occasionally, until

the vegetables begin to soften. Add the garlic and thyme and cook for 2 minutes. Add the swede and lentils and stir to coat. Add the beetroot juice and leave to bubble for 1 minute before adding the canned tomatoes, vegetable stock and tomato purée. Season well with salt and pepper, bring to the boil, and then reduce the heat to a simmer and cook for 30–35 minutes until the sauce has thickened.

Add the Worcestershire sauce for the final 5 minutes of cooking, if using.

4. Transfer the filling to an ovenproof baking dish. Top with the mashed potatoes and bake for 30–40 minutes until bubbling and crispy on top.

Store any leftovers in the fridge for up to 4 days.

mushroom and mixed bean hotpot

Cosy evening, glass of vino, tele on. Uhuh. Also, go crazy on the different mushroom types – lots of supermarkets do mixed boxes now. Lisa x

1½ hours | Serves 4

13g per portion

11

allergens: *celery, gluten (check shop-bought stock cubes)*

Fibre – a side of broccoli
Variety – use a variety
of mushrooms
Ferments – a side of
sauerkraut *(see p.160)*

2 tbsp olive oil

1 onion, finely diced

1 carrot *(skin on)*, finely diced

2 celery sticks, finely diced

3 garlic cloves, crushed

500g (1 lb 2 oz) mushrooms *(any variety)*, roughly chopped

2 tsp dried rosemary

1 tbsp dried thyme

500ml (18 fl oz) mushroom or vegetable stock

1 x 400g (14-oz) can of black beans, drained and rinsed

1 x 400g (14-oz) can of cannellini beans, drained and rinsed

1 medium potato *(skin on)*, sliced into 5mm- (¼ in-) thick rounds

1 parsnip (skin on), sliced into 5mm- (¼ in-) thick rounds

salt and pepper

1. Preheat the oven to 180°C fan/200°C/400°F/gas mark 6.

2. Over a medium heat, add half the olive oil to a casserole dish. Add the onion, carrot and celery and cook for 5–10 minutes until softened. Add the garlic and cook for 2 minutes, stirring. Add the mushrooms, rosemary and thyme, season and cook, stirring, until browned.

3. Stir in the stock and the beans. Bring to the boil and then reduce to a simmer for 10–15 minutes. Meanwhile, bring a pan of salted water to the boil and parboil the potato and parsnip for 5 minutes.

4. Arrange the potato and parsnip on top of the mushroom mixture, brush with olive oil and season. Cook in the oven for 30–40 minutes until golden.

Store any leftovers in an airtight container in the fridge for up to 3 days.

red lentil dahl

Bit of cauliflower love: it is a source of vitamin C, per portion gives 7% of recommended daily fibre. If you like a bit more spice, like me, add a tsp of chilli flakes. Lisa x

50 minutes | Serves 4

9.1 g per portion

13

milk kefir yogurt

allergens: *cow's milk, nuts (cashews)*

250g (9 oz) split red lentils

3 tbsp coconut oil

4 small or 1 medium shallots, finely diced

5cm- (2 in-) piece of fresh ginger, peeled and finely grated

2 garlic cloves, finely grated or crushed

1–2 tsp chilli flakes

1 tsp ground turmeric

2 tsp ground coriander

2 tsp ground cumin

500ml (18 fl oz) vegetable stock

1 x 400ml (14-fl oz) can of coconut milk

1 small cauliflower, broken into florets

2 carrots *(skin on)*, roughly chopped

2 tbsp tomato purée

1 lime

40g (1½ oz) cashews, roughly chopped

milk kefir yogurt *(homemade, see p.168, or shop-bought)*

2 handfuls of fresh coriander

salt and pepper

1. Preheat the oven to 180°C fan/ 200°C/400°F/gas mark 6. Use a sieve to rinse the red lentils until the water runs clear. Set aside.

2. Heat 1 tablespoon of the coconut oil in a large pan over a medium heat. Add the shallots and cook for 5–10 minutes until softened, stirring occasionally. Add the ginger, garlic and chilli flakes and cook for 2 minutes. Add the turmeric, 1 teaspoon of the ground cumin and ground coriander, then stir in the lentils and vegetable stock and cook for 5 minutes until the lentils begin to soak up the stock.

3. Add the coconut milk and tomato purée, bring to the boil, then reduce to a simmer, stirring occasionally. Cook until the lentils are cooked through (30 minutes).

Recipe continued overleaf

4. Melt the remaining coconut oil in a small saucepan and pour into a mixing bowl with the remaining spices. Add the cauliflower, carrots and a squeeze of lime juice, stir to coat and then season. Transfer to a medium baking tray and roast for 25–30 minutes until golden. Add the cashews for the final 5 minutes of cooking.

5. To serve, divide the dahl between four deep bowls and top with the roasted vegetables and cashews, fresh coriander and dollop of milk kefir yogurt.

Store any leftovers in the fridge for up to 3 days.

Fibre – add a side of wholegrain rice

Variety – add 2 handfuls of frozen spinach to the dahl for the final 10 minutes

Ferments – top with kimchi *(see p.164)*

chickpea balls topped with tomato sauce and walnut pesto

These are also great as a tapas-style starter too... Alana x

1½ hours | Serves 2

15g per portion

minimum 9

sourdough

allergens: *cow's milk, gluten, nuts (walnuts), eggs*

2 tbsp olive oil

1 onion, finely diced

1 red pepper, deseeded and roughly chopped

1 x 400g (14-oz) can of chopped tomatoes

3 garlic cloves, smashed

1 tsp dried oregano

pinch of chilli flakes

1 slice of day-old sourdough (homemade, see p.160, or shop-bought), roughly torn

1 x 400g (14-oz) can of chickpeas, drained and rinsed

50g (1¾ oz) sun-dried tomatoes

¼ bunch of fresh basil, leaves only

1 egg

salt and pepper

TO SERVE

Pesto *(homemade, see p.137, or shop-bought)*

30g Parmesan cheese or cheddar, grated to serve

1. Preheat the oven to 180°C fan/ 200°C/400°F/gas mark 6 and line a medium baking tray with baking paper.

2. Next, make the tomato sauce. Add 1 tablespoon of olive oil to a medium saucepan, add the onion and cook for 5–10 minutes until softened. Add the pepper and cook for 2 minutes. Add the tomatoes, swill a splash of water around the can and add this too, together with two of the smashed garlic cloves, the oregano, chilli flakes and a pinch of salt.

Fibre – add 2 tbsp ground flaxseed to the chickpea mixture

Variety – top with a handful of rocket

Ferments – toasted sourdough on the side (*see p.156*)

3. Bring the sauce to the boil, then reduce the heat to low and keep at a gentle simmer for 25–30 minutes until the sauce has thickened. Stir occasionally and, after 15 minutes, use a wooden spoon to crush the tomatoes and garlic against the sides of the pan.

4. Next, add the sourdough to a blender and pulse to breadcrumbs. Transfer to a mixing bowl, then add the chickpeas, sun-dried tomatoes, basil leaves and remaining garlic clove to the blender and blitz to a paste. Add the paste to the sourdough crumbs in the mixing bowl, season generously and mix to combine. Create a well in the mixture, add the egg, use a fork to whisk and combine into the chickpea mixture. Separate the mixture into eight portions and roll into small balls.

5. Heat a medium frying pan over a medium heat and add the remaining tablespoon of olive oil. Tip in the chickpea balls and lightly brown on all sides for 3–5 minutes, before transferring to the lined baking tray and baking for 15 minutes.

6. Remove the tomato sauce from the heat and, using a stick blender, blend to a smooth sauce. Season to taste.

7. To serve, divide the chickpea balls between two plates and top with the tomato sauce, pesto and the Parmesan or cheddar, if using.

Leftover chickpea balls, sauce and pesto will keep in the fridge for up to 3 days.

mac 'n' cheese

Our Mum's go-to dish for us when we're home, here we've added some gut-loving twists to it. Lisa x

45 minutes | Serves 6

14 g per portion

5

allergens: *gluten, milk, nuts*

60g (2¼ oz) cashews

2 tbsp olive oil

3 shallots, quartered

1 medium butternut squash (*skin on*), cut into 2.5cm (1-in) cubes

1 parsnip (*skin on*), roughly chopped

300g (10½ oz) dried pasta

300ml (10 fl oz) water

2–4 tbsp nutritional yeast

1 tbsp dried sage

60g (2¼ oz) feta cheese, crumbled (optional)

salt and pepper

Fibre – use wholegrain pasta
Variety – top with rocket
Ferments – try with a side of sauerkraut (*see p.160*)

1. To soak the cashews, place them in a bowl and cover with 2.5cm (1 in) of boiling water for 15 minutes, then drain.

2. Preheat the oven to 200°C fan/220°C/425°F/gas mark 7.

3. Put the butternut squash and parsnip on a baking tray, coat in the olive oil and season. Bake for 30–35 minutes until tender and golden. After 15 minutes, stir the vegetables and add the shallots for the final 15–20 minutes of cooking.

4. Cook the pasta according to the packet instructions, then drain and set aside.

5. Add the butternut squash, parsnip and shallots to a blender, along with the cashews and water, and blitz to a smooth sauce. Add the nutritional yeast and the sage and blend. Taste the sauce, add more nutritional yeast if needed and blend. Season to taste.

6. Pour the sauce over the cooked pasta and stir thoroughly to combine. Divide between bowls and sprinkle with the feta, if using. Serve immediately.

chapter

5

sides 'n' sauces

kefir tzatziki and sweet potato wedges

Break away from the usual suspects of BBQ sides – so so fresh and perfect for sharing. Lisa x

40 minutes | Serves 2

1g per portion

7

milk kefir yogurt

allergens: *cow's milk*

KEFIR TZATZIKI

1 cucumber

1 small garlic clove, finely grated

squeeze of lemon juice

½ tsp paprika

½ x 400g (14-oz) can of chickpeas, drained and rinsed

handful of fresh flat-leaf parsley, roughly chopped

250g (9 oz) milk kefir yogurt *(homemade, see p.168, or shop-bought)*

SWEET POTATO WEDGES

2 sweet potatoes *(skin on)*, cut into wedges

1 tbsp olive oil

salt and pepper

1. Preheat the oven to 180°C fan/200°C/400°F/gas mark 6.

2. Scatter the sweet potatoes wedges over a baking tray, drizzle with olive oil, season and cook for 35–40 minutes until golden.

3. For the tzatziki, grate the cucumber and squeeze out the liquid, then mix with the garlic, lemon juice, paprika, chickpeas and most of the parsley and stir into the milk kefir yogurt until well combined. Season to taste and garnish with a little extra parsley and a drizzle of extra virgin olive oil. Serve with the sweet potato wedges.

Store in the fridge for up to 3 days.

hummus

Hummus – lots of ways – sometimes I like to make them all at once for the ultimate dip fest... The chocolate suggestion came from one of our followers, Misty – love it with strawberries! Alana x

5 minutes | Serves 4

3.2g per portion

minimum 5

milk kefir yogurt

BASE HUMMUS

1 x 400g (14-oz) can of
   chickpeas, drained and
   rinsed

2–4 tbsp extra virgin olive oil

1 small garlic clove, smashed

½ tsp ground cumin

1 tbsp tahini

4 tbsp milk kefir yogurt
   *(homemade, see p.168
   or shop-bought)*

zest and juice of ½ lemon

salt and pepper

1. Add the chickpeas and 2 tablespoons of the olive oil to a blender and blitz until smooth. Add the garlic, cumin, tahini, kefir and lemon juice and half the zest. Season before blending to a smooth paste, adding a little extra oil if required. Taste and add more lemon juice, zest and seasoning if required.

flavour combos

BEETS *Fibre – 3.5g per portion*

1 medium cooked beetroot

2a. Roughly slice the beetroot into wedges and add to the blender along with the chickpeas. Proceed as before.

....

BLACK BEAN AND
LIME *Fibre – 5.7g per portion*

½ x 400g (14-oz) can of black beans, drained and rinsed

½ tsp ground coriander *(to replace the cumin)*

zest and juice of ½ lime *(to replace the lemon)*

handful of fresh coriander, chopped

2b. Add the black beans to the blender with the chickpeas. Add the coriander and lime and proceed as in the main recipe. Top with the fresh coriander.

....

CHOCOLATE
Fibre – 4.4g per portion

1 tbsp cacao powder
2 tbsp honey or maple syrup

2c. Omit the garlic, cumin and lemon. Add the cacao and maple syrup with the tahini and kefir as for the base recipe.

GREEN *Fibre – 4g per portion*

handful of greens, such as spinach, rocket or watercress

50g jarred Jerusalem artichoke, drained

2d. Add the greens to the blender with the base ingredients and blend – an easy way to add variety!

....

TOMATO AND
BASIL *Fibre – 4.9g per portion*

50g (1¾ oz) sun-dried tomatoes
½ bunch of basil

2e. Add the sun-dried tomatoes and basil to the blender with the chickpeas and omit the cumin and tahini from the base recipe.

....

SMASHED WHITE
BEAN *Fibre – 4.9g per portion*

1 x 400g (14-oz) can of cannellini beans, drained and rinsed

2f. Add the cannellini beans to the blender with the chickpeas and proceed as for the main recipe.

Store in the fridge for up to 4 days.

citrus greens

The best thing about dinners is all the sides and I always take it so far that there's never enough room on the table. However, the following dishes are designed to increase variety and fibre so you've got to make room for 'em all. Lisa x

15 minutes | Serves 4

4.8 g per portion

5

200g (7 oz) cavolo nero

1 tbsp olive oil

2 handfuls of broccoli (fresh or frozen), cut into florets

1 garlic clove, finely sliced or crushed

1 red or green chilli, deseeded and finely sliced

zest and juice of 1 orange

handful of flaked almonds

salt and pepper

1. Pull the green leaves of the cavolo nero away from the woody stalks and roughly shred, then discard the stalks.

2. Add the olive oil to a medium saucepan over a medium heat. Add the broccoli and a splash of water, then cover and cook for 3 minutes. Add the garlic and chilli and fry for a minute, then add the cavolo nero and season. Cover with a lid, cook for 2 minutes, stir, then cover again and cook for a further 2–4 minutes until the broccoli is tender and the cavolo nero is wilted.

3. Add the orange zest, a squeeze of orange juice and top with the flaked almonds. Serve immediately.

sliced root vegetable bake

Follows the simplicity of a traditional roast and, as with all roasts, it's all in the timings baby! Alana x

1 hour | Serves 4–6 as a side

minimum 5.4g
per portion

5

allergens: *gluten (check shop-bought vegetable stock)*

2 tbsp olive oil

1 kg (2 lb 4 oz) mix of root vegetables, such as potatoes, sweet potatoes, turnips, beetroot or parsnips, cut into 5mm- (¼ in-) thick rounds *(using a mandolin will make slicing easier)*

5 garlic cloves, smashed

500ml (18 fl oz) vegetable stock or water

2 tbsp fresh or dried mixed herbs, such as rosemary, thyme or sage

salt and pepper

1. Preheat the oven to 180°C fan/200°C/400°F/gas mark 6.

2. Grease a medium baking dish with a little of the olive oil. Layer the root veg into the dish, alternating between the different types. Once they are tightly packed, add the stock or water to fill the dish halfway and slot the smashed garlic cloves in between the vegetables. Season well.

3. Brush the top of the vegetables with the remaining oil and sprinkle over the mixed herbs. Cover with foil and bake for 30–35 minutes. Once the vegetables have started to soften, remove the foil and cook for a further 20 minutes until golden.

potato salad with sauerkraut

This is your new BBQ go-to – the perfect cut-through for those sweet and smokey BBQ flavours. Lisa x

30 minutes | 2 as a main or 4 as a side

11g per mains portion

10 *(based on 3 different types in the mixed leaf bag)*

sauerkraut

small bunch of fresh basil, leaves picked

500g (1lb 2 oz) new potatoes

120g (4¼ oz) frozen peas

3–4 tbsp extra virgin olive oil

1 small garlic clove

2 handfuls of mixed leaf salad

2 spring onions, finely sliced

bunch of fresh flat-leaf parsley, chopped

6 radishes, sliced

120g (4¼ oz) sauerkraut *(homemade, see p.160, or shop-bought)*

salt and pepper

1. Bring a large pan of salted water to the boil, drop in the basil and blanch for 20 seconds, then remove with a slotted spoon and set aside to cool.

2. Slice any large potatoes in half and add along with the rest to the pan of boiling salted water and cook for 20 minutes until tender, adding the peas for the final 3 minutes. Drain and leave to steam-dry while you make the basil dressing.

3. Squeeze any liquid from the basil, then add the leaves to a blender along with the oil and garlic. Blitz until you have a vibrant green oil.

4. Put the potatoes, peas, mixed leaf salad, spring onions and parsley in a mixing bowl and toss with the basil oil. Add the sliced radishes and season to taste. Serve topped with sauerkraut.

Store any leftovers in the fridge for up to 3 days.

butternut squash and lentil stuffing

This filling is not just for Christmas... Alana x

1 hour+ | Serves 4–6 as a side

7.9g per portion

6

sauerkraut

allergens: *gluten, nuts*

2 tbsp butter or olive oil, plus extra for greasing

2 slices of day-old sourdough (homemade, see p.160, or shop-bought)

1 red onion, finely diced

1 tbsp dried sage

1 medium butternut squash, *(skin on)* cut into 2.5cm (1-in) cubes, seeds reserved

2–3 garlic cloves, crushed

1 250g pack cooked Puy lentils

400ml (14 fl oz) vegetable or chicken stock

2 sprigs of fresh thyme

4 tbsp dried cranberries *(optional)*

handful of walnuts, roughly chopped

salt and pepper

1. Preheat the oven to 180°C fan/ 200°C/400°F/gas mark 6 and grease a medium baking dish with butter or oil.

2. Lightly toast the sourdough before tearing it into small pieces. Set aside.

3. Add 1 tablespoon of the butter or olive oil to a large non-stick pan over a medium-high heat. Add the onion and soften for 5 minutes, then add the butternut squash. Season well and add the dried sage. Cook for 10 minutes until the squash begins to soften. Stir in the remaining butter or oil, add the garlic and cook for a further 2 minutes. Remove from the heat and transfer to a medium bowl. Add the toasted sourdough and lentils, then add the stock.

4. Transfer the mixture to the greased baking dish, add the thyme and cover with foil. Cook in the oven for 30 minutes, then remove the foil and scatter over the butternut squash seeds, walnuts and cranberries (if using) and cook for a further 15–20 minutes until golden and crispy.

mushy peas

You mustn't have your TGS fish and chips without it... Lisa x

15 minutes | Serves 4

9g per portion | 4 | milk kefir yogurt

1 tbsp butter

1 x 400g (14-oz) can of cannellini beans, drained and rinsed

400g (14 oz) frozen peas

squeeze of lemon juice

2 tbsp milk kefir yogurt (home-made, see p.168, or shop-bought)

handful of fresh mint leaves, roughly chopped

salt and pepper

1. Add the butter to medium saucepan over a medium-high heat, add the cannellini beans and season well. Reduce the heat and add the peas. Cook for 5 minutes until cooked through. Add the lemon juice.

2. Mash the beans and peas by hand until they have reached your desired consistency. Stir through the kefir yogurt and mint and season to taste before serving.

tartare sauce

Tartare sauce... but not as you know it... Lisa x

10 minutes | Serves 4

1g per portion | 5 | milk kefir yogurt and olives

1 small shallot, finely diced

6 tbsp milk kefir yogurt (home-made, see p.168, or shop-bought)

1 tsp capers, finely chopped

handful of stoned olives, finely chopped

handful of fresh parsley

squeeze of lemon juice

salt and pepper

1. Add the shallot, milk kefir yogurt, capers, olives and parsley to a bowl and mix to combine. Add a squeeze of lemon and season to taste.

Store in the fridge for up to 2 days.

slaw

I have coleslaw with EVERYTHING (it was always such a luxury when we were younger) and after this, you will too. Lisa x

15 minutes | Serves 4

4.1g per portion | **minimum 3** | **milk kefir yogurt**

2 carrots *(skin on)*
½ cabbage *(white, green or red or a mix)*
handful of fresh flat-leaf parsley

2–4 tbsp milk kefir yogurt *(homemade, see p.168, or shop-bought)*
1 tbsp apple cider vinegar
salt and pepper

1. Grate the carrots, shred the cabbage and roughly chop the parsley.

2. Add all the ingredients to a bowl, mix well and season to taste.

Store in the fridge for up to 3 days.

corn salsa

Who knew sweetcorn could add such pizzazz to salsa? A great add-on to our spiced bean and jackfruit tacos (see p.100). Alana x

5 minutes | Serves 4

2g per portion | **5**

2 handfuls of cherry tomatoes, halved
4 x spring onions, sliced
1 x 160g (5½-oz) can of sweetcorn, drained

1 red chilli, deseeded and finely chopped
squeeze of fresh lime juice
salt and pepper

1. Put all the ingredients in a mixing bowl, add a squeeze of lime juice, stir well and season to taste.

Store leftovers in the fridge for up to 3 days.

fermented tomato ketchup

For all the ketchup fiends in your house – your gut bugs will be hooked on it too. Makes perfect condi-sense. Lisa x

15 minutes prep | Serves 30+ *and up to 5 days fermentation*

 minimum 6

500g (1 lb 2 oz) passata

150g (5½ oz) jarred tomato purée

2 garlic cloves

2 tbsp kombucha *(with mother, homemade, see p.170, or shop-bought)* or brine from existing vegetable ferments

1 tsp onion powder

1 tsp allspice

½ tsp mustard powder

50ml (2 fl oz) apple cider vinegar

50ml (2 fl oz) maple syrup

½ tsp salt

pepper, to taste

1. Add all the ingredients to a large mixing bowl and stir to combine. Transfer to a 1-litre (1¾-pint) jar and seal with a burping lid. Leave at room temperature out of direct sunlight for five days. Begin taste testing from day three and, once the tomato ketchup has reached your desired flavour, replace the burping lid with a screw-top lid.

Store in the fridge for up to 3 months.

fermented hot sauce

Get this right on some cheese on toast... or anything really. In fact, keep a bottle in your handbag. Lisa x

10 minutes prep | makes 1 litre
+ 7–14 days fermentation

3

800ml (1½ pints) water

3 tbsp sea salt

500g (1 lb 2 oz) red chillies, stalks removed and halved

2 Scotch bonnet chillies, stalks removed and halved *(optional)*

6 garlic cloves, peeled

50g (1¾ oz) fresh or frozen fruit, defrosted, such as blueberries, strawberries or mixed berries

1. Wash a 1-litre (1¾ pints) jar in hot soapy water, then place it in the oven at 90°C fan/110°C/225°F/gas mark ¼ for 15–20 minutes to sterilize it. Leave it to cool.

2. Place the water and salt in a jug and stir to dissolve to create a brine. Add the chillies, garlic and fruit to the sterilized jar and pour in the brine, ensuring the chillies are submerged.

3. Cover the jar with a burping lid and leave it to sit at room temperature, out of direct sunlight, for 7–14 days until you can smell a pleasant sour smell.

4. Strain the brine and reserve it. Transfer the chillies, garlic and fruit to a blender with 100ml (3½ fl oz) brine. Blitz until you have a smooth sauce consistency, using the remaining brine to loosen if required. Return the hot sauce to a clean 1 litre (1¾-pint) jar and cover with a screw-top lid.

Store in the fridge for up to 3 months.

piccalilli

I was actually surprised at how many different types of veg are in Piccalilli, your variety sandwich GO TO. Lisa x

10 minutes prep | makes
+ 4 hours resting **1 litre**
+ 5–14 days fermentation

 10

1 small cauliflower, cut into florets

1 medium courgette, halved and sliced

2 handfuls of green beans, trimmed and halved

1 red pepper, cored, deseeded and sliced

80ml (2¾ fl oz) water

2 tbsp honey or maple syrup

20g (¾ oz) rice flour

1 tbsp mustard powder

1 tbsp mustard seeds

2 tsp ground cumin

1 tsp coriander seeds

1 tsp ground turmeric

sea salt

1. Wash a 1-litre jar in hot soapy water, then place it in the oven at 90°C fan/110°C/225°F/gas mark ¼ for 15–20 minutes to sterilize it. Leave it to cool.

2. Place a mixing bowl on a set of scales and zero the scales. Place the vegetables in the bowl and measure their weight. Calculate 2% of that weight (by multiplying by 0.02) and measure out the result in salt. Sprinkle the measured salt over the vegetables and gently mix. This will begin to draw water out of the vegetables. Leave to sit for 4 hours.

3. To make the sauce, add the water, honey and rice flour to a saucepan over a medium heat. Bring to the boil and leave to thicken. Remove from the heat and leave to cool.

4. Mix the spices together and add with the sauce to the vegetables, gently massaging through (it's a good idea to wear gloves here so the turmeric doesn't stain your hands!). Pack the vegetables into the sterilized jar, pressing down so that the spice sauce covers the vegetables.

5. Cover the jar with a burping lid and leave it at room temperature, out of direct sunlight. After 24 hours, press down the vegetables again. Begin to taste test after five days. Once the piccalilli has reached your desired tanginess, replace the burping lid with a screw-top lid, and securely cover.

Store in the fridge for up to 3 months.

crunchy seed and nut mix

Make em and shake em.. the easiest way to add variety to any dish. Alana x

25 minutes | Serves 10

2.7g per tbsp

minimum 7

allergens: *nuts (hazelnuts, walnuts, almonds, cashews or pistachios), sesame*

120g (3½ oz) mixed nuts, such as hazelnuts, walnuts, almonds, cashews or pistachios

100g (1¾ oz) mixed seeds, such as pumpkin, sunflower and flaxseed

2 tbsp sesame seeds

1 tbsp cumin seeds

1 tbsp coriander seeds

1 tbsp fennel seeds

pinch of chilli flakes *(optional)*

salt and pepper

1. Preheat the oven to 180°C fan/200°C/400°F/gas mark 6.

2. Spread the nuts and mixed seeds (except the sesame seeds) over a baking tray and cook for 10–15 minutes until toasted.

3. Put a small non-stick pan over a medium heat. Add the sesame, cumin, coriander and fennel seeds and toast for 2 minutes. Remove from the heat, roughly chop the nuts and grind the toasted spices with a pestle and mortar. Mix the spices into the nuts.

4. Sprinkle over hot dishes, traybakes, hummus, dips or salads.

Store at room temperature in an airtight container for up to 2 weeks.

walnut pesto

I always get a big jar and make a double batch to add to meals for a variety-filled taste sensation. Lisa x

10 minutes | Serves 2

2.1g per portion

5

allergens: *nuts (walnuts), cow's milk (if using Parmesan)*

60g (2¼ oz) walnuts

1 small garlic clove, peeled

small bunch of fresh basil, leaves only

zest and juice of ½ lemon

2–4 tbsp extra virgin olive oil

2 handfuls of rocket or spinach

2 tbsp grated Parmesan cheese or 3 tbsp nutritional yeast

salt and pepper

1. Add the walnuts to a small pan over a medium-high heat and toast for a couple of minutes on each side. Remove from the heat, leave to cool for 2 minutes and then add to a blender. Blitz until coarsely chopped, about 10 seconds, then add the garlic, basil leaves, lemon zest, salt and pepper and gradually add the extra virgin olive oil to bind. Season to taste.

Store in the fridge for up to 4 days or in the freezer for up to a month.

chapter

6

just
desserts

summer trifle

Trifle made with butterbeans – YEAH YOU HEARD IT. Alana x

30 minutes | Serves 4-6
+ cooling

 8.2g per portion

 minimum 6

 milk kefir yogurt

allergens: *cow's milk, nuts*

CAKE LAYER
1 x 400g (14-oz) can of
    butterbeans, drained and
    rinsed
2 tbsp maple syrup
2 eggs, beaten
50g ground almonds
1 tsp baking powder
½ tsp salt
25g coconut oil, melted

FRUIT JAM LAYER
300g (7 oz) fresh, frozen
    mango or frozen tropical
    fruit mix
2 tbsp chia seeds

TO SERVE
2 kiwis, sliced
8 tbsp milk kefir yogurt
    homemade, see p.168,
    or shop-bought)
2 tbsp pistachios, roughly
    chopped

1. To make the cake layer, preheat the oven to 180°C fan/200°C/400°F/gas mark 6. Line a 20cm (8-in) cake tin with baking paper.

2. Put the butterbeans and maple syrup into a food processor and purée until smooth, whilst gradually adding the eggs.

3. Transfer the puréed mixture to a mixing bowl and fold in the ground almonds, baking powder, salt and coconut oil. Once combined tip into the lined cake tin and place to the oven for 20 minutes until golden on top. Set aside to cool.

4. Meanwhile, make the fruit chia jam. Place the fruit in a small saucepan with 100ml (3½ fl oz) water over a low heat, stirring occasionally, until the fruit begins to break down. Use a masher to mash the fruit to your desired consistency (or a food processor to pulse the fruit if you prefer a smoother consistency). Stir in the chia seeds until combined. Remove from the heat and leave to cool to room temperature.

5. Once the cake has cooled, crumble half between 4–6 pots, then layer with half the fruit jam and a spoonful of milk kefir yogurt. Repeat with another layer of cake, fruit jam and kefir and then top with the sliced kiwis and chopped pistachios.

Store in the fridge for up to a day. The fruit chia jam can be stored for up to 5 days if stored separately in an airtight container.

banoffee pie with kefir

MY FAVOURITE DESSERT! The last time I made this, my dog ate the base as it was cooling in the garden, so keep it indoors ha! Lisa x

40 minutes | Serves 6

5.5g

6

milk kefir yogurt

allergens: *nuts (almonds),*

OATY BASE

80g rolled oats

2 tbsp coconut oil

1 ripe banana

1 tsp ground cinnamon

½ tbsp cacao powder

pinch of sea salt

2 tbsp smooth peanut butter

DATE FILLING

200g (7 oz) stoned Medjool or soft dates

TOPPING

4 tbsp milk kefir yogurt (homemade, see p.168, or shop-bought)

1 large ripe banana, sliced into rounds

20g (¾ oz) 70% cocoa solids dark chocolate, cut into shavings

1. Preheat the oven to 180°C fan/ 200°C/400°F/gas mark 6. Place the dates in a bowl and cover in warm water. Leave to soak for 15 minutes, then drain, add to a blender and blitz to a paste.

2. While the dates are soaking, place the oats in a food processor and pulse until roughly ground. Place the coconut oil in a small saucepan and melt over a low heat.

3. Place the oats, cinnamon, cacao and salt in a mixing bowl and stir to combine. Add the banana and mash with a fork, then add the coconut oil and peanut butter and stir to combine.

4. Once mixed, line a 20cm (8-in) cake tin with baking paper (if using a cake tin with a removable base, there's no need to line it). Add the cake mix and bake for 15–20 minutes until golden. Remove from the oven and leave to cool.

5. To build the pie, spread the date paste over the oaty base, top with the sliced bananas, drizzle with milk kefir yogurt and finish with a sprinkle of dark chocolate shavings. Cool in the fridge before removing from the tin and cut into slices before serving.

The banana will begin to brown quite quickly, so store in the fridge and eat within a day.

fruit crumble

The perfect end to a Sunday roast! Alana x

40 minutes | Serves 4-6

5.1g per portion

6

milk kefir yogurt

4 apples *(skin on)*, roughly chopped

1 pear *(skin on)*, roughly chopped

100ml (3½ fl oz) water

100g (3½ oz) rolled oats

1 tsp ground cinnamon

1 tbsp maple syrup

1 tbsp coconut oil, melted

milk kefir yogurt *(homemade see p.168, or shop-bought)* or dairy-free alternative, to serve

allergens: *gluten, cow's milk*

1. Preheat the oven to 180°C fan/200°C/400°F/gas mark 6.

2. Place the apple, pears and water in a deep, heavy-based pan over a low-medium heat. Cook gently for 15 minutes until softened.

3. Add the oats, cinnamon, maple syrup and coconut oil to a mixing bowl and stir to combine.

4. Spread the fruit mixture over the base of a baking dish. Top with the oat mix and bake for 15–20 minutes until the oats are golden. To serve, top the crumble with a spoonful of milk kefir yogurt.

 Fibre and Variety – *add a handful of frozen cranberries when you're cooking the apples and pears*

Leftover crumble can be stored in the fridge for up to 3 days and reheated before serving.

sauerkraut brownies

We know this is RANDOM, but don't knock 'em til you try 'em. Lisa x

10 minutes | Serves 8–10
+ 30 minutes cooling

6.2g

minimum 6

sauerkraut

60g (2¼ oz) sauerkraut (*homemade, see p.160, or shop-bought*), finely chopped

400g (14 oz) stoned Medjool or soft dates

80g (2¾ oz) ground almonds

3 tbsp cacao powder

½ tsp sea salt

handful of walnuts, roughly chopped

80g (2¾ oz) mixed seeds (*pumpkin, sunflower, sesame, flaxseed or linseed*)

allergens: *nuts (almonds)*

1. Using a chopping board, finely chop the sauerkraut. Use kitchen paper to remove any excess liquid.

2. Place the dates, ground almonds, mixed seeds, cacao and salt in a food processor and blend until the mixture starts to stick together. Mix in the sauerkraut.

3. Line a square brownie tin with baking paper. Tip in the brownie mix and press firmly into the dish with your hands until evenly distributed.

4. Once the mix is evenly distributed, press the walnuts into the top of the brownies. Transfer to the fridge to set for 20–30 minutes. Remove the brownies from the fridge and cut into 8–10 squares.

Store in an airtight container in the fridge for up to 3 days.

banana and raspberry cookies

An absolute WINNER with a cup of tea! Alana x

35 minutes | Makes 6

4g per cookie

5

allergens: *nuts (peanut, almond or cashew), gluten, cow's milk – milk kefir yogurt, if using*

2 medium, ripe bananas

135g (4¾ oz) rolled oats

1 tsp ground cinnamon

2 tbsp nut butter, such as peanut, almond or cashew

pinch of sea salt

2 handfuls of raspberries (fresh or frozen)

1. Preheat the oven to 170°C fan/190°C/ 375°F/gas mark 5 and line a baking tray with baking paper.

2. In a large bowl, use the back of a fork to mash the bananas, then add the oats, cinnamon, nut butter and salt and mix to combine. Finally add the raspberries and gently combine. Use your hands to roll the mixture into 6–8 balls, then transfer to the lined baking tray and press down into cookies.

3. Bake for 20–25 minutes until golden. Eat warm or leave to cool on a wire rack.

 Fibre – *add a handful of chopped walnuts*
Variety – *top with mixed seeds (pumpkin, sunflower, sesame, flaxseed or linseed)*
Ferment – *milk kefir yogurt (see p.168)*

Once cool, store in the fridge for up to 4 days.

'nICE' cream and toppings

Ice cream, you scream, everybody scream (nicely!). Alana x

5 minutes | Serves 2

4.8g per portion

2

milk kefir

allergens: *cow's milk – milk kefir, if using*

2 frozen ripe bananas

1 frozen ripe avocado

250ml (9 fl oz) milk *(dairy, nut or plant-based or milk kefir)*

2 tbsp maple syrup

1 vanilla pod, deseeded (optional)

2 handfuls of ice cubes

TOPPINGS

80g of raspberries
+ 5.4g fibre

80g of blueberries
+ 1.2 g fibre

80g of strawberries
+ 3g fibre

2 tbsp pumpkin seeds
+ 1.5g fibre

2 tbsp sunflower seeds
+ 1.4g fibre

2 tbsp chia seeds
+ 7.7 g fibre

2 tbsp chopped cashews
1.6g fibre

2 tbsp chopped almonds
+ 3.2g fibre

1. Add all the ingredients to a blender and blend until smooth. This forms an instant 'nice' cream texture.

Either eat immediately or store in the freezer for up to a week.

mocktails

Upgrade your soft drink with your gut in mind – take us to The Gut Stuff bar!!

Up to 3 days | Serves 4
*after following first step
fermentation (see
kombucha p.170)*

 2

 kombucha

beetroot and ginger kombucha

1 beetroot, peeled and
chopped into 1cm (½-in)
cubes (or 120ml/3¾ fl oz
pressed beetroot juice)

800ml (1½ pints) kombucha
from first fermentation
(see p.170)

2 tbsp freshly grated, peeled
ginger

1. Preheat the oven to 180°C fan/200°C/400°F/gas mark 6.

2. If using beetroot, place it in the centre of a piece of foil, drizzle with 1 tablespoon of water and bring the sides of the foil together to create a parcel. Cook for 40 minutes.

3. Once the beetroot has cooled, transfer to a blender and purée into a smooth paste, adding a splash of kombucha.

4. Add the beetroot paste/juice and grated ginger to a 1 litre (1¾-pint) clip-top bottle. Using a funnel, pour in the first fermentation kombucha, leaving 2.5–5cm (1–2 in) clear at the top.

5. Store at room temperature, out of direct sunlight, for up to 3 days, until it reaches the desired level of carbonation. Chill in the fridge before serving.

Store both drinks in the fridge, tightly sealed, for up to 2 weeks. Once opened, they are best consumed within 3 days.

up to 2 days | serves 4
after following first step fermentation (See water kefir p.169)

2

water kefir

strawberry and lemongrass

50g (1¾ oz) strawberries, crushed

1 lemongrass stick, finely sliced

800ml (1½ pints) water kefir from first fermentation *(see p.169)*

1. Add the strawberries and lemongrass to a 1 litre (1¾-pint) clip-top bottle. Using a funnel, pour in the water kefir, leaving 2.5–5cm (1–2 in) clear at the top.

2. Store at room temperature, out of direct sunlight, for up to 2 days until it reaches desired level of carbonation. Chill in the fridge before serving.

chapter

7

ferments

sourdough starter

7 days | Serves n/a
+ weekly feeds

allergens: *gluten*

500g (1 lb 2 oz) wholemeal
   flour
500g (1 lb 2 oz) strong white
   bread flour
1.03kg (2 lb 5oz) water

Weigh an empty 500ml (18-fl oz) jar and make a note of the weight.

Day 1 – To make the starter mixture, combine 50g (1¾ oz) wholemeal flour, 50g (1¾ oz) strong white flour and 125g (4½ oz) water (at 24°C/75°F) in a bowl. Transfer to the 500ml jar and cover with a two-part lid. Leave at room temperature for 24 hours.

Day 2 – Add 75g (2¾ oz) starter mixture to a bowl (discard the rest), followed by 50 g (1¾ oz) wholemeal flour, 50g (1¾ oz) strong white flour and 115g (4 oz) water (at 24°C/75°F). Mix well, return to the jar, cover and leave at room temperature for 24 hours.

Days 3 and 4 – Repeat day 2.

Day 5 – Increase the feed to twice a day. In the jar, reduce the starter (discard the rest) to 75g (2¾ oz), then add 50g (1¾ oz) wholemeal flour, 50g (1¾ oz) strong white flour and 115g (4 oz) water (at 24°C/75°F). Mix well, cover and leave at room temperature for 12 hours. After 12 hours, repeat the feed with the same ratio of ingredients and set aside for 12 hours.

Day 6 – Repeat day 5.

Day 7 – Reduce the starter to 50g (1¾ oz), add 50g (1¾ oz) wholemeal flour, 50g (1¾ oz) strong white flour and 100g (3½ oz) water (at 24°C/75°F). After 12 hours, repeat the feed with the same ratio of ingredients and set aside for 12 hours.

After day 7, if you are not baking on a regular basis, store your starter in the fridge until you are ready to, and follow our weekly feeding instructions:

We recommend feeding the starter once a week whilst refrigerated. Feed it by first discarding all but 50g (1¾ oz) of the starter, then add 50g (1¾ oz) of wholemeal flour, 50g (1¾ oz) of strong white flour and 100g (3½ oz) water. Stir the mixture together with a spoon before replacing it to the fridge.

We've set up all our ferments with dating profiles so you can choose which one you want to take to dinner first ;)

the gut stuff sourdough

Sophie Stensrud

We knew we HAD to ask Sophie to contribute to this book as she has cooked and baked all her life and runs baking classes via The Scandicook – there's nothin' she doesn't know about sourdough!

Name: Sourdough (say it right 'sour-doh').

What is it? Bread made using a live starter instead of yeast to help it rise.

Flavour? Sour and tangy.

Likes? Flour, salt and water.

Dislikes: Not being fed enough flour (flangry – flour hangry).

Describe yourself in a few words: I'm moreish, have a good ear and you can put anything on top of me and I'll taste good.

....

up to 36 hours | Serves 12-14 slices
including resting

allergens: *gluten*

100g (3½ oz) active starter

350g (12 oz) water

300g (10½ oz) strong white bread flour

150g (5½ oz) strong wholemeal flour

50g (1¾ oz) rye flour

10g (¼ oz) salt

Step 1 – Your starter needs to be active, stringy and bubbly and to have at least doubled when you start mixing the dough. Add the water and starter to a mixing bowl and mix well to dissolve the starter. Add the flour and mix until it is fully hydrated, and no dry bits remain. Cover the bowl and leave for 30 minutes–1 hour.

Step 2 – Sprinkle the salt over the dough, splash on a little water (about 1 tablespoon), and squish the salt into the dough with wet hands. You can then knead the dough on the counter for a few minutes using the 'slap and fold' method or mix really well in the bowl and then do a series of stretch and folds. To stretch and fold grab the dough at the top end of the bowl, pull it up then over towards the bottom of the bowl. Use the other hand to turn the bowl and repeat all the way round the bowl a few times until you feel the dough is uniform and starting to tighten up a little. Cover the bowl again and leave it to rest for about 30 minutes.

Step 3 – Roughly every 30 minutes (or when the dough has relaxed back into the bowl) do a set of stretch and folds around the bowl, 4-6 stretches. Repeat 3-6 times.

Step 4 – Leave your covered bowl to rest and finish bulk proving. How long this takes depends on temperature and how active your starter is, it could be anything from 3–8 hours in total from adding the salt. When finished your dough should have increased in size about 50% – it should dome a little, be glossy and have some visible air bubbles.

Step 5 – Pre-shape by tipping the dough onto the countertop and, using a damp dough scraper and damp hands, shape it into a round. Leave to bench rest for about 30 minutes.

Step 6 – Prep your banneton, or a bowl covered with a tea towel by dusting it well with rice flour to avoid the dough sticking.

Lightly flour the dough and the counter next to it, as well as your hands. Using a dough scraper, flip your round upside down onto the flour.

Shaping a batard (oval loaf):
Gently grab the top with both hands and fold $^2/_3$ down, then tug the left side across the middle and right side across the middle over the bit you just folded over. Finally, grab the bottom with both hands and pull over your folds. Turn it 90 degrees and roll into a sausage, then place into a banneton seam-side up.

Shaping a boule (round loaf):
Pull the sides of the dough into the middle, starting at the top and going all the way round until you get a tightened ball. Flip it and use the sides of your hands to spin it on the countertop tightening the skin. Then place in a banneton or bowl, seam-side up.

Step 7 – Leave to rest on the counter for up to 30 minutes – it should be nice and jiggly when you pop it into the fridge. Leave the loaf in the fridge uncovered for 10-24 hours before baking.

To bake, preheat a lidded pot (see equipment) in the oven for 30 minutes at 230°C fan/250°C/475°F/gas mark 9. Tip your loaf onto a piece of parchment, score and gently lift into your hot pot. Bake with the lid on for 45 minutes. Allow to cool completely (at least 1 hour) before slicing.

NOTES:

Using a finely milled wholemeal flour will give you a light loaf and yet all the fibre. If you find the dough too sticky and hard to work with, try making it with all white flour a few times to practice. Once you have mastered the basics, you can increase the proportion of wholemeal flour. Flours tolerate different levels of hydration; usually wholemeal can manage more water. If you are increasing your proportion of wholemeal flour, also increase water up to 400g (14 oz).

GUT-FRIENDLY ADDITIONS:

To boost your bread, you can make additions when you add the salt. If adding flax seeds or chia seeds note that they soak up quite a bit of water so you might want to add another 25g (1 oz) as you squish them in. Stick to about 50g (1¾ oz) flax or chia

Sunflower, pumpkin, sesame or poppy seeds are all great additions, as well as chopped nuts and dried fruit. You can add up to 100g (3½ oz) at the same time as adding salt. Note that they will firm up your dough a little but can make it more difficult to handle, so it is best to play with additions once you´ve nailed the basics.

EQUIPMENT:

- **Mixing bowl**
- **Dough scraper**
- **Digital scales**
- **Banneton** (suitable for 1kg/2lb 4 oz) dough) or a bowl or colander covered with a tea towel, plus rice flour to dust.
- **Lame** (razor blade in a holder) or a very sharp knife or serrated knife to score.
- **Baking vessel** a Dutch oven is best, about 5 litre capacity but a lidded Pyrex, or lidded enamel or ceramic roaster can also be used. Check maximum temperature tolerance before baking and reduce oven temperature if needed.

TROUBLESHOOTING:

My bread is gummy/flat/dense
The loaf could be underbaked, cut into too soon or, most common, under-proofed. This happens a lot to beginners, don't despair, make sure your starter is active and happily doubling and increase bulk proof next time.

My bread is flat as a pancake
A flat loaf will usually be due to either under-proofing or over-proofing the dough. Under-proofing is more common than over-proofing. Study your crumb, if dense and gummy, and maybe some large but irregular holes it is typically underproved. If webby and flat, it's most likely overproved. A well-fermented crumb will have a mixture of hole sizes, be quite 'lacey' in appearance and have

no dense areas. If very sticky to handle when shaping, or 'floating out' when tipping out to bake, the dough could be under- or over-fermented (your crumb will tell you which). However, it could also be a lack of tension and strength in your dough. Work on doing enough stretch and folds during bulk, and better shaping. Shaping is hard at first, but practice makes perfect.

My dough won't rise
If you struggle to judge fermentation, it can be a good idea to prove in a square see-through plastic container, allowing you to mark the side so you can track rise. Slow or lacking rise is often due to the starter not being strong and active enough. Feeding it twice a day for a couple of days can help give it a boost, as well as using finger warm water both for feeding and mixing the dough. Be mindful of temperature, if your kitchen is cold finding somewhere cosy to prove can help, like middle rack of the oven switched off with a bowl of just boiled water or put the pilot light on for 15 minutes to warm it up a little.

the gut stuff sauerkraut

Name: Sour cabbage (goes by 'sauerkraut').

Likes? Hummus, potatoes and toast.

Dislikes: Being left out on the side too long.

Describe yourself in a few words: I'm tangy, sweet-smelling and make any dish complete.

....

50 minutes prep | Serves 20 portions
+ 7–14 days fermenting

1 cabbage (*green or red*)
sea salt
1 tbsp fennel seeds
   (*optional*)

1. Wash a 1-litre (1¾-pint) jar in hot soapy water, then place it in the oven at 90°C fan/110°C/225°F/gas mark ¼ for 15–20 minutes to sterilize it. Leave it to cool.

2. Remove the outer leaves of the cabbage and, if you're not using a weight, set a cabbage leaf aside. Slice into quarters and remove the hearts. Finely slice the quarters into thin ribbons.

3. Place a mixing bowl on a set of scales and zero the scales. Place the sliced cabbage into the mixing bowl and measure its weight. Calculate 2% of that weight (multiplying by 0.02) and measure out the result in salt. Sprinkle the measured salt over the cabbage and add the fennel seeds, if using. Using your hands, begin to squeeze the cabbage and massage for 5–10 minutes. The salt will draw water out of the cabbage, creating its own brine. Leave the mixture to sit for 30 minutes.

4. Pack the cabbage into the sterilized jar, being sure to add in all the cabbage juices, then pack down the contents by compressing the reserved cabbage leaf over the top, or by using a weight. Ensure you're applying enough pressure so that the brine covers the shredded cabbage completely.

David Zilber
is a chef, fermenter, food scientist and co-author of the NYT bestselling cookbook, The Noma Guide to Fermentation. He's basically the Rhianna of the fermenting world.

5. Cover the jar with a burping lid and leave it at room temperature, out of direct sunlight. After 24 hours, press down the cabbage again using the weight or leaf to ensure that the cabbage is submerged beneath the brine.

6. Start to taste test after 7 days. Once the sauerkraut has reached your desired tanginess, replace the burping lid with a screw-top lid, cover securely.

Store in the fridge for up to 4 months. We like ours around day fourteen – it's just the perfect level of tang!

David Zilber: *If you start off making this sauerkraut recipe with white cabbage, you can easily liven it up and turn it into a carotene dream. You simply need 2 good nubs of turmeric root, 1 young carrot, and tiny sweet potato (or, roughly the same amount of sweet potato as carrot by weight). Peel the sweet potato (as its skin is fairly fibrous), but simply wash the carrot and turmeric, so you retain all of the potent nutrients that sit just below the surface. From there, brunoise or finely mince all three of the roots. Toss the glowing mix into the bowl with the shredded cabbage before you measure 2% of its weight in salt, but continue with the recipe as normal from that point on. Other, optional seasonings that would fare well in this recipe and sunny up any cloudy day include: a tablespoon of dill pollen, caraway seeds, or toasted yellow mustard seeds.*

kimchi

Name: Kimchi

Likes? Lactic acid, as many vegetables as possible, chilli, rice, cheese and buddha bowls... what a versatile soul.

Dislikes: Being left unattended somewhere warm and mould.

Describe yourself in a few words: Spicy, sour and smelly enough to clear a crowd (just what you're looking for from a date!).

....

20 minutes prep | Serves 20
+ 12 hours resting
+ 7-14 days fermenting

1 Chinese leaf cabbage
  (napa cabbage)
1 litre (1¾ pints) water
2 tbsp sea salt
2 carrots *(skin on)*
100g (3½ oz) radishes
bunch of spring onions
6 large garlic cloves

2 shallots
2 red chillies
100g (3½ oz) fresh ginger,
  peeled
1–3 tbsp Korean chilli flakes
  or cayenne pepper
2 tbsp tamari *(optional)*

1. Wash a 1 litre (1¾-pint) jar in hot soapy water, then place it in the oven at 90°C fan/110°C/225°F/gas mark ¼ for 15–20 minutes to sterilize it. Leave it to cool.

2. Remove the outer leaves from the cabbage and discard them, then rinse the rest of the cabbage head well and cut into thick (5–6cm/2–2½-in) strips.

3. Using a jug, make a brine by mixing the water and salt. Stir well to ensure the salt is well dissolved. Place the sliced cabbage into a large bowl and pour the brine over the leaves to cover. Cover the bowl with clingfilm or a lid if it has one and leave it at room temperature overnight.

4. The following day, drain the brined cabbage, reserving the brine.

Recipe continued overleaf

David Zilber: *While the above ingredients are considered near universal stalwarts of kimchi recipes around the world, kimchi can encompass so much more than cabbage (and can be considered an umbrella term for a style of pickling). To get at the 'roots' of that sentiment, try a kimchi with radishes as its star; 250g (9 oz) D'Avingnon radishes, 250g icicle radishes, 250g Shunkyo radishes and 250g mini mak (you can disregard the 100g/3½ oz radish the original recipe calls for, but keep everything else the same). Cut all the radishes into similar-sized quarters, lengthwise, and treat them as you would the cabbage in the original recipe. The finished product is a crunchily delectable variation that's enlivens any meal it's served with.*

5. Grate the carrots, chop the radishes into thin slices and roughly chop the spring onion. Peel the garlic and shallots, deseed the chillies.

6. In a blender (or using a knife to finely mince), make a paste with the ginger, garlic, deseeded red chillies, shallots and chilli flakes or cayenne pepper (depending on your desired spice level). Transfer the paste to a large mixing bowl with your brined cabbage leaves and add the grated carrots, sliced radishes, spring onions and tamari (if using). Using rubber gloves, massage the mixture into the vegetables for 5–10 minutes.

7. Pack the vegetables tightly into the sterilized jar and cover with a little reserved brine, if required, to ensure it sits beneath the level of the brine-line.

8. Place a weight on top to ensure that everything stays beneath the brine-line, and securely seal the jar with a burping lid.

9. Store your jar at room temperature for 7–14 days. Begin tasting your kimchi after 7 days. It should be salty, pleasantly sour and a bit crunchy with the flavours melding together harmoniously. When fermented to your liking, replace the burping lid with a screw top lid.

Store in the fridge for up to 4 months.

fermented garlic

Likes? Kissing.

Dislikes: The fact that nobody likes kissing me.

Describe yourself in a few words: Like a lava lamp, bubbly, mesmerising and hot ;)

....

This recipe could not be easier!

....

10 minutes prep | Serves 7
+ 5-7 days fermenting

allergens: *garlic*

2 heads of garlic
300ml (10 fl oz) room
    temperature water
½ tsp sea salt

1. Wash a 500ml (18-fl oz) jar in hot soapy water, then place it in the oven at 90°C fan/110°C/225°F/gas mark ¼ for 15–20 minutes to sterilize it. Leave it to cool.

2. Peel the garlic cloves and add them whole to the jar. Add the water to a jug with the salt and stir until it has dissolved. Cover the garlic with the brine. If the garlic is not submerged under the brine, add some baking paper to weigh it down. Add the burping lid and leave at room temperature for 5–7 days.

3. Begin tasting after 5 days. Once the ferment has reached your desired taste, replace the burping lid with a screw-top lid and move to the fridge.

Store in the fridge for up to 4 months.

milk kefir

Name: Kefir (key-feh).

Likes? Lactose.

Dislikes: Getting too hot (ooo-er).

Describe yourself in a few words: I've been around for centuries – I'm creamy, tangy and contain more microbes per ml/fl oz than yogurt.

MILK KEFIR YOGURT

To make milk kefir yogurt, follow the recipe below. After removing the grains, reseal the jar and store at room temperature for a further 12–24 hours to thicken. Once thickened, store in the fridge and use within 4 days.

....

2 minutes prep | Serves 20
+ 24-48 days fermenting

5g (⅛ oz) milk kefir grains
250ml (9 fl oz) whole milk

allergens: *cow's milk*

1. Wash a 500ml (18-fl oz) jar in hot soapy water, then place it in the oven at 90°C fan/110°C/225°F/gas mark ¼ for 15–20 minutes to sterilize it. Leave it to cool.

2. Add the milk kefir grains to the sterilized jar and pour the milk over the top. Gently stir with a clean spoon to evenly distribute the microbes. Cover with gauze and fix in place with a rubber band. Set aside at room temperature for 24 hours, away from direct sunlight.

3. After 24 hours, stir and judge its taste and consistency. When the milk has thickened and tastes pleasantly tangy, it's ready. If not, replace the gauze and rubber band and continue fermenting at room temperature for a further 24 hours.

4. Once ready, strain the jar's contents through a sieve over a bowl to catch the final kefir. Transfer the milk kefir to a clip-top bottle and cover tightly.

Store in the fridge for up to a week.

water kefir

Name: Water kefir (water key-feh).

Likes? Special grains, sugar and water.

Dislikes: Being abandoned or heated metal spoons and sieves.

Describe yourself in a few words: I'm hungry, a quick grower, effervescent, slightly fruity and definitely alive!

....

10 minutes prep | Serves 4
+ up to 4 days fermenting

20g (¾ oz) cane sugar
800ml (1½ pints) filtered
water *(room temperature)*
30g (1 oz) water kefir grains

1. Wash a 1 litre (1¾-pint) jar in hot soapy water, then place it in the oven at 90°C fan/110°C/225°F/gas mark ¼ for 15–20 minutes to sterilize it. Leave it to cool.

2. Add the sugar to the sterilized jar, followed by the water and stir until the sugar has completely dissolved. Then add the water kefir grains. Gently stir the liquid once more to distribute the microbes throughout, then cover the jar with gauze and secure it tightly with a rubber band. Set aside at room temperature for 48 hours, keeping the jar away from direct sunlight.

3. After 48 hours, strain the grains from the mixture using a sieve and reserve. Pour the brewed kefir water into a clip-top bottle, then either store in the fridge or leave it out for another 48 hours to carbonate further.

Store in the fridge for up to a month, unopened. Once opened, it is best consumed within 30 days.

kombucha

Name: Kombucha (kom-boo-cha, replacing sam-boo-ka), or 'booch' for short.

Likes? Fruity flavours and symbiotic cultures of bacteria and yeast.

Dislikes: Being left out too long and stainless steel.

Describe yourself in a few words: Fizzy, fruity and sometimes so tart I'll make you pucker up!

10 minutes prep | Serves 7
+ 1 hour cooling
+ 5-7 days fermenting

1.7 litres (3 pints) filtered water
120g (4¼ oz) cane sugar
4 black teabags
200ml (7 fl oz) finished kombucha from a previous batch (*or the liquid the SCOBY is packaged in*)
1 SCOBY

1. Wash a 2 litre (3½-pint) jar in hot soapy water, then place it in the oven at 90°C fan/110°C/225°F/gas mark ¼ for 15–20 minutes to sterilize it. Leave it to cool.

2. In a large saucepan, bring the water and sugar to the boil. Stir to dissolve the sugar, then remove the pan from the heat and add the teabags. Steep for 5–10 minutes. Remove the teabags and leave to cool to room temperature.

3. Add the mixture to the sterilized jar, followed by the finished kombucha and SCOBY and cover the jar with gauze, fixing it in place with a rubber band. Leave the jar at room temperature but out of direct sunlight.

4. Fermentation can take anywhere from 5–14 days, depending on your desired taste. Begin tasting the kombucha after five days. As the kombucha ferments, its sugary sweetness will diminish as its

acidity rises. Once it has reached your desired level of tanginess, remove the SCOBY and reserve 200ml (7 fl oz) of kombucha to brew your next batch.

5. Strain the finished kombucha through a sieve to remove any stray particles that may have formed during fermentation. Use a funnel to pour your brewed kombucha into a clip-top bottle, then either store in the fridge or leave it out for a further 48 hours to carbonate further.

Store in the fridge for up to a month unopened. Once opened, it is best consumed within 7 days.

6. Repeat the process using the SCOBY and reserved kombucha to make a fresh batch of kombucha.

index

a

Henihit
apples: fruit crumble 142
aubergines: aubergine and sweet
potato katsu curry
86–7
aubergine parmigiana 96–7
avocado, smashed 98–9

b

bacteria: fermented foods
22–3
gut microbes 9, 11, 12, 16–17
baked beans: veggie brunch
51
bananas: banana and raspberry
cookies 146
'nICE' cream 148
banoffee pie with kefir 140
beans 28
black bean and lime hummus
121
creamy mushrooms on
sourdough 50
mushroom and mixed bean
hotpot 108
one-pot butterbean, broccoli
and leeks 93
plant-based traybake 68–9
real 'gut' baked beans 52
smashed white bean hummus
121
spiced bean and jackfruit tacos
98–9
summer trifle 138–9
veggie chilli 92
beef: spaghetti bolognese
80–1
beetroot: beetroot and ginger
kombucha 150
beetroot burgers 82–4
hummus 121

bolognese sauce 80–1
bread see sourdough
breakfast 26, 29
broccoli: one-pot butterbean,
broccoli and leeks 93
brownies, sauerkraut 144
Brussels sprouts salad 64–5
bubble and squeak 48
burgers, beetroot 82–4
butternut squash: butternut
squash and lentil stuffing 127
mac 'n' cheese 116

c

cabbage: The Gut Stuff
sauerkraut 160–1
slaw 129
carbohydrates 17
cavolo nero: citrus greens 124
celeriac slaw 102–3
cheese: aubergine parmigiana
96–7
kim-cheese 74
mac 'n' cheese 116
sourdough pizza 88–9
veggie brunch 51
chia seeds: fruit chia jam 41
chicken: chicken goujon Caesar
salad 58–60
chicken noodle one pot
70–1
chicken nuggets 85
chickpeas: chickpea balls
112–13
hummus 120–1
tomato and chickpea soup
76–7
chilli: fermented hot sauce
131
veggie chilli 92
chips, root vegetable 82–4
chocolate: chocolate
hummus 121
sauerkraut brownies 144
citrus greens 124
cookies, banana and raspberry
146

corn salsa 129
courgettes, spicy 96–7
crackers, fibre 61
crumble, fruit 142
cucumber: kefir tzatziki 118
curry, aubergine and sweet potato
katsu 86–7

d

dairy-free recipes 36
dates: banoffee pie 140
sauerkraut brownies 144
dietary requirements 36–7
digestive system 9–17

e

eggs 36–7
oMEGA salad 62–3
enzymes 12–14

f

fermented foods 22–3, 26,
153–71
fibre 20–1, 28–9
fibre crackers 61
fibre-cracker croutons
58–60
fishcakes, pantry 102–3
FODMAPs 37
freezers 32–3, 35
French toast, sourdough 46–7
fries, loaded 104
frozen food 32–3, 35
fruit 32, 35
fruit chia jam 41
mixed berry compote 46–7

g

gallbladder 10
garlic 32
fermented garlic 167
gastrointestinal tract 9–17
gluten-free recipes 36
grains: sunshine bowl 66
green hummus 121
gut microbes 9, 11, 12, 16–17

The Gut Stuff sauerkraut
160–1
The Gut Stuff sourdough
156–9

h

habit forming 24–6
herbs 30–1, 32, 34
hot sauce, fermented 131
hummus 120–1
hydrochloric acid 12, 13

i

ice cream 148

j

jackfruit: spiced bean and
jackfruit tacos 98–9
jam, fruit chia 41

k

kefir: banoffee pie with 140
    kefir tzatziki 118
    milk kefir 168
    water kefir 169
ketchup, fermented tomato
    130
kimchi 164–6
    kim-cheese 74
    kimchi grain bowl 72
kombucha 170–1
    beetroot and ginger kombucha
    150

l

large intestine 11, 16–17
leeks: one-pot butterbean,
broccoli and leeks 93
lentils: butternut squash and
lentil stuffing 127
    lentil shepherd's pie 106–7
    red lentil dahl 109–10
liver 10
loaded fries 104

m

mac 'n' cheese 116

mangoes: summer trifle 138–9
milk kefir 168
mindful eating 27
mocktails 150–1
mouth 12, 14
mushrooms: creamy mushrooms
on sourdough 50
    mushroom and mixed bean
        hotpot 108
    veggie brunch 51

n

'nICE' cream and toppings 148
noodles: chicken noodle one
    pot 70–1
nuts: crunchy seed and nut
    mix 133
    nut butter 41

o

oats: banana and raspberry
cookies 146
    overnight oats 40–1
oesophagus 10, 15
oils 35
oMEGA salad 62–3
onions 32

p

pancakes, spiced green 44
pancreas 11, 12
pantry fishcakes 102–3
pasta 29
    mac 'n' cheese 116
    spaghetti bolognese 80–1
peas 32
    mushy peas 128
peppers: real 'gut' baked beans 52
pesto, walnut 135
pharynx 10
piccalilli 132
pizza, sourdough 88–9
planning meals 26, 29
plant-based foods 19–21, 26
plant-based traybake 68–9
polyphenols 19
potatoes: bubble and squeak
    48–9

lentil shepherd's pie 106–7
mashed potato 48–9
potato salad with sauerkraut
    126
probiotics 23

q

quinoa: shredded Brussels
sprouts salad 64–5

r

ratatouille mix 32
rice: kimchi grain bowl 72
    veggie chilli 92
root vegetables: loaded fries
    104
    root vegetable chips 82–4
    sliced root vegetable bake
        125

s

salads: chicken goujon Caesar
salad 58–60
    oMEGA salad 62–3
    potato salad with sauerkraut
        126
    shredded Brussels sprouts
salad 64–5
salmon: baked salmon 94
    pantry fishcakes 102–3
salsa, corn 129
sauerkraut: The Gut Stuff
sauerkraut 160–1
    potato salad with 126
    sauerkraut brownies 144
seeds: crunchy seed and nut
    mix 133
    fibre crackers 61
shepherd's pie, lentil 106–7
shopping 34
slaw 129
    celeriac slaw 102–3
small intestine 11, 13, 16
soup, tomato and chickpea
    76–7
sourdough: creamy mushrooms
    on sourdough 50

The Gut Stuff sourdough
156–9
sourdough bread 23
sourdough French toast
46–7
sourdough pizza 88–9
sourdough starter 154–5
spaghetti bolognese 80–1
spices 34
spinach 32
stomach 10, 12, 15–16
strawberries and lemongrass
151
stuffing, butternut squash
and lentil 127
summer trifle 138–9
sunshine bowl 66
sweet potato wedges 118
sweetcorn: corn salsa 129

t
tacos, spiced bean and jackfruit
98–9
tartare sauce 128
tinned foods 35
tofu: kimchi grain bowl 72
tomatoes: aubergine parmigiana
96–7
chickpea balls 112–13
fermented tomato ketchup
130
real 'gut' baked beans 52
sourdough pizza 88–9
tomato and basil hummus
121
tomato and chickpea soup
76–7
traybake, plant-based 68–9

trifle, summer 138–9
tzatziki, kefir 118

V
vagus nerve 13
vegetables 35
bubble and squeak 48–9
kimchi 164–6
piccalilli 132
plant-based traybake 68–9
veggie brunch 51
veggie chilli 92
vinegars 35

W
walnut pesto 135
water kefir 169

UK/US Glossary

Aubergine – Eggplant

Baking paper – parchment paper

Baking tray – baking sheet

Beetroot – beet

Black-eyed beans – black-eyed peas

Butter beans – lima beans

Cake tin – cake pan

Chestnut mushrooms – cremini
mushrooms

Chickpeas – garbanzo beans

Clingfilm – plastic wrap

Coriander – cilantro

Courgettes – zucchini

Frying pan – skillet

Little Gem lettuce – Boston lettuce

Loaf tin – loaf pan

Pak choi – bok choy

Passata – strained tomatoes

Pepper (red, yellow, green) – bell pepper

Rocket – arugula

Tomato purée – tomato paste

Wholemeal – whole wheat

HUGE thank you to our in-house foodie, Lauren, who chopped, mixed and stirred her way through lockdown to make these recipes come to life, and to Kristy Coleman once again, for co-writing the nutrition bits and generally holding our hands.

And to the rest of The Gut Stuff team – there's ALOTTA cooks in this kitchen and they never spoil the broth.